Lecture Notes in Computer Science 12845

More information about this subseries at https://link.springer.com/bookseries/7411

Halima Elbiaze · Essaid Sabir ·
Francisco Falcone · Mohamed Sadik ·
Samson Lasaulce · Jalel Ben Othman (Eds.)

Ubiquitous Networking

7th International Symposium, UNet 2021
Virtual Event, May 19–22, 2021
Revised Selected Papers

 Springer

Editors
Halima Elbiaze 🆔
University of Quebec at Montreal (UQAM)
Motreal, QC, Canada

Essaid Sabir 🆔
ENSEM, Hassan II University of Casablanca
Casablanca, Morocco

Francisco Falcone 🆔
Universidad Publica de Navarra (UPNA)
Pampelune, Spain

Mohamed Sadik 🆔
ENSEM, Hassan II University of Casablanca
Casablanca, Morocco

Samson Lasaulce 🆔
University of Lorraine
Nancy, France

Jalel Ben Othman 🆔
Sorbonne University
Villetaneuse, France

ISSN 0302-9743   ISSN 1611-3349 (electronic)
Lecture Notes in Computer Science
ISBN 978-3-030-86355-5   ISBN 978-3-030-86356-2 (eBook)
https://doi.org/10.1007/978-3-030-86356-2

LNCS Sublibrary: SL5 – Computer Communication Networks and Telecommunications

This Springer imprint is published by the registered company Springer Nature Switzerland AG
The registered company address is: Gewerbestrasse 11, 6330 Cham, Switzerland

Preface

The International Symposium on Ubiquitous Networking (UNet) is an international scientific event that highlights new trends and findings in hot topics related to ubiquitous computing/networking. Given the travel restrictions and potential health risks due to the COVID-19 outbreak, UNet'21 was held virtually.

Ubiquitous networks sustain development of numerous paradigms/technologies such as distributed ambient intelligence, the Internet of Things (IoT), the Tactile Internet, the Internet of Skills, context-awareness, cloud computing, wearable devices, and future mobile networking (e.g., B5G and 6G). Various domains are then impacted by such a system, one can cite security and monitoring, energy efficiency and environment protection, e-health, precision agriculture, intelligent transportation, home care (e.g., for elderly and disabled people), etc. Communication in such a system has to cope with many constraints (e.g., limited capacity resources, energy depletion, strong fluctuations of traffic, real-time constraints, dynamic network topology, radio link breakage, interferences, etc.) and has to meet the new application requirements. Ubiquitous systems bring many promising paradigms aiming to deliver significantly higher capacity to meet the huge growth of mobile data traffic and to accommodate efficiently dense and ultra-dense systems. A crucial challenge is that ubiquitous networks should be engineered to better support existing and emerging applications including broadband multimedia, machine-to-machine applications, IoT, and sensors and RFID technologies. Many of these systems require stringent Quality of Service including better latency, reliability, higher spectral, and energy efficiency, but also some Quality of Experience and Quality of Context constraints.

The UNet conference series is a forum that brings together researchers and practitioners from academia and industry to discuss recent developments in pervasive and ubiquitous networks. This conference series provides a venue to exchange ideas, discuss solutions, debate identified challenges, and share experiences among researchers and professionals. UNet aims also to promote the adoption of new methodologies and to provide the participants with advanced and innovative tools able to catch the fundamental dynamics of the underlying complex interactions (e.g., game theory, mechanism design theory, learning theory, SDR platforms, etc.).

Message from the General Chairs

On behalf of the organizing committee, it is our great pleasure to welcome you to the proceedings of the 2021 7th International Symposium on Ubiquitous Networking (UNet 2021), which will be held virtually, during May 19–21, 2021.

The UNet conference series is a forum that aims to bring together researchers and practitioners from academia and industry to discuss recent developments in pervasive systems and ubiquitous networks. This conference series provides a venue to exchange ideas, shape future systems, discuss solutions, debate identified challenges, and share experiences among researchers and professionals. UNet aims also to promote the adoption of new methodologies and provide the participants with advanced and innovative tools able to catch the fundamental dynamics of the underlying complex interactions (e.g., artificial intelligence, game theory, mechanism design, learning theory, SDR platforms, etc.). Papers describing original research on both theoretical and practical aspects of pervasive computing and future mobile computing (e.g., 5G, 6G, AI-driven communications, IoT, TI, etc.) were invited for submission to UNet 2021.

Technically sponsored by Springer Nature, and co-organized by the NEST Research Group, LATECE Laboratory, ENSEM, the Hassan II University of Casablanca, and the University of Quebec at Montréal, the 2021 UNet followed five very successful events held in France, Tunisia, and Morocco. Over the past editions, the reputation of UNet has rapidly grown and the conference has become one of the most respected venues in the field of ubiquitous networking and pervasive systems.

The conference would not have been possible without the enthusiastic and hard work of a number of colleagues. We would like to express our appreciation to the Technical Program Committee (TPC) Chairs, Francisco Falcone, Samson Lasaulce, Mohamed Sadik, and Jalel Ben-othman, for their valuable contribution in building the high-quality conference program. We also thank the Track Chairs and all the organizing committee. Such an event relies on the commitment and the contributions of many volunteers, and we would like to acknowledge the efforts of our TPC members and reviewers for their invaluable help in the review process. We are also grateful to all the authors who trusted the conference with their work.

Special thanks to our keynote speakers, the best in their respective fields, Octavia Dobre, Mischa Dohler, Walid Saad, Xue Steve Liu, Roch Glito, and Richard Li, for sharing their expert views on current hot research topics. We also would like to thank Mohamed-Slim Alouini, Mehdi Bennis, Boon S. Ooi, and Abderrahmen Trichili for the outstanding tutorials they delivered at UNet 2021.

We hope that you enjoyed the rich program we built this year, that you made the most out of your participation, and that you come back to UNet for many years to come!

May 2021

Halima Elbiaze
Essaid Sabir

Message from the TPC Chairs

It is with great pleasure that we welcome you to the proceedings of the 2021 International Symposium on Ubiquitous Networking (UNet 2021). The conference featured an interesting technical program comprising 5 technical tracks reporting on recent advances in ubiquitous communication technologies and networking, The Tactile Internet and the Internet of Things, mobile edge networking and fog-cloud computing, artificial intelligence-driven communications, and data engineering, cyber security and pervasive services.

UNet 2021 also featured six keynote speeches delivered by world-class experts, shedding light on future 6G mobile standards, the Internet of skills, AI-driven communications, the Tactile Internet, wireless extended reality over 6G Terahertz, and the technical considerations behind the new IP technology. Moreover, two tutorials covering the new trends of communication-efficient and distributed machine learning over wireless networks and a comprehensive roadmap to free space optics, were also delivered.

In this edition, the UNet conference received 38 submitted manuscripts from authors 14 countries, out of which 16 papers were selected to be included in the final program with an acceptance rate of 42%. The selection of the program of UNet 2021 was possible in the first place thanks to the thorough reviews performed by our TPC members. Overall, the average quality of the submissions respected the fairly high standards of the event. The selection process, we believe, was conducted in a rigorous and fair manner. In particular, each paper received at least three independent reviews made by TPC members, taking into consideration the quality of presentation, the technical soundness, the novelty, and the originality of the manuscripts. The evaluation scale for each aspect of the evaluation was set to range from 1 to 5. UNet 2021 also featured a special session on machine learning for complex networks, for which three papers were accepted, and an invited papers session including six additional papers.

Building this excellent program would not have been possible without the dedication and the hard work of the different chairs, the keynote speakers, the tutorial speakers, and all the Technical Program Committee members. We grasp the opportunity to acknowledge their valuable work, and sincerely thank them for their help in ensuring that UNet 2021 will be remembered as a high-quality event.

We hope that you enjoy this edition's technical program, and we look forward to meeting you at the next conference.

May 2021

Francisco Falcone
Samson Lasaulce
Mohamed Sadik
Jalel Ben-Othman

Organization

Honorary Chairs

Aawatif Hayar	Hassan II University of Casablanca, Morocco
Christian Agbobli	University of Quebec at Montréal, Canada
Badreddine Benameur	ENSEM, Hassan II University of Casablanca, Morocco

General Chairs

Halima Elbiaze	University of Québec at Montréal, Canada
Essaid Sabir	ENSEM, Hassan II University of Casablanca, Morocco

TPC Chairs

Francisco Falcone	Universidad Publica De Navarra, Spain
Samson Lasaulce	CNRS/ENSEM, Lorraine, France
Mohamed Sadik	ENSEM, Hassan II University of Casablanca, Morocco
Jalel Ben Othman	University of Paris 13 Paris, France

Track Chairs

Vahid Meghdadi	University of Limoges XLIM-SRI, France
Muhammad Zeeshan Shakir	University of the West of Scotland, UK
Shuai Han	Harbin Institute of Technology, China
Francesco De Pellegrini	Avignon University, France
Oussama Habachi	University of Limoges XLIM-SRI, France
Elarbi Badidi	UAE University, Al-Ain, UAE
Diala Naboulsi	ETS, University of Quebec, Canada
Tembine Hamidou	University of New York, USA
Mohamed El Kamili	EST, Hassan II University of Casablanca, Morocco
Alexandre Reiffers	IMT Atlantique, Brest, France
Slim Rekhis	CN&S, Sup'Com, University of Cathage, Tunis, Tunisia

Special Session Chair

Abdellatif Kobbane	ENSIAS, Mohammed V University of Rabat, Morocco

Special Session: Machine Learning Meets Complex Networks

Ahmed Drissi El Maliani	Mohammed V University of Rabat, Morocco
Dounia Lotfi	Mohammed V University of Rabat, Morocco

Publicity Chairs

Antonio Jara   HOPU, Spain
Hajar Elhammouti   KAUST, Saudi Arabia

Local Arrangement Team

Ahmed Errami   ENSEM, Hassan II University of Casablanca, Morocco
Mohamed Khaldoun   ENSEM, Hassan II University of Casablanca, Morocco
Abdelhadi Ennajih   ENSEM, Hassan II University of Casablanca, Morocco

Steering Committee

Mohamed-Slim Alouini   KAUST University, Saudi Arabia
Eitan Altman   Inria Sophia Antipolis, France
Francesco De Pellegrini   University of Avignon, France
Rachid El-Azouzi   University of Avignon, France
Halima Elbiaze   University of Québec at Montréal, Canada
Mounir Ghogho   International University of Rabat, University of Leeds, UK
Marwan Krunz   University of Arizona, USA
Essaid Sabir   ENSEM, Hassan II University of Casablanca, Morocco
Mohamed Sadik   ENSEM, Hassan II University of Casablanca, Morocco

Technical Program Committee

Abdelkrim Abdelli   USTHB University, Algeria
Laila Abouzaid   ENSEM, Hassan II University of Casablanca, Morocco
Abdelkaher Ait Abdelouahad   LAROSERIE, Chouaib Doukkali University, Morocco
Noura Aknin   Abdelmalek Essaadi University, Morocco
Brahim Alibouch   LabSIV, Ibn Zohr University, Morocco
Wissal Attaoui   ENSEM, Hassan II University of Casablanca, Morocco
Imran Shafique Ansari   University of Glasgow, UK
Elarbi Badidi   UAE University, UAE
Abdelmajid Badri   FSTM, Hassan II University of Casablanca, Morocco
Asma Ben Letaifa   SupCom, Tunisa
Salah Benabdallah   University of Tunis, Tunisia
Mustapha Benjillali   INPT, Morocco
Yahya Benkaouz   FSR, Mohammed V University of Rabat, Morocco
Fatma Benkhelifa   Imperial College London, UK
Olivier Brun   Laboratoire d'Analyse et d'Architecture des Systemes, France
Stefano Chessa   Universita' di Pisa, Italy
Domenico Ciuonzo   University of Naples Federico II, Italy
Hamza Dahmouni   INPT, Morocco

Deepak Dasaratha Rao	Sysintel Inc, USA
Sabrina De Capitani di Vimercati	Università degli Studi di Milano, Italy
Yacine Djemaiel	University of Carthage, Tunisia
Safaa Driouech	ENSEM, Hassan II University of Casablanca, Morocco
Ahmed Drissi El Maliani	Mohammed V University of Rabat, Morocco
Schahram Dustdar	Vienna University of Technology, Austria
Loubna Echabbi	INPT, Morocco
Hajar El Hammouti	KAUST, Saudi Arabia
Mohamed El Kamili	EST, Hassan II University of Casablanca, Morocco
Mourad El Yadari	FPE, UMI, Morocco
Halima Elbiaze	University of Quebec at Montréal, Canada
Oussama Elissati	INPT, Morocco
Moez Esseghir	Technology University of Troyes, France
Francisco Falcone	Universidad Publica de Navarra, Spain
Dieter Fiems	Ghent University, Belgium
Rosa Figueiredo	University of Avignon, France
Giancarlo Fortino	University of Calabria, Italy
Alexandros Fragkiadakis	Institute of Computer Science, FORTH, Greece
Miguel Franklin de Castro	Federal University of Ceará, Brazil
Yacine Ghamri-Doudane	University of La Rochelle, France
Alireza Ghasempour	ICT Faculty, USA
Hicham Ghennioui	LSSC, University of Sidi Mohammed Ben Abdellah, Morocco
Majed Haddad	University of Avignon, France
Ridha Hamila	Qatar University, Qatar
José Luis Hernandez Ramos	European Commission - Joint Research Centre, Belgium
Amal Hyadi	McGill University, Canada
Khalil Ibrahimi	University of Ibn Tofail, Morocco
Tawfik Ismail	Cairo University, Egypt
Carlos Kamienski	Universidade Federal do ABC, Brazil
Vasileios Karyotis	Ionian University, Greece
Donghyun Kim	Georgia State University, USA
Hyunbum Kim	Incheon National University, South Korea
Jong-Hoon Kim	Kent State University, USA
Mohamed Koubaa	Université Tunis El Manar, Tunisia
Mohammed-Amine Koulali	Mohammed I University, Morocco
Rim Koulali	Hassan II University of Casablanca, Morocco
Samson Lasaulce	CRAN, CNRS, University of Lorraine, France
Shancang Li	University of the West of England, Bristol, UK
Marco Listanti	University of Rome "La Sapienza", Italy
Michael Losavio	University of Louisville, USA
Dounia Lotfi	Mohammed V University of Rabat, Morocco
Bala Krishna Maddali	GGS Indraprastha University, India
Zoubir Mammeri	Paul Sabatier University, France

UNet 2021 Keynote Speakers

From Cognition to Intelligence in Communications Networks

Octavia A. Dobre

Abstract. Since Mitola's idea of cognitive radio which arose close to 2000, significant advancements have been made toward applying intelligence in communications networks. While 2020 marks an important milestone in the deployment of 5G wireless networks, planning to deliver enhanced mobile broadband, massive connectivity, ultra-reliability and lower latency, beyond 5G wireless (B5G) aims to provide a major paradigm shift from connected things to connected intelligence. Besides the synergy between communications and computing, B5G seeks to integrate sensing and support a pervasive intelligence. After 20 years, we can state that the idea of extending cognition to artificial intelligence (AI) in the field of communications has arrived. The next decade is crucial for research and development activities to achieving a native AI-based 6G network, capable of not only advancing the digitalization of vertical industries, but also of addressing human challenges through a connected world.

This talk will provide a brief overview of advances in transitioning from cognition to intelligence in communications networks, with emphasis on the features of 5G, as well as on the envisioned 6G wireless. It will discuss the intelligence integration supported by mobile edge computing in both terrestrial and vertical dimensions of emerging communications networks, along with modalities to developing a deep learning network. Furthermore, applications of machine learning techniques to communications will be presented, e.g., to the identification of the signal types in both wireless and optical communications areas. Finally, the talk will highlight research directions for the application of AI to the field of communications.

Octavia A. Dobre is a Professor and Research Chair at Memorial University, Canada. Her research interests encompass various wireless technologies, such as non-orthogonal multiple access and intelligence reflective surfaces, blind signal identification, as well as optical and underwater communications. She has co-authored over 350 refereed papers in these areas.

Dr. Dobre serves as the Editor-in-Chief (EiC) of the IEEE Open Journal of the Communications Society. She was the EiC of the IEEE Communications Letters, as well as Senior Editor, Editor, and Guest Editor for various prestigious journals and magazines.

Dr. Dobre was a Royal Society Scholar and a Fulbright Scholar. She obtained Best Paper Awards at various conferences, including IEEE ICC, IEEE Globecom, IEEE WCNC, and IEEE PIMRC. Dr. Dobre is a Fellow of the Engineering Institute of Canada and a Fellow of the IEEE.

Wireless Extended Reality over 6G Terahertz Networks: A Tale of Two Rs

Walid Saad

Abstract. Unleashing the true potential of extended reality (XR) applications, encompassing virtual reality (VR), augmented reality (AR), and mixed reality, requires providing them with seamless and pervasive connectivity over wireless cellular networks such as 5G and 6G. However, deploying wireless XR applications will impose new visual and haptic requirements that are directly linked to the quality-of-experience of XR users. These requirements can only be met by wireless 6G connectivity that offers high-rate and high-reliability low latency communications (HRLLC), unlike the low rates usually considered in vanilla 5G ultra-reliable low latency communication scenarios. Therefore, in this talk, after a brief overview on our vision on the role of XR in 6G systems, we will explore the potential of using wireless 6G networks operating at the terahertz (THz) frequency bands for meeting HRLLC requirements of VR applications. We first quantify the risk for an unreliable VR performance through a novel and rigorous characterization of the tail of the end-to-end (E2E) delay. Then, we perform a thorough analysis of the tail-value-at-risk to concretely characterize the behavior of extreme wireless events crucial to the real-time VR experience. We use this analysis to derive system reliability for scenarios with guaranteed line-of-sight (LoS) as a function of THz network parameters. We then present simulation results that show how abundant bandwidth and low molecular absorption are necessary to improve the VR application reliability, although their effect remains secondary compared to the availability of LoS. Subsequently, we summarize some of our key results in two related areas: a) the reliability of AR over THz systems and b) the role of machine learning can play in enabling wireless VR applications. We conclude our talk with an overview on other key open problems in the area of cellular-connected XR.

Walid Saad (S'07, M'10, SM'15, F'19) received his Ph.D degree from the University of Oslo in 2010. He is currently a Professor at the Department of Electrical and Computer Engineering at Virginia Tech, where he leads the Network sciEnce, Wireless, and Security (NEWS) laboratory. His research interests include wireless networks, machine learning, game theory, security, unmanned aerial vehicles, cyber-physical systems, and network science. Dr. Saad is a Fellow of the IEEE and an IEEE Distinguished Lecturer. He is also the recipient of the NSF CAREER award in 2013, the AFOSR summer faculty fellowship in 2014, and the Young

Investigator Award from the Office of Naval Research (ONR) in 2015. He was the author/co-author of ten conference best paper awards at WiOpt in 2009, ICIMP in 2010, IEEE WCNC in 2012, IEEE PIMRC in 2015, IEEE SmartGridComm in 2015, EuCNC in 2017, IEEE GLOBECOM in 2018, IFIP NTMS in 2019, IEEE ICC in 2020, and IEEE GLOBECOM in 2020. He is the recipient of the 2015 Fred W. Ellersick Prize from the IEEE Communications Society, of the 2017 IEEE ComSoc Best Young Professional in Academia award, of the 2018 IEEE ComSoc Radio Communications Committee Early Achievement Award, and of the 2019 IEEE ComSoc Communication Theory Technical Committee. He was also a co-author of the 2019 IEEE Communications Society Young Author Best Paper. Dr. Saad received the Dean's award for Research Excellence from Virginia Tech in 2019. He currently serves as an editor for the IEEE Transactions on Mobile Computing and the IEEE Transactions on Cognitive Communications and Networking. He is an Editor-at-Large for the IEEE Transactions on Communications.

6G and the Internet of Skills

Mischa Dohler

Abstract. This keynote explains the roadmap towards 6G, what are the new features and breakthrough technologies. It then positions the Internet of Skills in that emerging ecosystem. The Internet of Skills is a novel internet enabling a complete democratisation of skills, and is underpinned by advancements in robotics, networking and artificial intelligence.

Mischa Dohler is full Professor in Wireless Communications at King's College London, driving cross-disciplinary research and innovation in technology, sciences and arts. He is a Fellow of the IEEE, the Royal Academy of Engineering, the Royal Society of Arts (RSA), the Institution of Engineering and Technology (IET); and a Distinguished Member of Harvard Square Leaders Excellence. He is a serial entrepreneur with 5 companies; composer & pianist with 5 albums on Spotify/iTunes; and fluent in 6 languages. He sits on the Spectrum Advisory Board of Ofcom, and acts as policy advisor on issues related to digital, skills and education. He has had ample coverage by national and international press and media. He is featured on Amazon Prime.

He is a frequent keynote, panel and tutorial speaker, and has received numerous awards. He has pioneered several research fields, contributed to numerous wireless broadband, IoT/M2M and cyber security standards, holds a dozen patents, organized and chaired numerous conferences, was the Editor-in-Chief of two journals, has more than 300 highly-cited publications, and authored several books.

He was the Director of the Centre for Telecommunications Research at King's from 2014–2018. He is the Cofounder of the Smart Cities pioneering company Worldsensing, where he was the CTO from 2008–2014. He also worked as a Senior Researcher at Orange/France Telecom from 2005–2008.

The Road to the Tactile Internet: from 5G to 6G

Roch Glito

Abstract. The Tactile Internet is foreseen as the next step of the Internet. Internet has first moved from fixed to mobile, then from mobile to the Internet of Every Thing. In sharp contrast with the Internet, the Tactile Internet will enable haptic communications, in addition to traditional voice, audio and video communications. It will actually enable skill set delivery over communication networks, and make possible a host of fascinating applications such as remote robotic surgery, vehicle fleet and industrial process automation. However, the road to the tactile Internet might not be as smooth as expected. A lot was expected from 5G, the first stop on the road, but it happens that the early 5G deployments are now indicating that the Ultra Reliable and Low Latency Communications (URLLC) services are short of meeting all the stringent requirements of Tactile Internet. All eyes are now on 6G, the next stop, but 6G is still at the vision level. In this keynote speech, we will introduce the Tactile Internet, discuss 5G as Tactile Internet enabler along with the limitations. We also will elaborate on the current visions of 6G which may make Tactile Internet a reality.

Roch H. Glitho (M'88–SM'97) received the M.Sc. degree in business economics from the University of Grenoble, Grenoble, France, M.Sc. degrees in pure mathematics and computer science from the University of Geneva, Geneva, Switzerland, and the Ph.D. degree (Tech.Dr.) in tele-informatics from the Royal Institute of Technology, Stockholm, Sweden. He is a Full Professor and a Canada Research Chair with Concordia University, Montréal, QC, Canada. He also holds the Ericsson/ENCQOR Senior Industrial Research Chair on Cloud and Edge Computing for 5G and Beyond. He has performed research in industry and has held several senior technical positions, such as a Senior Specialist, a Principal Engineer, and an Expert with Ericsson, Stockholm, Sweden, and Montréal, QC, Canada. Dr. Glitho has served as the Editor-in-Chief for the IEEE Communications Magazine and IEEE Communications Surveys and Tutorials. He has also served as an IEEE Distinguished Lecturer. R.H. Glitho is with the

Concordia Institute for Information Systems Engineering, Concordia University, Montréal, QC H3G 1M8, Canada, and also with the Computer Science Programme, University of Western Cape, Cape Town 7535, South Africa (e-mail: glitho@ece.concordia.ca).

New IP: Motivations and Technical Considerations

Richard Li

Abstract. Many new applications enabled by 5G/B5G/6G require new features and new functionality for the network protocols, and the networking challenges are shifting from the radio access network to the fixed network. I start with requirements for emerging applications such as industrial manufacturing and control, driverless vehicles, space-terrestrial integrated networks, and holographic type communications. Then I will discuss a new network protocol design, called New IP. In particular I will discuss (1) a free-choice addressing mechanism to connect and converge various vertical communication networks; (2) a contract mechanism for application KPI and sender's intent for business critical and life critical applications; (3) qualitative communication mechanism for volumetric holographic type communications. New IP is being designed as an evolution of IPv4/IPv6 to get the Internet ready for the next wave of upcoming applications and emerging industry verticals.

Dr. Richard Li is Chief Scientist and Vice President of Network Technologies at Futurewei, USA. Richard served as the Chairman of the ITU-T FG Network 2030 from 2018 to 2020, and as the Vice Chairman of the Europe ETSI ISG NGP (Next-Generation Protocols) from 2016 to 2019. He has also served as Chair of steering committees and technical program committees of some academic and industrial conferences. Richard is extremely passionate about advancing ICT infrastructure technologies and solving problems in their entirety, thus creating a bigger and long-term impact on the networking industry. During his career, Richard spearheaded network technology innovation and development in Routing and MPLS, Mobile Backhaul, Metro and Core Networks, Data Center, Cloud and Virtualization. Currently he leads a team of scientists and engineers to develop technologies for next-generation network architectures, protocols, algorithms, and systems in the support of forward-looking applications and industry verticals in the context of New IP and Network 2030.

Towards Ubiquitous Intelligence: A Machine Learning Based Wireless Sensing Approach

Xue Steve Liu

Abstract. Ubiquitous computing refers to the paradigm that computing is available everywhere and to every activity. Location awareness is a fundamental requirement for ubiquitous computing. Recent advances in Device-free Passive indoor (DfP) localization release the users from the burden of wearing sensors or carrying devices such as smartphones. Instead of locating devices, DfP technology directly locates human bodies. This promising technology enables many intelligent services, such as home automation and elderly care. Using wireless fingerprints and machine learning, new DfP approaches can achieve both high accuracy and high resolution. In this talk, I will discuss this exciting technology, its associated challenges, and corresponding solutions.

Dr. Steve Liu is a VP R&D, Chief Scientist, and Co-Director of the Samsung AI Center Montréal. He is also a Professor and William Dawson Scholar at McGill University. He received his Ph.D. with multiple honors from the University of Illinois at Urbana-Champaign. He has also worked as the Samuel R. Thompson Chaired Associate Professor in the University of Nebraska-Lincoln, as a visiting scientist at HP Labs in Palo Alto, California, and as the Chief Scientist of Tinder Inc.

Dr. Liu is a Fellow of the IEEE and an ACM Distinguished Member. He has received many awards and recognitions, including the Mitacs Award for Exceptional Leadership – Professor, Outstanding Young Canadian Computer Science Researcher Prize, the Tomlinson Scientist Award, and several IEEE or ACM Best Paper Awards. He serves/has served as an Editor/Associate Editor for several prestigious ACM and IEEE Transactions and has served on the organizing committees of many IEEE or ACM conferences, including INFOCOM, IWQos, CPS-IoT Week, ICCPS, e-Energy, RTSS, RTAS, SenSys, etc.

Communication-Efficient and Distributed ML Over Wireless Networks

Mehdi Bennis

Abstract. Breakthroughs in machine learning (ML) and particularly deep learning have transformed every aspects of our lives from face recognition, medical diagnosis, and natural language processing. This progress has been fueled mainly by the availability of more data and more computing power. However, the current premise in classical ML is based on a single node in a centralized and remote data center with full access to a global dataset and a massive amount of storage and computing. Nevertheless, the advent of a new breed of intelligent devices ranging from drones to self-driving vehicles, makes cloud-based ML inadequate. This talk will present the vision of distributed edge intelligence featuring key enablers, architectures, algorithms and some recent results.

Dr. Mehdi Bennis is an Associate Professor at the Centre for Wireless Communications, University of Oulu, Finland, an Academy of Finland Research Fellow and head of the intelligent connectivity and networks/systems group (ICON). His main research interests are in radio resource management, heterogeneous networks, game theory and machine learning in 5G networks and beyond. He has co-authored one book and published more than 200 research papers in international conferences, journals and book chapters. He has been the recipient of several prestigious awards including the 2015 Fred W. Ellersick Prize from the IEEE Communications Society, the 2016 Best Tutorial Prize from the IEEE Communications Society, the 2017 EURASIP Best paper Award for the Journal of Wireless Communications and Networks, the all-University of Oulu award for research, In 2019 Dr Bennis received the IEEE ComSoc Radio Communications Committee Early Achievement Award.Dr. Bennis is an IEEE Fellow.

Roadmap to Free Space Optics

Mohamed-Slim Alouini, Abderrahmen Trichili, and Boon S. Ooi

Abstract. Optical wireless communication (OWC) has received considerable attention for a variety of applications due to the broad unlicensed spectrum. OWC systems operate over different frequency bands to carry information on optical signals, which are then ultraviolet, visible, and infrared. In this tutorial, we will mainly focus on infrared OWC, commonly referred to as free space optics (FSO). FSO can guarantee a high-bit-rate line of sight transmission over long distances of up to several kilometers. As such, FSO is an attractive solution to the last-meter and last-mile connectivity problems in communication networks, mainly when fiber optics installation is unavailable. Installing FSO systems can significantly help to tackle the "digital divide" by lowering the installation time and cost. FSO is equally expected to be a significant part of the beyond 5G eras.

Throughout the tutorial, we will equally discuss from the experimentalist's point of view the primary channel and hardware challenges for FSO systems, including those employing structured light beams. We will also present the possible mitigation strategies of propagation effects and discuss their practicality. We will further give insights into our experimental work on how to potentially use structured light beams beyond laboratory test benches to establish real-world outdoor FSO communications. Other FSO applications, including satellite-to-satellite and ground–to satellite communication, will be discussed. Finally, we will identify open problems and provide future research directions.

Mohamed-Slim Alouini was born in Tunis, Tunisia. He received the Ph.D. degree in Electrical Engineering from the California Institute of Technology (Caltech) in 1998. He served as a faculty member at the University of Minnesota then in the Texas A&M University at Qatar before joining in 2009 the King Abdullah University of Science and Technology (KAUST) where he is now a Distinguished Professor of Electrical and Computer Engineering. Prof. Alouini is a Fellow of the IEEE and of the OSA. He is currently particularly interested in addressing the technical challenges associated with the uneven distribution, access to, and use of information and communication technologies in far-flung, rural, low-density populations, low-income, and/or hard-to-reach areas.

Abderrahmen Trichili received the Diplôme d'Ingénieur and PhD degree in Information and Communication Technology from l'École Supérieure des Communications de Tunis (SUP'COM, Tunisia) in 2013 and 2017, respectively. During his doctoral study, he received a mobility fellowship from the University of Padova (Italy), where he spent one year at the Information Engineering Department (DEI). In February 2018, he joined KAUST University as a Postdoctoral Fellow at the Computer, Electrical, and Mathematical Sciences & Engineering (CEMSE) division. His current areas of interest include optical wireless communication, space division multiplexing, simultaneous lightwave information and power transfer.

Boon S. Ooi received the B.Eng. and Ph.D. degrees in electronics and electrical engineering from the University of Glasgow, UK. He is currently a Professor of electrical engineering with the King Abdullah University of Science and Technology, Saudi Arabia. His research focuses on the study of semiconductor lasers, LEDs, and photonic integrated circuits for applications in energy efficient lighting and visible-light communication. He has served on the technical program committee or organizing committee of IEDM, OFC, CLEO, ISLC, and IPC. He is currently an Associate Editor for Optics Express, the IEEE Photonics Journal, and SPIE Journal of Nanophotonics. He is a fellow of OSA, SPIE, and IoP, UK. He is an Elected Fellow of the United States National Academy of Inventors.

Contents

Mobile Edge Networking and Fog-Cloud Computing

Artificial Intelligence-Driven Communications

Data Engineering, Cyber Security and Pervasive Services

Ubiquitous Communication
Technologies and Networking

Indoor Localization Techniques Based on UWB Technology

Youssef Ibnatta[⊠], Mohammed Khaldoun, and Mohammed Sadik

Department of Electrical Engineering, NEST Research Group ENSEM, Hassan II University,
Casablanca, Morocco
{youssef.ibnatta,m.khaldoun,m.sadik}@ensem.ac.ma

Abstract. Indoor positioning attracts a lot of attention because people spend their maximum time indoors. As well as the loss of GPS signal power through walls, which requires the integration of other approaches to locate passengers indoors. With the technological growth of telecommunications systems such as 5G and the development of the Internet of Things technique, indoor location is becoming an applicable reality, in order to improve the services offered indoors. In addition, ensuring security in public environments such as airports, train stations, shopping malls, supermarkets…

In this article, we focus on the analysis of the advantages and disadvantages of UWB, and then the exposure and evaluation of different indoor location techniques based on UWB. The document is structured around the following points:

- We expose the advantages and the disadvantages of UWB technique
- We present and evaluate the indoor positioning techniques based on the UWB

Keywords: UWB · RSS · PDR · IMU · OFDM · TOA · TDOA · AOA · PDOA · RFID · Filter de Kalman · RMSE

1 Introduction

The indoor location has attracted a lot of attention because people spend a lot of time indoors, so GPS is unable to locate passengers indoors due to the constraints of GPS signal penetration through walls. For this reason, the use of other indoor positioning tools is an applicable reality. Currently, several positioning techniques are used to infer passenger positions. Among these techniques, RSS (Received Signal Strength) is the most used technique in interior positioning systems, as it uses Wi-Fi or Bluetooth, which facilitates their deployment indoors. Triangulation and Trilateration techniques such as TOA (Time of Arrival), TDOA (Time Difference of Arrival), AOA (Angle of Arrival), ADOA (Angle Difference of Arrival) are also offered. With the technological development of smartphones, the use of IMU (Inertial Measurement Unit) inertial measurements of sensors integrated into mobile devices such as accelerometers, gyroscope, magnetometers, barometers, etc. Are more reliable in the case of CROWDSOURCING/CROWDSENSING.

© Springer Nature Switzerland AG 2021
H. Elbiaze et al. (Eds.): UNet 2021, LNCS 12845, pp. 3–15, 2021.
https://doi.org/10.1007/978-3-030-86356-2_1

Appel has built passive boxes called iBeacons which are based on low-energy Bluetooth (BLE) capable of communicating with the outside environment. RFID radio wave identification can also be used to identify the positions of passengers inside a building by a simple TAG/READER communication. The majority of approaches use radio waves, such as Wi-fi, Bluetooth, RFID, RADAR, ZigBee, UWB… Despite the diversity of localization techniques in the literature, these systems remain limited under specific conditions of use, due to the positioning constraints that show their positioning qualities. For example, the RSS method suffers against the calibration constraints of the database, heterogeneity of devices, change of environment… Otherwise, techniques based on inertial measurements are still confronted with problems of measurement instability, heterogeneity of mobile devices… The precision of techniques based on triangulation and trilateration decreases because of the multiple path constraints, undetected direct path, and signal interference. To solve these problems, researchers have proposed to integrate some mathematical tools into their systems. These tools are divided into two categories, one probabilistic and the other deterministic, for probabilistic approaches, the Kalman filter is used to reduce measurement instability and noise errors, Bayesian filtering, Map (Maximum a posteriori), maximum likelihood, Gaussian filter, Viterbi algorithm, least-square algorithm, for deterministic methods such as Dijkstra algorithm, particle filter, nearest neighborhood algorithm KNN etc. The UWB very short pulse radio modulation technique has attracted the attention of researchers because this tool can improve the quality of positioning systems.

Thanks to certain positive properties, for example, low energy consumption, low cost, simple to deploy, low communication time (less than nanoseconds), centimetric precision. In this article, we focus on the analysis of the advantages and disadvantages of UWB, and then the exposure and evaluation of different indoor location techniques based on UWB. Section 2 presents the advantages and disadvantages of UWB, Sect. 3 presents the exposure and evaluation of the different indoor locating techniques based on UWB, Sect. 4 presents the results and discussion, for the rest Sect. 5 presents the future work, Sect. 6 presents the conclusion.

2 Advantages and Disadvantages of UWB Technique

Ultra-wideband radio communication: this is a technology developed to transfer large amounts of data wirelessly over short distances, over a very wide frequency spectrum, in a short period of time. UWB technology has the capacity to handle the very wide band required to carry multiple audio and video streams. The UWB reel is ideally suited for data transmission between consumer electronics, PC peripherals and short-range mobile devices at very high speeds while consuming little power. This technology operates at a level that allows most systems to interpret noise and therefore does not cause interference with other radios such as mobile phones.

In this framework we quote some advantages of UWB:

- Extremely difficult to intercept: wideband pulsed radar spreads the signal to allows more users access to a limited amount of scarce frequency spectrum.

- Multipath Immunity: A low path loss and low energy density minimizes interference to other services, UWB is very tolerant of interference enabling operation within buildings urban areas.
- Precision: The continuous localization of the position in real-time with up to one-centimeter resolution gives good results.
- Low cost: Requires minimal components resulting in smaller size and weight.
- Low power: Typical consumption is in microwatt.

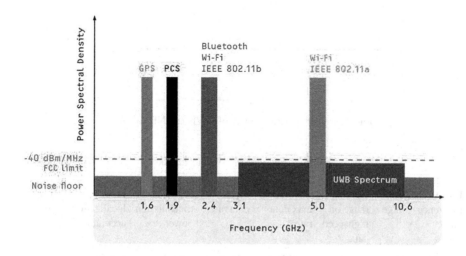

Fig. 1. UWB frequency spectrum

Figure 1 shows the UWB frequency spectrum with a width between 3.1 and 10.6 GHz. In general, [15] UWB technology is divided into two parts: narrowband (impulse radio) and multiband using some type of modulation such as OFDM (Orthogonal frequency-division multiplication). Figure 2 shows the power spectral density of the wideband and narrowband, where W_{NB} is the width of the N.B and W_{UWB} is the width of the wideband.

Despite of large advantage of UWB but, this technique stays in front of the constraints of shadow effect caused by multiple problems, amplitude variation, timing variation and shoulders effect. Challenges in developing such a system include UWB pulse generation, [8] pulse dispersion due to antennas, modeling complex propagation channels with severe multipath effects, the need for extremely high sampling rates for digital processing, synchronization between transmitter and receiver clocks, clock jitter, local oscillator (LO) phase noise, frequency offset between transmitters and receivers, and antenna phase center variation. The UWB system is sensitive to channel fading and will generate a non-negligible number. of outliers under NLOS conditions (Table 1).

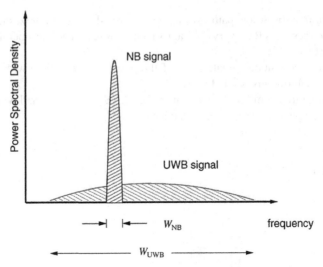

Fig. 2. Power spectral density of UWB and NB signals

Table 1. Features of UWB technique

Usable frequency range	Max range	Optimal range of highspeed data	Theoretical max data rate	Practical data rate	Max transmission power	Indoor localization accuracy	Duty cycle
3.1–10.6 GHz	200 m	<10 m	480 Mbit/s	27 Mbit/s	<1 mW	Centimetric	Low (max on-time 5 ms)

3   Exposure and Evaluation of the Different Indoor Locating Techniques Based on UWB

With the availability of Ultra-Wide-Band in smartphones, as well as the positive influence of UWB indoor positioning systems. The realization of a high-quality indoor positioning system becomes less complex. [11] An ultra-wideband based time- delay (TOA) indoor human localization scheme has proposed to provide indoor human localization with time-delay measurements. The author proposed an extended finite impulse response (EFIR) estimated employing the time delay localization model in purpose to solve the problem of EKF (Extended Kalman Filter). Which EFIR does not require the noise statistics. The experimental results have shown that the EFIR estimation is more robust than the extended Kalman filter. The average error of UWB only is between 0,19 m and 0,72 m, EKF based method error is between 0,21 m and 0,58 m. EFIR his accuracy is higher than EKF his average error is between 0,19 m and 0,54 m.

In [1] author has presented the results of the measurement and modeling of Ultra-Wide-Band time of arrival (TOA) based ranging in different indoor multipath environments. The author provided the characterization of the spatial behavior of ranging, where the author focused on the statistics on the spatial of the ranging error in the presence and absence of the direct path (DP) and evaluated the path loss behavior in the former case, which is important for indoor localization coverage characterization. The approach used two different bandwidths 500 MHz and 3 GHz with a nominal frequency of 4,5 GHz. The author used three different ranging scenarios ITI (Indoor to Indoor), OTI (Outdoor to Indoor) and RTI (Roof to Indoor). The method showed that the ranging coverage is inversely related to the bandwidth of the system and the harshness of the ranging scenario and environment. In addition, the statistics of the measured the ranging error showed that they follow normal and lognormal distributions in the presence and absence of DP. [5] A short-range UWB indoor localization system with millimeter-range accuracy has many promising applications. The author has proposed a system architecture similar to available commercial systems, sub-sampling the incoming pulse train and detecting the main LOS peak. The author has addressed the main challenges being faced in building this system, including sampling limitations, multipath interference, phase center error, and timing errors due to clock jitter, temperature effects, etc.

Subsampling techniques, sophisticated receiver- side leading edge detection increased number of base stations, phase-center calibration, and high fidelity PRF (pulse repetition frequency) crystals combined with a TDOA approach have been proposed as solutions to these problems, while the experimental results show the feasibility of achieving millimeter-range accuracy with a UWB indoor positioning system is highly reflective in indoor environments. The sub-sampling mixer is a usable option for sampling the incoming pulse train with a high sample rate. The effects of clock jitter can be mitigated by using PRF clocks with low phase noise and temperature compensation, although the total effect of PRF clock jitter on the sub-sampling process can cause substantial errors on the order of 1 mm. Time scaling originating from PRF clock stability has been shown through simulation to not impact final system accuracy by using a modified version of the TDOA algorithm.

The designed peak subtraction algorithm is robust to multipath interference. System performance in dense indoor environments can be further increased by a greater some base stations and optimal base station placement. The mean error in the unsynchronized 1-D experiment is 3,07 mm.

In [2] the experimental investigations and analysis of Ultra-Wide-Band localization of body-worn antennas in an indoor environment has proposed. Simple and effective techniques for identifying and mitigating NLOS situations have been applied and analyzed and the UWB localization scheme for the human body, tracking has been proposed using TOA technique, various features such as RMS delay spread, Kurtosis and signal amplitude has been used to classify the channel type between each antenna location and base station. GDOP (Geometric Dilution of Precision) analysis has been performed for validating the compact base-station configuration used with results showing GDOP values in the range of 1 to 2 which are considered as high accuracy values. Numerical analysis has been carried out on the effect of body-worn antenna localization. It has been observed that the radiation patterns are more directive in the presence of the human body and the area of the patterns decreases when the antenna is placed on the thick muscular region (torso) in comparison to the upper limbs. Hence the localization accuracy will be higher for the limbs in comparison to the torso. High accuracy 3D localization results in the range of 1 to 2 cm are obtained with the antennas placed on the limbs and 1 to 3 cm in the torso region as there will be more interference in the signal propagation by the torso. Best results are obtained when the antenna is placed on the elbow (0,5 to 1,5 cm). [9] UWB ranging measurements is influenced by the human body shadowing effect with biased ranging error up to 1,6 m and the error has a close relationship with RHA between Tag and ANC.

A UWB ranging error model addressing the problem has proposed based on measurement data obtained from three measurement campaigns covering both the typical environment and outdoor open space. The model is further integrated into a particle filter pedestrian tracking algorithm with gyroscope information fusion. The proposed algorithm is then evaluated in two indoor walking tracks which reduce mean positioning error up to 41,94% and demonstrate the robust and accurate tracking performance compared to existing solutions. It is noted that human body obstruction is the main cause for NLOS between TAG and Anchors in the tracking experiment setup. In scenarios with both the human body and environment obstruction such as walls, a more complex measurement model may be required. The mean error for T1 and T2 12,48 cm and 16,42 cm respectively. [6] The author has proposed an analytical approach to optimized ANs placement for efficient TDOA UWB-based localization of a TN moving along a corridor in large indoor scenarios. The approach imposed the realistic design constraints that the ANs are equally spaced and placed at the same height. Assuming that the TN moves along a straight line in the middle of the corridor, the author derived a closed-form expression for the optimal distance between consecutive ANs that minimizes the average MSE (Mean Square Error) of the TN position estimates the validity of the closed-form expression has been confirmed by simulations, which also show that the proposed placement strategy is also effective even when the TN follows other paths different from the linear one in the middle of the corridor.

A [13] novel architecture for UWB positioning systems has presented, which combines the signal-channel carrier-based UWB system and traditional energy detection (ED) based UWB positioning system. The UWB localization system is equipped with the low phase-noise carrier at both the transmitter and receiver and the advanced subsampling of the incoming pulse train. A proper modulation factor is intentionally chosen between the transmitter and receiver carrier and is combined with an ED step to eliminate the requirement of carrier synchronization. The approach has addressed step by step the main challenges the I/Q mismatch jitter errors due to phase noise in the carrier offsets, the Shoulder effect in static and dynamic scenarios, etc. Both simulation and measurement results show the robustness of the proposed system architecture with reduced timing jitter error and improved system dynamic range. By comparing two 1-D experiments, the ranging error has been improved significantly with the reduced timing jitter and Shoulder effect through the application of a low phase noise carrier-based UWB architecture together with advanced sub-sampling and ED. To further validate the theories, extensive 3-D static and dynamic experiments have been performed, including a tag moving randomly in a 3-D space and a tag attached to a robot arm with preplanned motion, where constant millimeter range accuracy in both static and dynamic scenarios has been demonstrated. The RMSE for Tag-free random motion is 6,37 mm, for robot dynamic tracking is 5,24 mm. A [8] joint TOA and AOA estimator has proposed for accurate indoor UWB localization applications. The device employs an array of antennas, each feeding a demodulator consisting of a square and low-pass filter. The signal samples from the filter outputs are processed to produce TOA and AOA estimates. Simulation has been run, assuming transmitted pulses with a bandwidth of either 0,5 GHz (type-2 pulses) or 1,5 GHz (type-1 pulses), requiring sampling rates of 1 GHz and 3 GHz, respectively. Ranging accuracies of about 20cm and angular accuracies of about 0,8° are achieved at an SNR of practical interest with type-1 pulses and two antennas at a distance of 50cm. Some degradations are incurred with type 2-pulses. [3] An improved PDR-UWB integrated system based on the VNV Kalman filter algorithm was proven to be able to accurately provide pedestrian locations in indoor environments. The first contribution refers to initial sensors is a complete gait detection based on the dual-frequency Butterworth filter and the multi-feature linear combination model involving the step frequency, the amplitude of acceleration. The second contribution refers to UWB is that they use the positioning information of a UWB system to estimate parameters of the linear combination model in real-time based on the L-nearest neighbor gradient descent method. The author used the drift-free heading direction of UWB to calibrate the heading angle of PDR processed by the periodic heading calculation function. In the improved PDR-UWB integrated structure, UWB system plays a crucial role in term of system position accuracy, the NLOS assessment function could accurately reflect the attenuation of received signals, and ensure the accuracy of systems under short-term NLOS conditions.

The improved system fusion strategy that dynamically adjusts the noise variance according to the probability of signal, attenuation can provide a robust and accurate positioning trajectory when the UWB signal is blocked in a short period of time by obstacles for indoor navigation applications. The average error is 0,326 m.

[10] The received signal strength (RSS) as a function of the distance, a localization simulator for an RSSI-based fingerprint positioning technique has carried out with conventional wireless USB sticks using OFDM HDR (High Data Rate) UWB radio technology. The results have been compared to simulation results using TOA-based positioning. With a measured log-normal fading process with a standard deviation of 0,53 dB the RSSI-based positioning provided that the synchronization in the accuracy of the TOA process is larger than 1ns. The weakness of the RSSI-based approach is the decreasing ranging accuracy with increasing distances between transmitter and receiver. The applied least square (LS) trilateration seems therefore not to be the best localization approach and can be further improved by evaluating the estimated distances to the anchor node with respect to their different reliabilities which depend on the RSSI. However, the main advantage of the RSSI-based positioning systems can easily be implemented in the software when using conventional low-budget UWB hardware. The mean estimation error depends on the number of anchor nodes, in all bases it remains below 0,2 m. In [4] author has analyzed a localization in MB OFDM UWB systems based on the TDOA method. The author proposed a new space-temporal signal model in IEEE 802.15.3a channel in which cluster delays in the channels between the transmitter and each sensor

in the sensor array are correlated due to the scattering on the scatters with a known position. The approach showed that this correlation decreases localization accuracy significantly. If the position estimates with significant error, MB OFDM UWB systems are suitable for indoor localization based on TDOA.

[14] PDOA assisted UWB positioning method (PDOA-UWB) for location-based user service in the smart home has proposed. The author has calculated the phase difference of arrival from PDOA chip integrated in the UWB BSs to obtain a coarse location of the elderly. This is used to distinguish which nearby BSs are in a LOS environment and those in an NLOS environment combined with the UWB positioning method. The approach proposed a PDOA assisted UWB (PDOA-UWB) positioning method to improve the positioning accuracy of the elderly. The Fig. 3 shows the workflow of PDOA-UWB method.

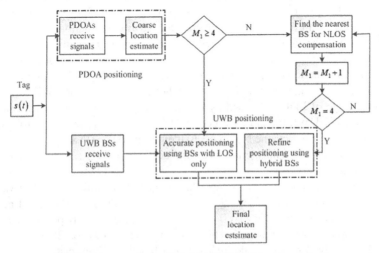

Fig. 3. The workflow of PDOA-UWB positioning method

Compared with some existing methods, this method can achieve higher accuracy with less NLOS compensation, and is easier to be implemented in complex practical indoor environments. The proposed PDOA-UWB method can efficiently select the minimal and optimal BSs for positioning, thus avoiding the blind compensation and the calculation burden of traditional UWB positioning methods. The proposed method is mainly designed for fast and robust, practical engineering applications, which reduce the computational burden of the convex-based methods greatly without remarkable performance loss the proposed positioning scheme can not only solve the problem of elderly care in smart homes, it also has better application. The probability of RMSE is less than 0,45m for 95,38%.

[7] the author has presented an experimental evaluation of three commercially available UWB positioning systems Ubisense, Decawave, and BeSpoon. The evaluation has been done in an NLOS environment is similar to an industrial warehouse with a diverse

equipment, which perturbates UWB radio propagation. Under these conditions, the performance of the Decawave system is slightly better than the BeSpoon System and significantly more reliable, in terms of accuracy and outlier content, then the Ubisense system. The conclusion that Decawave is more accurate than BeSpoon system these results are somehow logical since Decawave is using a more advanced antenna system than the BeSpoon equipment. The performance results for the Ubisense equipment are lower than Decawave and BeSpoon, and this occurs in case of only using TDOA data and also when using the integrated localization solutions that fuse TDOA and AOA. With Ubisense (TDOA and AOA) the AOA is more information and accurate for correct positioning, and contains fewer outliers, than TDOA data. Decawave is based on TOF (Time of Flight), it's fair to mention that Ubisense system dates from 2009 and BeSpoon from 2015, while Decawave is from 2016. The RMS is 0,59 m for Decawave, 0,86m for BeSpoon, 2,266 m for Ubisense, and 1,82m for Ubisense (AOA).

In [12] WUB-IP is a high precision positioning scheme using a UWB ultra-wideband telemetry system, recently solutions for accurate positioning in NLOS multipath and non-line-of-sight conditions have attracted a lot of attention, on the other hand, it is expected that WDMA Waveform Division Multiple Access technologies for multi-user UWB positioning applications will be indispensable soon, in this respect, a positioning scheme based on WDMA-UWB has studied. The author has used the TOA method to infer user positions using a communication (BS-User) a base station and user. The author has developed an approach based on information entropy to detect the primary paths, while entropy is used to measure the randomness of received signals. Simulation results show that the position error in channels CM1 to CM4 are 3,44 m, 7,42 m, 4,21 m and 5,04 m.

4   Results and Discussion

In this section, we evaluate the different techniques of indoor positioning systems based on the UWB on certain criteria such as Precision, Energy consumption, Cost, Ease to deploy, Stability, Response time, Adaptation to changes in the environment, and heterogeneity of devices, and complexities. Table 2 presents the evaluation of different approaches to indoor location-based on UWB. In this table, some criteria remain unchangeable such as energy consumption, cost, simplicity of deployment, response time. Because these depend on the UWB communication techniques serve to correct the errors produced by indoor positioning systems. The rest of the changeable criteria in the table are highly dependent on the UWB localization tools and type of implementation. It can also be said that the complexity criterion relates to all evaluation criteria. In general, the choice of a good indoor positioning system depends on the localization objective, which determines the nature of the criteria and thus the achievement of a high-quality system.

Table 2. Evaluation of the different techniques of indoor positioning systems based on the UWB

Approach title	Accuracy	Energy consumption	Cost	Simple to deploy	Stable	Response time	Adapting to a changing environment and device heterogeneity	Complexities
UWB-Based Indoor Human localization [11]	The error is between 0,19 m to 0,58 m	Low	Low	Yes	No	Low	No/–	Medium
Measurement and Modeling of UWB TOA based Ranging [1]	The error is less than 0,6m	Low	Low	Yes	No	Low	No/–	Low
Investigation of High-Accuracy Indoor 3Dpositioning [5]	The error in 1-D is 3,07 mm, in 3-D mean error is 5,77 mm	Low	Low	Yes	Yes	Low	Yes/–	Low
Experimental investigation of 3-D Human Body Localization [2]	The error is between 1 to3 cm	Low	Low	Yes	No	Low	– /–	Medium
Human body shadowing effect on UWB-based [9]	The mean error for T1 and T2 are 12,48 cm and 16,42 cm respectively	Low	Low	Yes	No	Medium	No/No	Medium

(*continued*)

Table 2. (*continued*)

Approach title	Accuracy	Energy consumption	Cost	Simple to deploy	Stable	Response time	Adapting to a changing environment and device heterogeneity	Complexities
UWB-based localization in large indoor scenarios [6]	–	Low	Low	Yes	No	Low	No/–	Medium
Real-Time Non-coherent UWB positioning [13]	3-D RMSE is 6,37 mm	Low	Low	Yes	Yes	Low	No/–	Low
Joint TOA and AOA [8]	1-pulse 10 cm, 2-pulses 35 cm	Low	Low	Yes	Yes	Low	No/–	Low
An improved PDR-UWB Integrated system [3]	The average error is 0,326 m	Low	Low	Yes	No	Low	– /No	Low
Positioning in Multiband OFDM-UWB utilizing RSS [10]	The error is less than 0,2 m	Low	Low	Yes	Yes	Low	No/–	Low
Localization of users in multiuser MBOFDM-UWB [4]	The SNR is 30 dB	Low	Low	Yes	–	Low	No/–	Medium
Toward Elderly [14]	The RMSE is 0,4 5m in 95,38%	Low	Low	Yes	–	Low	No/–	Low

5 Future Works

We have three types of UWB implementations: Impulse Radio, Ds-UWB (Direct sequence), and Mc-OFDM (Multiband). In our future perspective, we will elaborate on a fingerprint RSS-based localization system, we will improve the different handling criteria (accuracy, stability, simplicity of deployment, response time, cost...) to have a high-performance system, for this, we will integrate the MB-OFDM-UWB technique into the system.

6 Conclusion

In this article, we have focused on different positioning tools such as PDR, RSS, TOA, AOA, TDOA, PDOA based on UWB. First, we have analyzed the characteristics of UWB, then their advantages and disadvantages. In the second part, we have outlined some of the UWB-based localization techniques presented in the literature. In the third part, we have examined these approaches based on the criteria such as accuracy, power consumption, cost, simplicity of deployment, stability... As a result, the UWB method succeeded in reducing errors for the majority of the systems studied, with low power consumption, simplicity of deployment, low cost, low response time, and low complexity. Despite the quality of UWB, stills limited under precise conditions which determine its quality.

References

1. Alsindi, N.A., Alavi, B., Pahlavan, K.: Measurement and modeling of ultrawideband toa-based ranging in indoor multipath environments. IEEE Trans. Veh. Technol. **58**(3), 1046–1058 (2008)
2. Bharadwaj, R., Parini, C., Alomainy, A.: Experimental investigation of 3-d human body localization using wearable ultra-wideband antennas. IEEE Trans. Antennas Propag. **63**(11), 5035–5044 (2015)
3. Guo, S., Zhang, Y., Gui, X., Han, L.: An improved PDR/UWB integrated system for indoor navigation applications. IEEE Sens. J. **20**, 8046–8061 (2020)
4. Gvozdenovic, N., Eric, M.: Localization of users in multiuser mb OFDM UWB systems based on TDOA principle. In: 2011 19thTelecommunications Forum (TELFOR) Proceedings of Papers, pp. 326–329. IEEE (2011)
5. Mahfouz, M.R., Zhang, C., Merkl, B.C., Kuhn, M.J., Fathy, A.E.: Investigation of high-accuracy indoor 3-d positioning using UWB technology. IEEE Trans. Microw. Theory Tech. **56**(6), 1316–1330 (2008)
6. Monica, S., Ferrari, G.: UWB-based localization in large indoor scenarios: optimized placement of anchor nodes. IEEE Trans. Aerosp. Electron. Syst. **51**(2), 987–999 (2015)
7. Ruiz, A.R.J., Granja, F.S.: Comparing Ubisense, BeSpoon, and DecaWave UWB location systems: indoor performance analysis. IEEE Trans. Instrum. Meas. **66**(8), 2106–2117 (2017)
8. Taponecco, L., D'Amico, A.A., Mengali, U.: Joint TOA and AOA estimation for UWB localization applications. IEEE Trans. Wireless Commun. **10**(7), 2207–2217 (2011)
9. Tian, Q., Kevin, I., Wang, K., Salcic, Z.: Human body shadowing effect on UWB-based ranging system for pedestrian tracking. IEEE Trans. Instrum. Meas. **68**(10), 4028–4037 (2018)

10. Waadt, A., et al.: Positioning in multiband OFDM UWB utilizing received signal strength. In: 2010 7th Workshop on Positioning, Navigation and Communication, pp. 308–312. IEEE (2010)
11. Xu, Y., Shmaliy, Y.S., Li, Y., Chen, X.: UWB-based indoor human localization with time-delayed data using EFIR filtering. IEEE Access **5**, 16676–16683 (2017)
12. Yin, Z., Jiang, X., Yang, Z., Zhao, N., Chen, Y.: WUB-IP: A high precision UWB positioning scheme for indoor multiuser applications. IEEE Syst. J. **13**(1), 279–288 (2017)
13. Zhang, C., Kuhn, M.J., Merkl, B.C., Fathy, A.E., Mahfouz, M.R.: Real-time noncoherent UWB positioning radar with millimeter range accuracy: theory and experiment. IEEE Trans. Microw. Theory Tech. **58**(1), 9–20 (2009)
14. Zhang, Y., Duan, L.: Toward elderly care: a phase-difference-of arrival assisted ultra-wideband positioning method in smart home. IEEE Access **8**, 139387–139395 (2020)
15. Chiani, M., Giorgetti, A.: Coexistence between UWB and narrow-band wireless communication systems. Proc. IEEE **97**(2), 231–254 (2009)

Performance Analysis of RPL Protocol for Advanced Metering Infrastructure (AMI): Objective Functions Impact on Data and Control Traffic

Aisha Bouani[1(✉)], Driss Benhaddou[2], Yann Ben Maissa[1], Ahmed Tamtaoui[1], and Ahmed Hammouch[3]

[1] STRS Laboratory, National Institute of Posts and Telecommunications - INPT Rabat Morocco, Rabat, Morocco
{bouani.aisha,benmaissa,tamtaoui}@inpt.ac.ma
[2] Department of Engineering Technology, University of Houston, Houston, TX 77204, USA
dbenhadd@central.uh.edu
[3] Laboratory in Electrical Engineering (LRGE) ENSET Rabat, B.P 6207 Rabat, Morocco

Abstract. Smart grid (SG) has emerged to address most of the shortcomings of the existing electrical grid by integrating information and communication technologies to improve its performance in terms of reliability, efficiency, and security. The smart grid enables a two-way flow of electricity and data using digital communication technology. Advanced Metering Infrastructure (AMI) is a fundamental component of smart grid that provides a two-way communication flow between the power utilities and meters at the customer side. In recent years, there has been a great deal of interest in the design of an efficient routing protocol to meet the requirements of AMI networks. The IPv6 routing protocol for low power and lossy networks (RPL) has been recently proposed and standardized by the IETF ROLL working group to meet the requirements of Low power and Lossy Networks (LLNs) involved in different application domains. In RPL, routes are constructed based on an Objective Function (OF) and a variety of metrics and constraints. Given the importance of RPL protocol in AMI networks, this paper provides a comprehensive study of the performance analysis of the two main objective functions commonly used in RPL (OF0 and MRHOF) in the context of AMI networks.

Keywords: RPL Routing Protocol · Smart Grid (SG) · Advanced Metering Infrastructure (AMI) · Low Power and Lossy Networks (LLNs) · Objective Function (OF) · OF0 · MRHOF · Contiki-OS · Cooja

© Springer Nature Switzerland AG 2021
H. Elbiaze et al. (Eds.): UNet 2021, LNCS 12845, pp. 16–30, 2021.
https://doi.org/10.1007/978-3-030-86356-2_2

1   Introduction

Smart Grid (SG) has been a topic of much interest recently. The modern smart grid aims to address most of the limitations of the existing electrical grid by integrating information and communication technologies to improve its performance. Smart Grid implementation requires a variety of communication networks that allow SG sub-systems, such as the advanced metering infrastructure, to incorporate a number of devices and technologies to enable improvement in the electric power system in terms of reliability, efficiency, security and environment.

Advanced Metering Infrastructure (AMI) [7] is the most fundamental and critical part of SG, allowing two-way communication between smart meters and utility companies. It is designed to collect, measure, gather and analyze energy consumption and energy use patterns. The AMI is expected to be implemented on networks with a dense number of smart meters that connect to several data collectors. Therefore, the AMI network should provide suitable and efficient routing functionalities that ensure a reliable and efficient data transmission. In AMI networks, smart meters are resource-limited embedded devices with restricted processing power and storage capacity, and the links connecting these devices are generally characterized by low bandwidth, high packet loss rates and instability. These types of networks are typically called Low power and Lossy Networks (LLNs).

Routing in LLNs represent one of the critical challenges that requires further investigation. The routing protocol is basically responsible for forwarding the traffic and making routing decisions. If the routing decisions are not made efficiently, more retransmissions will occur across the network, which would consume more energy and cause additional delay on the network, and would also waste the limited available bandwidth in the network. Accordingly, an extensive performance analysis is required for the routing protocols used by any low power and lossy network.

Recently, many research have been devoted to the design and development of a reliable and low-latency routing solution for LLNs networks; however, the most preferred solution is the IPv6 Routing Protocol for LLN (RPL) [3], which was standardized on March 2012 by the Internet Engineering Task Force (IETF). RPL is a flexible routing protocol designed to satisfy the needs of a vast range of LLN application domains, including building automation, home automation, and Urban Low-Power and Lossy Networks (U-LLNs) such as AMI networks [7]. The key element that ensures the flexibility of RPL is the Objective Function (OF). The OF is used by RPL to specify how routing metrics and constraints should be applied to meet specific objectives.

Up to now, the Routing Over Low power and Lossy networks (ROLL) working group has specified two standard Objective Functions namely Objective Function Zero (OF0) [5] and Minimum Rank with Hysteresis Objective Function (MRHOF) [6] which are both considered suitable for AMI deployments [7].

In view of the importance of RPL applications, RPL's performances have been extensively studied in the context of Wireless Sensor Networks (WSN). However, few results are available about the ability of RPL to address the requirements of AMI networks. The lack of published papers focusing on how RPL's OFs affect the primary requirements of AMI infrastructures motivates authors to conduct this study. The purpose of this paper is to investigate the performance of RPL in an AMI network. More accurately, we aim at investigating the efficiency of the existing OFs in order to identify their shortcomings and to resolve them in the future OF designs.

The reminder of this paper is organized as follows: Section 2 summarizes existing studies evaluating the performance of RPL's objective functions. Section 3 presents a detailed overview of RPL protocol and its main objective functions. Section 4 describes a detailed implementation of RPL adapted for AMI networks and discusses the simulation results. Finally, Sect. 5 summarizes the results of this work and draws conclusions.

2   Related Work

In recent years, several research studies have been conducted to investigate the performance of RPL in different environments.

Parnian et al. [9], focused on AMI networks in smart grid communication. Contiki COOJA simulator is used to evaluate the two OFs in AMI network. The simulated AMI network is organized of one gateway and 1000 smart meters randomly dispersed in 300 * 300 m^2 area communicating with IEEE 802.15.4 radio. Smart meters send packets with 200 byte payload every 30 s toward the root. The scenario is simulated for 1300 s (20 min). Results show the superiority of the Hop Count Objective Function in terms of packet delivery ratio and average end-to-end delay. One of the limitations of this study is that it evaluates the two OFs in terms of only two metrics that are PDR and Latency.

Another work [10] was done to evaluate the performance of MRHOF and OF0 in the context of IoT. In this paper, authors used mobile-random and static-grid topologies with 25, 49, and 81 of which one is a sink node. Each topology was evaluated with three transmission ranges of 11, 20, and 50 m. The simulation performed in this paper conclude that: –OF0 is better than MRHOF in terms of convergence time and energy consumption in the static grid topology, Listen Duty Cycle, and Transmit Duty Cycle. –There is not much difference between the two objective functions under Mobile-Random topology, only that OF0 outperforms MRHOF in terms of power consumption.

Pradeska et al. [11], focused on the performance analysis of the two objective functions of RPL, namely MRHOF and OF0. Based on simulations, authors found that MRHOF performs better than OF0 in terms of network reliability, while OF0 provides faster network convergence and consumes less energy than the MRHOF.

The work in [12] examines the impact of the OF selection on the packet delivery ratio (PDR) for different network topologies. The evaluation has been preformed based on Packet Reception Ratio (RX) and topology and has been compared for both OF0 and MRHOF. The results of this study have revealed that MRHOF can provide better performance that OF0 could not provide.

Table 1. Summary of the related work

Reference	RPL Environment	Network Scale	Network Topology	Performance metrics	Findings
[9]	AMI	1000	Random Topology	- Average End-to-End Delay - PDR	- OF0 outperforms MRHOF in case of Average E-to-E Delay and PDR
[10]	IoT	25, 49, 81	Fixed Grid/Mobile Random Topology	- Convergence Time - Network Churn - Power Consumption	- OF0 is better than MRHOF with respect to convergence time and power consumption in the Static-Grid Topology
[11]	6LowPAN	25, 49, 81	Grid/Random	- Latency - PDR - Power Consumption - ETX / - HC - Convergence time	- OF0 outperforms MRHOF in terms of Convergence time, PC, and ETX - MRHOF is better in terms of Latency
[12]	WSN	20, 30, 40, 45	Grid/Random	- PDR - Power Consumption	- OF0 is better than MRHOF in terms of PDR - MRHOF is better than OF0 in terms of power consumption
[14]	6LowPAN	40, 80, 100, 200	Random Topology	- PDR - Control Overhead - Power Consumption - ETX	- MRHOF outperforms OF0 for all radio models and scaled networks
[13]	IoT	5, 50, 75	Random Topology	- PC - PDR - E-to-E-delay - Control traffic	- OF0 provides better performance in terms of PC, Latency, Control Traffic overhead and PDR as compared with MRHOF
Our Evaluation	AMI	20, 40, 60, 80, 100	Random Topology	- Latency - Packet Loss Ratio - Power Consumption - ETX - Hop Count - Control traffic overhead	- OF0 outperforms MRHOF with ENERGY metric in terms of latency, PC, Packet Loss Ratio, HC and ETX. - MRHOF based ETX provides almost the same performance as OF0 when the network consists of less than 80 but when the network exceeds 80 nodes, OF0 outperforms ETX. - MRHOF provides higher value of control overhead in the dense network.

The primary limitation of this analysis is that it involves a small number of metric studied under a small number of nodes.

The authors in [14] propose an evaluation of the performance of RPL based on the objective function. They compared OF0 and MRHOF in order to determine which one gives better performance of RPL. Based on the simulation results, it is concluded that the performance of the objective function based on ETX metric (MRHOF) is better as compared to the OF0 for all radio models and scaled networks. The major limitation of this study is the simulation time, each scenario is performed for only 10 min.

As summarized above, most of the previous studies usually involves a small number of metrics studied under a limited number of scenarios. In this study, we compare the two objective functions OF0 and MRHOF in terms of Latency, Power Consumption (PC), Packet Loss Ratio (PLR), Hop count (HC), Expected Transmission Count (ETX) and Control traffic overhead, and we investigate a significant number of scenarios. MRHOF is used as a two-metric OF to make routing decisions based on ETX as a link metric or energy as a node metric. Table 1 shows a comparison of our evaluation with other related studies.

3 RPL Overview

RPL is an IPv6 based distance-vector routing protocol specified in the standards document RFC 6550. RPL organizes the nodes in a topology as Directed Acyclic Graph (DAG). Each DAG created in RPL has a root. The DAG root is usually the gateway in the AMI network. The DAG is divided into one or more Destination Oriented DAGs (DODAGs), one DODAG per root. Each node in a DAG has a rank, which determines the position of node in relation to a DODAG root. A network may be composed of one or multiple DODAGs, which form together an RPL instance. A node can join one single DODAG, but it can participate in multiple instances to simultaneously carry different types of traffic. An RPL instance is associated with an objective function.

In order to define and maintain the topology RPL uses four main identifiers:

- **RPLInstanceID:** Which identifies an RPL instance. An RPL instance is composed of one or more Destination Oriented DAGs (DODAGs). All DODAGs in the same RPL Instance use the same OF.
- **DODAGID:** Which identifies one DODAG within an RPL instance. The combination of DODAGID and RPLInstanceID uniquely identifies one DODAG in the network.
- **DODAGVersionNumber:** A DODAG is sometimes reconstruct from the DODAG root. DODAGVersionNumber is incremented each time DODAG is rebuilt.
- **Rank:** identifies the position of a node in relation to the DODAG root.

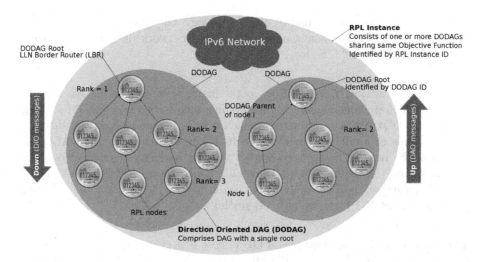

Fig. 1. Architecture of RPL Routing Protocol

RPL uses four ICMPv6-type control messages for creating and maintaining RPL topology and routing table:

- **DIO (DODAG Information Object)**: which contains information that enables a node to find an RPL instance, determine its configuration parameters, select a DODAG parent set and maintain the DODAG.
- **DIS (DODAG Information Solicitation)**: Which a node sends to its neighbors to solicit DIO.
- **DAO (Destination Advertisement Object)**: which is used by a node to spread destination information upward along the DODAG.
- **DAO-ACK (Destination Advertisement Object Acknowledgement)**: that is sent by a DAO recipient in response to a DAO message.

In order to construct and maintain the topology, RPL nodes periodically exchange routing information: in the down direction, through DIO messages; and, in the up direction, through DAO messages. DAO messages are used to populate the routing tables of ancestor nodes in the DAG, in support of point-to-point and point-to-multipoint traffic. Routes are reconstruct based on an Objective Function and a set of metrics and constraints. Figure 1 presents the architecture of the RPL routing protocol.

3.1   RPL Objective Function

OF is the fundamental concept that ensures the flexibility of RPL. OF defines how different metrics should be combined and translated into a rank, so that the protocol be able to use the rank to construct efficient routes. RPL OF determines, which parent will each node select, therefore it is directly responsible for the route establishment process and resultant topology. OF allows adapting RPL to a broad range of deployments, applications, and network designs. At present, there are two standard OFs for RPL:

Objective Function Zero (OF0): is the first objective function released by IETF in [5]. Hop count is used as the default routing metric in this OF. When using OF0, DODAG is constructed in such a way that nodes find the shortest path in terms of number of hops to reach the root. During the DODAG construction, the rank of nodes is computed and the parents are selected by each node based on the minimum rank value. The rank of a node R(N) is calculated by adding a strictly positive scalar value (rank_increase) to the rank of a selected preferred parent R(P) according to Algorithm 1 [5].

The Minimum Rank Hysteresis Objective Function: is another standard OF released by IEFT in [6]. MRHOF relies on hysteresis to select the path with the smallest path cost. It uses the metric that is specified in the DIO Metric Container. MRHOF is based on dynamic link metrics [4] like Expected transmission count (ETX) and Energy are the criteria for selecting the shortest path. Using MRHOF with the ETX as a link metric enables RPL to find the minimum stable number of ETX paths from the nodes to a root. Using MRHOF with Energy as a node metric, nodes select a route composed of nodes with high battery level.

For the rank computation, MRHOF introduces the concept of path cost that measures the path's property to the RPL root in relation to the metric used. The path cost is calculated by summing up the selected link metric to the path cost announced by the parent. The transformation of a path cost into a rank depends on the metric, as demonstrated in Algorithm 2 [6].

Algorithm 1: Rank computation for OF0

$R(N) = R(P) + rank\_increase$

$rank\_increase = (R_f * S_p + S_r) * MinHopRankIncrease \ Where :$

- R(P): rank of preferred Parent
- S_p: step_of_rank normalized scalar between 1 and 9 to represent the link properties.
- S_r: stretch_of_rank the maximum augmentation to the step_of_rank of a preferred parent to permit the selection of an additional successor. If none has been configured to the device, then the step_of_rank is not stretched.
- R_f: rank_factor that amplifies the rank_increase to indicate the relative preferences between different types of links that would be used in the single RPL Instance.

Algorithm 2: Rank computation for MRHOF

$path_{cost} = parent_{path\_cost} + link\_cost\ rank = func_{metric}(path_{cost})$ **Where:**

- $link\_cost$ is the cost of the parent's link regarding to the selected metric
- $parent_{path\_cost}$ is advertised by the parent and represents the path_cost of the parent itself.

---

4 Performance Evaluation

In order to evaluate the performance of both OF0 and MRHOF in AMI networks, a simulation study using Cooja simulator [2] has been conducted. Cooja is a flexible java-based simulator developed to simulate networks of sensors running the Contiki Operating System [1], it offers the possibility to simulate each node independently using either software or hardware. It allows simulating various levels of the system. It can operate at the network level, the operating system level, and the machine code instruction level. Contiki is a flexible and portable open source operating system. It provides powerful low-power Internet communication. It fully supports IPv4 and IPv6 standards, as well as the recent low-power wireless standards: 6LoWPAN, CoAP, and RPL. It is dedicated for WSNs and widely used for IoT applications.

4.1 Simulation Setup

In this study we have simulated scenarios with a single sink node, assuming a squared sensing area with a side L = 300 m. The nodes have been randomly dispersed in the sensing area. We have created an RPL network by performing the experiments under different network densities: RPL network with 20, 40, 60, 80, and 100 nodes. We did these experiments for the two OF's: OF0 and MRHOF (ETX and Energy metrics). We have also considered a transmitting range of 120 m and an interference range of 140 m for all nodes, including the sink. In each simulation, each RPL router periodically sends one data packet to the root each 60 s. We use Unit Disk Graph Medium (UDGM) with Distance Loss as the radio model. The simulated platform is Tmote Sky. We run each scenario for a sufficient time (60 min) to make sure that simulations converge to a stable state. The main settings of the scenarios studied are detailed in Table 2.

Table 2. Simulation parameters

Parameter	Value
Simulator	Cooja Contiki 3.0
Radio Model	Unit Disk Graph Medium (UGDM) distance loss
Mote type	Tmote sky
Number of motes	20, 40, 60, 80, 100
Simulation area	300 m × 300 m
Topology	Random
Transmission range	120 m
Interference range	140 m
Transport Layer	UDP
TX Ratio/ RX Ratio	100%
Objective function	OF0; MRHOF_ETX; MRHOF_ENERGY
Simulation time	60 min

4.2   Performance Metrics

For evaluating the performance of the two standard objective functions of RPL, the metrics must be chosen accurately to show the pros and cons of each OF. Thus, the metrics listed below have been chosen to evaluate OF0 and MRHOF. The results obtained according to the analysis of these metrics allow distinguishing which OF can be more suitable for the AMI network. Following is a brief description of the performance metrics that we have used in this study.

Network latency
It refers to time a transmitted packet consumes from sender node to sink node. The following equation can be used for calculating the network latency:

$$Network\ latency = \sum_{k=1}^{n} recv\ time(k) - send\ time(k) \tag{1}$$

where n is the total number of packets successfully received.

Power Consumption (PC)
PC is the amount of power used in each node. There are four types of power measurement: Low Power Mode (LPM), CPU power, radio listen, and radio transmit. Power consumption is a total of all calculations of all type above. LPM is a power consumption parameter that shows the power consumed in sleep mode. CPU power is a power parameter that indicates the processing level of the nodes. While radio listen and transmit is parameter related with node communication (transmit and receive). The following equation can be used for calculating the PC.

$$PC = \frac{(Transmit * 19,5\,\text{mA} + Listen * 21,5\,\text{mA}) * 3\text{V}}{32768} +$$

$$\frac{(CPU * 1,8\,\text{mA} + LPM * 0,0545\,\text{mA}) * 3\,\text{V}}{32768} \quad (2)$$

Packet Loss Ratio (PLR)

The PLR refers to the number of the packets dropped during the transmission to the total number of packets sent. It can be calculated as below:

$$PLR(\%) = \frac{\sum_{k=1}^{n} SentPackets - \sum_{k=1}^{n} ReceivedPackets}{\sum_{k=1}^{n} SentPackets} * 100\% \quad (3)$$

Hop Count (HC)

HC refers to the number of hops between node and its neighbor towards root. Application that requires to be done in real-time consider the lower possible number of hops to join the destination.

Expected Transmission Count (ETX)

ETX is the measure of total number of retransmission necessary for successful reception of data packet at the receiver node. Network with less ETX offers good link stability, which directly indicates that there will be less retransmissions of data packets and therefore less consumption of resources.

Control Traffic Overhead

refers to the total number of control messages exchanged between nodes in order to construct the DODAG and to select the best parent between candidate neighbors. The control messages contain the DIO, DIS and DAO messages. It can be calculated as follow:

$$Control\ Traffic\ Overhead = \sum_{k=1}^{n} DIO + \sum_{k=1}^{n} DIS + \sum_{k=1}^{n} DAO \quad (4)$$

The control traffic overhead is an important routing feature in LLNs. It can be used to determine the stability of the network, higher value of control traffic overhead means that the link between nodes is not stable. Due to large number of control packets flooded in the network, there will be congestion, packet collision and packet delay in the network.

4.3   Simulation Results and Analysis

Network Latency: Figure 2 depicts the variation of the latency in terms of network size. MRHOF with ENERGY metric exhibits higher latency as the number of nodes increases. Network latency is affected by the distance between nodes, retransmission time and buffering time. For a small network of less than 50 nodes the primary causes of the average end-to-end delay are buffering time and the nodes distance. As the network gets denser, more than 50 nodes, packet retransmission has a major impact on the network traffic and consequently the overall latency.

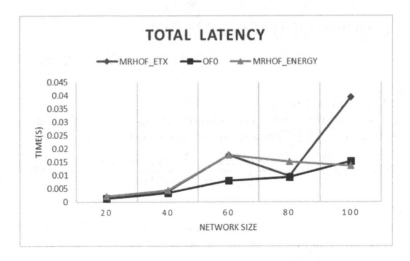

Fig. 2. Total latency as a function of network size

Packet Loss Ratio (PLR): Figure 3 shows the average PLR versus the network size. The PLR is higher in MRHOF_ENERGY, compared to MRHOF_ETX and OF0, because of the battery level energy metric it uses to build the DODAG routes. The OF will always select the next hop that has the higher energy level. As the network get denser, the traffic will be forwarded to a limited number of nodes that have high energy which create packet contention and therefore the number of packet loss is high in MRHOF_ENERGY. On the other hand, MRHOF_ETX and OF0 use ETX and Hop-Count, which enable the OF to take advantage of the network density and improve packet delivery.

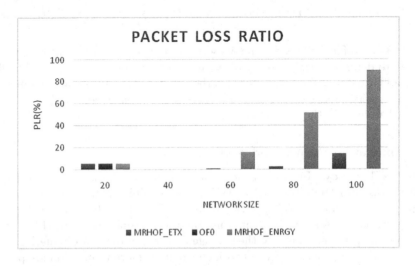

Fig. 3. Average Packet Loss versus network size

Power Consumption (PC). As can be seen, when the network density is between 20–40 nodes, the average PC is almost the same for all objective functions, however, as the network density increases it can be observed that MRHOF_ENERGY consumes much more power than OF0. The high level of power consumption in MRHOF can be explained by the fact that MRHOF_ENERGY exhibit higher PLR in high density network. As packet are being dropped the high level protocols will use it reliability functionality to retransmit packets and therefore the nodes will consume more energy as they need to transmit more packets. The power consumed by transmission is much higher than computation as shown in Eq. 2.

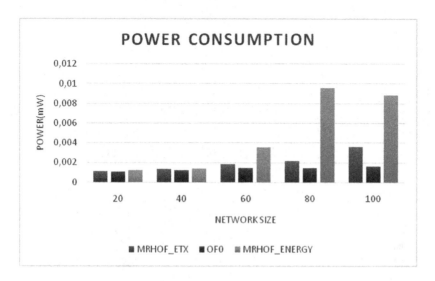

Fig. 4. Power consumption

Hop Count. Figure 5 shows the average hop count of MRHOF with ETX, MRHOF with ENERGY, and OF0. The three networks show similar results in a sparse network composed of less than 50 nodes. This is because the limited number of neighbors makes the choice of another parent very limited. However, it is quite obvious that OF0 has a lower average hop count, compared with MRHOF with ETX metric and MRHOF with ENERGY metric, in large-scale network of more than 50 nodes.

Average Expected Transmission Count (ETX). Figure 6 shows the comparison of average ETX between OF0, MRHOF_ETX and MRHOF_ENERGY. As can be seen in the Fig. 6, both MRHOF and OF0 provide approximately similar number of ETX in a small-scale network (composed of less than 50 nodes), but when the network starts to get wider, the performance of MRHOF with ENERGY metric declines more in comparison to the OF0 and MRHOF with ETX metric.

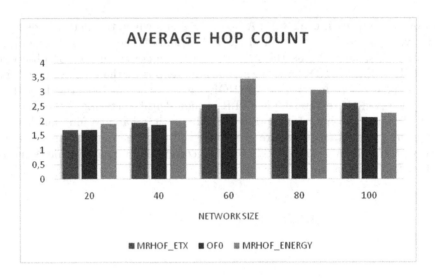

Fig. 5. Average Hop Count

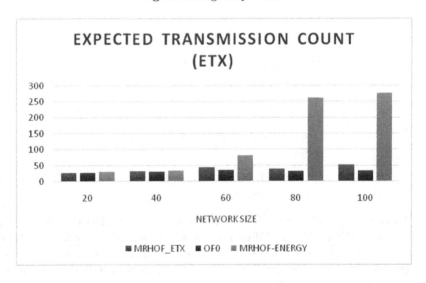

Fig. 6. Average Expected Transmission Count

Control Traffic Overhead. Figure 7 presents the RPL Control Traffic overhead versus the network size. When RPL uses MRHOF to construct the DODAG routes, it generates more control traffic compared to when it uses OF0. This is because MRHOF exchanges metrics for the path selection procedure while OF0 does not exchange any metric and it only selects the paths according to the number of hops to the root. Accordingly, since the probability of path updates by MRHOF is higher, more control traffic is generated. Since OF0 does not use any additional metrics, no control traffic is generated if there is no change in the parent network.

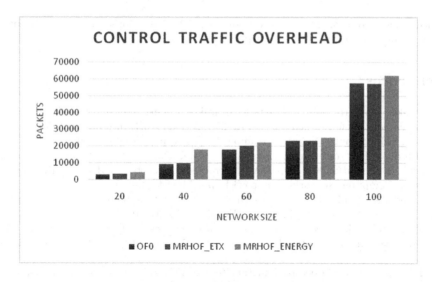

Fig. 7. Control traffic overhead vs. network size

5 Conclusion

RPL is a flexible and powerful routing protocol for LLNs and is considered as a preferred solution for AMI networks. One of the main issues within rpl is the selection of the objective, function, which highly influences routing performance and path selection process. In this paper, we have evaluated the impact of choosing OF on the performance of AMI network in terms of latency, Power consumption, Packet Loss Ratio, Hop Count, ETX, and control traffic overhead. Two OFs were evaluated: OF0 and MRHOF. Our results clearly indicate that the performance of RPL using OF0 is better in terms of latency, reliability, power consumption and Control traffic overhead compared to MRHOF based Energy metric. MRHOF based ETX provides almost the same performances as the OF0 when the network consists of less than 80 but when the network exceeds 80 nodes, OF0 outperforms ETX OF.

The two OFs have some limitations because of the use of a single metric and need more enhancements to deal with AMI Networks. Choosing hop count metric might generate shorter paths, but it could also lead to node failure due to depletion of the battery, as battery level is not taken into account in the decision making process. In the same manner, ETX might make the network more reliable but it comes at the cost of high routing latency, high power consumption and high control traffic overhead. In general, OFs based on single metric can perform well for one metric but poorly for others. As a future work, to address the single metric problem, we intend to design a new RPL OF that takes multiple metrics into account to efficiently satisfy the requirements of AMI networks.

Acknowledgements. This work was supported by The Moroccan National Center for Scientific and Technical Research (CNRST).

References

1. Dunkels, A., Gronvall, B., Voigt, T.: Contiki - a lightweight and flexible operating system for tiny networked sensors. In: 29th Annual IEEE International Conference on Local Computer Networks, Tampa, FL, USA, pp. 455–462 (2004)
2. Osterlind, F., Dunkels, A., Eriksson, J., Finne, N., Voigt, T.: Cross-level sensor network simulation with COOJA. In: Proceedings. 2006 31st IEEE Conference on Local Computer Networks, Tampa, FL, pp. 641–648 (2006)
3. Brandt, A., et al.: RPL: IPv6 routing protocol for low-power and lossy networks. In: Winter, T., Thubert, P. (eds.) RFC 6550, March 2012
4. Pister, K., Dejean, N., Barthel, D.: Routing metrics used for path calculation in low-power and lossy networks. In: Vasseur, J.P., Kim, M. (eds.) RFC 6551, March 2012
5. Thubert, P. (ed.): Objective Function Zero for the Routing Protocol for Low-power and Lossy Networks (RPL). RFC 6552, March 2012
6. Gnawali, O., Levis, P.: The Minimum Rank with Hysteresis Objective Function. RFC 6719, September 2012
7. Hui, J., Popa, D.: Applicability statement for the routing protocol for low-power and lossy networks (RPL) in advanced metering infrastructure (AMI) networks. In: Cam-Winget, N. (ed.) RFC 8036, January 2017
8. Ancillotti, E., Bruno, R., Conti, M.: The role of the RPL routing protocol for smart grid communications. IEEE Commun. Mag. **51**(1), 75–83 (2013)
9. Parnian, A.R., et al.: RPL Routing Protocol in Smart Grid Communication (2014)
10. Mardini, W., et al.: Comprehensive performance analysis of RPL objective functions in IoT networks. Int. J. Commun. Networks Inf. Secur. **9**, 323–332 (2017)
11. Pradeska, N., et al.: Performance analysis of objective function MRHOF and OF0 in routing protocol RPL IPV6 over low power wireless personal area networks (6LoWPAN). In: 2016 8th International Conference on Information Technology and Electrical Engineering (ICITEE) (2016)
12. Qasem, M., et al.: Performance evaluation of RPL objective functions. In: 2015 IEEE International Conference on Computer and Information Technology; Ubiquitous Computing and Communications; Dependable, Autonomic and Secure Computing; Pervasive Intelligence and Computing, pp. 1606–1613 (2015)
13. Safaei, B., et al.: Effects of RPL objective functions on the primitive characteristics of mobile and static IoT infrastructures. Microprocess. Microsyst. **69**, 79–91 (2019)
14. Sharma, R., Jayavignesh, T.: Quantitative analysis and evaluation of RPL with various objective functions for 6LoWPAN. Ind. J. Sci. Technol. **8**, 1 (2015)

Efficient Performance Evaluation of VANET Routing Protocol Using a 2^k Full Factorial Design

Souad Ajjaj[1]($\boxtimes$), Mohammed-Alamine El Houssaini[2], Mustapha Hain[1], and Souad El Houssaini[3]

[1] ENSAM, Hassan II University, Casablanca, Morocco
`SOUAD.AJJAJ-ETU@etu.univh2c.ma`
[2] ESEF, Chouaib Doukkali University, El Jadida, Morocco
`elhoussaini.m@ucd.ac.ma`
[3] Faculty of Sciences, Chouaib Doukkali University, El Jadida, Morocco
`elhoussaini.s@ucd.ac.ma`

Abstract. Performance analysis of routing protocols in Vehicular Ad hoc Networks is a crucial step towards apprehending the factors that influence the routing process either positively or negatively, along with finding out reliable approaches to optimize the existing protocols or implement more suitable ones in the future. In this context, this study proposes a novel option for the performance analysis tasks by applying the Statistical Design of Experiments Methodology (DOE). The goal is to investigate the effects of some traffic conditions and routing security attacks on the performance of the AODV routing protocol in VANETs. In this paper, we selected a two-level Full Factorial design (2^k-FFD) aiming to assess the influence of four factors namely the Node Density, the Number of Connections, the Black Hole and the Worm Hole Attacks over the following performance metrics called responses: Throughput and End to End delay. The objectives of our study are summarized as follows: (1) measuring the effects of factors on the considered responses (2) performing mathematical equations to model the responses (3) Analyzing the obtained results using the statistical method Pareto ANOVA (Analysis of Variance). For VANET simulations, we opted for the Network Simulator NS-3 and SUMO to generate a realistic vehicular mobility model. The findings of this study state that the AODV throughput was severely affected by the Black Hole and the Worm Hole Attacks along with the increment in the Node Density. Furthermore, the results prove that the high traffic conditions lead to the augmentation of the AODV End To End Delay.

Keywords: VANETs · Performance analysis · NS-3 · SUMO · AODV · Design of Experiments (DOE) · Two-level Full Factorial Design (2^k-FFD) · Pareto ANOVA

1 Introduction

Vehicular Ad Hoc Networks are a specific case of Mobile Ad Hoc Networks where mobile nodes are smart vehicles. VANETs are characterized by particular features such as: the

© Springer Nature Switzerland AG 2021
H. Elbiaze et al. (Eds.): UNet 2021, LNCS 12845, pp. 31–41, 2021.
https://doi.org/10.1007/978-3-030-86356-2_3

high and the predictable mobility, the dynamic topology, the intermittent connectivity, the delay constraints and the absence of power limitations [1]. Therefore, designing efficient routing protocols in such extremely dynamic environments is a crucial requirement. In fact, several works in the literature have dealt with the performance analysis of routing protocols in VANETs, wherein the commonly used strategy is to investigate the effect of each factor individually by varying one factor at a time while the other factors are held constant. Hence, in this approach the required number of experiences grows as the number of studied factors increases [2]. In this respect, our study suggests a new approach for the performance evaluation of VANET routing protocols by applying the Design Of Experiments Methodology (DOE). The implementation of DOE approach will allow to simultaneously appraise the effect of multiple factors on the performance metrics while making use of a reduced number of experiments. This approach is undemanding and less time consuming [3]. In this article, a two-level full factorial design (2^k FFD) was planned with four factors ($k = 4$) mainly the Node Density, the Number of Connections, the Black Hole Attack and the Worm Hole Attack. Accordingly, we select Throughput and Average End to End delay to operate as the system outputs or the responses. Furthermore, we have adopted NS-3 for the Network simulation and SUMO for the mobility model generation. The first goal of the present work is to measure and analyze the factor effects on the responses. Secondly, a mathematical model is given for each response mentioned earlier. Afterwards, Pareto ANOVA technique was applied to statistically analyze the achieved outcomes.

The rest of this paper is divided into five sections. Section 2 gives a brief overview of the related works. The third section details the proposed methodology to implement our work. Section 4 deals with the selected materials and methods. Experimental results and analysis of the acquired findings are detailed in Sect. 5. Finally, we conclude with a synthesis of the achieved results and the future research directions.

2 Related Work

In the literature, numerous studies have focused on investigating the effects of various factors on the performance of routing protocols in Vehicular Ad hoc Networks. For instance, the authors in [4] examined the influence of node density on Throughput, Packet Delivery Ratio (PDR), End to End delay and Packet Loss Ratio of three routing protocols specifically DSDV, OLSR and AODV. Moreover, the study [5] involved various speed and various number of nodes to analyze the performance of AODV, DSR, OLSR and AODVUU, with regard to packet delivery ratio, normalized routing overhead and average delay. The authors of [6] compared the performance of DSR, AODV and DSDV routing Protocols with varying pause time and node density over TCP and CBR Connections in VANETs. Besides, the authors of paper [7] studied the effect of Black Hole attack and vehicle density on AODV average Throughput, Packet Delivery Ratio, End-to-End Delay, Normalized Routing Load and Average Path Length. In the paper [8], authors evaluated the effect of Worm Hole Attack on AODV, and proposed a method to detect malicious nodes and react against wormhole attacks.

3 Methodology

Design Of Experiments (DOE) is a statistical methodology widely used in both scientific and engineering areas. They are practical methods to plan and structure experiments, used to study and analyze the effects of input variables (i.e. factors) on output variables (i.e. responses) by conducting the minimum number of experiments while extracting the maximum information. This paper makes use of a two-level full factorial design (2^k-FFD) to investigate the influence of four factors on the performance metrics of AODV routing protocol in VANETs. In fact, a two-level full factorial design (2^k-FFD) allows studying the effect of k factors, where each factor has two levels, a low level coded $(-)$ and a high level denoted $(+)$. Moreover, 2^k-FFD requires conducting 2^k number of experiments. For instance, if we want to study the effect of four factors, then $2^4 = 16$ experiments are required [3].

The implementation of our work follows the guidelines below:

- Define the Factors and their levels (the low and the high levels);
- Identify the performance measures called Responses;
- Build the 2^k-FFD matrix design, which is the table where columns represent the Factors and rows indicate the number of experiments. All possible combinations for factor levels are considered and for each combination the response is measured.
- Compute the main effect for each Factor, which refers to the difference between the average responses at the high level (+) and the average responses at the low level (−).

$$E_A = \frac{\sum y_+}{n_+} - \frac{\sum y_-}{n_-} \tag{1}$$

where n number of experiments at each level, and y the measured responses.
- Perform the Regression model of the 2^k design, in this study the mathematical model chosen is expressed in the form:

$$\hat{y} = b_0 + b_1 x_1 + b_2 x_2 + b_3 x_3 + b_4 x_4 \tag{2}$$

where $\hat{y}$ is the predicted response, factors are represented with the coded variables $x1$, $x2$, $x3$ and $x4$. b_0 is the constant of the model, b_1, b_2, .. b_4 are the coefficients of the variables $x1$, $x2$…$x4$.
This equation can be written in a matrix form as follows:

$$Y = BX \tag{3}$$

Y is the matrix of measured responses, B is the vector of coefficients, and X is the matrix of effects. The coefficients are determined by the method of least squares [9]:

$$B = (X^T X)^{-1} \left(X^T Y \right) \tag{4}$$

X^T: is the transposed matrix of X.
- Analyze the obtained results by using the statistical method: Pareto Analysis of Variance [10]. Pareto ANOVA method is a simple tool based on the calculation of the percent contribution of each factor expressed as follows:

$$P\% \text{ (Factor A)} = \frac{E_A^2}{\sum_{i=1}^{k} E_i^2} \tag{5}$$

where E_A is the effect of factor A and E_i the effect of factor i among the k factors.

4 Materials and Methods

4.1 AODV Routing Protocol

Ad hoc On Demand Distance Vector (AODV) is a reactive protocol in which routes are established only when needed. The AODV uses three important concepts: the route discovery mechanism, the route maintenance and the sequence number.

In the route discovery process, a Route Request (RREQ) message is broadcasted by the source node to all its neighbors. This RREQ is then relayed by the intermediate nodes until reaching the destination or an intermediate node that has a valid route. Afterwards, a Route Reply (RREP) is unicasted to the source node in the reverse path. In Route maintenance, AODV maintains routes as long as they are active. A route is considered active if the data packets periodically transit from source to the destination. The AODV uses the HELLO messages to check the connectivity of the routes. The AODV also applies the sequence numbers which are time stamps indicating the freshness of a route. The details of the AODV working are given in [11].

4.2 Selection of Factors and Responses

The main aim of our study is to evaluate the influence of some Factors related to traffic conditions and routing security attacks on the performance metrics of the AODV routing protocol in VANETs. This is precisely why we have considered the following factors (Table 1).

- The Node Density (ND) referring to the number of vehicles present in the network.
- The Number of Connections (NC) indicating the number of communicating nodes (source/Sink).
- The Black Hole attack (BKH) where the malicious node pretends having the shortest and the freshest route to the destination during the AODV route discovery; once it captures the data packets forwarded to it, the malicious node then drops them [7].
- The Worm Hole attack (WMH) where two malicious nodes collude and form a tunnel between them; the first end of the tunnel captures packets and sends them to the second end positioned at a remote location. Virtual routes are created causing the change of the network topology and the disturbance of the routing information [1].

The Node Density is ranging from 50 to 150 vehicles, while the Number of Connections varies between 4% and 20% of the total number of vehicles. For the Black

Table 1. The values for levels (−) and (+) of all factors.

Label	Factor	Level (−)	Level (+)
ND	Node Density	50	150
NC	Number of connections	4%	20%
BKH	Black Hole attack	0	1
WMH	Wormhole attack	0	1

Hole and the Worm Hole attacks, the level (−) refers to the absence of the attack and its value is set to 0. The level (+) is set to 1 when the attack is launched.

We picked the Throughput (Th) and the Average End to End Delay (E2E delay) as the responses of the study:

- Throughput (TH) is the total number of bits successfully received during the simulation time. It is measured in kilobits per second (kbps).
- Average End to End Delay (EED) is the average time of all successfully received packets delay, measured in (ms)

4.3 VANET Simulation Setup

In order to have a realistic scenario for VANET simulations, we opted for NS-3 as a Network simulator and SUMO (Simulation of Urban Mobility) for mobility model generation [12]. A real road map of El Jadida city from Morocco was imported in SUMO (see Fig. 1).

Fig. 1. View of the simulation zone in SUMO

Other simulation parameters are shown in the table bellow (Table 2).

Table 2. Simulation parameters in NS3.

N	Parameter	Value
1	Network simulator	NS3.29
2	Mobility simulator	SUMO-0.32.0
3	Propagation model	TwoRayGroundPropagationLossModel
4	Wifi channel	YansWifi
5	Mac and physic layer	IEEE 802.11p
6	Simulation time	200 s
7	Packet size	1024
8	Routing protocol	AODV

5   Results and Discussion

5.1   The Design Matrix

The matrix of experiments and the measured Throughput (TH) and Average End To End Delay (AEED) are tabulated bellow (Table 3).

5.2   Main Effects of Factors

The main effects of factors are computed according to the tables bellow and are graphically plotted.

From Table 4 and Fig. 2, we observe that the Node Density, the Black Hole and the Worm Hole Attacks have a negative effect on the Throughput, while The Number of Connections has a slight positive effect. This implies that the AODV Throughput cuts down with an increase in the number of vehicles as well as when the Black Hole and the Worm Hole attacks are launched, whereas the increment in the number of Connections raises slightly the AODV throughput. Indeed, in the presence of attacks, the degradation of the AODV Throughput is due to the behaviour of malicious nodes that act either by dropping packets in case of Black Hole Attack or capturing and forwarding the packets to a distant location in case of Worm Hole Attack. This results in reducing the number of successfully received packets and degrades the AODV routing performance. Similarly, the AODV throughput lowers when the Node Density grows, which can be explained by the frequent link breakages due to the high mobility of vehicles that generates more route error packets (RERR) causing the failure of the routing process.

Table 3. The matrix of experiments

N°	ND	NC	BKH	WMH	TH	AEED
1	−	−	−	−	30,89	41,68
2	+	−	−	−	25,47	58,96
3	−	+	−	−	27,24	92,80
4	+	+	−	−	20,85	103,76
5	−	−	+	−	18,89	11,41
6	+	−	+	−	15,56	51,69
7	−	+	+	−	22,46	72,68
8	+	+	+	−	15,96	76,91
9	−	−	−	+	14,40	59,58
10	+	−	−	+	16,75	63,43
11	−	+	−	+	19,67	121,87
12	+	+	−	+	17,28	126,74
13	−	−	+	+	18,97	23,90
14	+	−	+	+	10,99	39,93
15	−	+	+	+	15,08	33,53
16	+	+	+	+	14,03	177,21

Table 4. Main effects of factors on Throughput

Factors	ND	NC	BKH	WMH
Average TH in level (−)	20,95	18,99	21,57	22,17
Average TH in level (+)	17,11	19,07	16,49	15,90
Main effect	−3,84	0,08	−5,07	−6,27

In summary, the results revealed by applying the 2^k-FFD design approve with other works in the literature. For example, the authors in [4] stated that the throughput decreases when incrementing the network density. Likewise, the authors of [7] argued that the AODV throughput degrades under the Black Hole attack. [13] concluded that the AODV throughput is severely degraded in the presence of the Worm Hole Attack.

The Factors can then be ranked according to their main effects. The effect of the Worm Hole Attack comes first, then the Black Hole Attack, the Node Density and finally the Number of Connections.

Figure 3 and (Table 5) show the effect of Factors on the AODV End To End delay. Apparently, the effect of the Node Density, the Number of Connections and the Worm Hole Attack has a positive trend, unlike the effect of the Black Hole holding a negative trend. In other words, the AODV End To End delay goes up in the high level of all

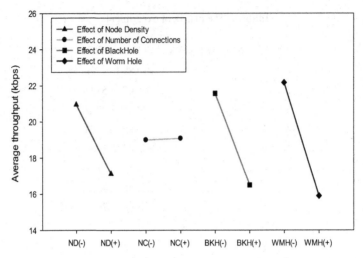

Fig. 2. Plot of main effects of factors on Throughput

Table 5. Main effects of factors on Average End to End Delay

Factors	ND	NC	BKH	WMH
Average TH in level (−)	57,18	43,82	83,60	63,73
Average TH in level (+)	87,33	100,69	60,91	80,77
Main effect	30,15	56,86	−22,69	17,04

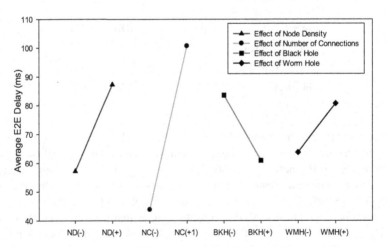

Fig. 3. Plot of main effects of factors on Average End to End Delay

factors except for the Black Hole Attack. These outcomes suggest that the E2E Delay increases with the rise of the network density, the number of communicating pairs and when the Worm Hole Attack is initiated. These results are clearly logical because the AODV relies on the route discoveries before sending the data packets. Increasing the number of vehicles or connections therefore results in raising the time spent in searching valid routes which leads to high values of delay. Additionally, in the Worm Hole Attack, the packets are tunneled through the malicious nodes that are located at remote positions; leading to higher End To End Delay. On the contrary, the AODV E2E Delay decreases in the presence of the Black Hole Attack. This can be explained by the malicious behavior of the Black Hole node that pretends having the freshest path to destination and fast Route Reply (RREP) to the source node. This significantly decreases both the route discovery process and the delay. This conclusion copes with the results of [7] where it is confirmed that the delay under the Black Hole is better than in a scenario free of attack. Again, [14] and [15] confirms the increase of the AODV End To End delay with the rise in the number of nodes and the number of connections. The authors in [16] highlighted the effect of the Worm Hole on delay and proposes a protocol enhancement to secure the AODV against the Worm Hole attacks.

5.3 The Regression Models of the 2^k Design

The coefficients of the models were calculated using the method of least squares (see Eq. 4 above).

$$\hat{y}_1(TH) = 28,48 - 0,04x_1 + 0,52x_2 - 5,07x_3 - 6,27x_4$$
$$\hat{y}_2(EED) = 2,29 + 0,3x_1 + 355,40x_2 - 22,69x_3 + 17,04x_4$$

The plots below are used to check the correlation between the experimental values of the responses and the predicted ones (from the mathematical model). X-axis represents the experimental values and Y-axis shows the predicted values.

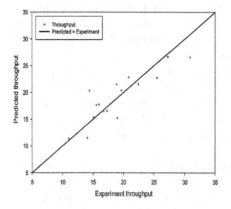
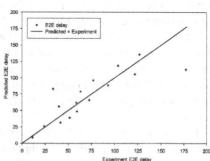

Fig. 4. Experiment vs predicted Throughput   **Fig. 5.** Experiment vs predicted E2E Delay

From Fig. 4 and Fig. 5, it is seen that the model performed is accurate; there's an important correlation between the model's predictions and the experimental results.

5.4 Pareto Analysis of Variance (ANOVA)

The percentage contribution of each factor in affecting the responses was computed. The results are shown in Fig. 6 and Fig. 7 for Throughput and Average End To End Delay respectively.

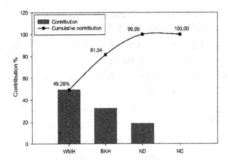 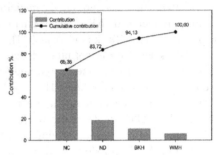

Fig. 6. Pareto chart for Throughput   **Fig. 7.** Pareto chart for average E2E Delay

From Fig. 6, it is concluded that the Worm Hole and the Black Hole attacks have strong influence on the AODV Throughput followed by the Node Density. However the factor NC (the Number of Connections) has lesser contribution.

Figure 7 presents the Percentage contribution (P%) of each factor with respect to the AODV Average End To End delay, it is observed that the Number of Connections has the most significant effect with 65,35% contribution, followed by the Node Density, then the Black Hole and finally the Worm Hole attack.

6   Conclusion

In this research, a new approach for the performance analysis of VANET routing protocols based on the Design Of Experiments methodology is proposed. A 2^k Full Factorial method was applied so as to measure the impact of Factors related to traffic conditions and two routing security attacks on the AODV Throughput and the Average End To End Delay performance metrics. Mathematical models were performed describing the relationship between each response and the considered Factors. Moreover, the experimental results were analyzed using the simplified statistical method: Pareto Analysis Of Variance (ANOVA). The findings of our study reveal that the application of statistical based methodologies are a simple and practical alternative for the performance analysis studies.

The outcomes state that the presence of the Black Hole and the Worm Hole attacks lowers extremely the AODV Throughput, along with the increment in the Node Density. Moreover, increased Node Density and Number of Connections raises the AODV End to End delay. Consequently, it would be very interesting to implement additional features for ensuring more scalability and security in VANET routing protocols.

In our future work, we will try to investigate the effect of other Factors on other types of VANET routing protocols particularly the proactive and geographic routing protocols.

Further, we intend to perform an optimization method addressing the security and the scalability issues in VANETs.

References

1. Arif, M., Wang, G., Bhuiyan, M.Z.A., Wang, T., Chen, J.: A survey on security attacks in VANETs: Communication, applications and challenges. Veh. Commun. **19**, 100179 (2019). https://doi.org/10.1016/j.vehcom.2019.100179
2. Law, A.M.: A tutorial on design of experiments for simulation modeling. In: Proceedings of the Winter Simulation Conference 2014, pp. 66–80 (2014). https://doi.org/10.1109/WSC. 2014.7019878
3. Jones, R.: Design and analysis of experiments (fifth edition), Douglas Montgomery, John Wiley and Sons, 2001, 684 pages, £33.95. Qual. Reliab. Eng. Int. **18**, 163 (2002). https://doi. org/10.1002/qre.458
4. Gupta, P., Chaba, Y.: Performance analysis of routing protocols in vehicular ad hoc networks for CBR applications over UDP connections. Int. J. Eng. Comput. Sci. **3**, 6418–6421 (2014)
5. Hu, S., Jia, Y., She, C.: Performance analysis of VANET routing protocols and implementation of a VANET terminal. In: 2017 International Conference on Computer Technology, Electronics and Communication (ICCTEC), pp. 1248–1252 (2017). https://doi.org/10.1109/ ICCTEC.2017.00272
6. Paul, B., Roy, A., Paul, S.K.: Comparison of DSR, AODV, and DSDV routing protocols with varying pause time node density over TCP CBR connections in VANET. In: 2014 International Conference on Computational Intelligence and Communication Networks, pp. 374–379 (2014). https://doi.org/10.1109/CICN.2014.90
7. Purohit, K.C., Dimri, S.C., Jasola, S.: Mitigation and performance analysis of routing protocols under black-hole attack in vehicular ad-hoc network (VANET). Wireless Pers. Commun. **97**(4), 5099–5114 (2017). https://doi.org/10.1007/s11277-017-4770-6
8. Narayanan, S.S., Gurusamy, M.: Modified secure AODV protocol to prevent wormhole attack in MANET. Concurr. Comput. Pract. Exp. **32**, e5017 (2018). https://doi.org/10.1002/cpe.5017
9. Dodge, Y., Rousson, V.: Alternative Methods of Regression. A Wiley-Interscience Publication, New York (1993)
10. Taghizadegan, S.: Road map to lean six sigma continuous improvement engineering strategies. In: Taghizadegan, S. (ed.) Essentials of Lean Six Sigma, pp. 107–174. Butterworth-Heinemann, Burlington (2006). https://doi.org/10.1016/B978-012370502-0/50010-2
11. Das, S.R., Belding-Royer, E.M., Perkins, C.E.: Ad Hoc On-Demand Distance Vector (AODV) Routing. https://tools.ietf.org/html/rfc3561. Accessed 20 Dec 2020
12. Krajzewicz, D., Erdmann, J., Behrisch, M., Bieker-Walz, L.: Recent development and applications of SUMO - simulation of urban MObility. Int. J. Adv. Syst. Measur. **5**(3 & 4), 128–138 (2012)
13. Devi, S., Mamini, K., Bhargavi, Y.: Performance analysis of AODV under worm hole attack. Int. J. Adv. Res. Comput. Sci. Softw. Eng. **7**, 879–883 (2017). https://doi.org/10.23956/ija rcsse/V7I4/0116
14. Pranav, K., Kapang, L., Tuithung, T.: Simulation based analysis of adhoc routing protocol in urban and highway scenario of VANET (2011). https://doi.org/10.5120/1716-2302
15. Viswacheda Duduku, V., Chekima, A., Wong, F., Dargham, J.: A study on vehicular ad hoc networks, 1 December 2015. https://doi.org/10.1109/AIMS.2015.73
16. Kumar, V., Kush, A.: Worm_secure protocol for wormhole protection in AODV routing protocol. Int. J. Comput. Appl. **44**, 15–21 (2012)

A Classification Proposal of VANET Applications in the Road Safety

Brahim Driouch[1]([✉]), Mohammed-Alamine El Houssaini[2], Souad El Houssaini[1], and Jamal El Kafi[1]

[1] Faculty of Science, Chouaib Doukkali University, El Jadida, Morocco
{Driouch.b,Elhoussaini.s,Elkafi.j}@ucd.ac.ma
[2] ESEF, Chouaib Doukkali University, El Jadida, Morocco
Elhoussaini.m@ucd.ac.ma

Abstract. The increasing of accidents and fatalities on road lead to adopting the new ITS (Intelligent Transport System) based on VANET (Vehicular Ad hoc Network) technologies such as V2V (Vehicle-to-Vehicle) communication by broadcasting information and alerts to avoid car incidents. Also V2I (Vehicle to Infrastructure) communication by sharing data as well as information usually in a bidirectional way regarding the infrastructure conditions and alerts to avoid traffic incidents. The aim of the study is to provide an analysis of current application of VANET technologies in the road safety domain, as well as alert management system between vehicles and infrastructures to avoid accidents. Next, the proposed classification framework was analyzed to identify areas of improvement. Results have confirmed that, although the number of VANET applications in the safety road, still need improvement regarding the characterization and control of road incidents causes (due to infrastructure and vehicles, rules and codes or drivers and pedestrians behaviors). Further developments will be oriented towards developing a new system for proactive risk assessment framework and behavior control to support this analysis.

Keywords: VANET · ITS · Road safety · Proactive risk control

1 Introduction

Advancement on wireless communication technologies and vehicular communications have enabled the evolution of Intelligent Transport System that address several transportation issues such as traffic congestion, road accident, or non-safety application such as interactive communication, online games, payment services and information updates whilst vehicles are on move. Recent studies have proposed the use of VANET, a distinctive type of a MANET (Mobile ad-hoc Network), in which moving vehicles act as either a node or a router to exchange messages or alerts between vehicles, or an Access Point (AP) [3]. Several safety applications with different approaches were defined such as collision avoidance, alerts for other vehicles for distancing when an accident occurred in the same road, alerts for vehicles when the safety distance is not respected, pre-crash

H. Elbiaze et al. (Eds.): UNet 2021, LNCS 12845, pp. 42–53, 2021.
https://doi.org/10.1007/978-3-030-86356-2_4

sensing or lane changing by using traffic monitoring and management application to enable risk control and accident prevention on road [4]. It is essential to realize that the ITS aims to improve road safety and provides a comfortable travel experience to driver and passengers.

The aim of the study of the contributions on the application of VANET on road safety is to analyze different approaches in order to address conclusions and possible contributions to improve the safety on road with a more proactive and preventive approach.

In order to achieve this analysis we propose a classification framework represented by several criteria that describe the VANET aspect, the main accident root causes categories and the main challenges escalated in the reviewed papers.

The rest of this paper is organized as follows. In Sect. 2, we give a brief overview of VANET applications on accident prevention techniques, and then we present the proposed classification framework in Sect. 3. Section 4 will deal with the details of results and analysis of contributions based on the proposed framework. Finally, we conclude with synthesis of results and future research directions.

2 VANET Application on Road Safety

The road safety applications is a part of VANET technologies advancement where each vehicle takes on the role of sender, receiver, and router to broadcast information to the vehicular-lar network which then uses these information to ensure safe and flow traffic. For communication to occur between vehicles and RoadSide Units (RSUs), [5] vehicles must be equipped with some sort of radio interface or On Board Unit (OBU) [6] that enables short-range wireless ad hoc networks to be formed. Vehicles must also be fitted with hardware that permits detailed position information such as Global Positioning System (GPS) or a Differential Global Positioning Sys-tem (DGPS) receiver [7]. Fixed RSUs, which are connected to the backbone network, must be in place to facilitate communication.

In the safety domain, several approaches for road accident avoidance have been identified [8] such us:

- Collision warning
- Intersection collision warning
- Approaching emergency vehicle
- Approaching accident zone waring
- Work zone warning
- Distancing warning
- Traffic signal violation warning
- Overtaking warning

2.1 Approching Accident Zone Waring

One of the root causes of road accidents is the lack of visibility for drivers on both sides of the road in a large bend or following fog, which can reduce visibility on the road Fig. 1. By sending a warning to other drivers in the same time of accident occurrence can reduce the harmful impacts that the collision of several vehicles can have, even at the level of the highway which knows multiple collisions following a traffic accident [9, 10].

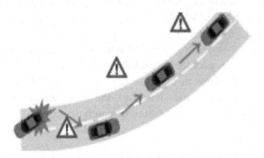

Fig. 1. Warning for accident occurrence

2.2 Overtacking Warning

When we try to overtake on a tow way-street we always think if the car in the other direction is far enough before making the decision to overtake the car in front of us [4]. The ITS can detect the speed of the car in the other direction and taking into account the speed of the vehicle number 2 and number 3 in the Fig. 2 can help the driver to make the decision whether to continue to overtake the car number 1 [11].

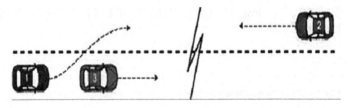

Fig. 2. Warning for vehicle initiates overtacking

2.3 Collision Warning

To avoid a To avoid a collision following an obstacle on the road which is generally only visible to the first driver, the ITS can send a warning message to all drivers in the coverage area of the VANET networks in order to brake at the right time and have sufficient braking distance or safety distance (SD) [12] (Fig. 3).

Fig. 3. Collision following an emergency breaking without warning

2.4 Intersection Collision Warning

At each intersection, the drivers sometimes confused between who will give up priority and who has priority to go first. with an RSU already arranged according to the applicable priority rule and can send warning messages to all the cars at the time of arrival at the intersection and only the car that will have priority to pass will be notified [11] (Fig. 4).

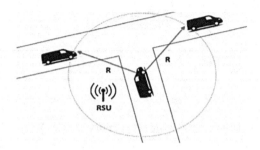

Fig. 4. Intesection collision warning

2.5 Approaching Emergency Vehicle

In the roads blocked by cars and in peak periods the passage of an ambulance becomes difficult especially having roads without reserved access for urgent cases. The fact of sending a warning message to several cars at a sufficient distance and each car transmitting the same message will greatly help to anticipate the passage of an emergency vehicle from its point of departure to the point of arrival [13] (Fig. 5).

2.6 Distancing Warning

Respecting the SD between two vehicles is always a difficult rule to control in highway traffic. In a VANET network, a warning message can be sent once:

$$x1 - x2 < SD$$

Fig. 5. Warning message to give priority for emergency vehicle

This warning will not be deactivated until the rule is respected [13] (Fig. 6).

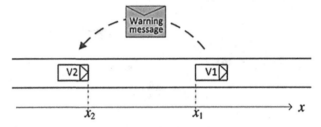

Fig. 6. Distancing warning between tow vehicles V1 and V2

2.7   Trafic Signal Violation Warning

Some drivers violates the rules of traffic signals especially at night when the traffic light stop to work. It is possible to control this rule by placing a RSU with a traffic light controller that broadcast traffic light information. The vehicles receive warning messages about the presence of a red light and another vehicle in the other side. These can avoid accidents in time [3] (Fig. 7).

2.8   Work Zone and Redirection Warning

Every time there is work on the road, the traffic becomes much more difficult to manage. What can be done is that the nearest RSU will broadcast warning messages to all vehicles circulating in the work area and each vehicle also transmits its warning with the direction of the traffic to be observed for a smoother traffic to avoid immediate braking due to obstruction caused by work zone [6] (Fig. 8).

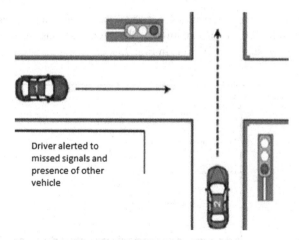

Fig. 7. Trafic light violation warning

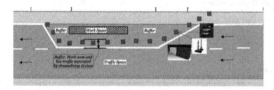

Fig. 8. Work zone and redirection warning for fluid and safe traffic

3 The Proposed Classification Framwork

Based on current applications of VANET in road safety domain, a framework for assessing the overall contributions on processes to avoid accident is proposed as follows. The aim is to propose a tool to support the control and effectivity of road safety processes as well as the assessment of current new applications. The framework is based on three main criteria, which are connected to the main features usually characterizing a VANET application (ITS, Main challenges and safety issue characterization. A detailed description is proposed as follows: The ITS criteria refer to the main components of the ITS based on the current topics mainly studied in the VANET applications which are characterized by the VANET communication mode, Quality of service (QoS) [14] and VANET reliability and VANET authentication and security. The Safety issues characterization criteria refer to main accident root causes classified on three main families of road accident causes: behavioral, technical and procedural causes, the safety issues is characterized by Human (drivers and pedestrian) behavior, vehicles and infrastructures defects and lows or code control. The Main challenges criteria refer to challenges that are escalated mainly by contribution on the VANET application on road safety which are characterized by the simulation system and real world, the VANET architecture and security and services cost-efficiently securely and reliably.

In order to depict the interactions between the three main criteria and their sub-categories, a three-axis representation of the proposed classification framework (including criteria and sub-categories) is in Fig. 9.

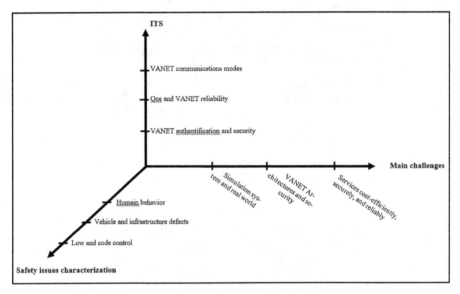

Fig. 9. The proposed framework reported in a 3-axis representation

In the next section, a state-of-the-art analysis is proposed aiming to apply the framework to analyze current practical studies published in the literature. The scope is to point out the criteria and applications witch need more studies in the road safety field.

4   The Literature Analysis Based on the Proposed Classification Framework

4.1   Contribution Analysis in the Road Safety Domain

The literature analysis has been developed by extracting a sample of articles from more well know database such us Scopus and Web of Science; both journal and conference papers have been included in the analysis. As the aim of the literature review focuses on the safety field, a combination of keywords "VANET AND road AND safety" has been adopted for the semantic search. The analyzed period started from 2008 and ended to 2020. In detail, articles dealt with a general analysis of VANET applications without referring explicitly to safety aspects and, vice versa together with theoretical studies and review papers (not involving the safety field) have been excluded, considering only applicative proposal and/or case studies on road safety. In Fig. 10, the distribution of studies sample for each year is proposed: an increasing trend in last years could be easily outlined even if the total number is not so high compared to studies focusing on VANET without a focus on safety.

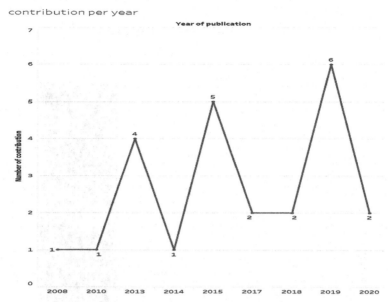

Fig. 10. Number of contribution published per year

Next, the specific field of VANET applications and architecture for road safety has been evaluated: results are in Fig. 11. The 75% of contributions studied the commu-nications and broadcasting modes in the VANET architecture. Almost 17% of papers address privacy, authentication and security in VANET and 8% of the papers covered the QoS and reliability of the VANET.

In the side of the safety criteria which were addressed in the reviewed papers, the distribution by safety criteria is presented in Fig. 12.

The major part of the safety criteria that were addressed in reviewed contributions is the vehicles and infrastructures defects and warning which represents **75%** of papers. For Human behavior just **4%** of papers that treat human decision and acts as safety criterion. For Codes and low control also **4%** of studies that escalate this issue and try to analyze this element. The tow criteria were less covered in the reviewed studies. The other papers representing **16%** treats VANET applications in the road safety without focusing on one of the three categories of accidents causes presented in the classification framework.

The last criterion is the main challenges witch are escalated in the reviewed papers, results presented in the Fig. 13. The VANET architecture and security represent **39%** of main challenges for VANET application on road safety, almost **35%** of addressed challenges are related to simulation system and application on real world, **17%** refers to service cost effeciently and reliabilily and almost 9% of contributions didn't escalt any specific challenges.

Contributions per studied ITS

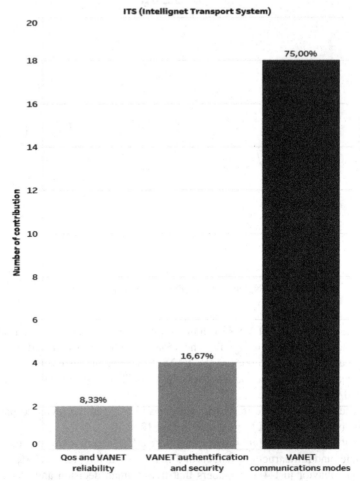

Fig. 11. Number of contributions per VANET aspects

According to Heinrich on the analysis of 75,000 of the industrial accidents causes, the human unsafe behavior represent 88% of causes, 10% accidents were causes by unsafe conditions or physical environment and only 2% of accidents were attributed to unresisting factors [11]. Heinrich research results indicated that 98% of accidents could be prevented and controlled within human ability.

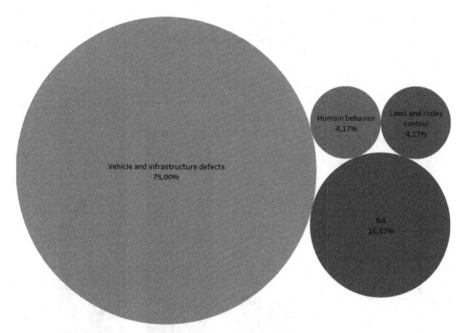

Fig. 12. Distribution of papers by safety criterion addressed

By analogy with Heinrich's analysis on the aspect of industrial accidents which is also valid for traffic accidents. According to the results of the analysis of the papers reviewed in our study, the behavior aspect is only treated at 4%. Knowing that it is the most domain aspect in the causes of accidents according to Heinrich. This aspect requires even more analysis and in-depth study to have a system based on ITS and VANET while controlling the behavior aspect. It is true the fact of having several warning message on the road conditions and the weather and on other vehicles in real time and on the road to avoid accidents but the driver behavior component and the pedestrians on the road is much more important to study and characterized in order to have a more robust system and allowing the prevention of accidents on the road.

In recent year a great deal of industrial accidents were also caused by human factors [2]. Therefore, it has become an important subject to prevent and control for accidents avoidance.

Main challenges per contributions

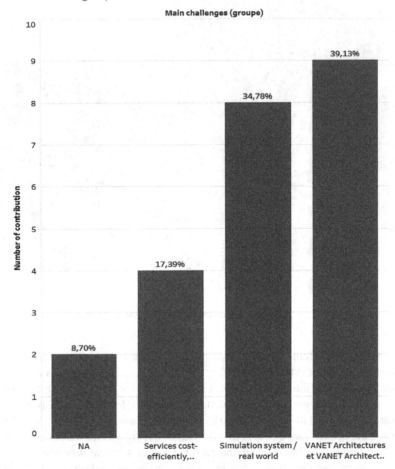

Fig. 13. Distribution of main challenges per contributions

5 Conclusion

In this paper, we presented a classification of papers that address applications of VANETs with a focus on applications regarding the accident prevention on road. Based on the classification framework and criteria that were used, we classified the papers on various categories. We made an analysis and comparative study of aspects that were addressed and discussed their strengths and weaknesses. Then, we discussed some of the open issues that remain to be addressed. We hope this classification will serve as ready reference for other researchers working in these areas, specifically in safety domain and help in addressing some of the open issues.

References

1. Outay, F., Kamoun, F., Kaisser, F., Alterri, D., Yasar, A.: V2V and V2I communications for traffic safety and CO_2 emission reduction: a performance evaluation. Procedia Comput. Sci. **151**, 353–360 (2019). https://doi.org/10.1016/j.procs.2019.04.049
2. Ranney, T.A.: Models of driving behavior: a review of their evolution. Accid. Anal. Prev. **26**(6), 733–570 (1994)
3. Gokulakrishnan, P., Ganeshkumar, P.: Road accident prevention with instant emergency warning message dissemination in vehicular ad-hoc network. PLoS ONE **10**(12), e0143383 (2015). https://doi.org/10.1371/journal.pone.0143383
4. Mari Kirthima, A., Verma, R., Hegde, C.R., Shanbhag, A.S.: Intelligent accident prevention in VANETs. Int. J. Recent Technol. Eng. **8**(2), 2401–2405 (2019). https://doi.org/10.35940/ijrte.B1805.078219
5. Loganathan, G.B.: VANET based secured accident prevention system. Int. J. Mech. Eng. Technol. **10**(06), 285–291 (2019). Article ID: IJMET_10_06_024. http://www.iaeme.com/ijmet/issues.asp?JType=IJMET&VType=10&IType=6
6. Martinez, F.J., Cano, J.-C., Calafate, C.T., Manzoni, P.: A VANET solution to prevent car accidents
7. Nekovee, M., Bie, J.: Rear-end collision: causes and avoidance techniques. In: Naja, R. (ed.) Wireless Vehicular Networks for Car Collision Avoidance, pp. 99–119. Springer, New York (2013). https://doi.org/10.1007/978-1-4419-9563-6_4
8. Premalatha, N., Kumaresan, M., Devi Raja, S., Loganathan, Y.: VANET based communication on vehicles for accident prevention. www.ijert.org
9. Qiong, W.U., Lucas, C.K., Hui, C.Y.Y., Chim, T.W.: Early car collision prediction in VANET. In: Proceedings of the 2015 International Conference on Connected Vehicles and Expo, ICCVE 2015, pp. 94–99, April 2016. https://doi.org/10.1109/ICCVE.2015.55
10. Al-Ani, R., Zhou, B., Shi, Q., Sagheer, A.: A survey on secure safety applications in VANET. In: Proceedings of the 20th International Conference on High Performance Computing and Communications, 16th International Conference on Smart City and 4th International Conference on Data Science and Systems, HPCC/SmartCity/DSS 2018, pp. 1485–1490, January 2019. https://doi.org/10.1109/HPCC/SmartCity/DSS.2018.00245
11. Bie, J., Roelofsen, M., Jin, L., van Arem, B.: Lane change and overtaking collisions: causes and avoidance techniques. In: Naja, R. (ed.) Wireless Vehicular Networks for Car Collision Avoidance, pp. 143–187. Springer, New York (2013). https://doi.org/10.1007/978-1-4419-9563-6_6
12. Taghizadeh, M., Biswas, S., Dion, F.: Chain collision accident: causes and avoidance techniques. In: Naja, R. (ed.) Wireless Vehicular Networks for Car Collision Avoidance, pp. 121–142. Springer, New York (2013). https://doi.org/10.1007/978-1-4419-9563-6_5
13. Chang, B.-J., Liang, Y.-H., Yang, H.-J.: Performance analysis with traffic accident for cooperative active safety driving in VANET/ITS. Wirel. Pers. Commun. **74**(2), 731–755 (2013). https://doi.org/10.1007/s11277-013-1318-2
14. Zeadally, S., Hunt, R., Chen, Y.S., Irwin, A., Hassan, A.: Vehicular ad hoc networks (VANETS): status, results, and challenges. Telecommun. Syst. **50**(4), 217–241 (2012). https://doi.org/10.1007/s11235-010-9400-5
15. Jehring, J.: Ind. Labor Relations Rev, vol. 4, no. 4, p. 609. Sage (1951)

Analyzing the Received Non Linear Noise in Asynchronous and Non Linear FBMC Systems

Brahim Elmaroud[(✉)]

Higher Institute of Maritime Studies, Casablanca, Morocco
b.elmaroud@isem.ac.ma

Abstract. Following the same developments as in our previous works where we have analyzed the joint effect of synchronization errors and High Power Amplifiers (HPA) non linear distortions on FBMC systems, in this paper we will evaluate the accuracy of some approximations related to the variance of the received non linear noise. We will show that theses approximations can be considered accurate over half the range of the values of the carrier frequency offset (CFO).

Keywords: Filter bank multicarrier · Cosine modulated multitone · HPA · Nonlinear distortion · Carrier frequency offset · SIR

1 Introduction

Filter Bank Multicarrier (FBMC) systems are very sensitive to synchronization errors caused by symbol timing offset (STO) and carrier frequency offset (CFO). The CFO is introduced by frequency mismatch in the transmitter and the receiver oscillators and the Doppler effect if the transmitter/receiver is moving. This causes system degradation by increasing intersymbol interference (ISI) and intercarrier interference (ICI) [1–3]. In addition to their sensitivity to synchronization errors, FBMC systems suffer from the high Peak-to-Average Power Ratio (PAPR) which makes the system very sensitive to nonlinear distortion (NLD) caused by high power amplifiers (HPA) [4–8]. In some of our previous works, we have investigated the joint effect of synchronization errors and HPA nonlinear distortions on FBMC systems [9–11]. In [9] and [10], we have considered a downlink FBMC based multi-cellular network for which we have derived an exact bit error rate (BER) expression by carrying out an analytical interference analysis in the presence of a frequency selective channel. In [11], we have studied the performance of an asynchronous and non linear Cosine Modulated Multitone (CMT) system in terms of signal to interference ratio (SIR). However, in all these works we made an approximation related to the received non linear noise where we have ignored the effect of the CFO. In this paper, we will simplify the expression of the received non linear noise in order to find a closed form expression of its variance and then derive the exact expression of the

H. Elbiaze et al. (Eds.): UNet 2021, LNCS 12845, pp. 54–61, 2021.
https://doi.org/10.1007/978-3-030-86356-2_5

SIR to be compared with the one obtained using the received non linear noise approximation.

The rest of this paper is structured as follows: Sect. 2 presents the FBMC considered system model. In Sect. 3, we derive the SIR expression using the non linear noise approximation. The closed form expression (of the variance) of the received non linear noise is proposed in Sect. 4. Simulation results are presented in Sect. 5 and conclusions are drawn in Sect. 6.

2 System Model

The considered CMT multicarrier system is presented in Fig. 1. According to this Figure, the CMT signal is given by

$$x(t) = \sum_{n=-\infty}^{\infty} \sum_{k=0}^{N-1} s_n^k h(t - nT) e^{j\frac{\pi}{2T}t} e^{jk(\frac{\pi}{T}t+\frac{\pi}{2})}$$

$$= \sum_{n=-\infty}^{\infty} \sum_{k=0}^{N-1} s_n^k \gamma_{k,n}(t) \tag{1}$$

where $\gamma_{k,n}(t) = h(t - nT) e^{j\frac{\pi}{2T}t} e^{j\Phi^k(t)}$ and $\Phi^k(t) = k(\frac{\pi}{T}t + \frac{\pi}{2})$.

h and T are, respectively, the prototype filter impulse response and the time symbols spacing. The CMT signal is affected by a HPA NLD, a CFO ϵ and a phase offset ϕ as shown by Fig. 2.

It is customary to model the NLDs, caused by HPA, using the Bussgang theorem which states that the output signal of the HPA block of Fig. 2 can be written as follows [12]

$$y(t) = \alpha x(t) + d(t) \tag{2}$$

where $\alpha = |\alpha| e^{\phi_\alpha}$ is a complex factor and $d(t)$ is a zero mean additive noise, which is uncorrelated to $x(t)$.

After the HPA block, the resulting signal $y(t)$ is then affected by ϵ, ϕ and an AWGN noise $n(t)$. Hence, the received signal can be written as

$$r(t) = \alpha x(t) e^{j(2\pi\epsilon t+\phi)} + d(t) e^{j(2\pi\epsilon t+\phi)} + n(t) \tag{3}$$

3 SIR Expression

In the following, we assume that the coarse frequency estimation and compensation has been already performed. Nevertheless, residual CFO ϵ still affect the transmitted signal even if it is small enough to warrant some approximations considered later in this paper. We will also assume that the phase offsets ϕ and ϕ_α are perfectly compensated within the channel equalization process.

Taking into account the above observations and following the same derivations as in [11], we can express the received and demodulated symbol at the lth subcarrier on the 0th time index (for simplicity's sake) as

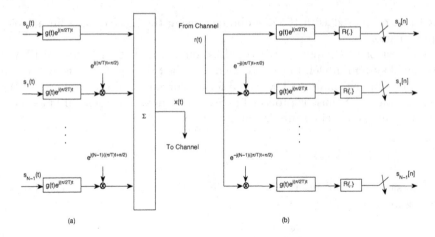

Fig. 1. Block diagram of a CMT transceiver: (a) transmitter; (b) receiver.

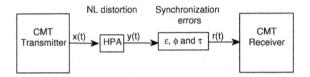

Fig. 2. System description with HPA NLD and synchronization errors.

$$\hat{s}_0^l = |\alpha| s_0^l Re \left\{ \int_{-\infty}^{\infty} h^2(t) e^{j2\pi\epsilon t} \right\} + \xi_{ici}^{isi}(\epsilon) + \hat{d}_0^l + \hat{n}_0^l \qquad (4)$$

where

$$\xi_{ici}^{isi} = |\alpha| Re \left\{ \sum_{n=-\infty}^{\infty} \sum_{k=0}^{N-1} s_n^k \int_{-\infty}^{\infty} h(t)h(t-nT) e^{j(\Phi^{k-l}(t)+2\pi\epsilon t)} dt \right\} \qquad (5)$$

is the interference term including ICI and ISI. $\hat{n}_0^l$ is the received AWGN noise and $\hat{d}_0^l$ is given by

$$\hat{d}_0^l = Re \left\{ \int_{-\infty}^{\infty} d(t) e^{j(2\pi\epsilon t+\phi)} \gamma_{l,0}^*(t) dt \right\} \qquad (6)$$

In the presence of HPA non linearities and CFO, the SIR can be expressed as follows

$$SIR(\epsilon) = \frac{P_s(\epsilon)}{P_i(\epsilon) + E\left[|\hat{d}_0^l|^2\right]} \qquad (7)$$

where $P_s(\epsilon)$, $P_i(\epsilon)$ and $E\left[|\hat{d}_0^l|^2\right]$ are the useful signal power, the interference power and the expectation of the non linear noise power $|\hat{d}_0^l|^2$, respectively. From (4), we can write the useful signal power as follows

$$P_s(\epsilon) = |\alpha|^2 \sigma_s^2 \left| \int_{-\infty}^{\infty} h^2(t) \cos(2\pi\epsilon t)\, dt \right|^2 \tag{8}$$

where σ_s^2 is the variance of the transmitted symbol.
On the other hand, the power of the interference is equal to

$$P_i(\epsilon) = E\left[|\xi_{ici,isi}|^2\right] = |\alpha|^2 \sigma_s^2 \sum_{n=-\infty}^{\infty} \sum_{\substack{k=0 \\ (n,k)\neq(m,l)}}^{N-1}$$

$$\left| \int_{-\infty}^{\infty} h(t)h(t-nT) \cos\left(\Phi^{k-l}(t) + 2\pi\epsilon t\right) dt \right|^2 \tag{9}$$

As in [2], we will consider the following observations. First, we assume that only adjacent subchannels overlap significantly. Therefore, the ICI is caused only by adjacent subcarriers $k = l - 1$ and $k = l + 1$. The same assumption can be made for the time index n since the prototype filter $h(t)$ is designed to minimize the effects of ISI beyond adjacent time symbols. Furthermore, we consider for simplicity that the signal is received on the subcarrier $l = 0$ which means that the summations over n and k in Eq. (9) will be limited to the values -1, 0 and 1. Finally, we assume that the CFO ϵ is very small and we can write $\sin(2\pi\epsilon t) \approx 2\pi\epsilon t$ and $\cos(2\pi\epsilon t) \approx 1$.

Using the above assumptions and following the same derivations as in [2], the useful signal power and the interference power can be rewritten, respectively, as follows

$$P_s(\epsilon) \approx |\alpha|^2 \sigma_s^2 \left| \int_{-\infty}^{\infty} h^2(t)dt \right|^2 = |\alpha|^2 \sigma_s^2 \tag{10}$$

and

$$P_i(\epsilon) \approx |\alpha|^2 \sigma_s^2 \lambda \epsilon^2 \tag{11}$$

with

$$\lambda = 8\pi^2 \sum_{n=-1}^{1} \left| \int_{-\infty}^{\infty} t\, h(t)h(t-nT) \cos\left(\frac{\pi}{T}t\right) dt \right|^2 \tag{12}$$

Therefore, the SIR expression (7) becomes

$$SIR(\epsilon) = \frac{1}{\lambda \epsilon^2 + \frac{\sigma_d^2}{|\alpha|^2 \sigma_s^2}} \tag{13}$$

with σ_d^2 is the variance of the non linear noise $d(t)$.

One may notice that expression (13) is obtained using the following approximation

$$E\left[\left|\hat{d}_0^0\right|^2\right] = E\left[\left|Re\left\{\int_{-\infty}^{\infty} d(t)e^{j2\pi\epsilon t}\gamma_{0,0}^*(t)dt\right\}\right|^2\right] \approx \sigma_d^2 \quad (14)$$

Actually, approximation (14) provides a reduced complexity but is not really rigorous. In order to examine its accuracy, the derivations of the next section are presented.

4   Variance of the Received Non Linear Noise

In this section, we will analyze the expression of the received non linear noise $\hat{d}$ in order to find a closed form expression of its variance $\sigma_{\hat{d}}^2 = E\left[\left|\hat{d}_0^0\right|^2\right]$.

Recall that the received non linear noise is expressed by

$$\hat{d}_0^0 = Re\left\{\int_{-\infty}^{\infty} d(t)h(t)e^{j(2\pi\epsilon + \frac{\pi}{2T})t}dt\right\} \quad (15)$$

We further consider PHYDYAS prototype filter whose impulse response is given by [13]

$$h(t) = \begin{cases} 2\sum_{k=0}^{K-1}(-1)^k H_k \cos\left(\frac{2\pi}{KT}kt\right) & \text{if } t \in [0, KT], \\ 0 & \text{elsewhere.} \end{cases} \quad (16)$$

where K is the overlapping factor and $H_k, k = 0,\ldots,K-1$ are the frequency coefficients of the filter.

Furthermore, the non linear noise $d(t)$ can be expressed as the sum of his real and imaginary components : $d(t) = d_r(t) + jd_i(t)$.

Therefore, the received non linear noise $\hat{d}_0^0$ can be rewritten as

$$\hat{d}_0^0 = 2\sum_{k=0}^{K-1}(-1)^k H_k \left[\int_0^{KT} d_r(t)\cos\left(\frac{2\pi}{KT}kt\right)\cos\left((2\pi\epsilon + \frac{\pi}{2T})t\right)dt\right.$$
$$\left. - \int_0^{KT} d_i(t)\cos\left(\frac{2\pi}{KT}kt\right)\sin\left((2\pi\epsilon + \frac{\pi}{2T})t\right)dt\right] \quad (17)$$

After a few steps of straightforward manipulations and by considering the following observations : (i) $d_r(t) = d_i(t) = d_r$ is constant in the interval $[0, KT]$, (ii) the overlapping factor $K = 4$, one can find that

$$\hat{d}_0^0 = -\frac{4T}{\pi}d_r \sin(4\pi T\epsilon)(\cos(4\pi T\epsilon) - \sin(4\pi T\epsilon))$$
$$\times \sum_{k=0}^{3}(-1)^k \frac{2H_k(4T\epsilon + 1)}{k^2 - (4T\epsilon + 1)^2} \quad (18)$$

Therefore, the variance $\sigma_{\hat{d}}^2$ can be expressed as

$$\sigma_{\hat{d}}^2 = 8\frac{T^2}{\pi^2}c^2\sigma_d^2(4T\epsilon+1)^2\sin^2(4\pi T\epsilon)(1-\sin(8\pi T\epsilon)) \tag{19}$$

where

$$c = 2\sum_{k=0}^{3}(-1)^k\frac{H_k}{k^2-(4T\epsilon+1)^2} \tag{20}$$

and the final SIR expression will become

$$SIR(\epsilon) = \frac{1}{\lambda\epsilon^2 + \frac{8\,T^2c^2\sigma_d^2(4T\epsilon+1)^2\sin^2(4\pi T\epsilon)(1-\sin(8\pi T\epsilon))}{\pi^2|\alpha|^2\sigma_s^2}} \tag{21}$$

5   Simulations

In this section, the accuracy of approximation (14) is evaluated via computer simulations. Furthermore, the sensitivity of the considered CMT system to the joint effect of CFO and NLD is also highlighted. The same results for OFDM and SMT (Staggered Modulated Multitone) systems (proposed by [2]) are also presented for comparison purposes.

Figure 3 shows the SIR curves corresponding, respectively, to a CMT system suffering from HPA NLD and CFO, and an SMT and an OFDM systems suffering from CFO. Moreover, we have plotted the SIR curves of the considered CMT system without NLD, an SMT system with CFO and NLD and an OFDM system with CFO and NLD. The results illustrated by Fig. 3 show that in the absence of NLD, the CMT signal is less sensitive to CFO than the SMT and OFDM ones. This can be explained by the high side lobes of the rectangular pulse shape used in OFDM and the presence of additional source of SIR degradation introduced by the mutual interference between real and imaginary parts of the transmitted SMT symbol. Figure 3 also shows that the SIR of the three systems is very sensitive to HPA non linear distortions. This sensitivity becomes less significant as the CFO increases. Such a result can be explained by the fact that for large values of CFO, this latter is the main source of distortions and the effect of HPA NLD becomes minor. Moreover, one can observe that in the presence of HPA NLD, the CMT system still perform better than SMT and OFDM systems.

The SIR curves presented in Fig. 3 are obtained using approximation (14) to be evaluated in the following. Figure 4 shows a comparison between the SIR expressions (13) and (21) obtained, respectively, using accurate and approximate expressions of $\sigma_{\hat{d}}^2$ ((19) and (14)). From this Figure, one can easily notice that the approximation (14) is not accurate for small values of CFO ϵ_N. However, when ϵ_N exceeds 0.25, the two curves tend to become closer because the CFO effect dominates over HPA NLD in this region and thus the system performance is not significantly affected by the variations of the non linear noise. Therefore, we can conclude that the approximation (14) can be considered accurate for half the range of the values of CFO.

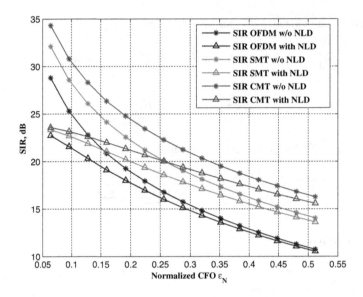

Fig. 3. SIR as a function of normalized CFO.

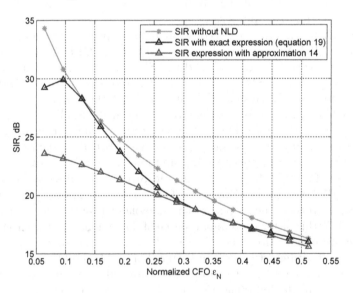

Fig. 4. SIR with exact and approximate expressions.

6   Conclusions

This paper was prepared to serve as a complement for our previous works [9,10] and [11] in which we investigate the joint effect of synchronization errors and HPA NLD on FBMC systems. In these works, we considered frequency errors and we derived the SIR expression of a CMT signal in the presence of CFO and NLD. The obtained expression was compared with other models designed for OFDM and SMT systems. In the present work, we showed that the approximation made on the received non linear noise variance is accurate over half the range of the values of CFO.

References

1. Sourck, H., Wu, Y., Bergmans, J., Sadri, S., Farhang-Boroujeny, B.: Effect of carrier frequency offset on offset QAM multicarrier filter bank systems over frequency-selective channels. In: Wireless Communications and Networking Conference (WCNC), pp. 1–6. IEEE, April 2010
2. Saeedi-Sourck, H., Wu, Y., Bergmans, J.W., Sadri, S., Farhang-Boroujeny, B.: Sensitivity analysis of offset QAM multicarrier systems to residual carrier frequency and timing offsets. Signal Process. **91**(7), 1604–1612 (2011)
3. Fusco, T., Petrella, A., Tanda, M.: Sensitivity of multi-user filter-bank multicarrier systems to synchronization errors. In: ISCCSP 2008, pp. 393–398, March 2008
4. Zayani, R., Shaiek, H., Roviras, D., Medjahdi, Y.: Closed-form BER expression for (QAM or OQAM)-based OFDM system with HPA nonlinearity over Rayleigh fading channel. IEEE Wirel. Commun. Lett. **4**(1), 38–41 (2015)
5. Yiming, L., O'Droma, M.: A novel decomposition analysis of nonlinear distortion in OFDM transmitter systems. IEEE Trans. Signal Process. **63**(19), 5264–5273 (2015)
6. Yiming, L., O'Droma, M., Ye, J.: A practical analysis of performance optimization in OSTBC based nonlinear MIMO-OFDM systems. IEEE Trans. Commun. **62**(3), 930–938 (2014)
7. Araujo, T., Dinis, R.: On the accuracy of the gaussian approximation for the evaluation of nonlinear effects in OFDM signals. IEEE Trans. Commun. **60**(2), 346–351 (2012)
8. Bouhadda, H., Shaiek, H., Roviras, D., Zayani, R., Medjahdi, Y., Bouallegue, R.: Theoretical analysis of BER performance of nonlinearly amplified FBMC/OQAM and OFDM signals. EURASIP J. Adv. Signal Process. **2014**(1), 1–16 (2014). https://doi.org/10.1186/1687-6180-2014-60
9. Elmaroud, B., Faqihi, A., Aboutajdine, D.: Sensitivity analysis of FBMC-based multi-cellular networks to synchronization errors and HPA nonlinearities. EURASIP J. Adv. Signal Process. **2017**(1), 3 (2017). https://doi.org/10.1186/s13634-016-0441-0
10. Elmaroud, B., Faqihi, M.A., Abbad, M., Aboutajdine, D.: BER analysis of FBMC based multi-cellular networks in the presence of synchronisation errors and HPA NLD. In: 2016 IEEE 84th Vehicular Technology Conference (VTC-Fall), pp. 1–6, September 2016
11. Elmaroud, B., Faqihi, A., Aboutajdine, D.: Performance analysis of asynchronous and non linear FBMC systems. In: Sabir, E., García Armada, A., Ghogho, M., Debbah, M. (eds.) UNet 2017. LNCS, vol. 10542, pp. 550–561. Springer, Cham (2017). https://doi.org/10.1007/978-3-319-68179-5_48
12. Dardari, D., Tralli, V., Vaccari, A.: A theoretical characterization of nonlinear distortion effects in OFDM systems. IEEE Trans. Comm. **48**(10), 1755–1764 (2000)
13. Bellanger, M.: Specification and design of a prototype filter for filter bank based multicarrier transmission. In: IEEE ICASSP 2001, vol. 4, pp. 2417–2420 (2001)

Resource Allocation for Multi-source Multi-relay Wireless Networks: A Multi-Armed Bandit Approach

Ali Al Khansa[1,2(✉)], Raphael Visoz[1], Yezekael Hayel[2], and Samson Lasaulce[3]

[1] Orange Labs, Chatillon, France
{ali.alkhansa,raphael.visoz}@orange.com
[2] LIA, Avignon University, Avignon, France
yezekael.hayel@univ-avignon.fr
[3] CRAN, CNRS, Nancy, France
samson.lasaulce@univ-lorraine.fr

Abstract. In this paper, we consider the problem of link adaptation (rate allocation) of Orthogonal Multiple Access Multiple Relay Channel (OMAMRC) using the Multi-Armed Bandit (MAB) online learning framework. The cooperative system is composed of a transmission phase where sources transmit in a round robin manner, and a retransmission phase where a scheduled node sends redundancies. We assume that we have no knowledge of the Channel State Information (CSI) nor of the Channel Distributed Information (CDI). Accordingly, rate allocation must be learned online following a sequential learning algorithm. We adapt to one variant of the MAB framework algorithms, the Upper Confidence Bound (UCB) family, and specifically the UCB1 algorithm. The UCB1 algorithm achieves a logarithmic regret uniformly over time, without any preliminary knowledge about the reward distributions. Due to the exponential growth of the number of arms, following the multiple sources included in the rate allocation, the UCB1 algorithm features a complexity problem. Thus, we propose a sequential UCB1 (SUCB1) algorithm which solves the complexity issue, and outperforms the UCB1 algorithm.

Keywords: Link Adaptation · Multi-Armed Bandit · Upper confidence bound · Multi-source multi-relay wireless network · Spectral efficiency

1 Introduction

One of the main objectives for 5G and 5G-beyond cellular networks is to allow heterogeneous services to coexist within the same network architecture. Some of these services need a very high peak data rates and a fast adaptation of the channel state, as in enhanced Mobile Broadband (eMBB). In order to meet those needs, we aim at improving the spectral efficiency. Cooperative communication [1] represents one of the key physical layer technologies which aims to optimize the spectral efficiency. The concept is to use the shared resources and

© Springer Nature Switzerland AG 2021
H. Elbiaze et al. (Eds.): UNet 2021, LNCS 12845, pp. 62–75, 2021.
https://doi.org/10.1007/978-3-030-86356-2_6

information of the users to improve the transmission and reception processes. The cooperation process can be performed by sources themselves (user cooperation), or by using some dedicated relay nodes. The difference between a relay node and a source node which implements user cooperation is the fact that the latter has its own message whereas the relay node does not.

Cooperative models have been analyzed extensively in the prior literature. These models depend on the number of source nodes, relay nodes, and destination nodes included. For example, we call the system Multiple Relay Channel (MRC) when we have multiple relays helping a single source to communicate with a single destination [2]. Other two examples are the Relay Broadcast Channel (RBC) [2] and the Multiple Access Relay Channel (MARC) [3]. In RBC, the system is composed of a single source, a single relay, and multiple destination nodes, whereas in the MARC, we have a single relay node helping multiple users to communicate with a single destination.

Here, we consider the Multiple Access Multiple Relay Channel (MAMRC), where we have multiple relay nodes, helping multiple users to communicate with a single destination. In addition, we consider user cooperation, where users that have no message to send, act as relays. Specifically, we consider a slow-fading half-duplex Orthogonal Multiple Access Multiple Relay Channel (OMAMRC), where orthogonality is achieved using Time Division Multiplexing (TDM) (check Fig. 1).

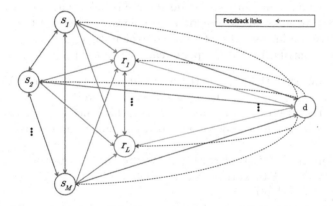

Fig. 1. Cooperative Orthogonal Multiple Access Multiple Relay Channel (OMAMRC) with feedback broadcast control channel to indicate the destination decoding set.

There are several relaying protocols widely used in cooperative communication. One category of these protocols is the linear relaying protocols, and its famous example the Amplify-and-Forward (AF) protocol [4]. Another category is the non-linear (regenerative) relaying protocols. Some examples of regenerative protocols are the Compress-and-Forward [5] and the Quantize-Map-and-Forward [6]. In our work, we use the Selective Decode-and-Forward (SDF) relaying protocol, where relays can forward only a signal representative of successfully decoded source messages. The error detection is based on Cyclic Redundancy

Check (CRC) bits that are appended to each source message. The used protocol is an updated version of the well known Decode-and-Forward (DF) protocol [7]. In DF, cooperative nodes are obliged to wait to successfully decode all the source messages before starting to cooperate, whereas in SDF, they can start cooperating before.

In this paper, we investigate the problem of Link Adaptation (LA) (rate allocation), where the destination is considered as the centralized node which allocates the rates for the multiple sources. In the prior art, several heuristic algorithms were presented. In [8], a Slow-Link Adaptation (SLA) algorithm was proposed. The algorithms proposed were heuristic, and based on the information available at the destination. When Channel State Information (CSI) is available, Fast Link Adaptation (FLA) algorithm is used, where allocation is performed once there is a change in the CSI. On the contrary, if CSI is not available (in high mobility scenarios), the SLA algorithm is used, where allocation is based on the Channel Distribution Information (CDI) (for example: the average Signal to Noise Ratio (SNR)) of the links.

In this work, we aim to solve the LA problem using a different perspective. First, we aim to use an algorithm which is not heuristic, and where the regret is bounded and tractable. Next, we want to solve the problem when no information is given at the destination. In other words, we aim to perform rate allocation using a learning algorithm, where the probability of transmission success at a certain rate is unknown (since the channel state is unknown) and rather needed to be learned. We adapt to the well known framework called Multi-Armed Bandit (MAB), where it addresses the exploration-exploitation dilemma.

The main contributions of the paper can be summarized as the following:

- To our knowledge, this work is the first which tackles LA for MAMRC with online learning perspective, using the MAB framework.
- We state the MAB problem based on the utility metric (spectral efficiency per frame), following the definitions of the common and individual outage events.
- We implement the UCB1 algorithm in the presented framework, and then, an approximated UCB1 algorithm was presented aiming to reduce the initialization step of the algorithm.
- We finally propose a sequential UCB1 algorithm which solves the problem of exponential dimension of the number of arms.

The rest of the paper is organized as follows: In the next section, the related work of the MAB literature is presented. In Sect. 3, the system model is presented. In Sect. 4, outage events are given, followed by the MAB problem formulation. In Sect. 5, the LA algorithms are described. Finally, numerical results and main conclusions are presented in Sects. 6 and 7 respectively.

2   Related Work

First, we state the main issue which MAB framework tackles, i.e., the exploration-exploitation dilemma. In scenarios where multiple choices are possible (multiple arms), each with an unknown average reward, MAB algorithms give sequential steps to decide whether we need to learn more (exploration), or to stay with the option that gave best rewards in the past (exploitation). There are different types of MAB problems, each based on the assumptions of the problem. In the survey [9], three different fundamental types of MAB problems were mentioned, stochastic, adversarial, and Markovian. In this paper, we are interested in the stochastic MAB problem, as it aligns with the case of rate allocation problem (the reward is stochastic). From a historical point of view, Lai and Robbins [10] introduced the first analysis of stochastic bandits with asymptotic analysis of regret. There, the principle of *optimism in the face of uncertainty* (to be optimistic while thinking about the not well explored choices) was used and the Upper Confidence Bound (UCB) algorithm was proposed. This concept is widely used in most of the MAB literature.

In UCB-like algorithms, we favor the exploration of actions with a strong potential to have an optimal value [11], and UCB measures this potential by an upper confidence bound of the reward value. Based on this type of literature, a lot of algorithms have been further proposed [12] (Sect. 2.2) and [13]. In [13], the authors proved that the proposed KL-UCB algorithm attains the optimal rate in finite-time. In addition, they proved that this algorithm is optimal for Bernoulli distributions (problems with reward of Bernoulli distribution).

Another type of algorithms widely used is based on Thompson Sampling (TS) (also known as posterior sampling and probability matching) [14]. Contrary to UCB-type algorithms, the TS algorithms are based on the assumption of posterior distribution for the unknown metric we are trying to learn. The algorithm chooses the arm which maximize the expected reward based on the current distribution. Then, after each iteration, the posterior distribution is updated. Although this type of algorithms was ignored in the academic literature until recently, several nowadays problems are using these strategies [15]. For interested readers, [16] gives a detailed discussion on when, why, and how to apply TS.

Besides UCB-type and TS-type algorithms, there are also different approaches tackling the MAB problem. In [17], rather than using the concept of *optimism in the face of uncertainty*, a new general algorithm is proposed aiming at matching the minimal exploration rates of sub-optimal arms as characterized in the derivation of the regret lower bound. In this algorithm, rather than only performing exploration and exploitation, a third process is taken into consideration as well: estimation. For simpler algorithms, ϵ-greedy is a well-known algorithm, where a fixed value $\epsilon \in [0,1]$, decides the percentage of time you spend on exploration and exploitation. Since, with a fixed value of ϵ, we will reach a linear (not logarithmic) regret, decreasing ϵ-greedy algorithms are used, taking ϵ as a decreasing variable with time (usually it is in the form of a fraction between a constant and time). We find in literature several papers comparing the previously mentioned algorithms, as in [18], where the power allocation problem was solved using several algorithms, as the UCB, TS and ϵ-greedy.

In our framework, there is a fixed set of Modulation and Coding Scheme (MCS) representing the available set of rates. These rates represent the possible choices of the MAB problem. Since we are considering MAMRC framework, at each frame transmission, the destination will allocate a rate for each given source. In other words, rather than selecting a single arm of the MAB, we need to select multiple arms, each corresponding to each of the multiple source nodes. Such kind of MAB problems is given under the name of Combinatorial MAB (CMAB), where a subset of arms is selected at each step, forming a *Super Arm*. In the literature, CMAB was investigated in several applications. In [19], the problem of beam selection in a vehicular network was solved using CMAB algorithms, based on TS. In [20], CMAB was also presented but this time using UCB-type algorithms. There, two applications were selected, online advertising and social influence maximization for viral marketing. In [21], Combinatorial Sleeping MAB model with Fairness constraints (CSMAB-F) was presented. The concept of sleeping arm is when some arms are not always available. In the next section, we present the system model, describing how a frame is transmitted. Then, based on this model, we present the CMAB rate allocation problem.

3   System Model

The system model is a slow-fading half-duplex OMAMRC. There are M source nodes, a single destination node, and L dedicated relay nodes. The source nodes belong to the set $\mathcal{S} = \{1, \ldots, M\}$, the relay nodes belong to the set $\mathcal{R} = \{M + 1, \ldots, M + L\}$, and we define the set of all source and relay nodes as $\mathcal{N} = \mathcal{S} \cup \mathcal{R} = \{1, \ldots, M + L\}$. In other words, a source s_i will be the node i in set $\mathcal{N}$, and a relay r_i will be the node $i + M$ in set $\mathcal{N}$. In order to explain a frame transmission in a cooperative system, the two steps of transmission should be explained, i.e., the transmission phase and the retransmission phase.

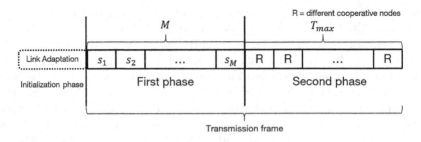

Fig. 2. Transmission of a frame: initialization, first and second phases.

As seen in Fig. 2, the frame transmission is composed of two steps, M time slots for transmission (each source of the M sources sends in one time slot), and several time slots for retransmission (up to $T_{\max}$ time slots). At the beginning of each time slot of the retransmission phase, the scheduler (at the destination) selects a relay node to send redundancies based on its correctly decoded source messages. We call the set of correctly decoded source messages the decoding set. The selection strategy used is based on maximizing the number of correctly decoded messages at the destination. This is done by choosing the node with the highest mutual information with the destination. Note that only the nodes which were able to decode at least one source from the set of non-successfully decoded sources at the destination are possible choices for selection (nodes which do not satisfy this condition cannot help no matter what the mutual information is). In [22], it is shown that this low-complexity strategy can reach the upper bound selection strategy (based on exhaustive search approach). For that reason, we retain to this selection strategy in the paper, although other strategies might also be used. Nevertheless, the LA problem and the proposed algorithms will not change.

The messages of all sources are mutually independent. A message $\mathbf{u}_s \in \mathbb{F}_2^{K_s}$ of a source s has a length of K_s information bits, where $\mathbb{F}_2$ represents the binary Galois field. In addition, the length K_s depends on the selected Modulation and Coding Schemes for that source. We assume that we have a finite set of possible rates of size n_{MCS}. These possible rates represent the arms of the MAB problem. In the initialization phase, the phase which comes before transmission and retransmission (check Fig. 2), the destination allocates M rates for the M sources. In other words, the destination chooses a set of M arms of the n_{MCS} arms, forming a *super arm*. As a results, our MAB problem is now a CMAB problem, with n_{MCS}^M arms.

In the prior art, the selection of the rates was based on the information available at the destination, i.e., CSI or CDI. Here, no information is available, and rather needed to be learned. Finally, for a given transmitting node $a \in \mathcal{S} \cup \mathcal{R}$, and a receiving node $b \in \mathcal{S} \cup \mathcal{R} \cup \{d\}$, at a given channel use k, the received signal $y_{a,b,k}$ can be written as:

$$y_{a,b,k} = h_{a,b} x_{a,k} + n_{a,b,k}, \tag{1}$$

where $x_{a,k} \in \mathbb{C}$ is the coded modulated symbol whose power is normalized to unity, $h_{a,b}$ are the channel fading gains, which are independent and follow a zero-mean circularly symmetric complex Gaussian distribution with variance $\gamma_{a,b}$, and $n_{a,b,k}$ represents the independent and identically distributed AWGN samples, which follow a zero-mean circularly-symmetric complex Gaussian distribution with unit variance. During the first phase, a given channel use k belong to $\{1, \ldots, U\}$, while during the second phase, k belongs to $\{1, \ldots, Q\}$, where U and Q represent the number of channel uses in each phase respectively.

4 Problem Formulation

4.1 Objective Function

Here, we define the utility function as the spectral efficiency per frame defined as the ratio between the total number of successfully received bits and the total number of channel uses in a given frame. The utility function depends on the vector of selected rates $\{R_i\}, i \in \{1, \ldots, M\}$ (rates we are allocating) chosen from a fixed set of possible rates. It also depends on the number of channel uses used at each transmission and retransmission phase. We define also the outage events $\mathcal{O}_{i,t}$ which occur when source i is not decoded correctly after the transmission phase ($t = 0$) and at each retransmission l up to t ($l = 1, \ldots, t$). We define, accordingly, the outage event indication $O_{i,t}$ which takes value 1 if the event $\mathcal{O}_{i,t}$ happens, and 0 otherwise. Or, in mathematical term, for any elementary event w, $O_{i,t}(w) = [w \in \mathcal{O}_{i,t}]$ where [P] denotes the Inverson bracket which takes the value 1 if P is true, and 0 otherwise. The spectral efficiency per frame can be written as

$$
\begin{aligned}
\eta^{frame}\left(\{R_i\}, \alpha\right) &= \frac{\text{nb bits successfully received}}{\text{nb channel uses}} \\
&= \frac{\sum_{i=1}^{M} K_i(1 - O_{i,T_{max}})}{MU + QT_{used}} \\
&= \frac{\sum_{i=1}^{M} R_i(1 - O_{i,T_{max}})}{M + \alpha T_{used}}
\end{aligned}
\tag{2}
$$

where

- $R_i = K_i/U$ represents the rate of a source i,
- $\alpha = Q/U$ denotes the ratio of the channel uses of retransmission phase Q and the channel uses of the transmission phase U,
- $O_{i,T_{max}}$ is the outage indication as defined above, i.e., $O_{i,T_{max}} = 1$ means that source i is not decoded correctly during a frame (since the maximum number of retransmissions is T_{max}),
- $T_{used} \in \{1, \ldots, T_{max}\}$ is the number of retransmissions activated for a frame.

The value of T_{uesd} depends on the number of retransmission rounds needed for the destination to decode all the source nodes, or to state an outage event (after T_{max} retransmissions). The outage indication $O_{i,T_{max}}$ is obtained from an information theory perspective. This means that we don't use practical decoding schemes (e.g., LDPC or Turbo codes), but we follow the ideal information theory assumptions. In other words, we use the knowledge of the links' states, assume as infinite codeword length with mutual information achieving (spatially distributed) channel coding codebooks, and a Maximum Likelihood (ML) decoding. Also, we assume that two successive frames are received with correlation time separation (to ensure no correlation). Finally, we formulate the analytical expression of the outage events. The detailed expressions of the common and individual outage, based on the results of [23], are presented in the Appendix A.

4.2   MAB Problem

After defining the utility metric, as well as the outage events, we can now formulate the considered rate adaptation problem as a MAB problem. We consider a finite set of possible arms of size n_{MCS}. At each step, a *super arm* of size M is selected for the M source nodes included. This leads us to an equivalent CMAB of arms size n_{MCS}^M. The reward of each arm is a stochastic random variable, with an unknown distribution and unknown average. We define the random variable $X_i(t)$ as the reward given when we select the *super arm* i at the tth transmission frame. The reward was defined before as the spectral efficiency per frame, and the randomness is within the variables T_{used} which varies between zero and T_{max}, and the outage event indications of each source node. We define the expected value of the reward of the *super arm* i as $\theta_i = \mathbb{E}[X_i(t)]$.

For a given online sequential algorithm π, where at each frame j, a decision I_j of a *super arm* i is selected ($I_j = i$), we define the regret as the difference between the rewards of the optimal algorithm (Oracle algorithm selecting the optimal arm each round) and the given algorithm. The regret of algorithm π up to transmission frame t can be written as:

$$\text{Reg}^\pi(t) = \theta^* t - \sum_{i=1}^{n_{MCS}^M} \theta_i \mathbb{E}[n_i^\pi(t)], \tag{3}$$

where θ^* represents the expected value of the optimal reward (i.e., the reward of the optimal *super arm* i^*), and $\mathbb{E}[n_i^\pi(t)]$ represents the expected value of the number of times arm i was selected after t rounds when using algorithm π. We aim to propose a rate allocation algorithm which performs exploration and exploitation in a way that minimizes this regret.

5   Algorithm

We retain here to a well-known algorithm in the literature, specifically, a UCB-like algorithm. Several types of UCB algorithms are seen in the prior art, each depending on the problem considered, the reward type, and the way we choose the upper bound. In this paper, we use the UCB1 algorithm [24], where it is known that it achieves a logarithmic regret uniformly over t and without any preliminary knowledge about the reward distributions. The only condition is to assume that the rewards are bounded in [0, 1], and this normalization can be assumed easily with no loss of generality. The sketch of the algorithm is presented in Algorithm 1.

Algorithm 1. UCB1

Initialization: For $t = 0, \ldots, n_{MCS}^M - 1$, for the $(t+1)^{th}$ transmission, select the super arm t+1 (play each super arm once).

UCB: For $t \geq n_{MCS}^M$, for the $(t+1)^{th}$ transmission, select the super arm i which maximizes $\overline{X}_i + \sqrt{\frac{2\ln t}{n_i}}$.

After the initialization step, where each arm is explored once, we start choosing the next arms based on the information collected. We see next that the choice is based on two terms summed together, $\overline{X}_i$ representing the average reward obtained from *super arm i* up to transmission t, and the upper confidence term represented by $\sqrt{\frac{2\ln t}{n_i}}$, where n_i represents the number of times *super arm i* was selected up to transmission t. The first term, i.e., $\overline{X}_i$, gives the exploitation term, where the history rewards of the arms are taken into consideration. On the other hand, the second term, i.e., $\sqrt{\frac{2\ln t}{n_i}}$, gives the exploration term. The ratio can be understood as, when a given arm i is not selected for enough time, compared to other arms, the fraction increases, and then the index of this arm composed of the sum of the two terms increases. In this way, we tend to compromise between the history of the rewards of each arm and the number of times this arm was selected. One final comment, about the logarithmic in the expression: In UCB1, we try to decrease the exploration coefficient as time increases, trying to set a limit to the exploration phase when enough information is collected through previously selected arms. The mathematical aspect of this result is based on the Hoeffding's Inequality, a theorem applicable to any bounded distribution. In theorem 1, the expected regret of the UCB1 algorithm when played t times is presented.

Theorem 1. *For all $n_{\text{MCS}}^M > 1$, if policy UCB1 is run on n_{MCS}^M machines having arbitrary reward distributions $P_1, \ldots, P_{n_{\text{MCS}}^M}$ with support in $[0,1]$, then its expected regret after any number t of plays is at most:*

$$8 \sum_{i:\theta_i < \theta^*} \left(\frac{\ln t}{\Delta_i} \right) + \left(1 + \frac{\pi^2}{3} \right) \left(\sum_{j=1}^{n_{\text{MCS}}^M} \Delta_j \right),$$

where $\theta_1, \ldots, \theta_{n_{\text{MCS}}^M}$ are the expected values of $P_1, \ldots, P_{n_{\text{MCS}}^M}$, and Δ_i is defined as:

$$\Delta_i = \theta^* - \theta_i.$$

Proof. The proof of the above upper bound is omitted and can be found in [24].

In practice, the proposed algorithm suffers mainly from the exponential growth of arms. Specifically, the initialization phase (pure exploration phase) will take too much time before reaching the exploitation-exploration phase. Thus, we propose an Approximated UCB1 (AUCB1) algorithm, which reduces the complexity of the initialization phase.

The goal of the initialization phase is to explore each *super arm* once, and to set its index, we call index the sum $\overline{X}_i + \sqrt{\frac{2\ln t}{n_i}}$. We propose here setting an approximated initial index in order to decrease the complexity of the initialization phase. One way in doing so is by removing the exponential relationship between the sources forming the *super arm*. In other words, rather than taking *super arms* initially, we take each arm by itself (each possible rate), and we test this arm with all the possible sources. In this case, when a source is sending with a given rate, other sources send nothing. We repeat this process for a given arm with all the given sources. Finally, we average for this arm the number of transmitted bits (Rate × success or failure), and we save the highest T_{used} needed with all the sources. We repeat this process for all arms (rates). Finally, for each *super arm* composed of M subset of arms, we calculate the reward (index) as the average of transmitted bits divided by the number of channel uses while using the highest T_{used} of the considered subset of arms (rates). Following these steps, we approximate the reward (recall Eq. 2). The complexity of the initialization phase is reduced from $O(n_{MCS}^M)$ to $O(n_{MCS} \times M)$. For brevity, we omit here the step-by-step AUCB1 algorithm, as it will only be an initialization step in the proposed Sequential UCB1 (SUCB1) algorithm presented next.

In SUCB1, the idea is to generalize the AUCB1 algorithm for all iterations rather than only the initialization step. After setting the indices of each arm using AUCB1, SUCB1 chooses each *super arms* successively, arm by arm. In other words, instead of choosing the *super arm* directly, we choose for each source of the M sources the arm with the highest index. After each selection, we update the indices' counter. Finally, we update the indices based on the cumulative reward, each based on decoding the signal of the related source. In SUCB1, we have n_{MCS} arms, rather than n_{MCS}^M arms, and this reduction will decrease the regret as we will see in the numerical results section. The sketch of the algorithm is presented in Algorithm 2.

Algorithm 2. SUCB1

Initialization: For $t = 0, \ldots, n_{MCS} \times (M-1)$, for the $(t+1)^{th}$ transmission, initialize the arms indices following the steps of *AUCB1*

SUCB: For $t \geq n_{MCS} \times M$, for the $(t+1)^{th}$ transmission, select the super arm i successively, arm by arm, for each of the M sources as:

  - select the arm which maximizes $\overline{X}_i + \sqrt{\frac{2\ln t}{n_i}}$.
  - update n_i
  - repeat for all sources within M to reach the super arm i

---

6   Numerical Results

In this section, we validate the learning algorithms with three source nodes and three relay nodes, while using 4 possible retransmissions in the second phase ($T_{max} = 4$) and $\alpha = 1/2$. We assume independent Gaussian distributed channel inputs (with zero mean and unit variance), with $I_{a,b} = \log_2(1 + |h_{a,b}|^2)$. Note that some other formulas could be also used for calculating $I_{a,b}$ but they would not have any impact on the basic concepts of this work. There are many factors to investigate: links configuration, SNR levels, and different MCS families.

Due to brevity, and after carefully checking different possible scenarios, we present the results of symmetric link configuration (SNR of all channel links is symmetric). Three different levels of SNR will be considered, specifically, SNR = $\{-4, 6, 21\}$ dB. The importance of choosing the different SNR links, is that the optimal rate allocation (the Oracle allocation) is different at each SNR level. Following the discrete MCS family whose rates belong to the set $\{0.5; 1; 1.5; 2; 2.5; 3; 3.5\}$ [b.c.u], the Oracle rate allocation of sources $\{s_1, s_2, s_3\}$ will be $\{1, 1, 1\}$, $\{3, 3, 2.5\}$, and $\{3.5, 3.5, 3.5\}$ respectively to the SNR set investigated.

In Figs. 3, 4, and 5, we see the regret analysis of the three different SNR levels. For clarity of the results, we present the regret in the form of percentage loss with respect to the optimal efficiency. In other words, we compare the efficiency of the algorithms as a ratio of the rewards of the algorithms and the Oracle. In Fig. 3, for SNR = -4 dB, we see that the three algorithms are featuring a close regret level (up to 25% loss after 1000 samples). Next, in Fig. 4, for SNR = 6 dB, we see a great improvement with using SUCB1 (reaching 90% of the optimal reward), as compared to UCB1 and AUCB1 which act closely as in the case when $\gamma = -4$ dB. In Fig. 5, the same result is seen for SNR = 21 dB, where SUCB1 is outperforms other algorithms, while AUCB1 is slightly better than UCB1. Finally, in Fig. 6, we present the Average Spectral Efficiency (ASE), for the different SNR levels between -5 and 15 dB after 500 samples (larger numbers of samples were investigated and gave the same results). We see that the proposed SUCB1 algorithm approaches the upper bound (the Oracle) while outperforming UCB1 and AUCB1.

7   Conclusion

In this paper, we investigate the LA of OMAMRC using an online learning framework, MAB. First, we formulate the system model as a MAB problem. Then, we adapt to the UCB-type family, specifically the UCB1 algorithm. In order to solve the problem of complexity of exponential number of arms included in the MAMRC system, a sequential algorithm SUCB1 is proposed. Within SUCB1, we use an approximated initialization phase AUCB1, then, we choose arms sequentially for the considered set of sources. The numerical results show that the proposed algorithm outperforms the traditional UCB1 algorithm in terms of regret and average spectral efficiency.

Appendix

A: Outage Events

Based on [23] proposition 1, we see a direct relation between the individual outage and the common outage. The individual outage is defined as the event that an individual source is not decoded correctly at the destination after T_{max} rounds. Similarly, common outage is defined for a set of sources, and it is declared when at least one of the sources within this set is not decoded correctly at the

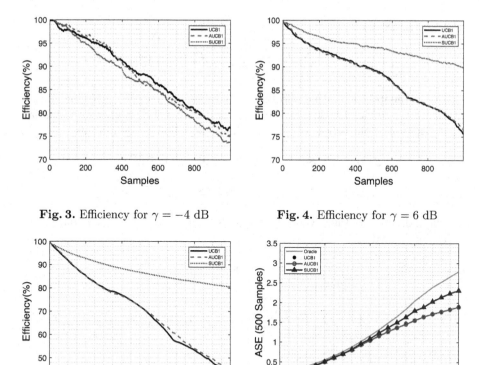

Fig. 3. Efficiency for $\gamma = -4$ dB

Fig. 4. Efficiency for $\gamma = 6$ dB

Fig. 5. Efficiency for $\gamma = 21$ dB

Fig. 6. ASE vs γ after 500 samples

destination. In other words, common outage of a set occurs when one or more of its source nodes are in an individual outage.

Both, the individual outage event $\mathcal{O}_{s,t}(a_t, \mathcal{S}_{a_t,t-1}|\mathcal{P}_{t-1})$ of a source s after round t, and the common outage event $\mathcal{E}_t(a_t, \mathcal{S}_{a_t,t-1}|\mathcal{P}_{t-1})$ after round t, depend directly on the rate being scheduled. In addition, they depend on the selected node $a_t \in \mathcal{N}$ and its associated decoding set $\mathcal{S}_{a_t,t-1}$. They are conditional on the knowledge of $\mathcal{P}_{t-1}$, where $\mathcal{P}_{t-1}$ denotes the set collecting the nodes $\hat{a}_l$ which were selected in rounds $l \in \{1, \ldots, t-1\}$ prior to round t together with their associated decoding sets $\mathcal{S}_{\hat{a}_l, l-1}$, and the decoding set of the destination $\mathcal{S}_{d,t-1}$ ($\mathcal{S}_{d,0}$ is the destination's decoding set after the first phase).

Analytically, the common outage event of a given subset of sources is declared if the vector of their rates lies outside of the corresponding MAC capacity region. For some subset of sources $\mathcal{B} \subseteq \overline{\mathcal{S}}_{d,t-1}$, where $\overline{\mathcal{S}}_{d,t-1} = \mathcal{S} \setminus \mathcal{S}_{d,t-1}$ is the set of non-successfully decoded sources at the destination after round $t-1$, and for a candidate node a_t this event can be expressed as:

$$\mathcal{E}_{t,\mathcal{B}}(a_t, \mathcal{S}_{a_t, t-1})$$

$$= \bigcup_{\mathcal{U} \subseteq \mathcal{B}} \left\{ \sum_{i \in \mathcal{U}} R_i > \sum_{i \in \mathcal{U}} I_{i,d} + \alpha \sum_{l=1}^{t-1} I_{\hat{a}_l, d} \mathcal{C}_{\hat{a}_l}(\mathcal{U}) + \alpha I_{a_t, d} \mathcal{C}_{a_t}(\mathcal{U}) \right\}, \tag{4}$$

where $I_{a,b}$ denotes the mutual information between the nodes a and b (the mutual information is defined based on the channel inputs, check Sect. 6 for Gaussian inputs example), and where $\mathcal{C}_{\hat{a}_l}$ and $\mathcal{C}_{a_t}$ have the following definitions:

$$\begin{aligned}
\mathcal{C}_{\hat{a}_l}(\mathcal{U}) &= \left[(\mathcal{S}_{\hat{a}_l, l-1} \cap \mathcal{U} \neq \emptyset) \wedge (\mathcal{S}_{\hat{a}_l, l-1} \cap \mathcal{I} = \emptyset) \right], \\
\mathcal{C}_{a_t}(\mathcal{U}) &= \left[(\mathcal{S}_{a_t, t-1} \cap \mathcal{U} \neq \emptyset) \wedge (\mathcal{S}_{a_t, t-1} \cap \mathcal{I} = \emptyset) \right].
\end{aligned} \tag{5}$$

The individual outage event of a source s after round t for a candidate node a_t can be defined as:

$$\mathcal{O}_{s,t}(a_t, \mathcal{S}_{a_t, t-1}) = \bigcap_{\mathcal{I} \subset \overline{\mathcal{S}}_{d,t-1}, \mathcal{B} = \overline{\mathcal{I}}, s \in \mathcal{B}} \mathcal{E}_{t,\mathcal{B}}(a_t, \mathcal{S}_{a_t, t-1}),$$

$$= \bigcap_{\mathcal{I} \subset \overline{\mathcal{S}}_{d,t-1}} \bigcup_{\mathcal{U} \subseteq \overline{\mathcal{I}}: s \in \mathcal{U}} \left\{ \sum_{i \in \mathcal{U}} R_i > \sum_{i \in \mathcal{U}} I_{i,d} + \alpha \sum_{l=1}^{t-1} I_{\hat{a}_l, d} \mathcal{C}_{\hat{a}_l}(\mathcal{U}) + \alpha I_{a_t, d} \mathcal{C}_{a_t}(\mathcal{U}) \right\},$$

$$\tag{6}$$

where $\overline{\mathcal{I}} = \overline{\mathcal{S}}_{d,t-1} \setminus \mathcal{I}$.

References

1. Kramer, G., Marić, I., Yates, R.D.: Cooperative communications (2007)
2. Kramer, G., Gastpar, M., Gupta, P.: Cooperative strategies and capacity theorems for relay networks. IEEE Trans. Inf. Theory **51**(9), 3037–3063 (2005)
3. Sankaranarayanan, L., Kramer, G., Mandayam, N.B.: Hierarchical sensor networks: capacity bounds and cooperative strategies using the multiple-access relay channel model. In: 2004 First Annual IEEE Communications Society Conference on Sensor and Ad Hoc Communications and Networks, SECON 2004, pp. 191–199. IEEE (2004)
4. Laneman, J.N.: Cooperative diversity in wireless networks: algorithms and architectures. Ph.D. dissertation, Massachusetts Institute of Technology, Cambridge, MA (2002)
5. Lim, S.H., Kim, Y.H., Gamal, A.E., Chung, S.Y.: Noisy network coding. IEEE Trans. Inf. Theory **57**(5), 3132–3152 (2011)
6. Avestimehr, A.S., Diggavi, S.N., Tse, D.N.C.: Wireless network information flow: a deterministic approach. IEEE Trans. Inf. Theory **57**(4), 1872–1905 (2011)
7. Cover, T., Gamal, A.E.: Capacity theorems for the relay channel. IEEE Trans. Inf. Theory **25**(5), 572–584 (1979)
8. Khansa, A.A., Cerovic, S., Visoz, R., Hayel, Y., Lasaulce, S.: Slow-link adaptation algorithm for multi-source multi-relay wireless networks using best-response dynamics. To be presented at NetGCOOP (2021)
9. Bubeck, S., Cesa-Bianchi, N.: Regret analysis of stochastic and nonstochastic multi-armed bandit problems. arXiv preprint arXiv:1204.5721 (2012)

10. Lai, T.L., Robbins, H.: Asymptotically efficient adaptive allocation rules. Adv. Appl. Math. **6**(1), 4–22 (1985)
11. Weng, L.: The multi-armed bandit problem and its solutions. lilianweng.github.io/lil-log (2018)
12. Bubeck, S.: Bandits games and clustering foundations. Ph.D. dissertation, INRIA Nord Europe (2010)
13. Garivier, A., Cappé, O.: The KL-UCB algorithm for bounded stochastic bandits and beyond. In: Proceedings of the 24th Annual Conference on Learning Theory. In: JMLR Workshop and Conference Proceedings, pp. 359–376 (2011)
14. Thompson, W.R.: On the likelihood that one unknown probability exceeds another in view of the evidence of two samples. Biometrika **25**(3/4), 285–294 (1933)
15. Chapelle, O., Li, L.: An empirical evaluation of Thompson sampling. Adv. Neural Inf. Process. Syst. **24**, 2249–2257 (2011)
16. Russo, D., Van Roy, B., Kazerouni, A., Osband, I., Wen, Z.: A tutorial on Thompson sampling. arXiv preprint arXiv:1707.02038 (2017)
17. Combes, R., Magureanu, S., Proutiere, A.: Minimal exploration in structured stochastic bandits. arXiv preprint arXiv:1711.00400 (2017)
18. Ameur, W.B., Mary, P., Hélard, J.-F., Dumay, M., Schwoerer, J.: Autonomous power decision for the grant free access MUSA scheme in the mMTC scenario. Sensors **21**(1), 116 (2021)
19. Nasim, I., Ibrahim, A.S., Kim, S.: Learning-based beamforming for multi-user vehicular communications: a combinatorial multi-armed bandit approach. IEEE Access **8**, 219 891–219 902 (2020)
20. Chen, W., Wang, Y., Yuan, Y.: Combinatorial multi-armed bandit: general framework and applications. In: International Conference on Machine Learning. PMLR, pp. 151–159 (2013)
21. Kuchibhotla, V., Harshitha, P., Elugoti, D.: Combinatorial sleeping bandits with fairness constraints and long-term non-availability of arms. In: 2020 4th International Conference on Electronics, Communication and Aerospace Technology (ICECA), pp. 1575–1581. IEEE (2020)
22. Cerovic, S., Visoz, R., Madier, L., Berthet, A.O.: Centralized scheduling strategies for cooperative HARQ retransmissions in multi-source multi-relay wireless networks. In: Proceedings of IEEE ICC 2018, Kansas City, MO, USA, May 2018
23. Mohamad, A., Visoz, R., Berthet, A.O.: Outage analysis of various cooperative strategies for the multiple access multiple relay channel. In: IEEE 24th Annual International Symposium on Personal, Indoor, and Mobile Radio Communications (PIMRC). IEEE 2013, pp. 1321–1326 (2013)
24. Auer, P., Cesa-Bianchi, N., Fischer, P.: Finite-time analysis of the multiarmed bandit problem. Mach. Learn. **47**(2), 235–256 (2002)

Tactile Internet and Internet of Things

Huber Estimator and Statistical Bootstrap Based Light-Weight Localization for IoT Systems

Yaya Etiabi[1]([✉]), El Mehdi Amhoud[1], and Essaid Sabir[2,3]

[1] School of Computer Science, Mohammed VI Polytechnic University,
Ben Guerir, Morocco
{yaya.etiabi,elmehdi.amhoud}@um6p.ma
[2] NEST Research Group, LRI Lab, ENSEM, Hassan II University Casablanca,
Casablanca, Morocco
[3] Department of Computer Science, University of Quebec at Montreal,
Montreal, QC H2L 2C24, Canada
e.sabir@ensem.ac.ma

Abstract. In this paper we study distributed cooperative localization algorithms for wireless sensor networks (WSN) and propose a novel approach that remarkably improves the accuracy of the localization in Internet of Things (IoT) systems. In our work, we focused on indoor localization problem in IoT infrastructures by investigating a two step position refinement method. We first utilize an iterative gradient descent method on the localization cost function based on Huber estimator. In the second step, we refine the position estimates given by the first step. We indeed use a statistical bootstrapping approach to deal with impairments due to Non-Line-Of-Sight (NLOS) disruptive effects and the wireless channel noise impact on range measurements; and once again, we run the gradient descent. The simulation results show up the robustness of our algorithm since it achieves better accuracy comparing to similar existing approaches.

Keywords: Cooperative localization · Distributed localization · Internet of Things · Sensor networks · Bootstrapping · Huber estimator

1 Introduction

The recent years have known an exponential growth of the number of connected devices leading to an unprecedented change pace in the internet of things domain. To deal with this rapid growth, numerous research projects have been initiated [1–3] to come up with up-to-date solutions that fit the new requirements induced by this new trend. In these works, the authors presented state-of-the-art solutions for IoT systems alongside challenges related to different IoT applications.

In particular, IoT localization is one of the most investigated subjects since it appears to be the cornerstone of location-based services, a key feature of IoT infrastructures. Indeed, in [4–6], the authors conducted literature reviews

© Springer Nature Switzerland AG 2021
H. Elbiaze et al. (Eds.): UNet 2021, LNCS 12845, pp. 79–92, 2021.
https://doi.org/10.1007/978-3-030-86356-2_7

of localization problems in IoT environments by summing up the different technologies used for specific applications and the related research challenges.

In addition, as the number of connected devices is exponentially growing, distributed cooperative localization is very promising to enhance the localization accuracy and to avoid a centralized processing. To this extent, many distributed localization algorithms [7–12] have been developed and recently machine learning algorithms [13–16] have been introduced.

However, there is a large gap between obtaining node position estimates and having accurate ones since the localization in IoT environments is subject to many impairments that need to be properly mitigated to have acceptable results.

In the paper [7], a NLOS error mitigation algorithm based on Bootstrapping M-estimator is proposed without prior knowledge of the NLOS error distribution. As in practice it is very difficult to determine NLOS conditions or to define a proper distribution of NLOS errors, the authors used the statistic bootstrap method to carry out NLOS biases in node positions estimation. This statistical approach requires high computational capability to correctly operate. So as presented in their work, this is suitable for only mobile network. Thus, this method needs to be tailored for conventional WSN with very constrained resources.

In the paper [8], authors introduced a non-parametric bootstrap multi-hop localization algorithm for large-scale WSNs in complex environments to build confidence intervals for multi-hop distance estimation, which can eliminate the risk of small sample size and unknown NLOS distribution. Since they are using multi-hop approach, this algorithm can be further improved by investigating its combination with range-based techniques such as ToA and RSSI.

In [9], the authors proposed a distributed cooperative localization algorithm derived from a centralized one proposed in the same paper. The previous work is in fact an improvement of the work proposed in [10], in which the authors developed a parallel projection method (PPM) algorithm based on the projection onto convex set (POCS) method. To have further improvement, they introduced an iterative parallel projection method (IPPM), and they focused on the mitigation of the NLOS effect. However, this mitigation approach relies on the full knowledge of channel NLOS conditions. Hence, in the case of the lack of the NLOS information, the algorithm cannot operate properly.

In [11], the authors proposed a more robust distributed cooperative localization scheme which is more tolerant to the NLOS bias and outliers in general. Their algorithm can relatively achieve good accuracy under some NLOS conditions without prior knowledge of the NLOS information, but needs further improvement since some location based services are very error-sensitive.

The work in [11] was the main foundation of our previous work in [12] where we investigated a distributed and cooperative localization algorithm based on a convex relaxation of the Huber loss function. The algorithm is iterative and based on the stochastic gradient descent (SGD) method which allows a fast convergence time, and hence makes it suitable for real-time applications. It has been shown that the presented algorithm has a relative low complexity but suffers from harsh NLOS effects although these have been handled by introducing a relaxation parameter.

In this paper, we differently address the localization problem in presence of NLOS impairments by proposing a two step distributed and cooperative localization algorithm based on a convex optimization of the Huber loss function. The algorithm first iteratively computes position estimates followed by a refinement step with bootstrapping method which leads to a very improved localization accuracy.

The remainder of this paper is organized as follows. In Sect. 2, we review the system model and describe the proposed localization algorithm. In Sect. 3, we present the performance analysis of our algorithm through simulations. In Sect. 4, we conduct an experimental validation of our results, and finally in Sect. 5 we conclude our work and present future research directions.

2 Bootstrapping Huber Estimator

2.1 System Model

In this part, we recall the system model from our previous work in [12], where we consider a wireless sensor network of size $[L \times W]m^2$ consisting of N sensor nodes denoted by $\theta_i \in \mathbb{R}^2$, for $i = 1, 2, 3, ..., N$, and M anchors $\theta_j \in \mathbb{R}^2$, for $j = N + 1, ..., N + M$.

In our work, we consider a Time of Arrival (ToA) based range measurements. We define $\mathbb{S}$ as the set of all index pairs (i, j) of all the neighbouring nodes that can communicate with each other and $\mathbb{S}_i$ as the index set of all the neighbouring nodes of the ith node by:

$$\begin{cases} \mathbb{S} = \{(i,j) \; : \; d_{ij} \leq R, \, i < j\} \\ \mathbb{S}_i = \{j \; : \; (i,j) \in \mathbb{S}\} \end{cases} \quad \text{and} \quad r_{ij} = \begin{cases} d_{ij} + n_{ij} & \text{if } (i,j) \in L \\ d_{ij} + n_{ij} + b_{ij} & \text{if } (i,j) \in N \end{cases}$$

$$\text{with} \begin{cases} L = \{(i,j) \in \mathbb{S} : \text{LOS link between } i^{th} \text{ and } j^{th} \text{ nodes}\} \\ N = \{(i,j) \in \mathbb{S} : \text{NLOS link between } i^{th} \text{and } j^{th} \text{ nodes}\} \end{cases}$$

where $\mathbb{S} = L \cup N$, r_{ij} is the pairwise range measurement and R the communication range. $n_{ij} \sim N(0, \sigma_{ij}^2)$ represents measurement noise terms. b_{ij} represents the NLOS bias between the corresponding pair of nodes. Furthermore, we assume that range estimates are symmetric, i.e., $r_{ij} = r_{ji}, \forall \, i, j$.

2.2 Performance Metrics

The objective is to find the optimal estimate $\hat{\Theta}$ of the true positions $\Theta = \{\theta_i\}_{i=1,2,...,N}$ such that the corresponding errors in the estimated locations are small. The localization problem is an optimization problem where we try to minimize the estimation errors as:

$$\hat{\Theta} = \arg\min_{\Theta} g(\Theta) = \arg\min_{\Theta} \sum_{(i,j) \in \mathbb{S}} (\|\theta_i - \theta_j\| - r_{ij})^2 \tag{1}$$

Where $g(\Theta) = \sum_{(i,j)\in\mathbb{S}}(\|\theta_i - \theta_j\| - r_{ij})^2$ is the cost function.

Furthermore, to measure the localization accuracy, we use the Root Mean Square Error (RMSE) defined by:

$$RMSE = \sqrt{\frac{\sum_{i=1}^{N} \mathbb{E}\{\|\hat{\theta}_i - \theta_i\|^2\}}{N}} \tag{2}$$

where $\mathbb{E}\{.\}$ denotes the expectation operation, and $\hat{\theta}_i = [\hat{x}_i, \hat{y}_i]^T$ denotes the ith node's estimated location in $\hat{\Theta}$.

As the accuracy is largely application dependant, it's important to make it reflect not only the positional error in terms of the distance, but also in terms of the geometry of the network. So, as in [17] another metric was introduced and known as the Global Energy Ratio (GER) which is defined by:

$$GER = \frac{1}{n(n-1)/2} \sqrt{\sum_{i=1}^{n}\sum_{j=i+1}^{n}(\frac{\hat{d}_{ij} - d_{ij}}{d_{ij}})^2} \tag{3}$$

The distance error between the estimated distance $\hat{d}_{ij}$ and the known distance d_{ij} is normalized by the known distance d_{ij}, making the error a percentage of the known distance.

In order to reflect the RMSE, the GER has been modified to define a new metric known as Global Distance Error (GDE) given by:

$$GDE = \frac{1}{R} \sqrt{\frac{\sum_{i=1}^{n}\sum_{j=i+1}^{n}(\hat{d}_{ij} - d_{ij})^2}{n(n-1)/2}} \tag{4}$$

where, R represents the average radio range of a sensor node. The GDE calculates the localization error represented as a percentage of the average distance nodes can communicate over.

2.3   Proposed Algorithm

We use the Huber cost function defined after a convex relaxation by:

$$H(\Theta) = \sum_{(i,j)\in\mathbb{S}} \rho(\|\theta_i - \theta_j\| - r_{ij}) \tag{5}$$

$$\text{where } \rho(e_{ij}) = \begin{cases} 0 & \text{if } e_{ij} \leq 0 \\ e_{ij}^2 & \text{if } 0 < e_{ij} < K \\ 2Ke_{ij} - K^2 & \text{if } e_{ij} \geq K \end{cases}$$

$e_{ij} = \|\theta_i - \theta_j\| - r_{ij}$, and $K = \alpha_n \times \sigma_{ij}$ is the Huber function cut-off parameter. K defines the degree of suppression of outliers and is chosen to be proportional to σ_{ij}, which make it highly data dependant.

First Step - Huber Estimator: At this stage, we try to minimize the cost function in the Eq. (5) using Gradient Descent algorithm. Thus position estimates are iteratively updated until convergence as follows:

$$\hat{\theta}_i^{n+1} = \hat{\theta}_i^n - \gamma \nabla H(\hat{\theta}_i^n) \text{ with } \nabla H(\hat{\theta}_i^n) = \sum_{j \in \mathbb{S}_i} \frac{\partial \rho(e_{ij})}{\partial \hat{\theta}_i^n}, \text{ for } i = 1, ..., N \qquad (6)$$

and the partial derivatives are given as:

$$\frac{\partial \rho(e_{ij})}{\partial \theta_i^n} = \begin{cases} 0 & \text{if } e_{ij}^n \leq 0 \\ 2e_{ij}^n \frac{\hat{\theta}_i^n - \hat{\theta}_j^n}{\|\hat{\theta}_i^n - \hat{\theta}_j^n\|} & \text{if } 0 < e_{ij}^n < K \\ 2K \frac{\hat{\theta}_i^n - \hat{\theta}_j^n}{\|\hat{\theta}_i^n - \hat{\theta}_j^n\|} & \text{if } e_{ij}^n \geq K \end{cases} \qquad (7)$$

Second Step - Bootstrapping: Based on the position estimates in the first step, we refine the position estimates using the statistical bootstrap method. At this stage, we refine the position estimates by processing as follows.

For each sensor i and every sensor j in its neighbourhood, we consider a set of L range measurements. Based on its position estimate $\hat{\theta}_i = [\hat{x}_i \ \hat{y}_i]^T$, we define the errors vector as:

$$E_i = \{\hat{e}_{ij}^l \ / \ j \in \mathbb{S}_i\} \text{ for } l = 1, 2, 3, ..., L$$

where

$$\hat{e}_{ij}^l = r_{ij}^l - \left\| \hat{\theta}_i - \hat{\theta}_j \right\|$$

Having these empirical samples of measurement errors, we build our bootstrap samples of the same size as the original one *i.e* L. To do so, we draw independently and identically distributed samples of size L denoted by:

$$E_i^\star = \left\{ e_{ij}^\star \ / \ j \in \mathbb{S}_i \right\}$$

where $e_{ij}^\star$ is randomly picked from the representative bootstrap sample obtained from the empirical distribution of $\hat{e}_{ij}$. We define the bootstrap samples of range estimates as

$$r_{ij}^\star = \left\| \hat{\theta}_i - \hat{\theta}_j \right\| + e_{ij}^\star$$

And the final refined positions are obtained by minimizing the new cost function defined by:

$$H^\star(\Theta) = \sum_{(i,j) \in \mathbb{S}} \rho(e_{ij}^\star) = \sum_{(i,j) \in \mathbb{S}} \rho(r_{ij}^\star - \left\| \hat{\theta}_i - \hat{\theta}_j \right\|) \qquad (8)$$

The resolution method is the same as in the first step an the overall process is describe by the Algorithm 1.

Algorithm 1: Two step positions refinement

Result: $\hat{\Theta} = \{\hat{\theta}_i\}$
Input: $R = \{r_{ij}\}$
Parameters initialization;
▷ Choose arbitrary positions $\hat{\theta}_i^0$ for all sensor nodes ;
▷ For anchor nodes : $\hat{\theta}_i = \theta_i \quad \forall i = N+1, N+2, ..., N+M$;
Begin step I:
▷n $= 0$;
while $n < maxIteration$ *and* $\max \left\| \hat{\theta}_i^{n+1} - \hat{\theta}_i^n \right\| > \varepsilon$ **do**

   for $i = 1$ *to* N *in parallel* **do**

      for *Data Exchange Time* **do**

         ▷ Broadcast Current Position Estimate $\hat{\theta}_i$;
         ▷Receive Position Estimates from Selected Neighbors;

      end

      ▷Update Position Estimate using GD : $\hat{\theta}_i^{n+1} = \hat{\theta}_i^n - \gamma \nabla \bar{H}(\hat{\theta}_i^n)$;
      ▷Compute $\left\| \hat{\theta}_i^{n+1} - \hat{\theta}_i^n \right\|$;

   end

   ▷ Compute $\max \left\| \hat{\theta}_i^{n+1} - \hat{\theta}_i^n \right\|$;
   ▷ n $\leftarrow$ n $+ 1$;

end
End step I
Begin step II: Bootstrapping
for $l = 1$ *to* L **do**

   ▷ For each sensor, Get range estimates form Neighbors;
   ▷ Compute the estimation Errors based on $\hat{\Theta}$: $\hat{e}_{ij}^l = r_{ij}^l - \left\| \hat{\theta}_i^l - \hat{\theta}_j^l \right\|$;

end
▷ Compute the empirical CDF of Errors $E_i = \{\hat{e}_{ij}^l \, / \, j \in \mathbb{S}_i\}$;
▷ *Construct bootstrap samples from the empirical CDF:*
for $ns = 1$ *to* N_{sample} **do**

   ▷ Random pick with replacement of $e_{ij_{ns}}^{\star}$ from E_i;

end
▷ Compute $e_{ij}^{\star} = mean(\{e_{ij_{ns}}^{\star}\})$;
▷ Set $E_i^{\star} = \{e_{ij}^{\star} \, / \, j \in \mathbb{S}_i\}$;
▷ Compute new range estimates based on bootstrap samples
$r_{ij}^{\star} = \left\| \hat{\theta}_i - \hat{\theta}_j \right\| + e_{ij}^{\star}$;
▷ *Repeat Step I*
End step II

2.4   Complexity Analysis

In this section, we investigate the complexity of the Algorithm 1 of the section above. We define n as the number of neighboring nodes of a given node and m the maximum number of iterations until convergence. Then for a given node, the complexity in terms of computation is defined by $\mathcal{O}(n \times m)$. Indeed, during the first step, for each iteration i out of m, the node updates its position by collecting the current position of each of its n neighbors leading to a complexity function $C_1 = n \times m$. The second step induces an additional complexity $C_2 = n \times m'$ with $m' \leq m$ since few steps of gradient descent are required in the refinement step. Therefore, the overall complexity function is defined by:

$$C = C_1 + C_2 = n \times m + n \times m' = n \times (m + m') \leq 2n \times m = \mathcal{O}(n \times m)$$

In terms of communication cost, with s as the size of the bootstrap samples for range estimation, the complexity is given by $\mathcal{O}(n \times s \times m)$.

3   Simulations and Discussion

The performance of our proposed algorithm is illustrated and compared with other algorithms through simulations. We consider $M = 4$ anchors and $N = 50$ sensors nodes in a network of size $L \times W = 10 \times 10\,\mathrm{m}^2$. The anchors are deployed such that $\theta_{N+1} = [0\ 0]$, $\theta_{N+2} = [0\ 10]$, $\theta_{N+3} = [10\ 10]$, $\theta_{N+M} = [10\ 0]$. For the position refinement using the bootstrap method, we set the size of samples to $L = 10$. The number of bootstrap samples has been set to $B = 1000$. With a communication range of $R = 3\,\mathrm{m}$, We assumed a uniform zero-mean Gaussian noise of standard deviation $\sigma_{ij} = \sigma_n = 0.5\,\mathrm{m}$ over all the network and an exponential distribution of the NLOS biases with parameter $\mu = 1\,\mathrm{m}$. Different NLOS levels have been considered: 5%, 50% and 95%.

The algorithms used for comparison are the non linear least squares (Original NLS) and its relaxed version (NLS relaxed), the relaxed Huber estimator (Stage I) followed by a refinement step using the original Huber estimator (Stage I + Stage II).

We first investigate the popular RMSE metric and the results are shown in Fig. 1, 2, 3.

Figure 1 and Fig. 2 show that with NLOS ratio up to 50% our algorithm presents a much better performance in terms of localization accuracy. From Fig. 3, we can conclude that the proposed two step refinement by bootstrapping method is at least as accurate as the simple two step refinement (Stage I + Stage II) and outperforms the other algorithms. Moreover, in order to give a meaningful understanding of the accuracy of our localization system, we conduct an analysis of the aforementioned performance metrics. The results are presented in the Table 1. We can notice that, in addition to being accurate in terms of RMSE, our algorithm keeps track of the network geometry by showing good GDE and GER in the different NLOS scenarios.

Ideally to improve the refinement accuracy in the bootstrapping step, the higher the number of samples, the better the accuracy. The restriction on the number of range estimates samples is due to its high communication cost for constructing bootstrap samples. So by simulating the estimation accuracy with respect to the number of samples used in bootstrapping step, we show in Fig. 4 that for small numbers of samples, the variation in accuracy is not that much.

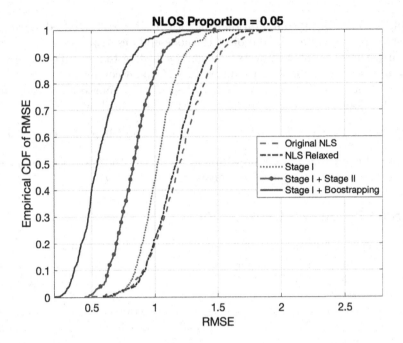

Fig. 1. RMSE for 5% NLOS links

Table 1. Performance measurements.

Algorithm	RMSE	GER	GDE	RMSE	GER	GDE	RMSE	GER	GDE
Stage I	1.0550	0.0119	0.1859	1.1358	0.0130	0.2011	1.2177	0.0151	0.2287
Stage I + Stage II	0.8761	0.0111	0.1708	1.1475	0.0131	0.2034	1.2080	0.0148	0.2260
Original NLS	1.2299	0.0129	0.1897	1.6856	0.0229	0.3206	2.0348	0.0322	0.4425
NLS relaxed	1.1928	0.0127	0.1991	1.3122	0.0147	0.2258	1.4066	0.0175	0.2637
Stage I + Bootstrapping	0.5936	0.0050	0.0802	1.0810	0.0140	0.2188	1.2039	0.0147	0.2251
(a) Algorithms	(b) 5% NLOS			(c) 50% NLOS			(d) 95% NLOS		

Thus, to save network resources, it is suitable to select that number as small as possible. With samples of size 5 we can achieve relatively good accuracy.

4   Experimental Validation

In this section we conduct an experimental validation of our algorithm using real data obtained from measurements campaign reported in [18].

The measurement environment was an office area of 14 m by 13 m containing Forty-four (44) device locations and partitioned by 1.8 m-high cubicle walls with hard partitioned offices, external glass windows, and cement walls on the outside of the area. The measurement system is composed of a wide-band direct-sequence spread-spectrum (DS-SS) transmitter (TX) and receiver (RX) (Sigtek model ST-515) which are battery-powered. The TX outputs an unmodulated pseudo-noise

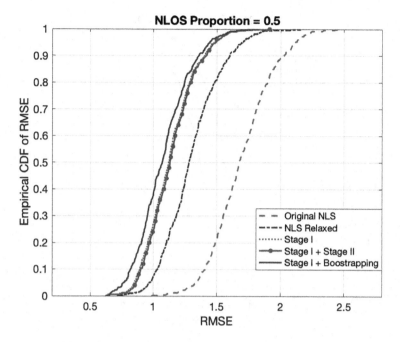

Fig. 2. RMSE for 50% NLOS links.

(PN) code signal with a 40-MHz chip rate and code length 1024. The center frequency is 2443 MHz, and the transmit power is 10 mW. Both TX and RX use 2.4-GHz sleeve dipole antennas kept 1 m above the floor. The antennas have an omnidirectional pattern in the horizontal plane and a measured antenna gain of 1.1 dBi.

Figure 5 shows the nodes' deployment pattern and the associated position estimates based on the experimental ToA data. We also investigate the RMSE of the localization system with the experimental data considering different NLOS scenarios and the results are shown in Fig. 6, 7, 8. We can see that the accuracy of our algorithm remains largely higher with NLOS link ratio up to 50 and even more (Fig. 6, 7), then presents similar accuracy with very high NLOS ratio (Fig. 8). In light of this, we can assert that our proposed localization method is a better choice.

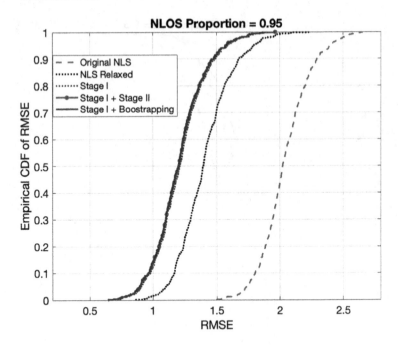

Fig. 3. RMSE for 95% NLOS links.

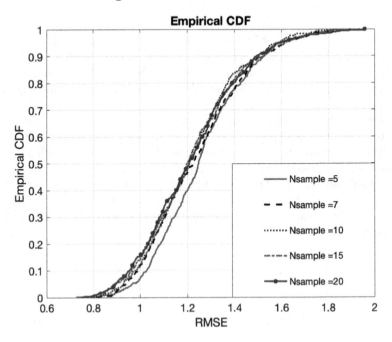

Fig. 4. CDF of RMSE for different sample sizes

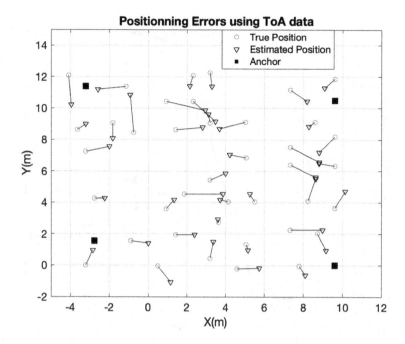

Fig. 5. Positioning errors with ToA range measurements

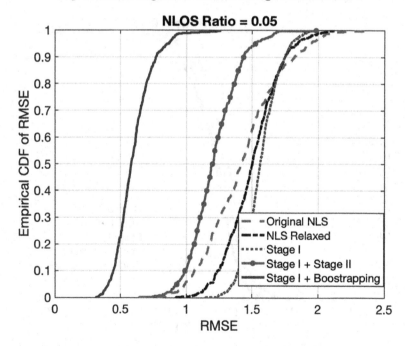

Fig. 6. RMSE for 5% NLOS links from experimental data.

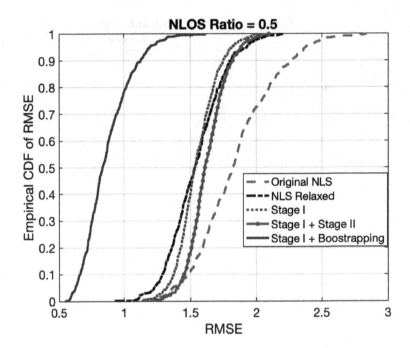

Fig. 7. RMSE for 50% NLOS links from experimental data.

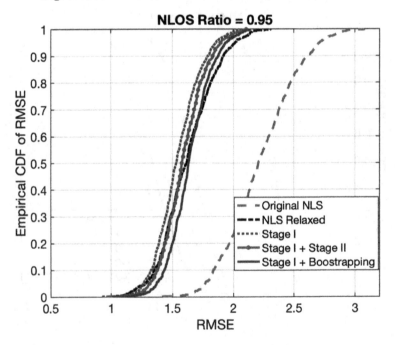

Fig. 8. RMSE for 95% NLOS links from experimental data.

5   Conclusion

In this paper we presented a bootstrapping-based distributed cooperative localization algorithm for IoT networks. Our algorithm addresses the issue of the NLOS effect on localization accuracy without prior knowledge of its distribution, while keeping better performance in NLOS-free environments. This has been proven through simulations and with experimental data and by comparison with the other algorithms mentioned above. We also deepened the performance analysis by investigation the so-called global distance error and the global energy ratio. It comes out that, our algorithm shows better performance in all the cases which makes it a better choice for IoT applications. However, the missing information of NLOS distribution slightly negatively impacts the global performance of the algorithm even if it has shown some robustness. Thus, building on the top of this algorithm a machine learning based NLOS identification method will lead to remarkable results and will enable the extension of this algorithm to massive IoT networks.

References

1. Sethi, P., Sarangi, S.: Internet of things: architectures, protocols, and applications. J. Electr. Comput. Eng. **2017**, 1–25 (2017)
2. Ray, P.: A survey on internet of things architectures. J. King Saud Univ. Comput. Inf. Sci. **30**(3), 291–319 (2018)
3. Khanna, A., Kaur, S.: Internet of things (IoT), applications and challenges: a comprehensive review. Wirel. Pers. Commun. **114**, 1–76 (2020)
4. Khelifi, F., Bradai, A., Benslimane, A., Rawat, P., Atri, M.: A survey of localization systems in internet of things. Mobile Netw. Appl. **24**, 06 (2019)
5. Zafari, F., Gkelias, A., Leung, K.K.: A survey of indoor localization systems and technologies. IEEE Commun. Surv. Tutor. **21**(3), 2568–2599 (2019)
6. Kordi, K., Alhammadi, A., Mardeni, R., Alias, M.Y., Abdullah, Q.: A review on wireless emerging IoT indoor localization, December 2020
7. Sun, G.L., Guo, W.: Bootstrapping m-estimators for reducing errors due to non-line-of-sight (NLOS) propagation. IEEE Commun. Lett. **8**, 509–510 (2004)
8. Ren, Y., Yu, N., Wang, X., Li, L., Wan, J.: Nonparametric bootstrap-based multihop localization algorithm for large-scale wireless sensor networks in complex environments. Int. J. Distrib. Sensor Netw. **2013** (2013)
9. Jia, T., Buehrer, R.M.: Collaborative position location with NLOS mitigation. In: IEEE International Symposium on Personal, Indoor and Mobile Radio Communications, PIMRC, vol. 1, no. 3, pp. 267–271 (2010)
10. Jia, T., Buehrer, R.M.: A set-theoretic approach to collaborative position location for wireless networks. IEEE Trans. Mob. Comput. **10**(9), 1264–1275 (2011)
11. Yousefi, S., Chang, X.W., Champagne, B.: Distributed cooperative localization in wireless sensor networks without NLOS identification. In: 11th Workshop on Positioning, Navigation and Communication, WPNC 2014 (2014)
12. Etiabi, Y., Amhoud, E.M., Sabir, E.: A distributed and collaborative localization algorithm for internet of things environments, pp. 114–118. Association for Computing Machinery (ACM), November 2020

13. Bhatti, G.: Machine learning based localization in large-scale wireless sensor networks. Sensors (Switzerland) **18**(12) (2018)
14. Weerasinghe, Y.S.P., Dissanayake, M.: Towards IoT; comparison of RSS based indoor localization using supervised learning and trilateration in WSN. In: 2019 14th Conference on Industrial and Information Systems (ICIIS), pp. 290–295 (2020)
15. Vidyapeetham, A.V., Sinha, S., Vidyapeetham, A.V.: Self - localization in large scale wireless sensor network using machine learning. In: 2020 International Conference on Emerging Trends in Information Technology and Engineering (IC-ETITE), pp. 1–5 (2020)
16. Ferrand, P., Decurninge, A., Guillaud, M.: DNN-based localization from channel estimates: Feature design and experimental results, March 2020
17. Priyantha, N., Balakrishnan, H., Demaine, E., Teller, S.: Anchor-free distributed localization in sensor networks. Technical report 892, MIT Lab For Computer Science, pp. 340–341, February 2004
18. Patwari, N., Hero, A., Perkins, M., Correal, N., O'Dea, R.: Relative location estimation in wireless sensor networks. IEEE Trans. Signal Process. **51**, 2137–2148 (2003)

Utility Maximisation in the Coordinator-Less IOTA Tangle

Mathilde Jay[1], Ambre Mollard[1], Ye Sun[1], Ruyi Zheng[1], Isabel Amigo[2],
Alexandre Reiffers-Masson[2(✉)], and Santiago Ruano Rincón[2]

[1] IMT Atlantique, Brest, France
{mathilde.jay,ambre.mollard,ye.sun,ruyi.zheng}@imt-atlantique.net
[2] IMT Atlantique, Lab-STICC, UMR-6285, 29238 Brest, France
{isabel.amigo,alexandre.reiffers-masson,
santiago.rincon}@imt-atlantique.fr

Abstract. Getting rid of the Coordinator in the IOTA Tangle is a challenging task, especially regarding the network trustworthiness. Using a customised testbed, we experimentally analyse the functioning of the GoShimmer, IOTA's current implementation of the decentralised Tangle, with respect to specific network performance metrics. We observe that a trade-off exists among such metrics. We thus propose to determine the optimal rate allocation through an optimization problem maximising network performance and user utility. We further propose a distributed and asynchronous scheme to allow nodes to solve such problem.

Keywords: Tangle · Utility maximisation · Distributed rate allocation

1 Introduction

IOTA is an open-source, fee-less, distributed ledger technology and cryptocurrency designed for the Internet of things (IoT). It uses a Direct Acyclic Graph (DAG) to store messages on its ledger, called the Tangle, motivated by a potential higher scalability over blockchain-based alternatives. IOTA does not use miners to validate messages, allowing them to be issued without fees, particularly interesting for micro-transactions. Moreover, the Tangle could be used to store data, and is already used by major actors, such as the Japanese government on NEDO project.

In the initial version of IOTA, the network achieves consensus through a coordinator node. Indeed, IOTA's definition of consensus requires a confirmed message to be referenced (either directly or indirectly) by a signed message issued by the Coordinator (see [11]). This makes the coordinator a single point of failure. To circumvent this problem, a new decentralised version of IOTA, that removes the need of the Coordinator, is being developed along with the GoShimmer node software[1] [11]. Being able to get rid of the Coordinator in IOTA is a

---

[1] GoShimmer: https://github.com/iotaledger/goshimmer/.

© Springer Nature Switzerland AG 2021
H. Elbiaze et al. (Eds.): UNet 2021, LNCS 12845, pp. 93–104, 2021.
https://doi.org/10.1007/978-3-030-86356-2_8

challenging task, at least from security and system performance points of view (synchronisation, validation rates, etc.). Initial answers have been given in [11], but a lot of questions remain open, especially regarding network management and control considerations.

Following IOTA's terminology, we call *nodes* the different actors participating in the ledger. Such actors will issue *messages* aiming to have them attached to the distributed ledger graph. In order to issue a message and get it attached, two actions must be done by the node: 1) perform a Proof Of Work (PoW) and 2) validate two messages already present in the graph. Once these two actions performed, the message is added to the graph, and it becomes a *tip*. A tip is thus a message that has not yet been validated by any other message.

Collaboration between the different nodes in the Tangle is essential for an IOTA ledger to be efficient and trustworthy. In addition to validate messages or tips, the nodes need to work together to resolve conflicts via the Fast Probabilistic Consensus (FPC) protocols [6,10]. More details about the Tangle, especially the performance metrics we are paying attention to, can be found in Sect. 2.1.

In this paper we first experimentally study the behaviour of the decentralised Tangle (Sect. 2). For that, we have built our own testbed based on publicly available software and study its performance under different scenarios. The main conclusion that can be thrown from these experiments is that a trade-off exists among different performance metrics according to nodes objectives.

In the second part of this paper (Sect. 3), we focus on finding a good trade-off for the evaluated metrics. We formulate the problem as an optimization one, which allows us to determine the optimal rate allocation. We further propose a distributed and asynchronous scheme to let the nodes reach the identified solution.

1.1 Related Work

Characterising the performance of the Tangle has drawn the attention of several research works, be it through theoretical models, simulations or empirical data. An initial paper [12] introduced the basis for a continuous time model, where several conjectures were presented, in particular regarding several performance metrics. These predictions have been verified through simulations in [8]. A discrete time model has been proposed in [5] where also performance metrics were deduced. In [8], the discrete time model is also validated through simulations and further analysis.

Empirical Analysis: The closest work to Sect. 2 is the work of [7] which focus exclusively on the analysis of empirical data in the public Tangle implementation. In this analysis, validation time and other metrics are shown to be more pessimistic than simulations and theoretical modes, while good or bad performance must be stated in regard of a given application. All cited works focused on IOTA's initial version, i.e. the one with a central coordinator. In our case, we focus on the Coordicide [11], the current under development version, which aims to get rid of such coordinator. Such a version is expected to be much more demanding for all performance metrics, since the network is now completely distributed. This constitutes a main difference of our work with current state-of-the-art.

Rate Control: Luigi Vigneri and Wolfgang Welz from the IOTA fondation proposed an Adaptive Rate Control Algorithm which adapted the PoW difficulty of a given node from its throughput and its reputation [15,16]. They explain that this algorithm allows every node to issue messages while penalising spamming actions. The authors claim that fairness is achieved and the issue of mining races is resolved. However, the notion of fairness is not tackled in [15], where authors argue that fairness and other properties must be achieved by properly tuning parameters, without giving further insight on how this tuning can be done neither on fairness measurements. In addition, the approach suggested in [15] does not allow users to add constraints such as a high transmission rate or very low CPU usage. In [16] authors revisit their previous work presenting now a fairness measurement, defined as "the ability of nodes to issue valid messages at a rate independent on their computational capabilities". While this property is doubtless desirable, we claim that a fairness measurement should also take into account the demand of each node, understood as the message rate each node needs to send to the network. We share with these works the objective of rate allocation, while in our problem we take into account the overall utility, understood as network performance and user experience.

Distributed Algorithm for Network Optimisation: A huge amount of work has been dedicated to the design of distributed algorithms for resource allocation and utility maximization. In our case, we will get inspired by the different methods proposed in network utility maximization [17], resource allocation in networks [9], distributed gradient [13] and in general distributed optimization [4,14].

2   Testbed and Empirical Findings

In our empirical study, we run several scenarios on a network of GoShimmer nodes, where we test different environment conditions. In this paper we focus on studying the impact of two variables: 1) the rate of generated messages, and 2) the PoW difficulty configured for each node.

The messages are generated by a customised spammer plugin. We have modified it to generate messages following a Poisson process, in order to match a common assumption in the literature [12]. Nodes are embedded in a network which is created using the docker-network tool included in the Goshimmer source code. All of the experiments have been run on an Intel Xeon E5-2630 v3 CPU @ 2.4 GHz server. Since all the GoShimmer nodes run on the same virtual server, we assign via docker two different CPU cores to each node, aiming to control and uniform their execution environment. For each experiment, we collect data from a specific GoShimmer plugin that dumps message-related data to disk.

The GoShimmer version that we are using can be found in our public git repository as well as the analysed data[2].

2.1   Relevant Performance Metrics

According to our use case (network's performance evaluation and utility optimisation), the most relevant metrics to consider are the following:

Throughput: Defined in this context as the number of messages that are attached to the Tangle per unit of time. A user is interested in maximising its throughput according to its current demand and hardware limitations.

Number of Tips: Tips are messages that have been attached to the Tangle but are not yet validated by any other message. In order to increase reliability of the network, it is desirable that the number of concurrent tips remains low. In addition, this quantity impacts the user experience since, for same input rate, the higher the number of tips, the longer it takes for one message to get approved.

Finality Time: The time elapsed between a message is issued and it is consider as irrevocable. The smaller this metric the fastest a user can have irrevocable messages attached to the Tangle. Determining finality of a message is however not implemented in the current version of GoShimmer (0.3.6), so we are not able to study this metric.

Solidification Delay: A message is considered solid by a node when the node knows it and all of its history [11]. An interesting metric describing the performance of the Tangle is the time span elapsed between the following two events: time at which a message is issued (event 1) and its solidification time (event 2). Indeed, the smaller this delay, the fastest nodes are synchronising.

2.2   Scenarios

We focus on homogeneous scenarios, i.e. all nodes have same input parameters, for this allows to see more clearly the impact of the parameters on network performance. The duration of each experiment is between 5 to 10 min. In all cases this was enough to see the metrics converging. These different scenarios allow us to measure the impact of the input rate (messages per minute) and the PoW difficulty, constituting 36 different scenarios. In particular, we can distinguish among scenarios of low, medium and high values for each parameter, where limits for PoW difficulty are given by GoShimmer (between 1 and 20) and for input rate from empirical limits.

---

[2] Our GoShimmer fork that includes customised plugins: https://gitlab.imt-atlantique.fr/iota-imt/goshimmer/.

2.3 Network Performance: Throughput, Solidification Delay and Average Number of Tips

Figure 1 shows the obtained results of our different experiments. We report on values about the whole network as seen by one of its nodes. We have checked thus consistency across the different nodes. For some scenarios, consistency was not always achieved, which suggests that nodes are not always able to synchronise. This was true for different scenarios (be it low, mid or high load), and varied across different runs of same scenario. Such inconsistencies can be seen in some of the reported results (e.g. input rate 3840 mpm for Pow 5). Results obtained still allow us to get the main trends of the metrics, and fully understanding the causes of such anomalies would be the subject of future work.

We can observe, in Fig. 1a that for low scenarios throughput matches the input rate, meaning that nodes are able to issue and send to the network as much as messages as demanded by application. For mid scenarios, this is less and less true since nodes spend more time solving the Pow. For high scenarios, throughput can drop dramatically with respect to input rate. These observations motivate the fact that the Pow can be used to regulate the throughput of each node.

In Fig. 1b, we observe an increase in the number of concurrent tips, when the number of transactions sent to the network or the PoW difficulty increase.

In Fig. 1c, we observe that the solidification delay remains small for mid and low scenarios (the median is less than 0.01 s), while in high scenarios the value increases up (the median is less than 0.05 s). This might have an impact in the increasing number of concurrent tips.

A general observation is that, for high scenarios, the node is not able to catch up with input rate, sending less messages to the network than asked by the application. Solidification delay also increases greatly due to the duration of the Pow. Same observations can be made for the number of concurrent tips.

2.4 Discussion

Previous results show that there is a trade-off between the different metrics, and that the best operation point given by the rate as well as PoW difficulty is not trivial to obtain, due to the fact that the metrics depend on these two inputs in a different way. In the next section, we consider that while input rate is determined by the application, PoW difficulty can be pertinently tuned to achieve an optimal trade-off between the different metrics.

3 Network Optimisation Scheme

This section is dedicated to the design of a rate allocation scheme which aims to determine the adequate Pow of each node taking into account performance metrics and nodes demands. Our solution is based on an optimisation problem, which we will first define after introducing the system model and assumptions.

Then we will design an iterative, distributed and asynchronous scheme which converges to the solution of the optimisation problem. We end the section with numerical results and discussion.

3.1 System Model

Let $\mathcal{I} := \{1, \ldots, I\}$ be the set of nodes in the system. We consider slotted time where at the beginning of each time slot $n \in \mathcal{N}_+$, a node i generates $0 < \lambda_i < +\infty$ new messages. $\boldsymbol{\lambda} := [\lambda_i]_{1 \leq i \leq I}$ is the associated vector. As already proposed in the

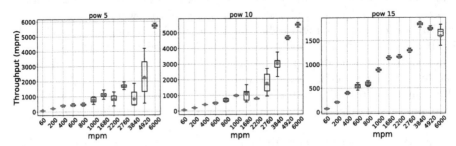

(a) Throughput per node (messages per minute) for different per-node input rates (messages per minute). For convenience, the figures are in different scales.

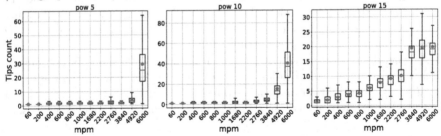

(b) Concurrent number of tips for different input rates.

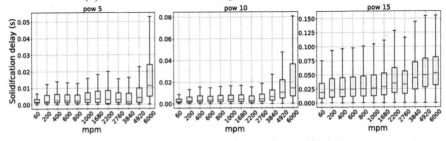

(c) Solidification delay for different input rates

Fig. 1. Experimental results for the different network performance metrics and scenarios. The number of messages per minute (resp. the metric studied) is represented on the x-axis (resp. on the y-axis). The title of each plot indicates the difficulty of the cryptographic puzzle. The result of each experiment is captured by a box plot.

literature [11, 15, 16] and in the current GoShimmer implementation, we consider that each node has to solve a cryptographic puzzle before sending a message to the network. We assume that if a node is not able to solve the cryptographic puzzle for a given message in $N \in \mathcal{N}_+$ time slots, then the message is rejected by the system. The success probability to solve a puzzle for any message sent by node i, during time slot n, is denoted by α_i. This assumption can be seen as the discrete version of the assumption that the time to solve a cryptographic puzzle follows an exponential law, as suggested in [1,2]. We assume that $\alpha_i \in [\underline{\alpha}_i, \overline{\alpha}_i]$ with $0 < \underline{\alpha}_i < \overline{\alpha}_i < 1$. We denote by $\boldsymbol{\alpha} := [\alpha_i]_{1 \leq i \leq I}$ the associated vector. Let x_i^n be the number of messages sent by node i in the network at the end of time slot n. These messages were still trying to solve the puzzle at the beginning of the time slot n. We call this quantity the *throughput* of node i at time slot n. The expectation of x_i^n, denoted by $\overline{x}_i := E[x_i^n]$ can be computed explicitly:

Lemma 1. *For all n, $n' \geq N$, $E[x_i^n] = E[x_i^{n'}]$ and*

$$\overline{x}_i(\alpha_i) := \overline{x}_i^N = \lambda_i \left(1 - (1 - \alpha_i)^N\right). \tag{1}$$

Observe that $\overline{x}_i(\alpha_i)$ is a strictly increasing concave function of α_i.

Proof. First note that the number of messages, from node i, that are currently solving a dedicated cryptographic puzzle at time slot n are only depending on the messages generated from the beginning of time slot $n - N + 1$ up to the end of time slot n. Moreover, due to the fact that λ_i and α_i are not varying over time, we have that $E[x_i^n] = E[x_i^{n'}]$ for all $n, n' > N$.

Let $z_i^{m,k} \in \{0, 1\}$ be a random variable which is equal to 1 when message m from node i sent at time $k \in \{n - N + 1, \ldots, n\}$ has been able to solve the cryptographic puzzle during time slot n. Otherwise $z_i^{m,k}$ is equal to 0. The probability that $z_i^{m,k} = 1$ is equal to $(1 - \alpha_i)^{n-k}\alpha_i$. We have $E[x_i^n]$ which is equal to:

$$E[\sum_{k=n-N+1}^{n} \sum_{m=1}^{\lambda_i} z_i^{m,k}] = E[\sum_{k=1}^{N} \sum_{m=1}^{\lambda_i} z_i^{m,k}] = \sum_{k=1}^{N} \sum_{m=1}^{\lambda_i} E[z_i^{m,k}] = \lambda_i \left(1 - (1 - \alpha_i)^N\right). \blacksquare$$

If we assume that the α_i is changing every N time slots, then this lemma is true for every $n = kN$ with $k \in \mathcal{N}$.

3.2   Modelling Network Performance Metrics

A first metric to observer is the average number of concurrent tips. As mentioned in Sect. 2, this is indeed an interesting metric to *minimize* as the less number of tips, the earlier a message can be validated. We assume that the average number of tips is a linear increasing function of the total throughput $\sum_{i=1}^{I} \overline{x}_i(\alpha_i)$. In particular, this agrees with our experimental findings as well as with state-of-the-art models and simulations [5, 8, 12]. We have thus that the mean number of tips in the Tangle at time slot n is given by $g(\sum_{i=1}^{I} \overline{x}_i(\alpha_i)) = c_1 \sum_{i=1}^{I} \overline{x}_i(\alpha_i)$, where c_1 is a constant depending on modelling assumptions.

Secondly, we consider each node's throughput as a metric to be *maximised*. We assume that every node i, at instant n, is interested in maximising a concave (to capture the diminishing returns effect) increasing and differentiable function $U_i(\overline{x}_i(\alpha_i))$ of the throughput rate $\overline{x}_i(\alpha_i)$. Note that $U_i(\overline{x}_i(\alpha_i))$ is concave in α_i as long as $U_i(\cdot)$ is an increasing concave function. We could assume that $U_i(\overline{x}_i(\alpha_i)) = w_i \log(\overline{x}_i(\alpha_i))$.

Finally, as aforementioned, finality time is an interesting metric to be optimised, however it is not yet available neither experimentally nor theoretically (no models exist in the literature). We thus consider an alternative metric, the average *confirmation time*, i.e. the average time elapsed between the following two events: the message is issued by the node (event 1) and the message is no longer a tip (event 2). Such metric is important in terms of quality of experience, since it considers the pace at which a user can add messages to the Tangle.

We assume that the confirmation time is a decreasing function of the total throughput which agrees with theoretical models (see [5]). The confirmation time is assumed to be given by a non linear decreasing convex function $h(\sum_{i=1}^{I} \overline{x}_i(\alpha_i))$. Note that this function is convex in the vector $\boldsymbol{\alpha}$ as the composition of a concave function (sum of concave functions) with a non-increasing convex function over an univariate domain. In particular, we can suppose that $h(\sum_{i=1}^{I} \overline{x}_i(\alpha_i)) = \frac{1}{\sum_{i=1}^{I} \overline{x}_i(\alpha_i)}$.

Note we are not considering solidification time as an objective to be optimised. Indeed, though this is an interesting metric, experimental results have shown not to be a stable one, and no models can be safely extracted from data. Considering such metric is thus left for future work.

3.3   Optimization Problem

Without loss of generality we define the utility maximization problem as a minimization cost problem. The instantaneous cost function, $J(\boldsymbol{\alpha})$, is the weighted sum of the quantities introduced in previous sub-section, described as follows:

$$J(\boldsymbol{\alpha}) := \lim_{n \to +\infty} \frac{1}{n} \sum_{k=0}^{n} c_1 \underbrace{\sum_{i=1}^{I} \overline{x}_i^n(\alpha_i)}_{\text{Inst. average tip count}} + \underbrace{h(\sum_{i=1}^{I} \overline{x}_i^n(\alpha_i))}_{\text{Inst. confirm. time}} - \underbrace{\sum_{i=1}^{I} U_i(\overline{x}_i^n(\alpha_i))}_{\text{Network Utility}}$$

$$= c_1 \sum_{i=1}^{I} \overline{x}_i(\alpha_i) + h(\sum_{i=1}^{I} \overline{x}_i(\alpha_i)) - \sum_{i=1}^{I} U_i(\overline{x}_i(\alpha_i)).$$

We thus propose to solve the following optimization problem:

$$\min_{\boldsymbol{\alpha}} \quad J(\boldsymbol{\alpha}),$$
$$\text{s.t.} \quad \alpha_i \in [\underline{\alpha}, \overline{\alpha}], \ \forall i \in \mathcal{I}. \tag{2}$$

This optimization problem can be solved in two steps. Indeed, due to the fact that for all $i \in \mathcal{I}$, $\overline{x}_i(\alpha_i)$ is strictly increasing in $\alpha_i \in [\underline{\alpha}, \overline{\alpha}]$, we can:

- Firstly, solve the following optimization problem:

$$\min_{\overline{x}} \quad c_1 \sum_{i=1}^{I} \overline{x}_i + h(\sum_{i=1}^{I} \overline{x}_i) - \sum_{i=1}^{I} U_i(\overline{x}_i),$$

$$\text{s.t.} \quad \overline{x}_i \in [\overline{x}_i(\underline{\alpha}), \overline{x}_i(\overline{\alpha})], \ \forall i \in \mathcal{I},$$

(3)

where $\overline{\boldsymbol{x}} := [\overline{x}_i]_{1 \leq i \leq I}$. This problem is a convex optimization problem.
- Secondly, if we denote by $\overline{\boldsymbol{x}}^*$ the solution of the optimization problem, then the optimal α_i^* is equal to $x_i^{-1}(\overline{x}_i^*) = 1 - (1 - \frac{\overline{x}_i^*}{\lambda_i})^{1/N}$, for all $i \in \mathcal{I}$.

In the next lemma, following the theory of convex optimization we derive an explicit solution of (3) for specific functions.

Lemma 2. *If for every $i \in \mathcal{I}$, $U_i(\overline{x}_i) = w_i \log(\overline{x}_i)$, $h(\sum_{i=1}^{I} \overline{x}_i) = \frac{c_2}{\sum_{i=1}^{I} \overline{x}_i}$, with $w_i > 0$ and $c_2 > 0$ and if $\overline{x}_i^* \in (\overline{x}_i(\underline{\alpha}), \overline{x}_i(\overline{\alpha}))$ for all $i \in \mathcal{I}$, then*

$$\overline{x}_i^* = w_i \frac{\sqrt{(\sum_{j=1}^{I} w_i)^2 + 4c_1 c_2} + \sum_{j=1}^{I} w_i}{2c_1 \sum_{j=1}^{I} w_i}.$$

Proof. Let us assume that $\overline{x}_i^* \in (\overline{x}_i(\underline{\alpha}), \overline{x}_i(\overline{\alpha}))$ for all $i \in \mathcal{I}$, then the first order optimality condition is equal to:

$$\frac{w_i}{\overline{x}_i^*} - c_1 + \frac{c_2}{(\sum_{j=1}^{I} \overline{x}_j^*)^2} = 0, \ \forall i \in \mathcal{I},$$

which is equivalent to $\overline{x}_i^* = \dfrac{w_i}{c_1 - \frac{c_2}{(\sum_{j=1}^{I} \overline{x}_j^*)^2}}$, for all $i \in \mathcal{I}$. By taking the sum over i, we obtain:

$$\sum_{j=1}^{I} \overline{x}_j^* = \frac{\sum_{j=1}^{I} w_i}{c_1 - \frac{c_2}{(\sum_{j=1}^{I} \overline{x}_j^*)^2}} \Leftrightarrow (\sum_{j=1}^{I} \overline{x}_j^*)^2 c_1 - (\sum_{j=1}^{I} \overline{x}_j^*) \sum_{j=1}^{I} w_i - c_2 = 0$$

$$\Rightarrow \sum_{j=1}^{I} \overline{x}_j^* = (2c_1)^{-1} \left(\sum_{j=1}^{I} w_i + \sqrt{(\sum_{j=1}^{I} w_i)^2 + 4c_1 c_2} \right).$$

The last implication is coming from the fact $\sum_{j=1}^{I} \overline{x}_j^* > 0$ and the fact that the solution $\frac{\sum_{j=1}^{I} w_i - \sqrt{(\sum_{j=1}^{I} w_i)^2 + 4c_1 c_2}}{2c_1}$ is always negative. We can now conclude our proof by plugging $\sum_{j=1}^{I} \overline{x}_j^*$ into $\overline{x}_i^* = \dfrac{w_i}{c_1 - \frac{c_2}{(\sum_{j=1}^{I} \overline{x}_j^*)^2}}$. ∎

3.4   Distributed and Asynchronous Algorithm

We now describe an asynchronous and distributed algorithm which will converge to the optimal solution of (3).

   We assume that every node updates their throughput at each kN time slot, for every $k \in \mathbb{N}$. We denote by $\overline{x}_i(k)$ the throughput adopted by node i, during time slots $\{kN, \ldots, (k+1)N - 1\}$. Only node i observes $\overline{x}_i(k)$ at every k. Let $Y(k)$ be the random subset of $\mathcal{I}$ indicating the subset of nodes which update their throughput at the beginning of the time slot kN. We assume that when a node i is active at time slot kN, it observes the total throughput $\sum_{j=1}^{I} \overline{x}_j(k)$. We also need to define the step sizes $\{a(k)\}, \{b(k)\} \in (0, 1)$ such that: (1) $\sum_k a(k) = \sum_k b(k) = \infty$, (2) $\sum_k a^2(k) + b^2(k) < \infty$ and finally (3) $\lim_{k \to \infty} \frac{a(k)}{b(k)} = 0$. For instance, the functions $b(k) = \frac{1}{k^{2/3}}$ and $a(k) = \frac{1}{k}$ satisfy the above mentioned conditions. We explain the importance of such assumptions over the step-size later on, when we discuss convergence. Let us first describe our algorithm.

Local iteration of node i

Initialization: Set $\overline{x}_i(0)$.

When $i \in Y(k+1)$:
(1) *Clock update step:* Node i observes $k + 1$.
(2) *Aggregation step:* Node i observes $\sum_{j=1}^{I} \overline{x}_j(k)$ and updates:

$$y_i(k+1) = y_i(k) + b(k+1)\left(\sum_{j=1}^{I} \overline{x}_j(k) - y_i(k) \right).$$

(3) *Gradient ascent step:* Update:

$$\overline{x}_i(k+1) = \left[\overline{x}_i(k) - a(k)\left(c_1 \overline{x}_i(k) + h'(y_i(k)) - U_i'(\overline{x}_i(k)) \right) \right]_{\overline{x}_i(\underline{\alpha})}^{\overline{x}_i(\overline{\alpha})},$$

where $[x]_a^b = \max\{\min\{x, b\}, a\}$.
Node i adopts throughput $\overline{x}_i(k + 1)$ during the instants $\{(k+1)N, \ldots, (k+2)N - 1\}$.

When $i \notin Y(k)$: $y_i(k+1) = y_i(k)$ and $\overline{x}_i(k+1) = \overline{x}_i(k)$. So node i adopts the strategy $\overline{x}_i(k+1) = \overline{x}_i(k)$ during the instants $\{k+1)N, \ldots, (k+2)N - 1\}$.

Convergence: The mathematical proof of the convergence of our algorithm is out of the scope of this paper. We will however briefly mention the different main ideas. Our algorithm is nothing more than an asynchronous stochastic gradient descent, with biased but consistent estimator of the gradient (see 10.2

in [3]). To prove the convergence almost surely of such scheme one needs to use the theory of stochastic approximation and more specifically two-time scale stochastic approximations and asynchronous stochastic approximations (see ch. 6 and 7 in [3]). The assumptions regarding the time-steps are standard and will ensure that every node i has a stable estimate of the total throughput $(\sum_{j=1}^{I} \bar{x}_j(k))$, decoupled of the gradient update $(\bar{x}_j(k+1))$.

The behaviour of our distributed/asynchronous scheme is illustrated in Fig. 2. We have 5 nodes. At each iteration, 2 nodes are randomly selected and perform an update of their throughput by following our scheme. The parameters are set to $w_i = i$, $c_1 = 1$, $c_2 = 1$ and $\lambda = 10$. We observe that our scheme converges to the optimal throughput in less that 75 iterations (see Fig. 2a and 2b).

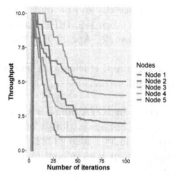
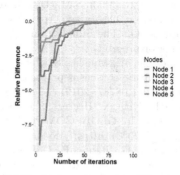

(a) Evolution of the throughputs.   (b) Evolution of relative difference.

Fig. 2. Convergence of proposed scheme. Parameters are set to $w_i = i$, $c_1 = 1$, $c_2 = 1$ and $\lambda = 10$. Figure 2a depicts the evolution of throughputs. The evolution of relative difference between the optimal throughput and the one generated by the asynchronous and distributed scheme is depicted in Fig. 2b.

4   Conclusion

We have focused on the study of the Tangle as an example of DAG-based ledgers. We have built a testbed and evaluated network performance under different input conditions, concluding that network's health and user experience depend on these input values, while a trade-off exists among the different considered metrics. A smart control is then needed in order to properly set such parameters.

We have thus defined a network optimisation problem which derives the optimal throughput for every node. For particular functions, we have provided a closed form solution. We have designed a distributed and asynchronous algorithm which converges to the optimum of our network optimisation problem.

This algorithm can be extended to a more complex set-up, e.g. noisy observations or exact shape of the function unknown by the nodes. This along with considering further constraints are among the directions of our future work.

Acknowledgments. Authors would like to thank the IOTA Foundation Team for their kind and prompt assistance, especially Angelo Capossele, who has helped us to understand a little bit the GoShimmer's guts.

References

1. Altman, E., et al.: Blockchain competition between miners: a game theoretic perspective. Front. Blockchain **2**, 26 (2020)
2. Altman, E., Reiffers, A., Menasche, D.S., Datar, M., Dhamal, S., Touati, C.: Mining competition in a multi-cryptocurrency ecosystem at the network edge: a congestion game approach. ACM SIGMETRICS Perform. Eval. Rev. **46**(3), 114–117 (2019)
3. Borkar, V.S.: Stochastic Approximation. TRM, vol. 48. Hindustan Book Agency, Gurgaon (2008). https://doi.org/10.1007/978-93-86279-38-5
4. Borkar, V.S., Shah, S.M.: Distributed algorithms: Tsitsiklis and beyond. In: 2018 Information Theory and Applications Workshop (ITA), pp. 1–9. IEEE (2018)
5. Bramas, Q.: The Stability and the Security of the Tangle, April 2018. Working paper or preprint
6. Capossele, A., Mueller, S., Penzkofer, A.: Robustness and efficiency of leaderless probabilistic consensus protocols within byzantine infrastructures. arXiv preprint arXiv:1911.08787 (2019)
7. Guo, F., Xiao, X., Hecker, A., Dustdar, S.: Characterizing IOTA tangle with empirical data. In: GLOBECOM 2020–2020 IEEE Global Communications Conference, pp. 1–6 (2020). https://doi.org/10.1109/GLOBECOM42002.2020.9322220
8. Kusmierz, B., Staupe, P., Gal, A.: Extracting tangle properties in continuous time via large-scale simulations. Technical report (2018)
9. Li, C., Yu, X., Huang, T., He, X.: Distributed optimal consensus over resource allocation network and its application to dynamical economic dispatch. IEEE Trans. Neural Netw. Learn. Syst. **29**(6), 2407–2418 (2017)
10. Popov, S., Buchanan, W.J.: FPC-BI: Fast Probabilistic Consensus within Byzantine Infrastructures. arXiv preprint arXiv:1905.10895 (2019)
11. Popov, S., et al.: The coordicide (2020). https://files.iota.org/papers/20200120_Coordicide_WP.pdf
12. Popov, S., Saa, O., Finardi, P.: Equilibria in the tangle. Comput. Ind. Eng. **136**, 160–172 (2019). https://doi.org/10.1016/j.cie.2019.07.025
13. Pu, S., Shi, W., Xu, J., Nedic, A.: Push-pull gradient methods for distributed optimization in networks. IEEE Trans. Autom. Control **66**, 1–16 (2020)
14. Shah, S.M., Borkar, V.S.: Distributed stochastic approximation with local projections. SIAM J. Optim. **28**(4), 3375–3401 (2018)
15. Vigneri, L., Welz, W., Gal, A., Dimitrov, V.: Achieving fairness in the tangle through an adaptive rate control algorithm. In: 2019 IEEE International Conference on Blockchain and Cryptocurrency (ICBC), pp. 146–148 (2019). https://doi.org/10.1109/BLOC.2019.8751358
16. Vigneri, L., Welz, W.: On the fairness of distributed ledger technologies for the internet of things. In: 2020 IEEE International Conference on Blockchain and Cryptocurrency (ICBC), pp. 1–3. IEEE (2019). https://doi.org/10.1109/ICBC48266.2020.9169465
17. Wei, E., Ozdaglar, A., Jadbabaie, A.: A distributed newton method for network utility maximization-I: algorithm. IEEE Trans. Autom. Control **58**(9), 2162–2175 (2013)

CSMA/CA Based Burst Transmission Algorithm for Medical-Healthcare Applications Using Wireless Body Area Networks

Imane Dbibih[1][(✉)] and Imad Iala[2]

[1] Laboratory of Engineering Sciences and Energy, Polydisciplinary Faculty of Ouarzazate Ibn Zohr University, Agadir, Morocco
i.dbibih@uiz.ac.ma
[2] LRIT Associated Unit to the CNRST-URAC N29, Faculty of Sciences, University Mohammed V, B.P.1014 RP, Agdal Rabat, Morocco

Abstract. Today, WBAN becomes one of the key networks in Medical-healthcare applications. These networks are derived from WSNs, but to be useful in healthcare, they have to deal with different and more constraints. Among the most important constraints facing WBANs is the traffic heterogeneity, which is due to the different monitoring functionalities ensured by the deployed sensors in the network. On the one hand, some sensors are dedicated to periodic monitoring where measurements are taken permanently. On the other hand, other sensors do critical monitoring, when it is necessary to send a critical vital sign, only if there is a trigger (a measurement that exceeds a threshold, etc.). These messages absolutely must be handled differently. In this paper, we tried to deal with the emergency of vital messages at the MAC layer. We propose CSMA/CA-based Burst Transmission algorithm that can ensure an emergency transmission along the path between sources and destinations, by using Gossip messages. Its objective is to inform other nodes having regular traffic to postpone their transmissions, and therefore, we get a clear channel. In this paper, we compared our algorithm with the IEEE 802.15.4 CSMA/CA and the MP-CSMA/CA algorithms. The results show that we have gained a lot in terms of latency and PDR.

Keywords: WBANs · Medical-healthcare · MAC layer · Slotted CSMA/CA · Traffic heterogeneity · Emergency traffic

1 Introduction

Recently, Wireless Body Area Networks (WBANs) have been attended in new communication technology for medical healthcare or lifecare services. These networks are an adapted new generation of WSNs, which are dedicated just to the healthcare utility. And thus, They are suffering from different constraints.

H. Elbiaze et al. (Eds.): UNet 2021, LNCS 12845, pp. 105–115, 2021.
https://doi.org/10.1007/978-3-030-86356-2_9

According to the utility of the deployed nodes in WBAN-based healthcare networks, we can find two types of heterogeneity. On the one hand, sensors may be implanted or only on the surface of the patient. On the other hand, they do not all monitor the same phenomena. Some nodes monitor organs in a way that they regularly send measurements to the sink. Some others are devoting to send a message only if there is a trigger. Consequently, in WBANs, we find two types of traffic; regular and triggered traffic.

In this paper, we deal with the traffic heterogeneity in WBAN-based medical healthcare at the MAC layer. This layer is considered as a key layer, when it is related to priority message transmission, power consumption, ensuring low latency, and good bandwidth management problems. Two standards could be used for WBAN systems, namely IEEE802.15.6 and IEEE.802.15.4. However, wireless UWB networks based on IEEE 802.15.4 offer the advantages of a large frequency range and low power spectral density, which makes it suitable for healthcare-related applications [1]. Therefore, our solution is IEEE 802.15.4 CSMA/CA algorithm-based. The proposed algorithm in this paper aims to ensure more efficient transmission for emergency traffic by reducing latency and avoiding collisions.

The remainder of this paper is organized as follows. In Sect. 2, we present the related work. In Sect. 3, we detail the proposed algorithm. When in Sect. 4, performance evaluation and results are described and analyzed. We conclude the paper and present the future scope in Sect. 5.

2   Related Work

Several studies have been conducted in the literature to analyze the performances of IEEE 802.15.4 CSMA/CA [2–7], and they all approve through simulations that it does not have mechanisms allowing it to deal with the traffic heterogeneity in either WSN or WBAN networks. Many works [8–11] have tried to propose QoS techniques for traffic heterogeneity in WBAN. Yoon et al. propose in [8] a new architecture for remote medical applications. To improve the delay and transmission time of critical vital signs, they try to differentiate services based on priority scheduling and data compression. Each type of vital signal receives a priority level and it is transmitted according to its priority. For the same purpose authors in [9,10] have modified the structure of IEEE802.15.4 to reduce the packet delay of emergency alarms. Also, to enhance the QoS of WBAN, they propose scheduling techniques utilizing prioritized retransmission of different physiological signals. In [11], authors have proposed a traffic adaptive MAC layer to deal with emergency and on-demand traffic; they modified the MAC superframe structure to include the configurable contention access period (CCAP); the rest of the superframe parts resemble the conventional IEEE 802.15.4 MAC. However, in this way they do not consider the emergency of some messages. A heterogeneous body area network [12,13] scenario is analyzed under CSMA/CA-based mechanism, in which channel switching is done by using a Markov chain model. An analysis has been performed to choose the contention window size randomly, according to the load on the channel. Also, many other works tried to propose CSMA/CA-based algorithms to improve QoS in BWANs since they are a special case of WSNs. While, in [14–18], authors propose to classify the traffic according to its priority to provide a quality of service to sensor networks. In [14], the authors handle the medium access according to the node priority. According to each level, we can set the minimum and the maximum of the backoff exponent ($macMinBE$, $aMaxBE respectively$) and the contention window (CW). Also, in [16] the authors create an analytic model of medium access contention, during the CAP period of IEEE 802.15.4. This study was carried out to evaluate the effect of the CW parameter on the medium contention of nodes having prioritized messages. To get the same purpose, [17] proposes a new CSMA/CA-based scheme called MP-based CSMA/CA that considers two priority levels; high priority assigned to critical-time messages and low priority assigned to non-real-time messages. Therefore, to differentiate services, authors specify two intervals from which nodes can choose their backoff times (Wait time), before accessing the medium.

3   CSMA/CA-Based Burst Transmission Algorithm

Our algorithm mainly targets the problem of heterogeneity in deployed WBANs for medical-healthcare applications. In these networks, we find two categories of traffic; periodic and emergency traffic. The last one is only generated if there is a trigger and mostly is of a critical-time nature. Our goal is to provide an urgent transmission to this traffic.

In this paper, we differentiate two types of source nodes: nodes periodically generating messages according to the observed measurements, and nodes generating messages only if an event has occurred (crossing a threshold, unexpected movement, etc.). To guarantee an emergency transmission to the second kind of traffic our algorithm uses Gossip messages. The objective of this control message is to inform neighboring nodes (which may be one of them, a relaying point) that there will be a transmission of emergency traffic, and therefore all nodes must collaborate and cooperate to succeed in this urgent transmission. Collaborating nodes have to free the channel as much as possible.

Once a node receives a Gossip message, firstly it retransmits it to its neighboring nodes (those located within its transmission range). Secondly, if the node receiving the Gossip message is free or preparing to transmit periodic traffic, it postpones its transmission for a time called Rollback time ($T_{rollback}$); this sensor is called a collaborating node. During $T_{rollback}$ time, it listens to the channel and remains in a state of readiness to receive and relay the emergency traffic. Otherwise, if the node receiving the Gossip message already has emergency traffic to send or relay, it ignores the $T_{rollback}$ and proceeds directly to the transmission of its emergency traffic, this sensor is called a selfish node. Gossip message is sent in broadcast mode to neighboring nodes, and it must be relayed along the path to the destination node. It acts as an ambulance to get an empty medium as much as possible.

Gossip message includes two important pieces of information, namely the identifier of the emergency data, and the estimated time needed to transmit the emergency data. This time is calculated based on the data size (see Eq. 1 [19]). And then, $T_{rollback}$ matches the estimated time in the Gossip message, provided that it should not exceed a limit time.

$$T_{rollback} = PacketSize/Bitrate \tag{1}$$

To get medium, the nodes use CSMA/CA-based Burst Transmission algorithm (BT-CSMA/CA), which provides to nodes having emergency traffic more chances to win contention and access the medium. BT-CSMA/CA algorithm mainly consists of differentiating two contention windows. The first is reserved for nodes having a gossip message to transmit. The second is for the transmission of either emergency or periodic traffic.

The purpose of this differentiation is to provide to Gossip messages more chance to be spread. Once Gossip messages are received, nodes with periodic data fall back during $T_{rollback}$. Therefore, only nodes with emergency data content to get the medium. We define a one contention window for both types of data to gain in terms of latency; if ever there is no emergency traffic to send, the other nodes with periodic traffic content directly during the second window.

To guarantee an interesting and rapid propagation of the Gossip message, BT-CSMA/CA algorithm offers privileged access by two measures; differentiating contention windows and carrying out the CCA procedure only once time. If the message to be transmitted was the Gossip message, then the node makes sure that the channel is free for only one time; otherwise, the node performs the CCA twice. Figure 1 illustrates the steps to get the medium according to the BT-CSMA/CA algorithm.

BT-CSMA/CA algorithm consists of six steps:

Step (1): define CW according to the Eq. (2), initialize the parameters $NB = 0$ and $BE = macMinBE$, where $macMinBE$ is the minimum value of BE.

$$CW = \begin{cases} 1 & \text{if Gossip message,} \\ 2 & \text{if data,} \end{cases} \tag{2}$$

Step (2): calculate the Wait time (backoff time) using Eq. (3).

$$Wtime = \begin{cases} random([0, B_{off}]) * BP & \text{if Gossip message,} \\ random([B_{off}, 2^{BE}]) * BP & \text{if data,} \end{cases} \tag{3}$$

Step (3): after the expiration of the wait time, the node performs CCA (determining whether the channel is free or busy), to assess whether the channel is idle. If the channel is assessed to be busy the node goes to Step (4), otherwise, it goes to Step (5).

Step (4): if the channel is busy, the values of NB and BE are increased by one. Then the node tests if the value of NB exceeds macMaxCSMABackoffs (the maximum number of backoffs the CSMA/CA algorithm will attempt before

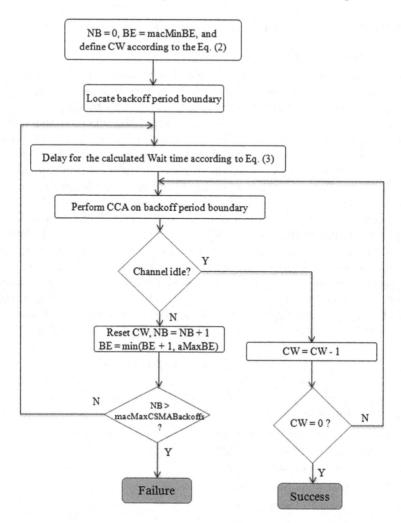

Fig. 1. CSMA/CA-based Burst Transmission algorithm

declaring a channel access failure), if this is the case, it declares a channel access failure. Otherwise, it goes to Step (2).

Step (5): if the channel is not busy, the value of CW is decreased by one, and then the node tests whether CW reaches 0, if this is the case it accesses the channel, otherwise it goes to Step (3).

Knowing that, in Eq. 3, $B_{off} = macMinBE$ is fixed, however BE is varying between $macMinBE$ and $aMaxBE$. In Eq. 2, CW parameter specifies the number of times the channel monitoring should be performed (CCA procedure) before accessing the medium. We differentiate two values of CW; $CW = 1$ in case of Gossip messages, and $CW = 2$ otherwise (periodic or triggered traffic), see Eq. (2).

4   Simulation, Results and Analysis

4.1   Simulation Parameters

We tested our solution using the implemented version of the standard IEEE 802.15.4 in NS-2 (Network simulator) [20]. It provides an implementation of this standard without sleep function (allowing devices to go to sleep state during the inactive period). So, we have implemented all the functions that put the transceiver in a sleep state periodically. In this simulation, we do not consider the CFP period, so we will extend the CAP period along the active time.

Many parameters may influence the behavior of the algorithm, and since the main objective of our algorithm is ensuring a burst transmission to emergency traffic along the path to the destination, we decide to simulate our algorithm in a multi-hops scenario. The number of nodes in the network is fixed to 20 nodes, deployed randomly in the network. We observe the behavior of our algorithm while increasing the number of hops between source and destination nodes. Our algorithm aims to differentiate emergency traffic over periodic one, and thus we use in our simulation two types of traffic load; CBR application layer to simulate the periodic traffic (generated by five nodes), and ON/OFF Exponential traffic to simulate sporadic emergency traffic (generated by five nodes). All results are the average of 10 simulations. The simulation parameters are cited in Table 1.

Table 1. Simulation parameters in NS-2

Parameter	Value
Duty-cycle	50%
Beacon interval	0.24576 s
Active period	0.12888 s
Inactive period	0.12888 s
Simulation time	800 s
Number of nodes	20
Source nodes	10
Network type	Multi-hop
Simulation area	10 m^2
Routing protocol	AODV
Application layer 1	CBR
Application layer 2	ON/OFF Exponential traffic source
Data packet size	100 Bytes

In the remainder of this section, we compare the results of our algorithm with those of Slotted CSMA/CA and MP-CSMA/CA algorithms, in terms of latency of emergency traffic, the latency of both periodic and emergency traffic, network throughput, and packet delivery ratio (PDR). All simulations are setting up in a beacon-enabled mode.

4.2   Emergency Traffic Latency

To evaluate the efficiency of our algorithm in terms of burst transmission, we calculate the average latency of all the emergency traffic transmitted between sources and destinations.

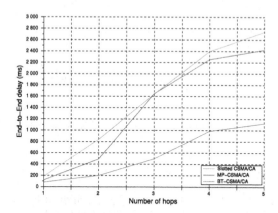

Fig. 2. Emergency traffic latency vs number of hops

Figure 2 shows that there is a significant difference between BT-CSAMA/CA and the others algorithm. BT-CASMA/CA ensures a very low latency compared to those of both algorithms slotted CSMA/CA and MP-CASMA/CA. BT-CSMA/CA provides a privilege to emergency traffic; Gossip messages can clear the medium, and only nodes having emergency traffic can content to access the channel. In this way, our algorithm ensures an emergency transmission even in 5 hops between sources and destinations.

4.3   Average Network Latency

In this experiment, we calculate the average latency of all the sent data, between source and destination.

Observing Fig. 3, we can see that the given results by our algorithm are reduced compared to those of both algorithms Slotted CSMA/CA and MP-CSMA/CA, which proves the efficiency of our algorithm. In our algorithm, nodes having emergency traffic get a clear medium along the path to the destination, which ensures low latency. On another side, when nodes are not informed by a Gossip message, they get access to the medium directly without additional Backoff time to send periodic traffic. However, in MP-CSMA/CA algorithm, there is a differentiation of the backoff time.

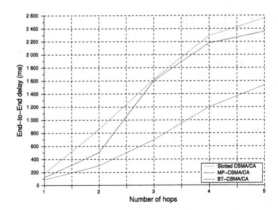

Fig. 3. Average network latency vs number of hops

4.4   Throughput

In this experiment, we calculate the throughput achieved by all nodes deployed in the network. We note in Fig. 4 that BT-CSMA/CA outperforms Slotted CSMA/CA and MP-CSMA/CA. Throughput shows the efficiency of an algorithm on how it manages the bandwidth and the access to the medium. The depicted results in Fig. 4 are justified by two reasons. The first is the reduced latency because once we reduce the transmission latency at each node we get more chance to send more data efficiently. The second reason is about collision; when there is emergency traffic to transmit, the relaying nodes get informed by Gossip message, so they do not content to get medium.

4.5   Packet Delivery Ratio

In this experiment, we evaluate the PDR of all transmitted traffic in the network.

According to the shown results in Fig. 5, we can confirm that our algorithm ensures an improved PDR compared to those of slotted CSMA/CA and MP-CSMA/CA algorithms. Our algorithm can efficiently manage medium access and gets a low collision rate, which offers more efficient transmission. Nodes having both, emergence or periodic traffic can get access and transmit successfully at the first attempt.

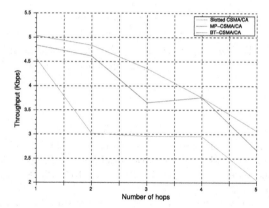

Fig. 4. Network throughput vs number of hops

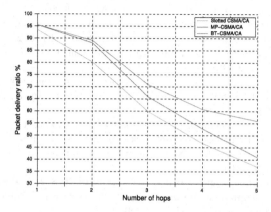

Fig. 5. Packet delivery ratio vs number of hops

5 Conclusion

In this paper, we proposed a new CSMA/CA-based transmission scheme (BT-CSMA/CA algorithm) that guarantees an emergency transmission. Generally, traffic in WBANs can be classified into two classes; periodic and sporadic emergency traffic. Our algorithm mainly privileges the second traffic class. By using, the Gossip messages, the channel gets clarified to transmit the emergency traffic, by consequence we are reducing to nothingness the collision rate, and at the same time, we offer a reduced latency emergency traffic. We proved the efficiency of our algorithm in a multi-hop network by the obtained results in the simulations. The shown results confirmed that through our algorithm, we can achieve improved packet delivery ratio and low emergency traffic latency that is a logical consequence of the proposed channel access mechanism. In addition, we proved the efficiency of our proposed mechanism in other performance criteria (PDR, network latency, and throughput). In this paper we have focused on traffic heterogeneity, however, there are a lot of other heterogeneity criteria that should be considered by communication protocols. Our future researches will concentrate to deal with the heterogeneity of WBAN sensors; take into consideration the position of nodes (implanted or not) in the chosen path to transmit the traffic.

References

1. Khssibi, S., Van Den Bossche, A., Idoudi, H., Azouz Saidane, L., Val, T.: Enhancement of the traffic differentiation architecture for WBAN based on IEEE 802.15.4. Wireless Pers. Commun. **101**(3), 1519–1537 (2018). https://doi.org/10.1007/s11277-018-5775-5
2. Anastasi, G., Conti, M., Di Francesco, M.: The MAC unreliability problem in IEEE 802.15.4 wireless sensor networks. In: Proceedings of the 12th ACM International Conference on Modeling, Analysis and Simulation of Wireless and Mobile Systems, Ser. MSWiM 2009, pp. 196–203. ACM, New York (2009)
3. Park, P., Di Marco, P., Soldati, P., Fischione, C., Johansson, K.: A generalized Markov chain model for effective analysis of slotted IEEE 802.15.4. In: IEEE 6th International Conference on Mobile Adhoc and Sensor Systems, MASS 2009, pp. 130–139, October 2009
4. Koubaa, A., Alves, M., Tovar, E.: A comprehensive simulation study of slotted CSMA/CA for IEEE 802.15. 4 wireless sensor networks. In: IEEE WFCS, vol. 6, pp. 63–70 (2006)
5. Liu, X., Leckie, C., Saleem, S.K.: Performance evaluation of a converge-cast protocol for IEEE 802.15.4 tree-based networks. In: 2010 Sixth International Conference on Intelligent Sensors, Sensor Networks and Information Processing (ISSNIP), pp. 73–78, December 2010
6. Lee, J.: An experiment on performance study of IEEE 802.15. 4 wireless networks. In: 10th IEEE Conference on Emerging Technologies and Factory Automation, 2005. ETFA 2005, vol. 2, p. 8, IEEE (2005)
7. Cuomo, F., Cipollone, E., Abbagnale, A.: Performance analysis of IEEE 802.15.4 wireless sensor networks: an insight into the topology formation process. Comput. Netw. **53**(18), 3057–3075 (2009)
8. Yoon, J.S., Ahn, G., Joo, S., Lee, M.J.: PNP-MAC: preemptive slot allocation and non-preemptive transmission for providing QoS in body area networks. In: 2010 7th IEEE Consumer Communications and Networking Conference, pp. 1–5 (2010)
9. Yaghmaee Moghaddam, M.H., Adjeroh, D.: A novel congestion control protocol for vital signs monitoring in wireless biomedical sensor networks. In: 2010 IEEE Wireless Communication and Networking Conference, pp. 1–6 (2010)
10. Kwak, K.S., Ullah, S.: A traffic-adaptive mac protocol for WBAN. In: IEEE GLOBECOM Workshops 2010, pp. 1286–1289 (2010)
11. Smart, G., Deligiannis, N., Surace, R., Loscri, V., Fortino, G., Andreopoulos, Y.: Decentralized time-synchronized channel swapping for ad hoc wireless networks. IEEE Trans. Veh. Technol. **65**(10), 8538–8553 (2016)
12. Hsiao, C., Lin, C., Kuo, J., Chen, W.: LAMP: load adaptive mac protocol for interban interference mitigation. In: IEEE Wireless Communications and Networking Conference (WCNC) 2018, pp. 1–6 (2018)
13. Li, N., Li, C., Zhang, B., Zhang, Y.: An interference mitigation mac protocol for wireless body area network. In: IEEE/CIC International Conference on Communications in China (ICCC) 2017, pp. 1–6 (2017)

14. Collotta, M., Scata, G., Pau, G.: A priority-based CSMA/CA mechanism to support deadline-aware scheduling in home automation applications using IEEE 802.15.4. Int. J. Distrib. Sensor Netw. (2013)
15. Severino, R., Batsa, M., Alves, M., Koubaa, A.: A traffic differentiation add-on to the IEEE 802.15.4 protocol: implementation and experimental validation over a real-time operating system. In: 2010 13th Euromicro Conference on Digital System Design: Architectures, Methods and Tools (DSD), pp. 501–508, September 2010
16. Ndih, E., Khaled, N., De Micheli, G.: An analytical model for the contention access period of the slotted IEEE 802.15.4 with service differentiation. In: IEEE International Conference on Communications, ICC 2009, June 2009, pp. 1–6 (2009)
17. Dbibih, I., Iala, I., Zytoune, O., Aboutajdine, D.: Message priority CSMA/CA algorithm for critical-time wireless sensor networks. In: El Oualkadi, A., Choubani, F., El Moussati, A. (eds.) Proceedings of the Mediterranean Conference on Information & Communication Technologies 2015. LNEE, vol. 381, pp. 265–274. Springer, Cham (2016). https://doi.org/10.1007/978-3-319-30298-0_28
18. Koubaa, A., Alves, M., Nefzi, B., Song, Y.: Improving the IEEE 802.15.4 slotted CSMA/CA MAC for time-critical events in wireless sensor networks. In: Proceedings of the Workshop of Real-Time Networks (RTN 2006), Satellite Workshop to ECRTS 2006. Jean-Dominique Decotignie, Dresden, Germany, July 2006
19. IEEE standard for information technology- local and metropolitan area networks-specific requirements- part 15.4: Wireless medium access control (MAC) and physical layer (PHY) specifications for low rate wireless personal area networks (WPANs), pp. 1–320
20. The network simulator - ns-2 (2020). https://www.isi.edu/nsnam/ns/

An IoT Framework for SDN Based City Mobility

Anas Al-Rahamneh[1,2]([⊠]), José Javier Astrain[1,2], Jesús Villadangos[3], Hicham Klaina[4], Imanol Picallo[3], Peio Lopez-Iturri[2,3], and Francisco Falcone[3]

[1] Statistics, Computer Science and Mathematics Department, Public University of Navarra, 31006 Pamplona, Spain
[2] Institute of Smart Cities, Public University of Navarre, 31006 Pamplona, Spain
[3] Electric, Electronic and Communication Engineering Department, Public University of Navarre, 31006 Pamplona, Spain
francisco.falcone@unavarra.es
[4] Department of Signal Theory and Communication, University of Vigo, 36310 Vigo, Pontevedra, Spain

Abstract. The Internet of Things (IoT) is becoming more widespread, with global application in a wide range of commercial sectors, utilizing a variety of technologies for customized use in specific environments. The combination of applications and protocols and the unique requirements of each environment present a significant challenge for IoT applications, necessitating communication and message exchange support. This paper presents a proposed SDN-based edge smart bypass/ multiprotocol switching for bicycle networks that supports functionalities of coordination of various wireless transmission protocols. A performance assessment will be presented, addressing a comparison between the different protocols (LoRaWAN vs. Sigfox) in terms radio coverage.

Keywords: Internet of Things · Smart mobility · SDN · Wi-Fi · LoRaWAN · Sigfox

1 Introduction

The Internet of Things (IoT) has gotten a lot of press lately because of the features it offers that could help humanity advance in terms of intelligence, automation, and convenience, among other things. The IoT has transformed objects that are entirely unrecognizable into distinct, recognized, interconnected intelligent things that are supported by high-quality communication protocols, which are referred to as sensible objects. The new devices collect environmental data and send messages over the Internet while being monitored and controlled remotely by a central network server. The IoT entails extending communication to a new range of physical devices and everyday objects beyond popular devices such as laptops and smartphones.

The IoT services utilize various network protocols depending on the IoT service's specific purpose [1]. Current popular wireless protocols include ZigBee [2] and Z-Wave [3], which are mesh network protocols and utilize the IEEE 802.15.4 [4] personal area

© Springer Nature Switzerland AG 2021
H. Elbiaze et al. (Eds.): UNet 2021, LNCS 12845, pp. 116–124, 2021.
https://doi.org/10.1007/978-3-030-86356-2_10

network standard. Alternatives to both standards include 6LowPAN [5], Thread [6], and Bluetooth Mesh [7], which also support IPv6 over mesh networks.

The IoT world is full of heterogeneous, often proprietary protocols, each tailored to a specific use case. This poses a challenge to the IoT's widespread adoption and evolution. The integration of multiple wireless communication protocols into a wireless sensor node provides flexible and expanded connectivity from the same device, also devices to be able to communicate seamlessly in ad-hoc environments.

Software-Defined Networking (SDN) is another new intelligent technology within the networking domain that increases network performance and provides better security, reliability, and privacy using dynamic software programs [8]. The SDN allows the control logic to be separated from the sensor nodes/actuators, which makes it a promising solution for inflexible management WSNs. The benefit of using SDN for WSN management is that it allows for centralized control of the entire network, making it easier to deploy network-wide management protocols and applications on demand.

Several works of literature have discussed how to deal with wireless communication multiprotocol in the heterogeneous network. Uddin et al. have proposed in [9] an SDN-based multiprotocol edge switching for largescale, heterogeneous IoT environments. The proposed system is based on the P4 programming language that lets end users dictate how networking gear operates to achieve this non-IP multiprotocol programmable forwarding capability. The proposed approach based on using a customized network switch to deal with different protocols requires availability throughout the city, which is a challenge in terms of cost and infrastructure.

Gao and Chang have presented in [10] a scalable and flexible communication protocol which is designed to work as a gateway between the Internet and various heterogeneous wireless networks. Froiz-Míguez et al. have presented in [11] a ZiWi gateway, a low-cost IoT fog computing home automation system that allows for carrying out seamless communications among ZigBee and WiFi nodes. Amiriyan and Nguyen have investigated in [12] the multiprotocol flow assignment in a smart home IoT network to the appropriate gateway interfaces. Kang et al. have proposed in [13] a self-configurable gateway featuring real-time detection and configuration of smart things over wireless networks. Chaudhary et al. have presented in [14] a smart home multiprotocol automation System using smart gateways. Kim et al. have proposed in [15] an Internet of Vehicles (IoV) access gateway to controls the incoming data traffic to the In-vehicle network (IVN) backbone and the outgoing data traffic to the IoV in the network environment. The challenges that face the gateways are that they are preconfigured, use vendor-specific APIs, and are limited to authorized devices and policies only.

This paper presents a proposed SDN-based edge smart bypass/multiprotocol switching for bicycle networks that supports functionalities of coordination of various wireless transmission protocols, whether they be legacy, mainstream, or emerging solutions.

The proposed implementation benefits from the protocols' advantages, allowing it to perform better in various scenarios. When Wi-Fi connectivity is available, it will allow for more extensive data payloads and more frequent uplink transmissions. LoRaWAN, on the other hand, will take advantage of its low energy consumption and associated long-range coverage to cover a large area at once.

The rest of the paper is organized as follows. Sect. 2 presents the architecture of the proposed SDN-based edge. The system description is presented in Sect. 3. The measurement results are given in Sect. 4. Finally, Sect. 5 concludes the paper.

2   System Architecture of SDN-Based Smart Bypass for Bicycle Network

We proposed an SDN-based Smart edge bypass solution/multiprotocol switching to forwarding data coming from wireless IoT devices and sensors over different wireless communication standards. This proposal aims to use public/open access points (AP) or gateways that are distributed throughout the city for various wireless communication protocols to transmit data to the cloud.

In our case, the mobility node (bicycle) is equipped with several wireless communication modules. So, when the node gets close to one of the APs or gateways, the SDN controller implements several pre-defined rules to match the AP's protocol with the wireless communication modules' protocols, then chooses the proper protocol to flow the data through it. In the case of a group of the different APs or gateways, the SDN controller determines the appropriate protocol to transmit data depending on the data type, size, etc. (see Fig. 1).

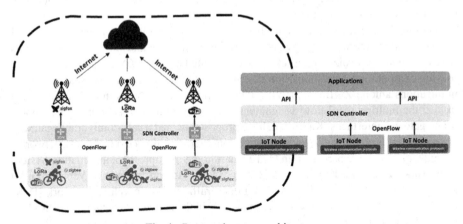

Fig. 1. Proposed system architecture

3   System Implementation/Use-Case/System Description

This section describes the proposed SDN's functionality and how we can implement it in our use case, Bicycle Network. Each of the bicycles will be equipped with several wireless communication modules and different sensors for sensing and gathering information about the environment. This data varies in size and formats, so selecting the appropriate protocol to send this data is essential to ensure that it reaches the destination. For instance, multimedia files such as video, pictures, and audio files require high-bandwidth wireless protocols due to these files' large size. In contrast, the small size of sense data like temperature measurements, humidity, or gas levels does not need this ability. Therefore, the functionalities of coordination of various wireless transmission protocols need to be handled well. For overcoming the problem of partial node death due to exhaustion of energy, energy harvesting was used through the use of a dynamo installed in a bicycle hub.

The proposed SDN will be provided by a set of pre-defined IF-This-Then-That (IFTTT) rules that regulate the protocols selection process and responsible for a set of tasks such as file transfer queuing, message queuing, and confirmation of receipt - acknowledgment packet (ACK) and negative acknowledgment (NAK).

In this respect, if the bicycle becomes close to a group of access points, the proposed SDN will first determine the protocol for each access point and the signal strength. Secondly, it will group the sense data based on its type and size. In case that there is multimedia data between that data, it is first ascertained that there is a Wi-Fi net-work within the networks. Secondly, it measured the Received Signal Strength Indicator (RSSI) and then attempted to connect to the strongest open network available. Once the connection is established, the proposed SDN dividing each file into one or more messages and transmitting the messages. The proposed SDN will wait until it receives an ACK from the recipient. If the ACK is not sent or the recipient returns a NAK, the proposed SDN will either try again from the same access point or send it from another access point. Figure 2 shows a flow diagram that illustrates the different tasks performed based on pre-defined IFTTT rules.

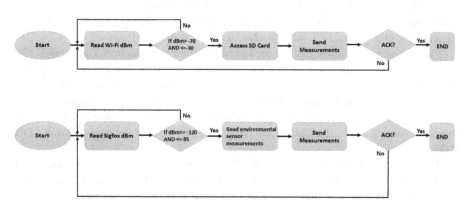

Fig. 2. Flow diagram of the simplified IFTTT rules to send for sensing information.

4 Experiments/Performance Assessment

This section presents the experimental setup and the experimental results of the RSSI and packet loss measurements that have been carried out within an urban test scenario in the city of Pamplona for the wireless protocols Sigfox, LoRaWAN, and Wi-Fi. The Sigfox and LoRaWAN are operating at 868 MHz, while the Wi-Fi operates within 2.4 GHz/5.5 GHz bands. Figure 3 shows the employed hardware.

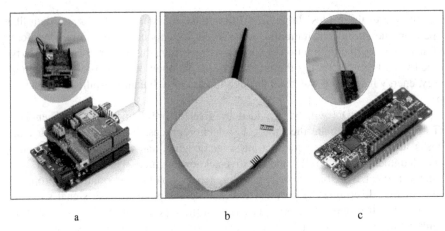

a   b   c

Fig. 3. Employed LoRaWAN and SigFox hardware for measurements; a) Dragino LoRa shield with GPS, b) The Things Networks LoRaWAN Gateway; and c) Arduino MKR FOX 1200.

The Dragino LoRa shield with GPS mounted on an Arduino UNO board has been employed to assess LoRaWAN technology. The TTN Gateway has been deployed within the Electric, Electronic, and Communications Engineering Department building of the Public University of Navarre (UPNA), and it is represented by a blue circle named "GW" in Fig. 4. The gateway has been located on the second floor, near a window, in order to increase link visibility. The Arduino MKR FOX 1200 device has been used for SigFox technology assessment. In this case, no gateway deployment is needed since the SigFox alliance provides the network infrastructure and coverage, so unlike.

Figure 4 shows a map where the measurement campaign has been carried out. The blue circle represents the LoRaWAN Gateway location, and the 26 measurement points where the mote based on Dragino LoRa shield has been deployed are shown with different colors. LoRaWAN, there is no need to establish and maintain the wireless communication network infrastructure. Values are in general above the sensitivity values (in the case of Dragino LoRa of −148 dBm and in the range of −126 dBm in the case of MKR FOX 1200).

The blue circle represents the LoRaWAN Gateway location, and the 7 measurement points where the mote based on Dragino LoRa shield has been deployed are shown with different colors. The green color represents that no packet has been lost in the communication; the yellow color means that some packets have been lost, and the red color that all packets have been lost. For each measurement point, 4 packets have been transmitted from the mote to the TTN Gateway. The packets have been sent every 30s, which is the shortest interval between packets allowed by LoRaWAN. The equivalent measurement set for the case of SigFox setup is depicted in Fig. 5.

The high elevation zone (marked in DarkOrange in Fig. 5, which is higher than the tallest building of the University) causes significant losses in the communication with the nodes deployed across the hill, even for short distances from the Gateway (e.g. measurement points 2 and 3).

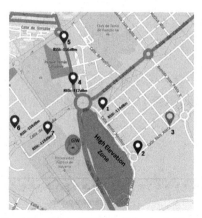

Fig. 4. LoRaWAN measurements results. Green: No packet losses. Yellow: some packet losses. Red: All packets lost (Color figure online).

Fig. 5. SigFox measurements results. Green: No packet losses. Yellow: some packet losses. Red: All packets lost (Color figure online).

In order to gain insight in relation with quality of service metrics in relation with the operation of the proposed LPWAN systems, Signal to Noise ratio values have been measured within the area under analysis previously described. The measurement results for both SigFox SNR values as well as LoRaWAN are depicted in Fig. 6. As a function of node location, SNR values exhibit variations in the order of 10 dB, with higher values in the case of SigFox, owing in principle to larger values of transmit power employed.

As previously indicated, the system will make use of wireless connectivity as a function of network availability and bandwidth requirements. In the case WLAN is required, it will be employed as a function of coverage availability. Figure 7 shows the map of public Wi-Fi hotspots locations within the city of Pamplona where people may obtain Internet access [16]. Work is currently underway in terms of traffic characterization, in order to aid in Quality of Services/Quality of Experience metrics, related with inter radio access technology traffic handling, achievable transmission rate and overall end to end delay, among others.

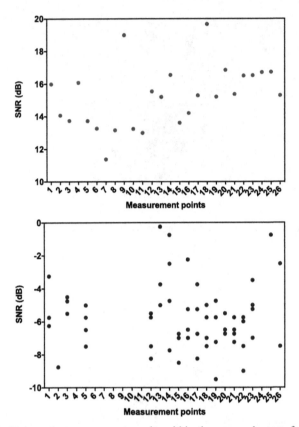

Fig. 6. Signal to Noise ratio measurement results within the area under test, for SigFox (upper image) and LoRaWAN (bottom image).

Fig. 7. Locations of public Wi-Fi hotspots within the city of Pamplona.

As it can be seen, the mobile node continues to search for APs while moving to transmit the information. Each wireless interface module on the mobile node keeps measuring the RSSI of its protocol. The node applies the pre-defined IFTTT rules over the received RSSI. Once any of the IFTTT rules are met, the mobile node performs that rule. The rule determines which kind of information is best suited to the capability of each wireless communication protocol to transmit the data over it.

5 Conclusions

This work presents a proposed SDN-based Smart bypass solution to switch between heterogeneous wireless communications protocols that are equipped to a mobile IoT node. The proposed system gives the node the flexibility and ability to choose the appropriate protocol between these protocols to transmit the data based on several factors such as packet loss, RSSI, file size, etc. Work is going in relation with traffic end to end characterization within the scenario under analysis.

References

1. Al-Fuqaha, A., Guizani, M., Mohammadi, M.: Internet of things: a survey on enabling technologies protocols and applications. IEEE Commun. Surv. Tutorials **17**(4), 2347–2376 (2015)
2. Alliance, Z.: ZigBee specification. ZigBee Document 05347r17, pp. 1–576, January 2008
3. Z-Wave Alliance: Z-Wave device class specification. Z-Wave Document SDS1042, pp. 1–195, March 2018
4. IEEE 802 Working Group: IEEE standard for local and metropolitan area network – Part 15.4: low-rate wireless personal area networks (LR-WPANs). IEEE Std 802.15.4TM-2011, pp. 1–314, June 2011
5. Kushalagarent, N. et al.: IPv6 over low-power wireless personal area networks (6LoWPANs): overview, assumptions, problem, statement and goals. IETF RFC 4919, August 2007
6. Thread Group. https://www.threadgroup.org. Accessed 16 Apr 2021.
7. Bluetooth SIG: Bluetooth mesh networking. Bluetooth SIG Document, pp. 1–28, July 2017
8. Kreutz, D., Ramos, F.M.V., et al.: Software-defined networking: a comprehensive survey, In: Proceedings of the IEEE, vol. 103, pp.14–76 (2015)
9. Uddin, M., Mukherjee, S., Chang, H., Lakshman, T.V.: SDN-Based multiprotocol edge switching for IoT service automation. IEEE J. Sel. Areas Commun. **36**(12), 2775–2786 (2018)
10. Gao, R., Chang, C.H.: A scalable and flexible communication protocol in a heterogeneous network. In: 2014 IEEE/ACIS 13th International Conference on Computer and Information Science (ICIS 2014) pp. 49–52, Septemper 2014
11. Froiz-Míguez, I., Fernández-Caramés, T., Fraga-Lamas, P., Castedo, L.: Design, implementation and practical evaluation of an IoT home automation system for fog computing applications based on MQTT and ZigBee-WiFi sensor nodes. Sensors **18**(8), 2660 (2018)
12. Amiriyan, M., Nguyen, K.-K: Multiprotocol Flow assignment in smart home IoT network. In: 2020 IEEE International Conference on Communications (ICC) (2021)
13. Kang, B., Kim, D., Choo, H.: Internet of everything: a large-scale autonomic IoT gateway. IEEE Trans. Multi-Scale Comput. Syst. **3**(3), 206–214 (2017)
14. Chaudhary, S.K., Yousuff, S., Meghana, N.P., Ashwin, T.S., Guddeti, R.M.R.: A multiprotocol home automation system using smart gateway. Wireless Pers. Commun. **116**(3), 2367–2390 (2020). https://doi.org/10.1007/s11277-020-07795-0

15. Kim, D.-Y., Jung, M., Kim, S.: An internet of vehicles (IoV) access gateway design considering the efficiency of the in-vehicle ethernet backbone. Sensors **21**(1), 98 (2020)
16. Buildings and Wi-Fi Areas in Pamplona. https://www.pamplona.es/ayuntamiento/varios/edificios-y-zonas-wifi-en-pamplona. Aaccessed 16 Apr 2021

Analysis of Inter-train Wireless Connectivity to Enable Context Aware Rail Applications

Imanol Picallo[1,2(✉)], Peio López Iturri[1,2], Mikel Celaya-Echarri[3], Leyre Azpilicueta[3], José Javier Astrain[2,4], and Francisco Falcone[1,2]

[1] Electrical, Electronic and Communication Engineering Department, Public University of Navarre, 31006 Pamplona, Spain
[2] Institute of Smart Cities, Public University of Navarre, 31006 Pamplona, Spain
[3] School of Engineering and Sciences, Tecnologico de Monterrey, 64849 Monterrey, Mexico
[4] Statistics, Computer Science and Mathematics Department, Public University of Navarre, 31006 Pamplona, Spain

Abstract. Train systems are fundamental players within multi-modal transit systems, providing efficient transportation means for passengers and goods. In the framework of Smart Cities and Smart Regions, providing context aware environments is compulsory in order to take full advantage of system integration, with updated information exchange among Intelligent Transportation system deployments. In this work, inter-train wireless system connectivity is analyzed with the aid of deterministic 3D wireless channel approximations, with the aim of obtaining estimations of frequency/power volumetric channel distributions, as well as time domain characteristics, for different frequency bands. The results show the impact of the complex inter-train scenario conditions, which require precise channel modelling in order to perform optimal network design, planning and optimization tasks.

Keywords: Inter-train communication · 3D Ray Launching simulation · Wireless communication systems

1 Introduction

Intelligent Transportation Systems are one of the main elements within the framework of Smart Cities and Smart Regions [1–3], with the aim of enabling secure, energy efficient and reduced contamination transportation of passengers and goods. Different transportation systems are considered and optimal use in general takes advantage of multi-modal use schemes. This is particularly relevant in the case of dense urban scenario, in which user travel can be enhanced by the combined use of different transportation systems, such as bicycles, shared cars, taxis, urban buses, trams, metro lines or trains, among others. In order to take full advantage of these different transportation means, information exchange combined with user preferences can be employed in order to implement adaptive route planning mechanisms. In this context, data collection and transmission is

H. Elbiaze et al. (Eds.): UNet 2021, LNCS 12845, pp. 125–132, 2021.
https://doi.org/10.1007/978-3-030-86356-2_11

relevant in order to implement context aware environments that enable effective multi-modal transportation schemes. This is extensible to the case of train transportation, in which communication system integration is gaining increased interest [4–8].

Given inherent mobility requirements, wireless communication systems are mainly considered in order to enable the aforementioned data exchange. Different types of wireless communication systems can be employed, depending on the coverage/capacity requirements (i.e., required received power levels as a function of transceiver sensitivity thresholds, which at the same time, are given by transmission bit rate, modulation/coding schemes and electronic parameters, such as noise factor values), such as Low Power Wide Area Networks (LPWAN, such as LoRa/LoRaWAN), Public Land Mobile Networks (such as 4G/5G), Satellite Networks or Wireless Local Area Networks. Given the different operating conditions, such as transmission rates, coverage, number of nodes or cost, one of these systems or a combination of them can be employed. In general, currently the operation frequency is below 6 GHz, except for VSAT satellite communication systems or 5G NR Frequency Range 2 (initially in the 28 GHz frequency band), owing to larger coverage extension and lower system cost, as compared with higher frequency millimeter wave systems.

The selection of the corresponding wireless systems is strongly dependent on the frequency of operation, as this defines path loss (higher as frequency increases) and interference dependence (in principle higher as frequency ranges are lower, owing to spectrum congestion). Propagation losses are given by multiple factors, such as distance and interaction with the surrounding environment with multiple mechanisms, such as diffraction, diffuse scattering or multipath propagation, among others. Estimation of propagation losses can therefore be a complex task, especially for scenarios with large obstacle densities, which is the case of urban train environments.

In this work, wireless channel analysis for the case of inter-train communications is presented, with the aid of precise deterministic channel models. Different frequencies of operation are analyzed within the below 6 GHz. Time domain results are also presented, in order to gain insight on the impact of multi-path propagation within the train scenario under test.

2   Inter-train Wireless Communication Scenario Analysis

In order to analyze coverage/capacity conditions within inter-wagon train wireless communication links, a deterministic geometric simulation approach has been employed. An in-house implemented 3D Ray Launching code has been used, based on the approximation of Geometric Optics with Uniform Theory of Diffraction, applied within the complete volume of the scenario under analysis. An arbitrary number of transmitter sources can be placed within any given location of the scenario. Once these sources (which are equivalent to active transmitters) have been defined, they launch rays with given volumetric angular resolution, as well as with specific reflection conditions (i.e., maximum number of reflections of any given ray until ray suffers power extinction). The volumetric representation of the scenario considers the shape, size and material characteristics (i.e., frequency dispersive dielectric constant and electric conductivity) of all the elements within the scenario. The code in implemented in Matlab and the parameters employed in terms of angular resolution, cuboid size and maximum number of reflections until ray extinction (given be previous convergence analysis studies [7, 8]) are the following: angular resolution $\Delta\varphi = \Delta\theta = 1°$, Δcuboid $= 1$ m, N (maximum reflections enabled) $= 6$. A schematic representation of the scenario is depicted in Fig. 1. The scenario is given by two trains located within the landing platform of an urban train station. Full details of the trains are provided, including seats, wagon enclosures, doors, windows, etc.

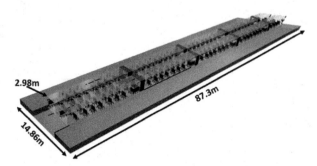

Fig. 1. Schematic representation of the inter-train communication scenario under analysis, which represents an urban train landing platform, with two trains located within the train station.

In order to analyze wireless channel performance of different communication systems which can be integrated within the inter-train scenario, a specific transmitter location has been included within the scenario. The location can be modified in order to consider any potential transmitter node, a task that can be further undertaken within a system deployment design and optimization phase as required. In this case, a central position within the rooftop of the train convoy has been chosen. The operating frequency has been subsequently varied in order to consider the potential use of different systems such as LPWAN, WLAN and 5G NR Frequency Range 1 (i.e., below 6 GHz) communication systems. Estimation of received power levels have been obtained for the complete volume of the scenario under test. In order to provide a comprehensive overview, results have been particularized for different cut plane heights (2 m, 3.5 m and 6 m). The results obtained for each one of the frequencies under consideration (f @ 868 MHz, f @ 2.4 GHz, f @ 3.5 GHz, f @ 5.6 GHz) are depicted in Figs. 2, 3, 4 and 5 for each one of the 3 cut plane heights. The results show that propagation losses increase as frequency increases, which is inherent to the frequency dependent nature of path loss estimation. In relation with cut-plane height variations, the highest received power level distributions are given for cut-plane heights of 3.5m. This is given by the fact that fading effects owing to non-line of sight links are stronger in the case of lower height (i.e., h = 2 m), whereas distance effects are larger as distance increase (h = 6m). It is worth noting that despite the relatively small distance differences, variations in received power level distributions are non-uniform, affected by the surrounding environment (i.e., train structure). In this sense, the main propagation mechanisms are given by shadowing by the train wagons, as well as by multi-path propagation effects, supported by the large density of scatterers present within the scenario under analysis.

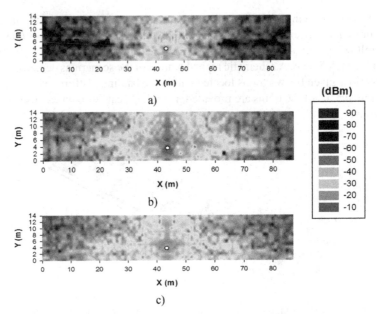

Fig. 2. Estimation of received power level distribution, with a frequency of operation of f @868 MHz within the inter-train scenario, based on volumetric 3D Ray Launching approximation, for different 2D cut-plane heights: a) cut plane height = 2 m, b) cut plane height = 3.5 m, c) cut plane height = 6 m

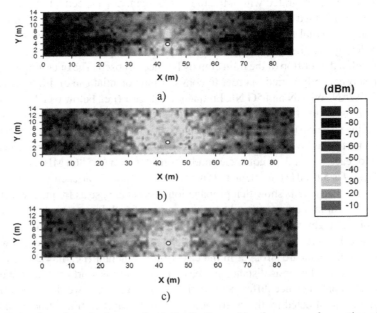

Fig. 3. Estimation of received power level distribution, with a frequency of operation of f @2.4 Ghz within the inter-train scenario, based on volumetric 3D Ray Launching approximation, for different 2D cut-plane heights: a) cut plane height = 2 m, b) cut plane height = 3.5 m, c) cut plane height = 6 m

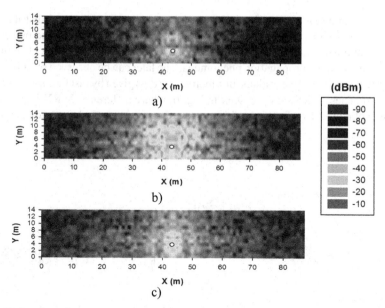

Fig. 4. Estimation of received power level distribution, with a frequency of operation of f @3.5 Ghz within the inter-train scenario, based on volumetric 3D Ray Launching approximation, for different 2D cut-plane heights: a) cut plane height = 2 m, b) cut plane height = 3.5 m, c) cut plane height = 6 m

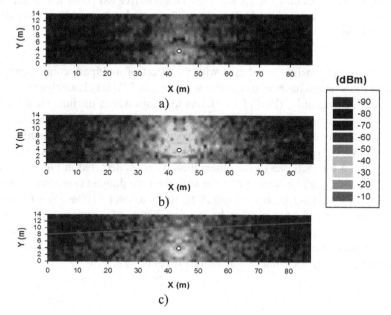

Fig. 5. Estimation of received power level distribution, with a frequency of operation of f @5.6 Ghz within the inter-train scenario, based on volumetric 3D Ray Launching approximation, for different 2D cut-plane heights: a) cut plane height = 2 m, b) cut plane height = 3.5 m, c) cut plane height = 6 m

From the previous results, it can be seen that received power level distribution is strongly influenced by the surrounding environment, given mainly by the presence of multiple scatterers, which give rise to shadowing losses owing to non-line of sight links as well as to multipath propagation phenomena. The later can be observed by considering linear transmitter to receiver radials, in which strong dips given by fast fading components are present. These effects can be seen in Fig. 6, where different TX-RX linear radials have been obtained, as a function of frequency of operation and observation height.

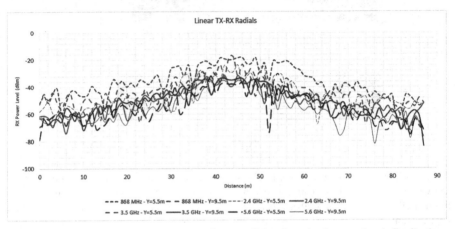

Fig. 6. Representation of different TX-RX linear radials of received power level distributions, as a function of frequency and height. Fast fading effects can be observed, owing to multipath propagation components within the inter-train wagon scenario.

In order to gain insight in relation with the effect of multipath components, time domain analysis results have been obtained with the aid of 3D Ray Launching simulation code. Power delay profiles (PDP) for different locations within the inter-train scenario, specifically for three different arbitrary positions of potential transceivers. The PDP represent all the time domain components detected within the receiver volume, which is given equivalently by the corresponding cuboid within the simulation scenario. The results obtained for each one of the observation points is depicted in Fig. 7. As it can be seen, variations can be seen in relation with the time domain components, leading to delay spreads ranging from approximately 100ns to over 1100ns, as a function of the observation points. This is given by the distribution of scatterers, which in term define the field components that propagate within the inter-train scenario and which can be employed in order to analyze system dependence on coherence time and on the definition and design of channel equalization elements.

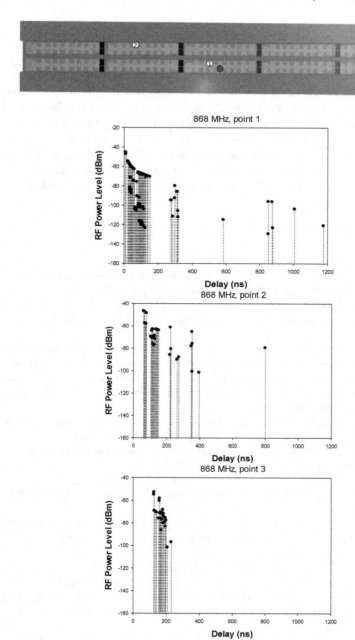

Fig. 7. Estimation of power delay profiles, with a frequency of operation of f @ 868 MHz within the inter-train scenario, based on volumetric 3D Ray Launching approximation, for 3 different locations (points 1, 2 and 3, as depicted in the schematic scenario description provided in the top image).

3 Conclusions

The implementation of context aware environments within train applications takes advantage of the connection capabilities delivered by wireless communication systems. The presence of the train wagons as well as by the surrounding infrastructure determine the performance of wireless communication systems, in terms of path loss as well in time domain characteristics. Wireless channel behavior in power/frequency distributions as well as time domain characterization results have been obtained with the aid of deterministic 3D RL simulation method, providing results for the complete volume of the scenario under test. The proposed simulation technique provides precise coverage/capacity estimations, which can be employed in order to optimize network design and implementation phases.

References

1. Kirimtat, A., Krejcar, O., Kertesz, A., Tasgetiren, M.F.: Future trends and current state of smart city concepts: a survey. IEEE Access **8**, 86448–86467 (2020)
2. Du, R., Santi, p., Xiao, M., Vasilakos, A.V., Fischione, C.: The sensable city: a survey on the deployment and management for smart city monitoring. In: IEEE Commun. Surv. Tutor. **21**(2), pp. 1533–1560, Secondquarter (2019)
3. Mehmood, Y., Ahmad, F., Yaqoob, I., Adnane, A., Imran, M., Guizani, S.: Internet-of-things-based smart cities: recent advances and challenges. IEEE Commun. Mag. **55**(9), 16–24 (2017)
4. Wang, H., Yu, F.R., Zhu, L., Tang, T., Ning, B.: Finite-state markov modeling for wireless channels in tunnel communication-based train control systems. IEEE Trans. Intell. Transp. Syst. **15**(3), 1083–1090 (2014)
5. Wang, X., Liu, L., Zhu, L., Tang, T.: Train-centric CBTC meets age of information in train-to-train communications. IEEE Trans. Intell. Transp. Syst. **21**(10), 4072–4085 (2020)
6. Lazarescu, M.T., Poolad, P.: Asynchronous resilient wireless sensor network for train integrity monitoring. IEEE Internet Things J. **8**(5), pp. 3939–3954 (2021)
7. Briso-Rodríguez, C., Fratilescu, P., Xu, Y.: Path Loss modeling for train-to-train communications in subway tunnels at 900/2400 MHz. IEEE Antennas Wirel. Propag. Lett. **18**(6), 1164–1168 (2019)
8. Liu, Y., Wang, C., Huang, J., Sun, J., Zhang, W.: Novel 3-D nonstationary MmWave massive MIMO channel models for 5G high-speed train wireless communications. IEEE Trans. Veh. Technol. **68**(3), 2077–2086 (2019)
9. Song, H., Schnieder, E.: Availability and performance analysis of train-to-train data communication system. IEEE Trans. Intell. Transp. Syst. **20**(7), 2786–2795 (2019)
10. Azpilicueta, L., Rawat, M., Rawat, K., Ghannouchi, F.M., Falcone, F.: 'A ray launching-neural network approach for radio wave propagation analysis in complex indoor environments.' IEEE Trans. Antennas Propag. **62**(5), 2777–2786 (2014)
11. Azpilicueta, L., Rawat, M., Rawat, K., Ghannouchi, F., Falcone, F.: 'Convergence analysis in deterministic 3D ray launching radio channel estimation in complex environments.' ACES J. **29**(4), 256–271 (2014)

Load Balancing and Network Life in Linear Wireless Sensor Networks

Rachid Aouami$^{(\boxtimes)}$, Rashedul Hoque, and Sébastien Roy

GRIMM Lab, Institut Interdisciplinaire d'Innovation Technologique (3IT),
Université de Sherbrooke, Sherbrooke, QC J1K QA5, Canada
{rachid.aouami,rasr2701,sebastien.roy13}@usherbrooke.ca

Abstract. The distributed management of residual energy among sensor devices within wireless sensor networks is a crucial technique that can be leveraged to maximize network lifetime. This paper proposes an approach towards this goal based on an ultra-low-power Medium Access Control (MAC) protocol and a geographical multi-hop routing protocol according to a given metric. The best node for the next hop is selected as a function of the minimum hop count and a link cost function. This is done in a manner which minimizes the overall energy consumption of the network, while balancing the load according to the residual energy at each node. To achieve this, the cost function accounts for residual energy, free buffer size, and link reliability to neighbouring nodes. It is designed to balance energy consumption, network life and QoS requirements in terms of end-to-end delay and reliability. Simulation results are presented, obtained through the Castalia framework based on the Omnet++ simulator. These results demonstrate the viability of the proposed scheme through observation of key performance parameters as a function of consumed energy, active time ratio of each node, and packet delivery ratio.

Keywords: Linear wireless sensor network · Residual energy · Best neighbour discovery · Energy-balancing scheduling · Hop count

1 Introduction

In the current state of things, wireless sensor networks (WSNs) play a key role in the development of smart environments and smart industry where everyday new categories of small objects are fitted with computational capabilities and different types of communications [1–3]. Furthermore, autonomous wireless sensors have been widely used in several fields such as medical, disaster warning, industrial, aerospace, smart grid, and others.

One area of interest is the structural health monitoring (SHM) of large structures such as bridges where WSNs can be advantageously leveraged to avoid costly wired infrastructures. However, this is a particularly demanding application due to the need for high frequency synchronized sampling of vibration data across the entire structure with sufficient spatial resolution. Furthermore,

© Springer Nature Switzerland AG 2021
H. Elbiaze et al. (Eds.): UNet 2021, LNCS 12845, pp. 133–146, 2021.
https://doi.org/10.1007/978-3-030-86356-2_12

WSNs having a linear or quasi-linear topology (e.g. such as for bridge health monitoring) form a specific class with specific characteristics which affect routing strategies and power management. Such linear WSNs (henceforth referred to as LWSNs) are applicable to many environments in addition to bridges, such as tunnels, pipelines, railroads, [4] etc.

Typically, a wireless sensor node comprises a sensor (and/or actuator), a small computer (such as an ultra-low-power microcontroller), a power source, and a wireless communication interface. In many cases of interest, the power source is a battery and the environment is such that it is costly and/or inconvenient to perform manual maintenance (such as battery replacement). In such cases, it is important to maximize the operation lifetime of the network before battery replacement becomes necessary. This is done by optimizing energy consumption at the node level, but also by finding ways to distribute the power burden intelligently since a minimum density of operating nodes is required for routing purposes.

The focus of this paper is on the maximization of the operating life of battery-powered LWSNs, taking into account key limitations of such devices, such as limited processing power, memory, and bandwidth. In terms of specific topology, we can distinguish three categories of LWSNs, i.e.

- Thin: Nodes are deployed strictly along a straight or curved line.
- Thick: A partially linear network where some of the nodes are deployed along a line while others are located at some small distance from the line in a random manner.
- Very thick: Nodes are randomly deployed between two parallel lines.

The nodes in a typical LWSN perform three main tasks: 1-acquisition of sensor data, 2-aggregation of the data acquired throughout the network at a single data sink. For this latter task, the nodes can collaborate and relay packets in a manner which maximizes network life. This requires a routing approach which is energy efficient and allows some degree of load balancing. Unless load balancing is made a specific objective, some nodes will naturally incur a larger portion of the routing burden and thus drain their batteries quicker. This problem is compounded in a linear topology where nodes that are close to the data sink will tend to be more solicited. For a specific source-destination pair, we can choose to have a small number of long hops or a large number of short hops. The latter will typically incur a lower average network energy cost, but a longer end-to-end delay. In this context, numerous works which study energy efficiency and delay rely on point-to-point communication approaches such as response time, distance and LQI (Link Quality Indicator) [5,6]. They do not take residual node energy into account.

Asynchronous MAC protocols include receiver-initiated and sender-initiated schemes. In receiver-initiated protocols, which are in general known to be more energy efficient, each node periodically wakes up to send a short beacon signaling its availability to forward packets to potential senders [7–9]. The beacon can contain useful routing information, such as residual energy. This allows the sender node to intelligently select its receiver according to some distributed load balancing criterion and thus maximize network life. A key challenge in this context resides in finding an appropriate combination of MAC and routing protocols. To the best of our knowledge, the integration of multi-hop neighbour discovery and link quality estimation as a distinct phase has not been the object of a detailed study to date.

In this paper, we present an effective method to balance the energy consumption of each node and enhance the lifetime of the network in linear wireless sensor networks with a static topology. To improve energy efficiency and reduce the number of exhausted nodes, a collaborative model is postulated based on energy-balancing scheduling. Each node transfers the arrival and sensed packets to other nearby nodes until they reach the sink node or vice versa. Unlike the other nodes, it is assumed that the sink is not limited in terms of energy or processing power, i.e. it is a larger device connected to a continuous power source. Each node forwards its data according to the energy consumption as well as residual energy of its neighbours. Furthermore, a novel sending receiving hello message iteration process is designed and a predicted scheduling algorithm is provided. Through this paper, we show the benefits of our proposed cost function design guideline by performing a detailed simulation study of the possibility of choosing the best neighbouring node in a large-scale and dense linear network based on multi-hop or single-hop scenario.

The paper is structured as follows. Section 2 describes the background and some previous work about the existing neighbour discovery protocols. Section 3 presents the proposed system model and algorithm, while Sect. 4 provides numerical results and the associated discussion. Finally, Sect. 5 consists in a conclusion, including avenues for future work.

2   Background

In many industrial applications, sensor nodes are deployed according to a linear or quasi-linear topology with a total span of hundreds of meters or, in some cases, kilometers (such as along a bridge or road). Sensor nodes are tasked with the collection and forwarding of data to one or more sink nodes, while consuming as little energy as possible. Energy is consumed when collecting, receiving and forwarding data, conditioned by network topology and data scheduling. For this reason, the maximization of the active lifetime of wireless sensor networks has attracted considerable research attention. Furthermore, locating the affected area in case of damage or malfunction in a WSN requires collection and forwarding of a larger amount of data than during normal operation. This entails a higher aggregate throughput and higher energy consumption [2]. To this end, a sustainable rendezvous protocol is provided, as well as optimal sleep/wake-up periods.

The main constraints in WSNs in general and LWSNs in particular are energy reserve, storage capacity, and processing power. Single-hop transmissions are generally not an energy efficient strategy in LWSNs given the distances involved. However, naive implementation of multi-hop routing strategies will lead to uneven energy usage amont the nodes. A routing approach incorporating a form of load balancing would therefore constitute an appropriate, yet little studied in this context, approach to equalize energy consumption and therefore maximize useful network life. Indeed, the network life would then not be constrained by the life of one over-solicited, thus making the network operational and reliable for the longest possible time.

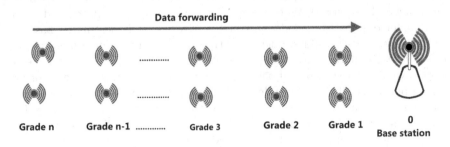

Fig. 1. Schematic model of regular linear topology.

2.1 Related Works

Over the past decade, several neighbor discovery protocols have been proposed to discover initial network connectivity and dynamically detect topological changes as they occur [5,10]. In asynchronous communication protocols, the birthday-protocol-based energy-efficient deployment approach is the first neighbor discovery technique to propose random transitions between sleep, listen, and transmission states during the neighboring discovery process [11].

It is well known that medium access and routing schemes have a huge impact on energy efficiency, latency, and other network performance metrics. However, the selection of an efficient routing scheme is constrained by multi-hop networking issues [12].

Power consumption is an interesting challenge to prolong the lifetime of wireless sensor networks. All of the collected data must reach a sink node through single or multi-hop communication, in which nodes closest to the sink carry heavier traffic loads and would be depleted of their energy faster [13]. In conformity with these rules, a hierarchical multi-path routing protocol has been proposed in [14]. Therein, each node has a hop value count that indicates the distance to the sink. During an initial "layer construction" phase and assuming that all node positions are fixed for the life of the network, the nodes construct a hierarchical system of paths in an autonomous fashion by exchanging these hop count values. The resulting routing map looks like a tree with the sink as the root node, with several nodes having multiple paths to the sink. This scheme has the benefit of achieving some degree of load balancing while being very simple to implement.

Other works determine the optimal transmission range based on the physical channel characteristics. Chen et al. [15] define the optimal one-hop length for multi-hop communications that minimizes the total energy consumption and analyze the influence of channel parameters on this optimal transmission range in a linear network [16]. In [17], a mobility-based network lifetime maximization scheme for WSNs is proposed based on a balanced-tree approach.

Many papers focus on asynchronous communication protocols in improving energy efficiency [8,9]. However, neighbor discovery and the impact of unreliable channels has not been fully explored, especially in linear wireless multi-hop networking with the evolution of structural health monitoring applications. In the literature, many techniques based on communication protocols may help conserve the energy of each node. Typically, their main objective is the maximization of the network lifetime, by relying on metrics such as received signal strength indicator (RSSI) and link quality indicator (LQI), both of which being obtained from neighbor nodes at the time of synchronization. Other sources of information are often ignored, such as residual energy, geographic location, etc., therefore limiting the potential development of multi-hop communications. Another asynchronous neighbor discovery algorithm is presented in [6]. In this protocol, nodes calculate the probability of beacon transmission at each slot before initializing neighbor discovery based on an accurate estimate of the number of their neighboring nodes. Since all parameters are determined based on a fixed node density, this algorithm is ill-suited for irregular densities. Recently, a number of asynchronous MAC protocols have been tailored specifically for energy-efficient wireless sensor networks, such as TMAC, XMAC and RIMAC.

Timer-based contention schemes enable nodes to select the best neighbor for routing according to some parameters without any a priori information about the neighborhood. They offer the benefit of simplicity, and work across the MAC and network layers. To reduce network discovery time while promoting energy efficiency, two such schemes were proposed at the MAC level designated 1-hopMAC [18] and OPWUM [7]. The first one is semi-asynchronous transmitter initiated and the second on is received initiated. In both cases, the nodes wake up periodically to communicate as either a sender or receiver, in such a way as to minimize power consumption. Indeed, unless special measures, idle listening and overhearing are the dominant sources of energy consumption in WSNs. This is because a lot more time is normally spent in listening mode (whether receiving data or not) than in the transmit mode (which consumes more power, but only in short bursts) [19]. This can be remedied through duty cycling, in which the transceiver is periodically turned ON and OFF according to the traffic flow [20]. It is a delicate problem to minimize the time a node spends in idle listening mode while ensuring that nodes are awake and listening with high probability when they are needed for reception or forwarding. Any scheme attempting to resolve this problem must do so in a manner which is adapted to the degree and nature of the traffic. For example, a duty-cycle parameter controlling the ratio of the activity period to the sleep period can be implemented and adjusted according to traffic [21,22].

3 Analytical Evaluation and Methods

In this section, we aim to explore the proposed algorithm and protocols requiring predictable communication to select an efficient next hop, in order to comply with the residual energy level and scheduling phase, which is considered as appropriate route to choose the best destination node.

3.1 System Model and Assumption

As shown in Fig. 2, we consider a thick wireless network deployed in linear fashion comprised of n sensor nodes. Nodes are assumed statically deployed (i.e., all nodes are stationary and have the same transmission range), without any external synchronization or positioning system. The sink is outside the range of most nodes, so that more than one hop is typically required, and nodes cannot detect collisions.

Nodes are disciplined according to a fixed sampling interval. Once per sampling period, they wake up, collect data and forward it to the sink using an appropriate multi-hop route. They are assumed to be equipped with a half-duplex radio transceiver which cannot transmit and receive concurrently. Thus, each device sends or receives on one channel in a given time slot. Additionally, all nodes at any given time are able to calculate their residual energy and free queue size, and are also able to determine the channel reliability between themselves and their neighbors.

When each node on the network starts to forward packets to the neighboring nodes, a given MAC protocol requires many steps, such as beacon frame, data frame, Acknowledgment, etc. Moreover, the frame is divided into three periods; Sleep period, waiting period and transmission period frame. To do that, the traditional standard communications in the wireless sensor network choose the time slots contention based, the short-hops neighboring discovery protocols and the queuing size to minimize energy consumption.

The proposed algorithm and the basic notations used in this work are summarized as follows:

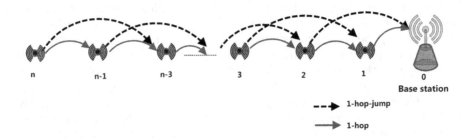

Fig. 2. Communication model.

- Depending on the application, there are one or two sinks located outside the field (i.e., right, left, and sometimes both);
- All nodes in the network have the same transmission range and can use more the single-hop-jump than single-hop transmission to choose the parent nodes;
- The failure of the network will happen only when the energy is exhausted;
- When sensor node has data to send in a specific time slot, it will receive a "Hello message" packet containing a residual energy, queue size and link quality as a metric from its neighboring nodes. This message will be used to learn how to route packets;
- Each node is equipped with one antenna that only permits a single node to receive or transmit data;
- The nodes in the grade i can receive/transmit data from the nodes in their range(grade i ± 1 or grade i ± 2).

3.2 Energy Model

Any node on the network can be a received or transmitted, but the hop count to the base station is based on three parameters as mentioned earlier. However, the priority will be based on the residual energy of each node in the network. The power consumption model used in this research work is based on the concept, where the energy consumption is directly proportional to the transmission distance. Equation (1) below shows the node energy consumption for transmitting bits of data for a distance (calculated by meters). The energy consumed for receiving of bits is given by [23]:

$$E_{Tx} = K * E_{ele} + K * E_{amp} * d^2 \tag{1}$$

$$E_{Rx} = K * E_{amp} * d^2 \tag{2}$$

where E_{ele} is the electronics energy in transceiver and E_{amp} is the amplifier energy.

In wireless sensor network topology, each node spends its life time in three modes, namely, receiving the sampling data from neighboring nodes, transmitting its own data (and/or neighbor node's data), and sleep mode. Let E_{ii} denote the initial energy, E_{th}, threshold energy, E_r energy consumed during reception, and E_t and energy consumed during transmission of one data sample. Further, we assume that each sampled data has a fixed size, therefore the transmitting time and the receiving time for each data sample are the same, namely, T_s. During each sampling interval, a parent node, with member nodes, spends T_t time for transmission, kT_t time for receiving samples, and remaining $T_s - (K + 1)T_t$ time in sleep mode. Therefore, the life of the each parent node can be calculated in terms of the number of sampling intervals, N, as

$$N = \frac{E_{in} - E_{th}}{E_t + KE_r + (T_s - (k + 1)T_t)P_s} \tag{3}$$

3.3   Technique to Select the Best Neighbor

When a transmitted node generates a collecting packets, it would be forwarded to the closely node by the shortest number of hops using the best routing algorithms taking into account many parameters. To do that, we consider residual energy of each node in the particular communication (i.e., one sender, two or three receivers) as the main metric to choose the best receiver node election between them.

The proposed algorithm goes through following phases:

Phase 1: Scheduling. Each sensor node generates "Hello messages" and broadcasts them periodically to its neighboring nodes. The most important fields of a hello message packet are shown in Fig. 3. When a node i has data to transmit to the active receiver, it does not send its beacon message in the corresponding active slot. Neighboring nodes can discover node i by overhearing the data message. In this technique, at every periodic slot time, a sender node turn on his radio to send the ready or related data. The node attempts to select an ultimate next hop node located in the next direction grade. In this case, the node turns his radio on receiving mode to receive the periodic hello message (e.g. ID, residual energy, queue size) from all receivers in his range. This is in contrast with the work presented in [18] where a sender node attempts to transmit to a received node who reply first as decided beforehand by the timer based algorithm.

Node's ID	Distance to sink	Energy level	Queue size	Packet 's ID
8bits	8 bits	16 bits	8 bits	16bits

Fig. 3. Hello message exchange structure.

- Where nodes produce relevant information periodically, the receiver node will send a beacon message to its neighbors containing residual energy and the free queue size capacity.
- After that, the sender calculates and compares the residual energy of each neighbor based on the cost function in order to make prediction and/or decision.
- The sender sends request containing the elected receiver to forward the data, all other receiver nodes receive this message then turn off their radios.
- This procedure is repeated until all the nodes in the network are dead.

Phase 2: Cost Function and Routing Data. The cost function is the relationship between the mean forward time and traffic flow on the wireless communication networks. When more than one of the neighbor nodes attempt to become the best parent simultaneously. The receiver node first computes the cost function for all its higher level nodes from the neighbor information. Indeed, a sender node can gives a good estimation based on residual energy, free queue size, and travel time on the link to reach to sink node, that decreases the number of intermediate nodes in the selection of optimal route.

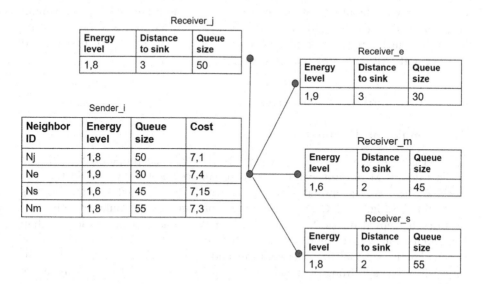

Fig. 4. Diagram of cost function of optimal parent selection.

In such routing algorithms, battery life of each node should be taken into account while selecting a destination node in the network. Therefore, a node currently having a packet to transmit decides locally which of its neighborhoods is the next hop based on a cost function. A well-designed cost function will lead to energy-efficient decisions and prolonged network lifetime.

The cost function is utilized in each node to find the next hop node. The optimal next hop is calculated from the cost function that node is known as the optimal parent or next hop during data forwarding. The value is approximately taken from every iteration and to find one node as optimal parent, it employs to select only the parent with highest energy level. Otherwise, it continues its iteration and tries to balance the load among several shortest paths. In addition, we suppose that each node has a battery level with a finite initial energy E_{tot} while the sink node is supposed to have unlimited energy. This mechanism includes residual energy of node and the free queue size of node s_j between nodes s_i and s_j. $Cost_{ij}$ is defined as follows:

$$Cos_{ij} = C_E * \frac{E_{resj}}{E_{totj}} + C_Q * \frac{Q_{empj}}{Q_{totj}} \qquad (4)$$

where E_{resj} = Estimated residual energy at the node, E_{totj} = initial energy, Q_{empj} = Estimated free size, and Q_{totj} denotes initial buffer size. C_E and C_Q are the cost energy required for transmitting one packet and its size, respectively.

The main goal of this algorithm is the discover the best receiver. The algorithm starts looking for the best value in terms of remaining energy, while the sender can detect dynamically which one is good the be the elected receiver. In conformity with the objectives, all nodes know the minimum and the maximum value of energy. To this end, a suitable comparison without any prior routing among the ultimate neighbors to choose one next hop to be the best elected receiver node with the cost function value.

4 Numerical Investigation

4.1 Simulation Parameters

This section presents a comparative study through the proposed work based on new design MAC protocol approach to balance the energy load in the network, and the work proposed in the 1-hopMAC. We simulated a system with as shown in the Fig. 2, on Castalia framework of Omnet++ simulator and based on work presented in [24,25]. In this regard, We considered a static multihop communication with 60 nodes and one sink node arranged in linear topology. Given that it is a multihop network, all nodes are in charge of collecting and forwarding packets from their neighboring nodes. In order to give this, every node generates periodically packets at an average frequency of one packet every 10s excepted the sink node, where the exact number of packets that each node will transmit is known in advance. Moreover, we ran various simulations for a fixed periods of time to analyze the performances, while the wake-up period as sender or receiver is fixed once for all at the deployment of the network. The intensive set of simulations performed based on the parameters which are given in Table 1.

Table 1. Simulation parameters

Name of parameter	Value
Network area	200×500
Number of sensor nodes	60
Data packet size	512 bytes
Control packet size	40 bytes
Initial energy	18720 J
Data packet size	Uniform
Simulation time	1800 s

4.2   Results and Analysis

Through the simulation, the proposed protocol has been analysed and compared with the work presented in 1-hopMAC [22]. The performance of the protocol based on various metrics such as energy consumption, network life time, packet delivery ratio, and average packet received without interference.

Average Energy Consumption. Is the average amount of energy consumed in the network doing the transmission and reception of any kind of data. The following results are illustrated in Fig. 5-a.

By considering altogether the graphs, we see that even though it is clear that the proposed protocol provides a good results in terms of average energy consumed per network in the case of proposed approach is lower comparing to 1-hopMAC, the energy is batter balanced among nodes in the network when increasing the number of nodes. On the other hand, in the 1-hopMAC approach, the network suffers from idle listening due to the contention among contenders when the retransmission packets are increased. We notice that, our proposed protocol performs better than 1-hopMAC.

Average Packets Received Without Interference Ratio. It is the ratio of successful packets received by the base station in the network. The comparison between the data received of each MAC protocol depicted in Fig. 5-b in same duration of simulation 1800 s. It is clear that, the proposed protocol provides the best results due to the synchronization time and the election of the best destination.

Duty Cycle: It is a period of activate radio followed by a sleep or deep sleep period of the main radio interface of the wireless device, it is provides and benefits in terms of energy remaining and throughput. In the network, the control packets are exchanged for neighbor maintenance, best node election, route discovery, establishment and maintenance. Additionally, it is clearly shown in the Fig. 5-d that, increase the duty-cycle in 1-hopMAC mechanism does not give a significant improvement in terms of reception packet without interference. Because, the nodes send the data to their parent nodes, while they are occupied to forwarding the data toward the sink. Otherwise, our proposed scheme is greater than the 1-hopMAC and do not suffers from collision and retransmission problems.

Network Lifetime. Lifetime is defined here as the total elapsed time from the beginning of network operation to the first node failure due to energy depletion. While each node in transmitting mode determines the relay node to be the next destination from the candidate nodes. Figure 5-c shows the network lifetime of protocols under various number of nodes, while the vertical axis shows the estimated life time and the horizontal shows axis shows the number of nodes. It is evident that, the network lifetime is defined as the number of rounds until of the first node die. In this figure, it is clearly seen that, the proposed approach outperforms 1-hopMAC in term of estimated life time for various number of nodes. In order to come up, 1-hopMAC protocol have equal lifetimes, it uses the multi-hop communication and contention time based to channel access. While, keep into account the closest nodes to the sink.

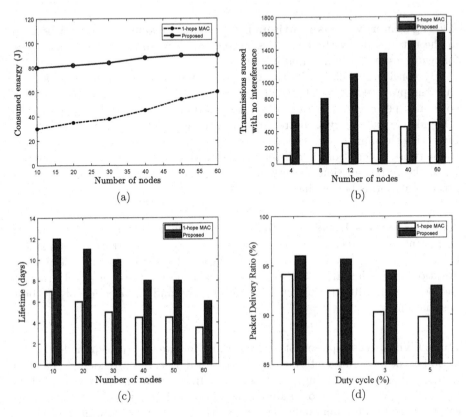

Fig. 5. Average energy consumed versus the number of nodes (a), Packets succeed without interference versus number of nodes (b), Packets succeed without interference versus duty-cycle (c), and (d) Estimated network lifetime.

5 Concluding Remarks

This paper proposes a solution based on the combination of an ultra low power MAC and geographical multi-hop routing according to the residual energy at each node for WSNs with a quasi-linear topology. This strategy avoids routes with an excessive number of hops while maximizing network lifetime through load balancing. Indeed, in order to maximize the operation lifetime of battery-powered LWSNs, a key concept put forth herein is to use residual node energy and the link cost function for the minimum hop count for choosing the next hop election needed in forwarding data to the sink node. Furthermore, the proposed algorithm uses a new strategy without energy suffering for the nodes located close to the sink. In future extension, we intend to develop and implement smart antennas at each node in the network to improve the best strategies for neighbor discovery in static topology through innovating design, where energy and reliability of sensor nodes will be taken into consideration. After all, we use our experience to extend with the real-world deployment in the bridge monitoring, taking into account the environment requirements (e.g., climate Canadian, longevity).

References

1. Abidoye, A.P., Obagbuwa, I.C.: Models for integrating wireless sensor networks into the Internet of Things. IET Wirel. Sens. Syst. **7**(3), 65–72 (2017)
2. Sethi P., Sarangi, S.R.: Internet of things: architectures, protocols, and applications. J. Electr. Comput. Eng. **2017** (2017)
3. Wan, J., Chen, B., Wang, S., Xia, M., Li, D., Liu, C.: Fog computing for energy-aware load balancing and scheduling in smart factory. IEEE Trans. Ind. Inform. **14**(10), 4548–4556 (2018)
4. Yousif, Y.K., Badlishah, R., Yaakob, N., Amir, A.: A review of data collection approaches in linear wireless sensor networks (LWSNs). J. Phys. Conf. Ser. **1019**, 012006 (2018)
5. Radi, M., Dezfouli, B., Bakar, K.A., Razak, S.A., Lee, M.: Network initialization in low-power wireless networks: a comprehensive study. Comput. J. **57**(8), 1238–1261 (2014)
6. Borbash, S.A., Ephremides, A., McGlynn, M.J.: An asynchronous neighbor discovery algorithm for wireless sensor networks. Ad Hoc Networks **5**(7), 998–1016 (2007)
7. Ait Aoudia, A., Gautier, M., Berder, O.: OPWUM: opportunistic mac protocol leveraging wake-up receivers in WSNs. J. Sens. **2016** (2016)
8. Sun, Y., Gurewitz, O., Johnson, D.B.: Ri-mac: a receiver-initiated asynchronous duty cycle mac protocol for dynamic traffic loads in wireless sensor networks. In: Proceedings of the 6th ACM Conference on Embedded Network Sensor Systems, pp. 1–14 (2008)
9. Lin, E.-Y., Rabaey, J.M., Wiethoelter, S., Wolisz, A.: Receiver initiated rendezvous schemes for sensor networks. In: GLOBECOM 2005. IEEE Global Telecommunications Conference, vol. 5, p. 6. IEEE (2005)
10. Yick, J., Mukherjee, B., Ghosal, D.: Wireless sensor network survey. Comput. Networks **52**(12), 2292–2330 (2008)
11. McGlynn, M.J., Borbash, S.A.: Birthday protocols for low energy deployment and flexible neighbor discovery in ad hoc wireless networks. In: Proceedings of the 2nd ACM International Symposium on Mobile Ad Hoc Networking and Computing, pp. 137–145 (2001)
12. Abo-Zahhad, M., Ahmed, S.M., Sabor, N., Sasaki, S.: A new energy-efficient adaptive clustering protocol based on genetic algorithm for improving the lifetime and the stable period of wireless sensor networks. Int. J. Energy Inf. Commun. **5**(3), 47–72 (2014)

13. Li, J., Mohapatra, P.: An analytical model for the energy hole problem in many-to-one sensor networks. In: VTC-2005-Fall. 2005 IEEE 62nd Vehicular Technology Conference, vol. 4, pp. 2721–2725 (2005)
14. Wang, Y., Tsai, C., Mao, H., et al.: HMRP: hierarchy-based multipath routing protocol for wireless sensor networks. Tamkang J. Sci. Eng. **9**(3), 255 (2006)
15. Ganesan, D., Krishnamachari, B., Woo, A., Culler, D., Estrin, D., Wicker, S.: Complex behavior at scale: an experimental study of low-power wireless sensor networks, Technical Report. Citeseer (2002)
16. Jaffres-Runser, K., Gorce, J.-M., Ubéda, S.: Multiobjective QoS-oriented planning for indoor wireless LANs. In: IEEE Vehicular Technology Conference, pp. 1–5. IEEE (2006)
17. Khatri, A., Kumar, S., Kaiwartya, O., Aslam, N., Meena, N., Abdullah, A.H.: Towards green computing in wireless sensor networks: controlled mobility-aided balanced tree approach. Int. J. Commun. Syst. **31**(7), e3463 (2018)
18. Walteyne, T., Bachir, A., Dohler, M., Barthe, D., Auge-Blum, I.: 1-hopmac: An energy-efficient mac protocol for avoiding 1-hop neighborhood knowledge. In: 2006 3rd Annual IEEE Communications Society on Sensor and Ad Hoc Communications and Networks, vol. 2, pp. 639–644. IEEE (2006)
19. Rault, T., Bouabdallah, A., Challal, Y.: Energy efficiency in wireless sensor networks: a top-down survey. Comput. Networks **67**, 104–122 (2014)
20. Schurgers, C., Tsiatsis, V., Ganeriwal, S., Srivastava, M.: Optimizing sensor networks in the energy-latency-density design space. IEEE Trans. Mobile Comput. **1**(1), 70–80 (2002)
21. Langendoen, K., Halkes, G.: Energy-efficient medium access control. Embedded Syst. Handb. **6000**, 1–34 (2005)
22. Demirkol, I., Ersoy, C., Alagoz, F.: Mac protocols for wireless sensor networks: a survey. IEEE Commun. Mag. **44**(4), 115–121 (2006)
23. Heinzelman, W.B., Chandrakasan, A.P., Balakrishnan, H.: An application-specific protocol architecture for wireless microsensor networks. IEEE Trans. Wirel. Commun. **1**(4), 660–670 (2002)
24. Boulis, A.: Castalia: revealing pitfalls in designing distributed algorithms in WSN. In: Proceedings of the 5th International Conference on Embedded Networked Sensor Systems, pp. 407–408 (2007)
25. Benedetti, D., Petrioli, C., Spenza, D.: Greencastalia: an energy-harvesting-enabled framework for the castalia simulator. In: Proceedings of the 1st International Workshop on Energy Neutral Sensing Systems, pp. 1–6 (2013)

Mobile Edge Networking and Fog-Cloud Computing

DDoS Attack and Defense
in SDN-Based Cloud

Safaa Mahrach[1]($\boxtimes$) and Abdelkrim Haqiq[1,2]($\boxtimes$) (iD)

[1] Faculty of Sciences and Techniques, Computer, Networks, Mobility and Modeling laboratory: IR2M, Hassan First University of Settat, 26000 Settat, Morocco
s.mahrach@uhp.ac.ma
[2] Machine Intelligence Research Labs (MIR Labs), Washington, D.C., USA
abdelkrim.haqiq@uhp.ac.ma

Abstract. Software defined networking-based cloud has many advantages over traditional network infrastructure, such as improved network flexibility, programmability, and scalability. However, new security concerns and especially new trends of Distributed Denial of Service (DDoS) attacks have been introduced during the integration of Software Defined Networking (SDN) and cloud computing. The good capabilities of SDN, such as software-based traffic analysis, centralized control and dynamic network reconfiguration, can significantly improve DDoS attack detection and mitigation in a cloud environment. However, SDN itself may be targeted by the attackers, which raise the risk of DDoS attacks in the SDN-based cloud environment. In this context, this paper aims to address the DDoS attacks which are intended to harm the scalability and availability of SDN-based cloud environment. We propose an efficient and secure SDN-based cloud architecture based on the Openstack cloud platform, Open Network Operating System (ONOS) controller, and Open vSwitch (OvS). To protect the proposed SDN-based cloud system, we incorporate the lightweight and convenient mitigation mechanism 'DDoS flooding attack mitigation in Software Defined Networks' into a reconfigurable data path. Our proposal leverages switch programmability, distributed packet processing, and centralized SDN control, to offer a secure and resilient SDN-based cloud system that can resist DDoS flood attacks.

Keywords: Cloud computing · Software Defined Networking (SDN) · Network security · DDoS flooding attacks · DDoS mitigation · P4 language · SDN-based CLoud

1 Introduction

Cloud computing has been introduced as the next-generation architecture of IT companies and it gives great capabilities that ensure improved productivity with minimal costs. Cloud computing provides an enhanced level of flexibility and scalability in comparison to the traditional IT systems.

The success and growth of cloud computing depends on supporting network infrastructure. With the growth of cloud computing, the problems facing

© Springer Nature Switzerland AG 2021
H. Elbiaze et al. (Eds.): UNet 2021, LNCS 12845, pp. 149–162, 2021.
https://doi.org/10.1007/978-3-030-86356-2_13

the supporting network infrastructure are also increasing. Problems faced by traditional cloud networks include limited management flexibility, performance issues, poor application deployment capability, lack of support for network innovation, increased security risks, and more [25,26]. To suffice the need of the hour, the cloud computing environment requires flexible, secure, dynamic, and programmable networks that can deal with these challenges.

SDN is an emerging networking architecture that is dynamic, cost-effective, programmable, and manageable. SDN technology has been developed to simplify the operational complexities of traditional networks by decoupling the control decisions from the forwarding devices. The benefits of SDN paradigm can also be used in the cloud environment to make it more scalable, easy to manage, and programmable [33].

SDN-based cloud or software-defined cloud networking is a new form of cloud networking in which SDN enables centralized control of the network, provides a holistic view of the network, and delivers network as a service (NaaS) in the cloud computing environment [27,28]. However, new security issues and particularly new trends of DDoS attacks have been introduced over the integration of SDN and the cloud computing [22,29,30]. DDoS attack may happen when an attacker forces a targeted cloud service to use excessive amounts of finite system resources like network bandwidth, memory, Central Processing Unit (CPU), or disk space, making services and computing resources unavailable.

The good capabilities of SDN, such as software-based traffic analysis, centralized control and dynamic network reconfiguration, can greatly improve the detection and mitigation of DDoS attacks in the cloud computing environment [12,31]. For example, the separation of the control plane from the data plane in SDN allows IT administrators to easily perform large-scale attack and defense experiments in a real environment, unlike traditional networks. However, SDN itself can be targeted by attackers, which increases the risk of DDoS attacks in the SDN-based cloud environment [15,34,37].

The SDN paradigm decouples the control plane from the data plane. The controller is the brain of the SDN architecture, responsible for implementing policies, retaining a global view of the network and providing a hardware abstraction layer to the control applications. Therefore, it can be considered a single point of failure if it is made unavailable by a DDoS attack. For example, an attacker can make the controller inaccessible by generating a series of new Transmission Control Protocol (TCP) SYN requests from distributed bots using spoofed Internet Protocol (IP) addresses, which involves the controller in a series of unnecessary processes. In this case, the controller will be saturated and thus unable to process legitimate requests. In addition, this type of attack also exhausts the bandwidth of the communication channel between the controller and the switches, as well as the flow tables of the switches with false flow rules [12,14,15]. This type of attack is different from the traditional DDoS attack which aims to deplete server resources in the target cloud environment. The control layer DDoS attack can affect the controller power process, the interface resources, and the switch flow table space in the SDN-based cloud environment.

This challenge motivated us to protect SDN components against DDoS attacks first. In the previous work [36], we have developed and proposed a new security solution 'DDoS flooding attack mitigation in Software Defined Networks' which aims to protect SDN architecture and create an efficient network system that can resist DDoS flood attacks.

In the present research work, we intend to protect the SDN-based cloud environment and make it more resilient to DDoS attacks. First of all, we provide an efficient and secure SDN-based cloud architecture based on the Openstack opensource cloud platform [1] and the ONOS controller [2]. In this proposal, we aim to activate a high-performance and reconfigurable data path based on the combination of the Programming Protocol-independent Packet Processors (P4) [3], the P4Runtime interface [9], and the OvS [6] software switch. Second, to protect the proposed SDN-based Openstack cloud architecture, we integrate the lightweight and convenient mitigation system that has been provided in [36]. Our approach leverages switch programmability, distributed packet processing, and centralized SDN control, to offer a secure and resilient SDN-based cloud system.

The present paper is organized as follows: In Sect. 2, we present the general architecture of SDN-based cloud environment, we discuss how the cloud characteristics make it more vulnerable to DDoS attacks, and we present some benefits and drawbacks of the usage of SDN in protecting the SDN-based cloud against DDoS attacks. In Sect. 3, we evaluate some of the existing research works which propose security solution to detect and mitigate DDoS threats in SDN-based cloud system. Before presenting the proposed approach, we present the methods and techniques used in our proposed mitigation solution in Sect. 4. We present the design and architecture of our approach 'DDoS defense in SDN-based cloud' in Sect. 5. Finally, we give our conclusion and perspectives in Sect. 6.

2   SDN-Based Cloud Computing Environment

SDN has emerged as the dominant programmable network architecture. It has been developed to simplify the operational complexities of traditional networks by decoupling the control decisions from the forwarding devices. SDN-based cloud is a new form of cloud networking in which SDN allows a centralized control of the network, gives a global view of the network, and provides NaaS in the cloud computing environments [27–29].

2.1   SDN-Based Cloud Architecture

The Fig. 1 indicates the architecture of the standard SDN-based cloud systems obtained from the literature [29].

Cloud Manager (CM) controls the cloud tenants and resources including compute, networking, etc. CM manages the tenant requests such as virtual machine (VM) creation and provisions cloud resources to supply the cloud services. It also controls energy-efficient resources and resource monitoring. OpenStack is an open-source instance of a CM widely used to create public and

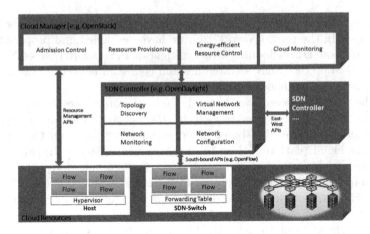

Fig. 1. SDN-based cloud architecture

private clouds. Network services are managed by *SDN controller* which communicates with the cloud manager using north-bound Application Programming Interface (APIs). SDN controller is responsible for performing the essential network functions such as network monitoring, network topology discovery, dynamic network configuration, and virtual network management. Scalability is possible using multiple SDN Controllers communicating through east/west-bound APIs. *Cloud resources* include compute and networking resources. Compute Resources (CRs) are the servers that host VMs using hypervisor such as Kernel-Based Virtual Machine (KVM), Xenserver, Vmware, etc. CRs are controlled by the cloud manager via resource management APIs. Networking Resources (NRs) are the switches that can support multiple virtual switches using OvS. Physical and virtual switches (i.e., both virtual switches hosted in switches and in hosts) are controlled by SDN controller by updating forwarding tables in switches via South-bound APIs (e.g., OpenFlow, P4 Runtime).

2.2 DDoS Attacks in SDN-Based Cloud

A combination of studies [15,29,30] shows how the key characteristics of cloud computing may be the reason for the increased rate of DDoS attacks in a cloud environment. Virtualization and multi-tenant technologies are the key development of cloud computing. Therefore, any vulnerability of these technologies can put the security of the cloud system and all services at significant risk. In combination with rapid elasticity, the pricing model can be exploited to financially affect a customer by generating fraud invoices or performing an Economic Denial of Sustainability attack (EDoS), which is a new form of DDoS attacks. Moreover, the on-demand self-service characteristic can be easily leveraged to build a powerful botnet and launch DDoS attacks in a short time, as it allows customers to independently obtain cloud services. In addition, the lack of security on most mobile devices used to access cloud services can be easily exploited to launch DDoS attacks in the cloud infrastructure.

SDN features present a great promise in terms of defending against DDoS attacks in cloud computing environment. In traditional networks, it was difficult to implement, experiment, and deploy new ideas on large-scale networks such as cloud environment. However, the separation of the control plane from the data plane in SDN enables experimenters to perform easily large-scale attack and defense experiments in a real environment [29]. This separation provides a programmable network in which network devices can operate and manage network traffic dynamically [31]. Hence, the programmability of SDN allows us to flexibly implement intelligent defense algorithms against DDoS attacks in cloud environment. A centralized control feature of SDN gives a network-wide knowledge, which helps to build a relevant security policy for the network. Characteristics like centralized control and programmability allow SDN to defend cloud computing against DDoS attacks [13]. In SDN, the network traffic can be analyzed innovatively using intelligent mechanisms and various types of software tools [12]. Hence, SDN can greatly enhance the DDoS detection and mitigation ability using the software-based traffic analysis.

Some significant characteristics of SDN approach help to defend the DDoS attacks in the cloud computing environment. However, SDN itself is vulnerable to different kind of security attacks including, flow-table overloading attack, controller-aimed DDoS attack, unauthorized access, Fraudulent flow rules, malicious applications, data leakage, etc. [12,14,15,22]. Therefore, it is important to discuss the vulnerabilities of SDN architecture which may raise the risk of DDoS attacks in the SDN-based cloud environment.

The SDN architecture is divided into three planes including, application plane, control plane, and data plane. All these planes and APIs can be targeted by the attackers to launch DDoS attacks. The controller is the brain of SDN architecture. Hence, it could be seen as a single point of failure if it is made unreachable by DDoS attack. In control plane, DDoS attacks can target controller services, northbound, southbound, eastbound, and westbound interfaces [12]. In the data plane, switches suffer from the limited storage capacity of the flow tables. This limitation may be exploited by the attackers to launch the flow table overloading attack [14,22]. In the application plane, unauthenticated and unauthorized applications pose a great challenge for SDN. Furthermore, the problem of isolation of applications and resources is not well solved in SDN; as a result, a DDoS attack on one application can affect other applications as well.

3 Related Work

SDN-based cloud has many advantages over traditional network infrastructure, such as improved network flexibility, programmability, and scalability. However, several security issues and especially new trends of DDoS attacks have been introduced [12–15,22]. Most of the research separately focuses on mitigating DDoS attacks in cloud computing or SDN. Therefore, research on mitigating DDoS attacks in the SDN-based cloud is limited.

For instance, DaMask was proposed in [12] as an architecture to protect the SDN-based cloud environment from DDoS attacks. It consists of two modules: a DaMask-D anomaly-based attack detection module and a DaMask-M attack mitigation module. The detection module is built on a graphical model of probabilistic inference and the attenuation module is a flexible control structure that enables rapid attack reaction. In [22], the authors proposed a new approach to improve the resiliency of the SDN-based cloud computing against flow table overload DDoS attacks. The approach uses the unused flow table-space of other switches to resist the attack at a switch currently under attack. ProDefense [13] provides an SDN-based DDoS defense framework for smart city data center. It uses a custom detection filter to meet the specific security requirements of smart city applications. Phan et al. [32] introduce a hybride machine learning model to classify DDoS attack, it relies on support vector machine and self organizing map algorithms. They came up with a solution combining both the hybrid machine learning algorithm and an enhanced history-based IP filtering scheme (eHIPF) to defend the SDN cloud against DDoS attacks. Chen et al. [35] used a machine learning based classifier named Extreme Gradient Boosting (XGBoost) to detect DDoS attack in SDN-based cloud. XGBoost is implemented in the SDN controller as a detection module. Authors focused on the controller resources saturation attacks and control channel congestion.

Machine learning methods have been widely used to detect DDoS attack in SDN and cloud environment. However, the machine learning process is so complex and requires a lot more steps before and after predictive analytics. In contrast, our proposed solution uses simple methods to control the new incoming packets, and classify the benign requests from flood attacks at an early stage (i.e., at the switch level). As a result, it reduces the traffic load on the control channel bandwidth and the controller.

Most of the proposals for DDoS attack detection and mitigation are implemented at the SDN control plane, which increases the involvement of the SDN controller in each operation. Consequently, the data-control channel quickly goes into a bottleneck, which may affect the performance of the network and limit its scalability and reactivity. In addition, they used a fixed data plane such as an openflow-enabled switch, which is limited and does not allow dynamic reconfiguration of the network infrastructure.

Frameworks, compilers and programming languages [16–18,20,21,23] were designed to leverage the SDN data plane with a means to dynamically implement specific operations (e.g., monitor, detect, react) inside the switch.

Our proposal exploits the SDN data plane capabilities to design an efficient and secure SDN-based cloud architecture using the programming protocol independent packet processors - P4. P4 is a network programming language for describing how packets are processed by switches. This language enables the implementation of novel applications which operate with new header fields in a reconfigurable data path (i.e., P4-enabled switch).

4   Methods and Techniques

4.1   SYN Flooding Defense Method

The most efficient mitigation methods against spoofed SYN flood attacks are various variations and combinations of the SYN Cookie method. The SYN cookie [4] is a state-less technique to prevent the memory consumption caused by the half-open Synchronize (SYN) attacks (SYN flood attacks). The system (i.e., server or switch) enabling the SYN cookie technique intercepts the SYN request received from a client and sends back a SYN-ACK packet with a pre-generated Initial Sequence Number (ISN). The cookie or ISN is generated using some details of the initial SYN packet and cryptographic hashing function to make the decoding of the cookie more complicated (cf. Subsect. 4.2). If the mitigating system receives an Acknowledge (ACK) packet from the client (with pre-generated cookie +1), it checks the validation of the TCP sequence number (i.e., is the ACK-1) as shown in Subsect. 4.2.

4.2   Pre-generated Cookie

Referring to [11], the implementation of the SYN cookie technique must fulfill the following basic requirements:

- Cookies should contain some details of the initial SYN packet and its TCP options.
- Cookies should be unpredictable by attackers. It is recommended to use a cryptographic hashing function in order to make the decoding of the cookie more complicated. To this end, we select the recommended Linux SYN cookie method for generating and validating cookies [24].

Cookie generation:

$$H_1 = hash(K_1, IP_s, IP_d, Port_s, Port_d) \tag{1}$$

$$H_2 = hash(K_2, count, IP_s, IP_d, Port_s, Port_d) \tag{2}$$

$$ISN_d(cookie) = H_1 + ISN_s + (count \times 2^{24}) + (H_2 + MSS)2^{24} \tag{3}$$

Cookie validation:

$$ISN_d = ACK - 1 \tag{4}$$

$$ISN_s = SEQ - 1 \tag{5}$$

$$count(cookie) = (ISN_d - H_1 - ISN_s)/2^{24} \tag{6}$$

$$MSS(cookie) = (ISN_d - H_1 - ISN_s)2^{24} - H_2 2^{24} \tag{7}$$

As we can see above and in Table 1, we calculate the two hash values H_1 and H_2 (based on TCP options, secret keys k_1, k_2 and count) then we use them with ISN_s and MSS to generate the cookie (ISN_d), as it is shown in (3). For the cookie validation, there are 2 integrity controls (count(cookie) and MSS(cookie)). The first one checks the age of the cookie. The second evaluates whether the value of the MSS is within the 2 bit range (0–3). If the cookie meets both integrity controls, it is considered valid, and the connection can be accepted.

Table 1. Parameters of the Linux implementation [24]

Parameter	Description
K_1, K_2	Secret keys
IP_s, IP_d	Source and destination IP addresses
$Port_s$, $Port_d$	Source and destination ports
ISN_s, ISN_d	Source and destination initial sequence numbers
ACK	Acknowledgement number
SEQ	Sequence number
MSS	2 bit index of the client's Maximum Segment Size
Count	32 bit minute counter
Hash()	32 bit cryptographic hash

5   Proposed Approach

The purpose of our research work, is the design of an efficient and resilient SDN-based cloud environment that can resist DDoS threats. To this end, we firstly provide an efficient and a secure SDN-based cloud architecture based on the open source Openstack cloud platform, the ONOS SDN controller, and the Open vSwitch software switch. The proposal aims to activate a high-performance and reconfigurable data path based on the integration of the Programming Protocol-independent Packet Processors, the P4Runtime API, and the OvS software switch. Moreover, we use ONOS controller to get visibility and control over the entire network.

Since it offers a reconfigurable data path, the architecture allows administrators to easily activate new network operations such as monitoring, routing, virtualization, firewall, detection, mitigation, etc. In contrast to the traditional OpenFlow and OvS implementation which requires complex design and several lines to add and modify to implement new functions which operate with new header fields.

To defend the SDN-based cloud system against DDoS attacks, we integrate the lightweight and convenient mitigation system that has been provided in [36]. This latter protect the SDN components including the centralized controller, switches, and southbound interface, as well as the downstream cloud servers.

The goal of our proposed DDoS mitigation mechanism is to activate P4 or reconfigurable data path with smart and advanced functions to prevent and mitigate DDoS flood attacks in the SDN-based cloud environment. To reach this aim, we activate the reconfigurable data path with the classification and mitigation module to analyze and classify the new incoming packets and perform the adaptive countermeasures. In addition we incorporate the control application which will be implemented in the ONOS controller. This application allows the controller to interact with the P4 data path through the P4Runtime interface.

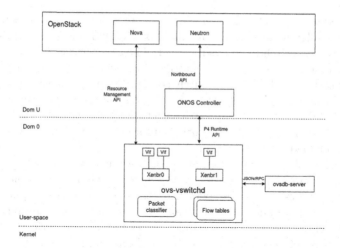

Fig. 2. Overall architecture

5.1 System Components and Architecture

The designed architecture and components of the proposed system are presented in Fig. 2 and 3.

CLoud Manager - In our proposed system, all major cloud-based OS, such as CloudStack, Xen Cloud Project (XCP), OpenStack, etc. can be compatible. We select Openstack as cloud manager to host and control cloud resources. Compute resources are managed using Nova service via resource management API (XenAPI). Networking resources are managed using Neutron networking service via northbound API. The Neutron communicates with the ONOS controller to control the entire physical and virtual network infrastructure. Compute servers host VMs using Xenserver hypervisor which is an efficient virtualization solution. There are two types of domains in Xenserver-based cloud including Domain0 (Dom0) and DomainU (DomU). The Dom0 is the management domain that owns the storage and networking hardware, the device drivers, and the main control software. The DomU is an unprivileged domain which is dedicated for administrative purpose to place the Openstack control software (nova and neutron), the SDN controller, and the rest of Vms.

SDN Controller - We use the open source ONOS SDN controller to manage the entire physical and virtual network infrastructure. It is the only SDN controller which supports both the P4 data path and the P4Runtime API. ONOS controller offers the flexibility to develop and implement new dynamic network functions with simplified programming interfaces such as P4Runtime API. It allows us to dynamically reconfigure the network and control network elements in real time.

Open vSwitch - OvS is the widely used software switch in cloud networking system. In our established system, OvS is natively implemented in the Dom0 of

XenServer hypervisor. The communication between VMs within the same server and those of different servers is controlled by the OvS. In user-space, there are two modules: ovs-switchd and ovsdb-server. The ovs-switchd module is the core component of OvS that supports multiple independent data paths (bridges). The ovsdb-server module holds switch configuration. As shown in Fig. 2, the ovs-switchd communicates with the ovsdb-server via the management protocol. The ovs-switchd module communicates with the ONOS controller via P4Runtime API. In our system, OvS operates entirely in userspace without changing kernel source code or loading kernel modules.

OvS is the software implementation of the OpenFlow switch. It can also operate as software implementation of P4-enabled switch. Our implementation is based on the *P4-OvS* project which extends the OvS with support for the P4-enabled data path and the P4Runtime API to create a high-performance P4 software switch [5]. We use this software implementation to perform the offered mitigation system in our proposed SDN-based Openstack cloud platform.

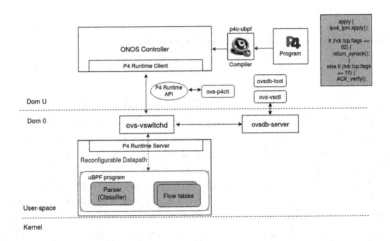

Fig. 3. OvS and P4 architecture

The *P4-OvS* project extends OvS with new blocks [5], as shown in Fig. 3:

- *Reconfigurable or P4 data path* treats the incoming packets using the packet processing pipeline generated from the P4_program, at runtime. The supported example of reconfigurable data path can be eBPF (Extended Berkeley Packet Filter) [8], XDP (eXpress Data Path) or uBPF (userspace BPF) [7].
- *P4Runtime API* allows communication between the reconfigurable data path and the ONOS controller. In particular, it implements gRPC server with P4Runtime protocol and allows users to control P4 data path.
- *P4 compiler (p4c-ubpf)* allows to create data path-specific binary from the P4_program and P4_Info metadata file for P4Runtime API.

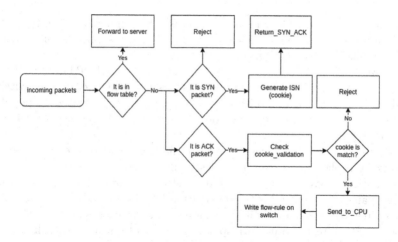

Fig. 4. TCP SYN flood defensive flowchart

– *Ovs-p4ctl* is the management tool for the P4 switch. It controls P4 programs and manages P4 objects (e.g. P4 tables, registers, etc.).

In this soft implementation, we use uBPF data path. uBPF is the userspace re-implementation of in-kernel eBPF VM which provides a user-space execution environment that is extensible at runtime [7].

5.2   DDoS Mitigation Solution

Classification and Mitigation module enables the reconfigurable data path (DP) to analyze and classify the new incoming packets. Data path will be able to classify the benign packets from the SYN flood attacks and perform adaptive countermeasures.

In first, DP checks if the incoming packet exists in the flow table if so, the packet will be immediately forwarded to the destination server. Otherwise, the DP checks if it is a TCP SYN or an ACK packet. If it is a SYN packet, the DP returns a SYN-ACK packet with a pre-generated ISN (cf. Subsect. 4.2). Otherwise, if the packet is not a TCP SYN packet or an ACK packet, it is rejected (cf. Fig. 4).

If the DP receives an ACK packet, as shown in Fig. 4, it checks the validation of the TCP sequence number (i.e., is the ACK-1), as shown in Subsect. 4.2. For the validation of the cookie, we control two integrities: count(cookie) for checking the age of the cookie (must be lower to 2 min), and MSS(cookie) for evaluating whether the value of the MSS is within the 2-bit range (0–3). If the cookie meets both integrity controls, it is considered valid, and the connection can be accepted.

If the TCP connection is validated the switch transmits the ACK packet as packet in message to the controller to write the required flow-entry. Optionally, the switch sends back a TCP-reset packet, with source IP of the original server, to the client in order to enable him to re-establish the connection directly with the server. In our system, we use a local controller that is responsible for controlling the P4 switches via the P4Runtime API in real time.

Control module enables the controller to interact with the P4 data path using the P4Runtime interface. The module connects the controller to the switch(s), installs the classification and mitigation P4-programs on the switch(s), populates the flow-tables with flow entries, and describes how the ONOS controller handles the incoming messages (packet-in).

Once the controller receives a packet-in message, it learns details of the validated ACK packet to create the requested flow rule. It extracts the IP source, IP destination, MAC source and MAC destination addresses, and the source and destination ports. It adds the destination IP address and the corresponding MAC address to its memory, if it does not exist. It also checks for the existence of the source IP address and its corresponding Mac address, and adds them if they do not exist. Then the controller is able to write automatically the requested flow rule to the switch. Each flow rule is installed with a timeout value, both hard and idle timeouts, to avert the growth of rules in the switch flow-tables.

6   Conclusion

The growing adoption of cloud and SDN technologies have highlighted the requirement to analyze and evaluate the benefits and vulnerabilities of these technologies. While DDoS attacks remain a top threat that is growing in size and frequency of reported incidents, SDN-based cloud opens the door for yet new vulnerabilities to this type of attacks. In this paper, we evaluated some of the existing research that offers solutions to detect and mitigate DDoS threats in SDN-based cloud environment. In this sense, we have proposed an efficient and secure SDN-based cloud system architecture which aims to enable a powerful and reconfigurable data path. In addition, we have integrated the lightweight and convenient mitigation mechanism 'DDoS flooding attack mitigation in Software Defined Networks' to protect the SDN-based cloud system against DDoS flood attacks. Compared to existing solutions, our approach activates DDoS attack mitigation in a reconfigurable (P4) data path unlike the fixed Openflow data path which required complex design and multiple lines to implement new applications that work with new header fields. Consequently, it prevents and reduces the risk of saturation attack in the SDN controller, south interface, switches, and cloud servers. In future work, we will simulate our proposed approach, create and implement new advanced functions in the reconfigurable data path.

References

1. Openstack. https://www.openstack.org/
2. Open Network Operating System (ONOS). https://opennetworking.org/onos/
3. The P4 Language Specification. https://p4.org/p4-spec/docs/P4-16-v1.0.0-spec.html

4. Bernstein, D.J.: SYN Cookies. http://cr.yp.to/syncookies.html
5. P4-OvS - Bringing the power of P4 to OvS! https://github.com/osinstom/P4-OvS
6. Open vSwitch (OvS). https://www.openvswitch.org/
7. Userspace BPF (uBPF). https://github.com/iovisor/ubpf
8. Extended Berkeley Packet Filter (eBPF). https://ebpf.io/
9. P4Runtime. https://p4.org/api/p4-runtime-putting-the-control-plane-in-charge-of-the-forwarding-plane.html
10. RFC 793 (TCP). https://tools.ietf.org/html/rfc793
11. Simpson, W.: TCP cookie transactions (TCPCT). RFC 6013, January 2011
12. Wang, B., Zheng, Y., Lou, W., et al.: DDoS attack protection in the era of cloud computing and software-defined networking. Comput. Netw. **81**, 308–319 (2015)
13. Bawany, N.Z., Shamsi, J.A., Salah, K.: DDoS attack detection and mitigation using SDN: methods, practices, and solutions. Arab. J. Sci. Eng. **42**(2), 425–441 (2017)
14. Yan, Q., GonG, Q., Yu, F.R.: Effective software-defined networking controller scheduling method to mitigate DDoS attacks. Electron. Lett. **53**(7), 469–471 (2017)
15. Mahrach, S., Haqiq, A.: DDoS defense in SDN-based cyber-physical cloud. In: Cybersecurity and Privacy in Cyber Physical Systems, p. 133 (2019)
16. Bosshart, P., Daly, D., Gibb, G., et al.: P4: programming protocol-independent packet processors. ACM SIGCOMM Comput. Commun. Rev. **44**(3), 87–95 (2014)
17. Moshref, M., Bhargava, A., Gupta, A., et al.: Flow-level state transition as a new switch primitive for SDN. In: Proceedings of the Third Workshop on Hot Topics in Software Defined Networking, pp. 61–66 (2014)
18. Bianchi, G., Bonola, M., Capone, A., et al.: OpenState: programming platform-independent stateful openflow applications inside the switch. ACM SIGCOMM Comput. Commun. Rev. **44**(2), 44–51 (2014)
19. Pisharody, S., Natarajan, J., Chowdhary, A., et al.: Brew: a security policy analysis framework for distributed SDN-based cloud environments. IEEE Trans. Dependable Secure Comput. **16**(6), 1011–1025 (2017)
20. Zhu, S., Bi, J., Sun, C., et al.: SDPA: enhancing stateful forwarding for software-defined networking. In: 2015 IEEE 23rd International Conference on Network Protocols (ICNP), pp. 323–333. IEEE (2015)
21. Arashloo, M.T., Koral, Y., Greenberg, M., et al.: SNAP: stateful network-wide abstractions for packet processing. In: Proceedings of the 2016 ACM SIGCOMM Conference, pp. 29–43 (2016)
22. Bhushan, K., Gupta, B.B.: Distributed denial of service (DDoS) attack mitigation in software defined network (SDN)-based cloud computing environment. J. Ambient Intell. Human. Comput. **10**(5), 1985–1997 (2019)
23. Sivaraman, A., Cheung, A., Budiu, M., et al.: Packet transactions: high-level programming for line-rate switches. In: Proceedings of the 2016 ACM SIGCOMM Conference, pp. 15–28 (2016)
24. Echevarria, J.J., Garaizar, P., Legarda, J.: An experimental study on the applicability of SYN cookies to networked constrained devices. Softw. Pract. Exp. **48**(3), 740–749 (2018)
25. Moura, J., Hutchison, D.: Review and analysis of networking challenges in cloud computing. J. Netw. Comput. Appl. **60**, 113–129 (2016)
26. Azodolmolky, S., Wieder, P., Yahyapour, R.: Cloud computing networking: challenges and opportunities for innovations. IEEE Commun. Mag. **51**(7), 54–62 (2013)
27. Son, J., Dastjerdi, A.V., Calheiros, R.N., et al.: SLA-aware and energy-efficient dynamic overbooking in SDN-based cloud data centers. IEEE Trans. Sustain. Comput. **2**(2), 76–89 (2017)

28. Cziva, R., Jouët, S., Stapleton, D., et al.: SDN-based virtual machine management for cloud data centers. IEEE Trans. Netw. Serv. Manage. **13**(2), 212–225 (2016)
29. Yan, Q., Yu, F.R., Gong, Q., Li, J.: Software-defined networking (SDN) and distributed denial of service (DDoS) attacks in cloud computing environments: a survey, some research issues, and challenges. IEEE Commun. Surv. Tutor. **8**(1), 602–622 (2016)
30. Somani, G., Gaur, M.S., Sanghi, D., et al.: DDoS attacks in cloud computing: issues, taxonomy, and future directions. Comput. Commun. **107**, 30–48 (2017)
31. D'cruze, H., Wang, P., Sbeit, R.O., et al.: A software-defined networking (SDN) approach to mitigating DDoS attacks. Inf. Technol. New Gener. 141–145 (2018)
32. Phan, T.V., Park, M.: Efficient distributed denial-of-service attack defense in SDN-based cloud. IEEE Access **7**, 18701–18714 (2019)
33. Son, J., Buyya, R.: A taxonomy of software-defined networking (SDN)-enabled cloud computing. ACM Comput. Surv. (CSUR) **51**(3), 1–36 (2018)
34. Xu, X., Yu, H., Yang, K.: DDoS attack in software defined networks: a survey. ZTE Commun. **15**(3), 13–19 (2019)
35. Chen, Z., Jiang, F., Cheng, Y., et al.: XGBoost classifier for DDoS attack detection and analysis in SDN-based cloud. In: IEEE International Conference on Big Data and Smart Computing (BigComp). IEEE 2018, pp. 251–256 (2018)
36. Mahrach, S., Haqiq, A.: DDoS flooding attack mitigation in software defined networks. Int. J. Adv. Comput. Sci. Appl. **11**(1), 693–700 (2020)
37. Dong, S., Abbas, K., Jain, R.: A survey on distributed denial of service (DDoS) attacks in SDN and cloud computing environments. IEEE Access **7**, 80813–80828 (2019)

Quantum Ecosystem Development Using Advanced Cloud Services

Lalitha Nallamothula$^{(\boxtimes)}$

Frisco, TX 75035, USA

Abstract. The four fundamental quantum phenomena of superposition, entanglement and tunneling are envisioned to give quantum computing the ability to solve complex problems in very low-resolution times as compared with classical computers. Quantum computing relies on various types of processors, frameworks, algorithms, and simulators which can be accessed using Cloud services. Quantum computers provide an incredible processing power to the users. Having these quantum capabilities as services over cloud to access through internet is called Cloud-based quantum computing. Many tech giants have connected their quantum computers to the cloud platform and provided access to internet users from various sectors to be able to build and run simple programs on them. Industry-leading companies have started capitalizing on the capabilities of quantum technologies. It is exciting to see potentially transformative applications in the quantum algorithm space. Quantum computing software projects have significantly increased in areas where complex problems could be solved in very low-resolution times. From computing to communications, signal processing, navigation systems, quantum solutions offer unprecedented level of performance, privacy, security, and speed. The existing single layer architecture of providing *Quantum as a service* is still very basic and makes it complicated for users to have a choice over the kind of applications they would like to implement. This is because the services are not distinct and relevant to the needs of the users. This paper attempts to study IBM's existing Quantum cloud platform and provides a multilayered enhanced approach with advanced quantum cloud services. This paper presents a new approach to develop a sophisticated quantum ecosystem to enhance the user base and quantum computing applications.

Keywords: Quantum computation · Quantum cloud services · Superposition · Entanglement · Quantum tunneling · Quantum annealing · Computational power

1 Introduction

Quantum computers get their phenomenal computing power by harnessing quantum properties namely, superposition, entanglement, tunneling, and annealing [1]. Quantum Cloud services are offered via the internet by many companies. Tech giants like Google, IBM, Microsoft, AWS began to offer cloud-based quantum computing services in hopes to herald the wave of this emerging technology [2]. Quantum Technologies are advancing way too fast and there is a clear need to revise the existing cloud computing models to suit

© Springer Nature Switzerland AG 2021
H. Elbiaze et al. (Eds.): UNet 2021, LNCS 12845, pp. 163–171, 2021.
https://doi.org/10.1007/978-3-030-86356-2_14

quantum computing. The existing single layer architecture of providing *Quantum as a service* is still very basic and makes it complicated for users to have a choice over the kind of applications they would like to implement. This is because the services are not distinct and relevant to the needs of the users. This paper provides a multilayered enhanced approach with advanced quantum cloud services to develop a quantum ecosystem to enhance the user base and quantum computing applications.

In quantum computers, data is processed as qubits as opposed to regular bits in classical computing. Quantum computers need special types of processors and simulators that operate using quantum phenomena and are a lot different to classical computers [4–6]. There is also a huge learning curve in adapting to the new quantum specific software components, platforms, and interfaces to be able to program and run quantum circuits, algorithms, and web applications. In regular cloud computing, the layers of services are categorized as IaaS (Infrastructure as a service), PaaS (Platform as a service), FaaS (Functions as a service), and SaaS (Software as a service) [3]. This paper attempts to create a new quantum ready SOA (Service Oriented Architecture) model replacing the existing layers with quantum ready scalable services, while virtualizing software and hardware components of quantum computing. This approach makes quantum ecosystem development a lot easier by enabling the users to have choice over application specific needs and reduces the learning curve. This paper attempts to put this analysis in a perspective and creates a multilayered approach to IBM's quantum ecosystem development roadmap [2, 3, 6, 7].

The main functional benefits for this approach are in the areas of research, developing commercial applications and in educating and preparing the industry to be quantum ready. This multilayered architecture empowers the users with tools to use and knowledge to take advantage of quantum computing.

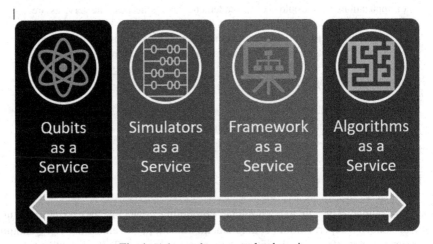

Fig. 1. Advanced quantum cloud services

Figure 1 shows the proposed multilayered architecture for advanced quantum cloud services.

The services include:

- *QuaaS – Qubits as a Service*
- *QsaaS – Quantum simulators as a Service*
- *QfaaS – Quantum framework as a Service*
- *QaaaS – Quantum algorithms as a Service*

2 Qubits as a Service

QuaaS – Qubits as a Service: A qubit is like a bit used in classical computing except that a qubit is a two-level quantum system with two possible quantum states. And these two basis qubit states are l0 > and l1 >. A qubit is essentially a carrier of quantum information. A variety of quantum processors have demonstrated the potential to control the quantum states using qubits. There are different types of qubits. The qubits that IBM uses are the superconducting transmon qubits made of superconducting materials. These qubits are fabricated by creating a difference in two isolated energy levels. Qubits developed in this manner are maintained at extremely low temperatures. The temperature is such that

$$k_B T \ll hf$$

where kB is Boltzmann's constant, h is Planck's constant, f is frequency of the qubit and T is temperature. We need a quantum gate to control the qubit. Quantum gates are essential to describe the evolution of a quantum state. Some quantum gates are different to classical gates such as Hadamard gate H, phase shift gates. These quantum gates operate on quantum mechanical phenomenon such as superposition and entanglement.

A Bloch sphere representation of a qubit state is shown below. X, Y, Z are the cartesian coordinates of a Bloch sphere of unit length 1 [2, 3, 6, 7, 12] (Fig. 2).

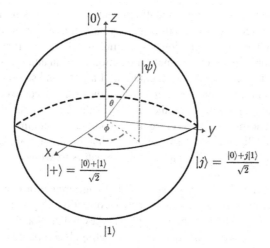

Fig. 2. Bloch sphere representation of a qubit

Quantum machines with qubits ranging from 5 to 5000 or more can be accessed by the users over the cloud. Whether the users are running IQP circuits (Quantum Polynomial Time) or QAOA circuits, (Quantum Approximate Optimization Algorithm), they would need a certain number of qubits. An array of different quantum computers with different qubit power can be networked over a quantum internet and can be accessed as cloud service. These quantum machines can either be a Q-network of photonic quantum computers, continuous variable quantum machines, annealer based machines or gate-based quantum machines [11, 12]. Having the potential to choose the number of qubits needed to run specific algorithms as a service would be an additional advantage to the users.

3   Simulators as a Service

QsaaS – Quantum simulators as a Service: Researchers and developers working on quantum algorithms and applications often need to simulate the operations of the quantum computation. A quantum simulator allows the users to simulate the behavior of quantum computer on a classical computer. The main drawback of a simulator is that it allows simulation for quantum computers with a smaller number of qubits. Since classical computers need complex numbers to store a computation based on n qubits. IBM currently has a variety of simulators for simulating quantum circuits and algorithms. There are different types of simulation strategies.

1. Schrodinger wavefunction based simulator
2. Clifford simulator
3. Extended Clifford simulator
4. Matrix product state simulator
5. General purpose simulator

These simulators use different simulation techniques such as simulating a quantum circuit using Schrodinger's wave function of the qubit's state vector as gates and applying instructions (Schrodinger wavefunction based simulator), or using a rank-based stabilizer decomposition technique to approximate the action of a quantum circuit, or a tensor network technique that uses MPS representation of a state, and so on.

Each of these simulators suit different needs of the users based on certain factors like number of qubits, noise modeling, number of shots per job, number of circuits to execute, input circuits and parameters. IBM currently supports a maximum of 300 circuits and 8192 shots per job. Clifford simulator supports a maximum of 5000 qubits. There is a current time limit of 10000 s job runtimes on simulators to avoid long running jobs [2, 3, 6, 7].

This service provides the users with the ability to run simulations on the encoding and decoding circuits in the process of quantum error correction. Physicists can make use of simulations to better formulate problems in physics beyond the Standard Model such that a way that they can be solved using quantum computing. If compared adiabatic quantum computing to gate-based quantum computing, it is equivalent in power to implement arbitrary unitary operations. The substantial difference between gate-based quantum computing and quantum annealers is that in gated based quantum computing, logical variables are mapped only to single qubits and not to chains (A. J. Abhari et al.) [16]. Quantum simulators provide a comprehensive and powerful service for these scenarios [18] (Fig. 3).

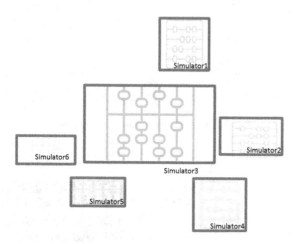

Fig. 3. Network of quantum simulators

4 Framework as a Service

QfaaS – Quantum framework as a Service: The design flow of a generic quantum architecture would consist of a technology independent optimizer followed by a technology dependent optimizer (QASM) and finally a quantum device/simulator (QPOL). The technology independent optimizer produces the QIR (quantum intermediate representation) and a technology dependent optimizer processes it into QASM (quantum assembly language). And finally, a quantum device/simulator processes it to a QPOL (quantum physical operations language) (Fig. 4).

QIR: quantum intermediate representation
QASM: quantum assembly language
QPOL: quantum physical operations language

IBM currently provides a secure environment to use cloud-based quantum services. It uses different programming tools, prebuilt application models and simulators accessible via the IBM cloud. IBM's Quantum system services are built upon cryogenic electronics and are all based on superconducting qubit technology. Providers are used to control the services. A provider is essentially a container unit of sublevels called hubs, groups, and projects. Hubs contain groups, and groups contain projects [2, 3, 6–8] (Fig. 5).

A job instance is created for every task that we attempt to run using a quantum service. These jobs can be used to track the tasks and to retrieve the results. Providers are categorized as private or open based on the user account.

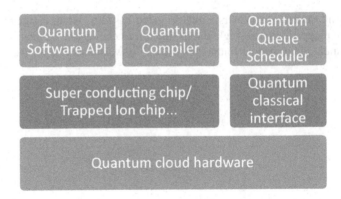

Fig. 4. Quantum architecture framework

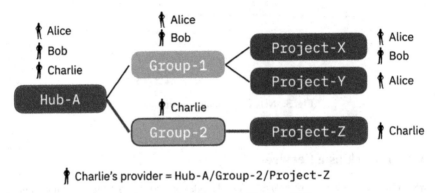

Fig. 5. Hubs, Groups and Projects [30]

IBM has created a transparent roadmap to enhance the current capabilities in quantum computing. Through an open-source collaborative vision, IBM is working on developing an advanced quantum computing stack with a robust cloud-based API. In the next two to five years, IBM's focus is on three areas with respect to quantum computing: Kernels, Algorithms and Models. Quantum Kernel developers focus more of hardware and developing circuit APIs that enhance features like faster runtimes, being able to store programs, and running more circuits in less time. Quantum Algorithm developers explore new applications of quantum circuits. Model developers essentially think in terms of creating families of prebuilt frameworks by combining the foundations provided by kernel and algorithm developers.

Quantum framework as a service provides a unified environment and programming choice of available frameworks for the users to perform classic-quantum hybrid programming. It provides quantum classical interfaces, underlying hardware options and software programming selection array to compiler options to find the suitable architecture framework for the users [12–17, 21–29].

5   Algorithms as a Service

QaaaS – Quantum algorithms as a Service: The application areas of quantum computing breakthrough spread across multiple industries such as Finance, quantum chemistry and many others. Having a set of prebuilt tools accelerates the development of quantum application. A variety of quantum software projects, quantum web applications, quantum games are deployed on a quantum cloud network. Gate-based projects and annealing based projects are being developed using different quantum devices, algorithms, frameworks, and quantum programming languages. It is not always easy to decide the right architecture for your project.

Firstly, there are three different types of quantum computing models.

a) Quantum annealing
b) Quantum simulations
c) Universal quantum computing

IBM uses its very own Qiskit, an open-source SDK needed to interact with Quantum systems and simulators. It has a library of quantum algorithms specific to the applications. Be it machine learning, which consists of algorithms like QSVM, VQC (Variational Quantum Classifier), or Nature in general which consists of quantum biology, quantum chemistry and physics related algorithms, or finance algorithms such as optimization algorithms, Qiskit together with Python are considered evolving ecosystems.

This *QaaaS – Quantum algorithms as a Service* provides a library of some important and basic algorithms such as quantum optimization algorithms, quantum gaming algorithms, and so on. There are many available quantum simulators grouped by programming language. Some examples are: OpenQASM, Q#, QML, QuTiP etc. Having access to such a library as a service gives the ability to accelerate the learning and development processes for the users [9, 10, 20, 29]. This service should provide the ability to access a set of well-defined circuits or building blocks of a more complicated model to explore quantum computational advantage (Fig. 6).

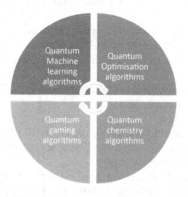

Fig. 6. Quantum algorithm library

6 Conclusion

In summary, with the rise of quantum computers, we need a network of Quantum computing software tools and cloud services to carry out extensive research and to provide effective solutions. From computing to communications, signal processing, navigation systems, quantum solutions offer unprecedented level of performance, privacy, security, and speed. The number of qubits quantum computers can support are increasing tremendously and so are the noise mitigation and correction strategies making quantum computing a rising field. The existing single layer architecture of providing Quantum as a service is still very basic and makes it complicated for users to have a choice over the kind of applications they would like to implement. This is because the services are not distinct and relevant to the needs of the users. This paper attempts to study IBM's existing Quantum cloud platform and provides a multilayered enhanced approach with advanced quantum cloud services. This paper presents a new approach to develop a sophisticated quantum eco-system to enhance the user base and quantum computing applications. As described in sections I to V, this approach to create a new quantum ready SOA (Service Oriented Architecture) model replacing the existing single layer of Quantum as a service with a multi layered quantum ready scalable services makes quantum ecosystem development a lot easier and incredibly faster. Section I provides an introduction about the current problem and the idea behind this model. Section II covers the first service *QuaaS – Qubits as a Service*. Section III covers the second service *QsaaS – Quantum simulators as a Service*. Section IV covers the third service *QfaaS – Quantum framework as a Service* Section V covers the fourth service *QaaaS – Quantum algorithms as a Service*. This model also increases the quantum user base from various industries, researchers, and academia considering its effective and plug and play services over the cloud. This model gives users a tremendous leap over existing cloud computing capabilities and thus helps increase usability.

References

1. Dirac, P.: The Principles of Quantum Mechanics, 4th edn. Oxford University Press, Oxford, p. 9 (1958)
2. IBM Quantum (2021). https://quantum-computing.ibm.com/
3. https://www.ibm.com/blogs/research/2020/09/ibm-quantum-roadmap, Jay Gambetta (2020)
4. D-Wave. D-Wave Sys Technical documentation (2020). https://docs.dwavesys.com/docs/latest/c_gs_2.html
5. Huawei cloud (2020) https://hiq.huaweicloud.com/en/index.html
6. https://qiskit.org/documentation/ (2021)
7. www.research.ibm.com/ibm-q
8. Gian; Nicholas (2020). https://iopscience.iop.org/article/10.1088/2058-9565/ab8505
9. IBM Q Experience: quantumexperience.ng.bluemix.net (2019)
10. Quantum in the Cloud. bristol.ac.uk (2017)
11. Proceedings of the National Academy of Sciences, vol. 114, no. 13, pp. 3305–3310. ISSN 0027-8424. https://doi.org/10.1073/pnas.1618020114. PMC 5380037. PMID 28325879.
12. Nallamothula, L.: Quantum Mechanics – Math Made Easy, Heisenberg's Uncertainty Principle, Frisco TX, USA ISBN: 1695038908, 9781695038905 (2019)

13. Nallamothula, L.: Selection of quantum computing architecture using a decision tree approach. In: 2020 3rd International Conference on Intelligent Sustainable Systems (ICISS), pp. 644–649. IEEE, December 2020

14. Nallamothula, L.: Selection of quantum computing architecture using a decision tree approach. In: 2020 3rd International Conference on Intelligent Sustainable Systems (ICISS), pp. 644–649 (2020)

15. Nallamothula, L.: Selection of quantum computing architecture using a decision tree approach. In: 2020 3rd International Conference on Intelligent Sustainable Systems (ICISS), pp. 644–649 (2020). https://doi.org/10.1109/ICISS49785.2020.9315893

16. Malik, P., Nallamothula, L.: Fourfold properties of light and its relevance to quantum computation. In: 2020 11th IEEE Annual Information Technology, Electronics and Mobile Communication Conference (IEMCON), pp. 0707–0711). IEEE, November 2020

17. Malik, P., Nallamothula, L.: fourfold properties of light and its relevance to quantum computation. In: 2020 11th IEEE Annual Information Technology, Electronics and Mobile Communication Conference (IEMCON), pp. 0707– 0711 (2020). https://doi.org/10.1109/IEMCON 51383.2020.9284871

18. Nallamothula, L.: The Story of my Quantum Quest. The Story of Light ISBN-13: 978-1731084446 ISBN-10: 1731084447 (2019)

19. Choi,C.Q.: September 2020. https://spectrum.ieee.org/tech-talk/computing/hardware/photonic-quantum

20. Devitt, S.J.: Performing quantum computing experiments in the cloud. Phys. Rev. A **94**(3), 032329. arXiv:1605.05709. Bibcode:2016PhRvA.94c2329D (2016). https://doi.org/10.1103/PhysRevA.94.032329

21. https://iopscience.iop.org/article/10.1088/2058-9565/ab9acb. Rigetti 2020

22. Cody Jones, N., et al.: Layered Architecture for Quantum Computing. https://doi.org/10.1103/PhysRevX.2.031007

23. Linke, N.M.: Experimental comparison of two quantum computing architectures

24. Brandl A.: Quantum von Neumann Architecture for Large-Scale Quantum Computing

25. Copsey, D., et al.: Toward a scalable, silicon-based quantum computing architecture. IEEE J. Sel. Top. Quantum Electron. **9**, 1552–1569 (2003)

26. Murali, P.: Full-Stack, Real-System Quantum Computer Studies: Architectural Comparisons and Design Insights arXiv:1905.11349v2

27. Schrödinger, E.: An Undulatory Theory of the Mechanics of Atoms and Molecules (PDF). Phys. Rev. **28**(6), 1049–1070 (1926). Bibcode:1926PhRv...28.1049S. https://doi.org/10.1103/PhysRev.28.1049

28. Dirac, P.A.M.: The Principles of Quantum Mechanics. Clarendon Press, Oxford (1930)

29. https://qutip.org/docs/latest/guide/qip

30. https://quantum-computing.ibm.com/lab/docs/iql/manage/provider/

Cloud Architecture Based Learning Kit Platform for Education and Research – A Survey and Implementation

Bramha S. Tripathi[✉], Ritu Gupta[✉], and S. R. N. Reddy

CSE Department, IGDTUW, Delhi, India
srnreddy@igdtuw.ac.in

Abstract. In today's scenario technology has become an important part of life. Technology plays a very vast and significant role in the tremendously increasing education system. Having technical education has become mandatory in current time for education and research. Every day new technologies and researches are coming up to improve the teaching methodologies providing a refined and easier way of learning and practical approaches. Cloud computing is a rapidly emerging technology for education 4.0 in recent years. Cloud computing is all about enabling resources to users according to their need over the internet. Cloud computing, mainly provides the services like servers, databases, networking, storage etc. This paper presents implementation of a learning kit consisting of cloud integration with computing platform i.e. raspberry pi; multiple sensors have been connected to it. The main aim of integration of cloud computing with raspberry pi is to collect and monitor the real time data generated via cloud. This paper describes the implementation, challenges and other aspects of cloud based learning kit in education and research area and how to use these types of kits for learner, educator and researcher.

1 Introduction

Technical education is one of the most important parts of the today's educational system, as it becomes the need of every human being to get upgraded technically for having their livelihood in technically smart way. Technical education cannot be provided by just teaching and explaining the things theoretically, it also requires hands – on working experience to be provided to the learners for their better understanding and learning perspectives. For the same purpose the technical educators and researcher continues to build some smart learning devices and applications for the students. Scientific researches in education promote the scientific strategies that ensure the development of innovative minds of the learners [1]. There are many online and offline solutions have been developed in past few years for the learning purpose.

Many universities and institutions providing technical education in different countries prefer smart way of learning i.e. providing the live practical demonstration of what they are teaching. Some of the technical courses ensure the practical learning approach as an essential part of learning. Many educational devices, learning kits and tablets have

H. Elbiaze et al. (Eds.): UNet 2021, LNCS 12845, pp. 172–185, 2021.
https://doi.org/10.1007/978-3-030-86356-2_15

also been developed in this scenario. A couple of technical courses like embedded systems, Internet of Things, embedded system design and development, mobile architecture and programming, cloud computing etc. requires both simulation based learning and real time interfacing and deployment, as they relates the real time data and are developed for working well with real life applications.

By taking one more step towards making the learning better and practically more feasible, this paper presents the design and development of a learning kit for practically teaching embedded systems, integration with IOT, Cloud computing with the aim of providing hands – on experience towards how they actually work in real time scenario.

This Paper is consists of the following major sections: Sect. 1 - introduction, Sect. 2 - Literature Survey, Sect. 3 - Cloud Computing based Learning Kit, Sect. 4 - Comparative study, Sect. 5 - Implementation, Sect. 6 - Deployment, Result, Challenges and Benefits and Sect. 7 - Conclusion.

2 Literature Survey

In today's world cloud computing is playing a vital role in every domain like sales and marketing, real state, medical facilitation, hospitality and management etc. It also becomes a need of educational institutions and universities for the purpose of managing their data and other resources as well as for improving the learning methodologies [2]. In current scenario it becomes the need of every student to learn the cloud computing technique and methodologies in order to improve their technical skills and up gradation.

Cloud computing is all about the providing the IT resources and services over internet. In simple words it refers to enabling computing resources, on-demand basis to user over internet. Cloud is widely used at global scale because of its low computing cost, high speed, enhanced productivity, better performance and reliability.

A cloud model is composed of five essential characteristics, three service model and four deployment models [11]. Five essential characteristics of cloud consist of on-demand self-service, broad network access, resource pooling, rapid elasticity and measured service [11]. Cloud services resides in three broad categories namely - Infrastructure–as–a–service (IaaS), Platform–as–a–service (PaaS) and Software–as–a–service (SaaS) [10] and deploys in four different manners as a public, community, private and hybrid cloud. Using cloud means fast implementation; there are no long procurement cycles and no complex implementation plans. It offers lower costs because it is a pay-as-you-go service; just like the electricity we use at our homes [3]. Cloud computing provides better performance, reliability and scalability. Also it promises to provide low environmental cost and high energy efficiency [12].

Similarly, sensors also come as an important need of today's technical world. Sensors play an important as well as vital role in our lives. Everyone is surrounded with several sensors in their daily life. There is network around all of us consisting of various sensors [7]. This network of sensors is active in almost every field related to the daily life; such a sensor network is referred as the wireless sensor network in technical terms. The application of wireless sensor network consists of various domains like whether and environmental monitoring, agriculture forecasting, production and delivery and healthcare [4].

Many of the learning kits have been proposed and developed so far in order to make the technical education and learning more easy and realistic. These kits also help the students to learn and gain the experience of actual practical implementation of the technology by providing the real world practical examples and demonstrations.

3 Cloud Computing Based Learning Kit

The cloud based learning kit designed and developed via means of making learning the technical aspects of cloud computing easier to the learners and students. The idea behind the development of the kit is to provide a real, practical experience to its user along with all the conceptual knowledge [8]. The model developed here consists of all the technical aspects from the very beginning followed by implementation of the techniques learned conceptually to the practical example. It also helps the users to better understand the feasibility and performance aspects also (Fig. 1).

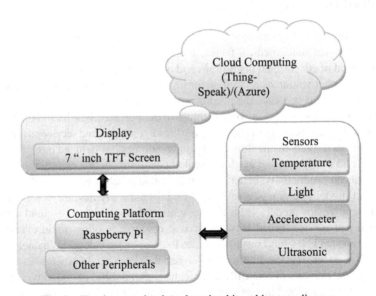

Fig. 1. Cloud computing base learning kit architecture diagram

3.1 Hardware Architecture

The hardware architecture consists of a computing platform of Broadcom series along with a Add-on board used for integrating various sensors to the computing platform.

a. **Computing Platform:** computing platform used here is Raspberry Pi 3 model B having a SoC BCM2837. The raspberry pi is basically a single board system of credit card size globally used for prototype development. This model consists of on-board 802.11n WiFi, Bluetooth 4.0 and a quad-core 64-bit ARM cortex A53 processor [16].

b. **Add-On Board**: Raspberry pi is associated with a add-on board consisting of various ICs and multiplexing technique which makes it capable of integrating multiple sensors and communication modules at a single time with the pi. This add-on board is also associated with built-in LEDs, buzzer and push button on it. Its feature of plug-in and plug-out of various sensing and communication modules makes it very easily operable.

c. **Sensors**: Digital sensors that are compatible with raspberry pi have been used here temperature and humidity sensor (DHT11), light sensor (TSL 2561), Accelerometer (ADXL345) and Ultrasonic sensor. DHT11 is ultra-low-cost digital sensor that generates calibrated digital output. DHT11 consists of a capacitive humidity sensor and a thermistor to measure the surrounding air. Basically, DHT11 is used to measure humidity of range 20–80% and temperature of range 0–50 °C [6]. TSL 2561 is an ambient light sensor that uses I2C interfacing and is ideal for a wide range light situations to measure the luminosity intensity. It works well to detect the light ranges from 0.1 to 40000 LUX [14]. ADXL345 is a small, thin, low-power 3-axis digital accelerometer with high resolution, accessible through both SPI and I2C digital interfaces. ADXL345 is best suitable for mobile device applications. It measures both static and dynamic accelerations. Ultrasonic SR04 is a distance measuring module consisting of ultrasonic transmitter, receiver and control circuit. The transmitter triggers the ultrasonic wave, the wave travel in air and get reflected back when it finds an object in its way. This reflected wave is received by ultrasonic receiver and then it calculates the distance measured [15].

3.2 Software Architecture

The software architecture consists of Operating System used, python as the programming language, Tkinter as GUI development toolkit and ThingSpeak as the cloud computing platform.

a. **Operating System:** Raspbian is an official operating system, freely available for Raspberry pi based on Debian. This operating system is basically a set of basic programs and utilities that make Raspberry pi operable [17]. The standard operating system is then further customized to make all the experiments and programs workable.

b. **Graphical User Interface:** The GUI of the proposed system is developed using the python's standard GUI package named as Tkinter. Tkinter is easily available and compatible on most of the

c. UNIX platforms. Python with Tkinter is the easiest and fastest way to develop GUI applications.

d. **ThingSpeak:** ThingSpeak is a freely available web service where one can collect and store the sensor data on order to develop it IOT based applications [5]. It is a freely accessible cloud computing web service provided by MathWorks in order to analyse, visualize and aggregates the live data streams from the computing devices. It also consists of feature of sending web alerts like twitter messages based on the visualisations from the computing devices. It also provides the service to write your own MATLAB code in order to do real-time analysis and visualisation of the data collected. ThingSpeak allows building applications for sensor collected data stored over its channels [13]. Thus, makes the prototype and system development easier and faster without setting up servers.

e. **Azure IOT Hub:** Microsoft Azure is Microsoft's IAAS and PAAS solution which relies on global network of data centres to provide a collection of services that facilitate development deployment and management of cloud based applications and services managed by Microsoft [18]. Azure IOT Hub is a cloud based service that works as a central message hub, for bidirectional communication between the IOT devices and IOT applications. Basically, it is used to build IOT based solutions that provide more reliable and secure communication between IOT devices using cloud. It supports multiple messaging patterns like telemetry, file uploads, request reply methods to control devices from cloud. It helps to build scalable, full- featured IOT solutions for managing industrial equipments in manufacturing, Tracking assets and monitoring office buildings.

3.3 Software Architecture

Comparative Study with My Smart Phone Kit: Cloud Architecture based learning kit is technically upgraded and updated model. In comparison with previous model, this model consists of upgraded hardware components as well as newly designed Add-On Board. Also this Model is more technically upgraded and faster than My Smart Phone Kit (Table 1).

Table 1. Comparative analysis between cloud architecture based learning kit and My Smart Phone Kit

Aspects	Cloud architecture based learning kit	My Smart Phone Kit [8]
SOC used	Raspberry Pi 3 Model B	Rasperry Pi Model 2
Add–On Board	Small board with simple to use	Large board with complex structure
GPS module	Older version	New Version
OS used	Raspbian OS compatible with pi 3	Raspbian Os compatible with pi 2
Sensors	DHT11, TSL2561, ADXL 345, Ultrasonic Sensor, IR, PIR, LDR	DHT11, TSL2561, ADXL345, Ultrasonic Sensor
Cloud Technology	Azure, ThingSpeak	None
Wi-Fi	In-Built	External module used
Size	Small tablet phone sized kit	Brief case sized kit
Mobile/Remote learning	Best-suited	Less-suitable
Optimization	Highly optimized	Less optimized

(*continued*)

Table 1. (*continued*)

Aspects	Cloud architecture based learning kit	My Smart Phone Kit [8]
Operability	Easy and fast operable	comparatively slow and little complex
Technology	Technically advanced version	Older versions
Usability	user friendly, simply understandable	Little complex structure, hard to understand

4 Implementation

This cloud computing based smart phone kit is an enhancement and improvement over the existing prototype named my smart phone kit. This improved model has been made more customised and optimised at both hardware and software end. All these customizations and optimizations results into a more compact hardware design which is technically faster and advanced version. All these implementations work well with the prospective of remote learning and mobile learning platforms. The implementation consists of Hardware and software implementation.

4.1 Hardware Implementation

In hardware implementation a new small add-on board has been developed so as to make the kit more compact and smaller in size. This board is quite easy to fix over the raspberry pi and also makes the sensor integration in easier way. This small board has a capacity to integrate more sensors, embedded system modules and communication modules.

a. **Component Selection**

Component Selection basically deals with choosing the best component for the project as per the requirements. This is done in order to avoid the unnecessary problems due to bad choice of component selection. Thus, component selection for a project may include selection of:

- Master board (SOC): A system on chip is an integrated circuit also known as a heart of the any hardware that assembles all components of a one electronic systems.
- Operating System: The Operating system is one of the important part for helping to operating the SOC.In this project we are customise the raspbion OS according to kit functionality requirements.
- Programming language: A programming language is an important part while developing a project as its ease of development makes the project as per needed.
- Sensors: A sensor is a device for detecting events or changes in its environment and sending the information to other electronic devices.

- Display: Display may include devices as a part of Input/output peripherals to show output
- Programming language: A programming language is an important part while developing a project as its ease of development makes the project as per needed.
- Communication Module: this is very important part for communication with internet and helping to sending the data on cloud (Table 2)

Table 2. Component selection

Features	Component name
Mother board SOC/Slave board	Raspberry Pi-4/customised designed board for sensor connect with SOC
Operating System	Customise Raspbion OS
Display	7 Inch capacitive touch screen
Programming language	Python
Sensor used	DHT-11, TSL-2561, ADXL 345, Ultrasonic sensor, IR/PIR
Cloud technology used	AZURE, Thinkspeak
Communication module	Wi-Fi, Bluetooth, GSM, GPS

5 Case Studies

A large number of cloud architecture platforms available that provide cloud computing services, this research article consists of two case studies based on two different cloud platforms for learning and teaching easiest way for higher education and basic fundamental knowledge research and development.

5.1 Case Study 1: Implementation with Thing Speak

Implementation with the cloud platform Thing Speak is divided into three major steps:

First step consists of creation of a channel over the web based cloud platform. For creating a channel using Thing Speak we only require to have a Thing Speak or MathsWork account. After signing in to the account user is required to click on the channel button in the menu bar and migrate to My Channels page. Now click the new channel button, the channel setting page will get open, the user is then require to fill all the attributes along with the channel name in order to create a channel (Fig. 2).

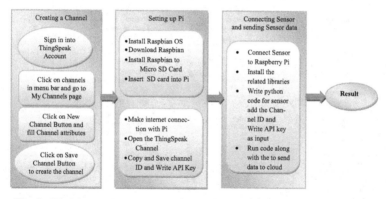

Fig. 2. Working flowchart of Thingspeak cloud architecture base learning kit

In the second step is all setting up raspberry pi and making necessary installations. This step involves installation of the operating system named Raspbian over the SD card followed by making internet connection and opening the ThingSpeak channel over the pi. In the last Step the user is required to connect the sensor with the raspberry pi and make necessary library installations to be done for making the sensor work. Finally, write the python code for sending sensor data over cloud for real time monitoring and visualizations.

5.2 Case Study 1: Implementation with Azure

There are three major steps for Azure implementation: the first step involves creation of an IOT Hub. For this purpose the user first needs to sign in to Azure portal, followed by opening the dashboard the then creating an IOT Hub from the resources. TheXFD2 creation IOT hub is then followed by registering the IOT device over it. After successful device registration the user is required to copy and save the connection string for future use.

The second step involves setting up raspberry pi. It also consists of two part: the first part involves installation of Raspbian operating system over the SD Card and the second part consists of enabling SH and I2C interfaces, followed by successful build and installation of azure sample application over the pi.

The last step involves connecting the sensor with the raspberry pi, making required sensor library installations. Then writing the python code for sending sensor data and then finally running the code along with the connection string in order to send data over azure IOT Hub (Fig. 3).

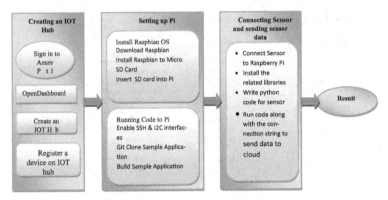

Fig. 3. Working flowchart of Azure cloud architecture base learning kit

6   Result, Discussion and Challenge and Benefits

6.1   Deployment and Result

The proposed system was deployed at Embedded Lab in the Department of Computer Science, IGDTUW under the supervision of Prof. SRN Reddy.It was showcased at the campus for visiting students to take valuable feedback regarding its effectiveness in learning purposes and found to be quite efficient and handy in terms of its usability. This Implementation is done in first phase second phase implementation is working (Fig. 4).

- **Hardware Design:**

Fig. 4. Hardware design (under evaluation process)

- **Performance Experience:**
  Based on the Lab workshop and project staff giving review on the different valuable parameters (Fig. 5).

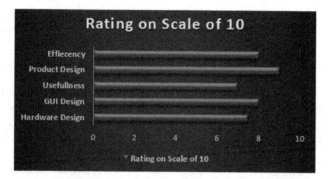

Fig. 5. Survey result (workshop students and project staff)

6.2 Result

After case studies, comparative analysis based on different parameters give the result to use different cloud architecture according to their properties and learning facilities will be provide and utilized (Table 3).

Table 3. Comparative analysis between cloud computing platforms i.e. ThingSpeak and Azure

Features	ThingSpeak	Azure
Developed BY	Mathworks	Microsoft
Deployment type	Saas	Paas
Operating Systems	Web Browser	Windows, Linux
License type	Open Source	Subscription
Software Category [6]	Application Enablement Platform	Application Enablement Platform
Storage	Permanent	Temporaryyktu6866
Database	MySQL	NOSQL, Relational, Big Data through HDI insight and Windows Azure Table
IOT Devices	Arduino, Particle photon and electron, ESP8266 WiFi, Raspberry Pi	Raspberry Pi 3, SparkFun-Things Dev, Intel NUC, Adafruit Feather MO WiFi, PMC 5231, and many more

(*continued*)

Table 3. (*continued*)

Features	ThingSpeak	Azure
Pricing	Pricing depends upon the license you have choosen	Pricing of Azure depends upon the services you have opted for
Getting Started	Being an open Source provides free access for non commercial usage	Provide Free trials for experimentation and learning
Type of Data can be stored	Only Numeric and Alpha Numeric	Apart from numeric and alphanumeric data values, can also store all kind of media files using Blob storage
Analytics [9]	Supports only MATLAB Analytics and Visualizations	Enables various data analytic services that include Azure Analysis Services, Data Lake Analytics, Machine Learning Studio and Stream analytics
Security	Can use HTTPS in order to get some security	Azure enables security services like Azure Active Directory Azure Information Protection
No. of devices Connected simultaneously	Less number of device connectivity simultaneously	Comparatively large number of device connectivity
Developer Friendly [5]	Highly developer friendly	Moderately developer friendly

6.3   Challenges of Cloud Architecture Based Learning Kits

Cloud computing research challenges come up to meet the requirement of upcoming new cloud platforms and architectures. There are some common challenges that every cloud computing service has to face like Networking challenges, data management, security, interoperability, access control, reliability and availability etc. During development of cloud based learning kits, main challenges that come across to the way of performance of the kit and affecting working of kits. Challenges that we are seeking with and trying to over come with this learning kit while using it a very large scale and for other industrial education and training purposes with more enhanced and accordingly customised design, are described as below (Fig. 6).

A. **Security and Privacy**
    Data security is a major concern with these cloud based learning kits because of complete dependency over the cloud service providers. Cloud service providers also don't have access to the physical security of the data centres, where the data actually get stored. For this service providers have to rely over infrastructure providers to achieve complete security [20].
B. **Powered management issues**
    Another big challenge arose, is power management i.e. developing energy efficient kits. Cloud computing uses a pool of resources working over different platforms

Fig. 6. Challenges for using cloud based learning kits

with different applications running over it. In order to maintain effective cost of the cloud based product it becomes very necessary to make it energy efficient without affecting its working and performance. The key challenge is to maintain a good trade-off between enery saving and performance of the system.

C. **Liability**

Liability is a key challenge of all newly developed products in terms of their performance and trust among users. Liability of these kits depends upon various factors that may result in improper working, incorrect data , missed data values , inaccurate and improper results etc. These factors include inaccurate or faulty sensors, networking problems like network congestion, lost or suspended network connections and other hardware related and networking challenges.

D. **Dependency on internet**

Cloud Architecture based learning kits are completely dependent on the availability, quality, speed and performance of the internet because network builds the main infrastructure of cloud computing services. Using internet one can easily create a pool of resources by connecting servers and databases at different locations via using a number of switches and routers. Due to complex interconnected networks with a large number of users working on a variety applications cloud networks poses various challenges related to networking [19].

6.4 Benefits of Cloud Architecture Based Learning Kits

A. **Benefits of Cloud Architecture based learning kit for Education 4.**0 are smart teaching, hands on practical based platform for learner and educators. This platform provides practical teaching for students to learn sensor interfacing and sending the data in different clouds and it calculates the various parameter performance. In these learning kits based platforms use different tools and techniques that promote the hands on based learning education & Provide the hands-on based learning outcomes & easy to practical teaching methodology for students and educators. These type cloud architecture based learning kits are objective to improve performance by enhancing educator's skills and improving student learning using Education 4.0.

B. **Benefits of Cloud architecture based learning kit for research students.** These type kits provide the important objective for all research students: to encourage the research on cloud based architecture and helping the basic fundamentals of different cloud and hands-on based practical to sensor working and data read write on cloud based systems. These learning kit outcomes improve learning as most of the tools and methodology that support Cloud based architecture and sensor interfacing for basic level understanding and learning for research students (Fig. 7).

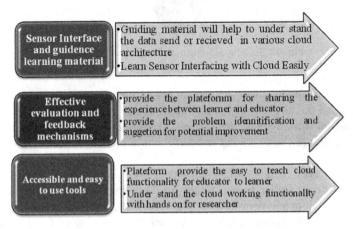

Fig. 7. Benefits for using cloud based learning kits

7 Conclusion

Cloud computing is an innovative technology, able to provide computational facilities according to user's requirement by creating a common platform where a lot can be done by sharing common resources without making lots of investment. In spite of all its limitations, cloud computing came as best to adopt solution in order reduce the expenses for developing technologies. The main objective of the paper is to introduce essential aspects of cloud computing to work with the embedded system technology, to higher education pupils. This paper shows implementation of cloud based learning kit consists of two web based cloud platforms i.e. Microsoft azure and ThingSpeak, successful integration of both technologies with sensors, visualization and monitoring of sensor data over cloud, finally ends with a comparative analysis among both cloud computing platforms. Also the Challenges discussed here describes the future scope and more enhancements needed to deal with the upcoming future works. Cloud computing is a new emerging technology that uses all existing technologies like internet,grid computing, distributed computing, virtualization etc., also it works well with almost all kind of existing hardware technologies. Hence, it came as a solution of the problems of increasing need of infrastructure, hardware, software and storage in this growing world of information.

Acknowledgement. We would like to express our gratitude to our Project Principal Investigator Prof. S.R.N. Reddy, Department of Computer Science & Engineering, IGDTUW, Delhi, India for giving us the guidance and mentoring us throughout the project. We acknowledge support from the Mobile education kit projects (MEK-1, MEK-2, MeK-3), funded by Nokia University relation and Microsoft university relation . Additional support was provided by Prof. M. Bala krishanan & Prof PVM Rao from IIT Delhi, Mr Suresh Chande from Microsoft.

References

1. Zea, C.M., Rodriguez, A., Bueno, N.A.: An innovation model in curriculum design for teaching engineering at Universidad EAFIT. IEEE Front. Educ. 1–6 (2014)
2. Encalada, W.L., Sequera, J.L.C.: Social cloud for information technology skills: an experience with universities in Ecuador. IEEE RevistaIberoamericana de Tecnologias del Aprendizaje **12**(2), 76–85 (2017)
3. Tepe, A., Yilmaz, G.: A survey on cloud computing technology and its application to satellite ground systems. In: 6th International Conference on Recent Advances in Space Technologies (RAST), pp. 471–481 (2013)
4. Romer, K., Mattern, F.: The design space of wireless sensor networks. IEEE Wirel. Commun. **11**(6), 54–61 (2004)
5. Nakhuva, B., Champaneria, T.: Study of various Internet of Things Platforms. Int. J. Comput. Sci. Eng. Surv. (IJCSES) **6**(6), 61–74 (2015)
6. https://www.iotone.com/software/thingspeak/compare/s288
7. Chowdhury, C.R.: A survey on cloud sensor integration. Int. J. Innov. Res. Comput. Commun. Eng. **2**(8) (2014)
8. Reddy, S.R.N., Kaur, J., Chande, S., Challa, R.K.: My smart phone kit: design and development of an integrated platform for innovation and product design in engineering education. Comput. Appl. Eng. Educ. **26**(3), 642–654 (2018)
9. Ray, P.P.: A survey on IOT cloud platforms. Future Comput. Inform. J. **1**(1–2), 35–36 (2016)
10. Midha, S., Kaur, G., Tripathi, K.: Cloud deep down – SWOT analysis. In: 2nd International Conference on Telecommunication and Networks (TEL-NET 2017) (2017)
11. Mell, P., Grance, T.: The NIST definition of cloud computing (2011)
12. Yang, H., Tate, M.: A descriptive literature review and classification of cloud computing research. Assoc. Inf. Syst. (AIS) **31**, Article 2 (2012)
13. Maureira, M.A.G., Oldenhof, D., Teernstra, L.: ThingSpeak– an API and Web Service for the Internet of Things (2014)
14. https://learn.adafruit.com/dht
15. https://learn.adafruit.com/tsl2561
16. https://www.sparkfun.com/datasheets/Sensors/Accelerometer/ADXL345.pdf
17. https://www.raspbian.org/
18. .https://www.microsoft.com/en-us/research/wp-content/uploads/2016/02/microsoft-azure-for-research-overview.pdf
19. Wei, D.S.L., Mukherjee, S., Naik, K., Nayak, A., Tseng, Y.-C., Wang, L.-C.: Guest editorial: networking challenges in cloud computing systems and applications. IEEE J. Sel. Areas Commun. **31**(12) (2013)
20. Nazir, M.: Cloud computing: overview & current research challenges. IOSR J. Comput. Eng. (IOSR-JCE) **8**(1), 14–22 (2012)

On Computing in the Network: Covid-19 Coughs Detection Case Study

Soukaina Ouledsidi Ali[1], Zakaria Ait Hmitti[1], Halima Elbiaze[1(✉)], and Roch Glitho[2]

[1] Université du Québec À Montréal, Montreal, Canada
elbiaze.halima@uqam.ca
[2] Concordia University, Montreal, Canada

Abstract. Computing in the network (COIN) is a promising technology that allows processing to be carried out within network devices such as switches and network interface cards. Time sensitive application can achieve their quality of service (QoS) target by flexibly distributing the caching and computing tasks in the cloud-edge-mist continuum. This paper highlights the advantages of in-network computing, comparing to edge computing, in terms of latency and traffic filtering. We consider a critical use case related to Covid-19 alert application in an airport setting. Arriving travelers are monitored through cough analysis so that potentially infected cases can be detected and isolated for medical tests. A performance comparison has been done between an architecture using in-network computing and another one using edge computing. We show using simulations that in-network computing outperforms edge computing in terms of Round Trip Time (RTT) and traffic filtering.

Keywords: In-Network Computing · Information-Centric Networking · Named Function Networking · Edge computing

1 Introduction

Over the years, the needs of users increase more and more, pushing our global Internet network architecture to its limits. Indeed, low latency, QoS, minimization of core network traffic and scalability have been very challenging to satisfy [6]. New approaches have emerged, based on data instead of addresses (IP addresses) such as Information-Centric Networking (ICN). The main idea of ICN is to ensure a communication not through the IP addresses, but rather by sending requests for data without specifying the destination, the network then takes care of retrieve this data in a reliable and secure way, without going each time asking the data to its producer, if the data has already been generated and sent to a closer node, the latter will play the role of the data source [1].

In addition, there is another approach that can be combined with ICN or with the current network protocols, which is in-network computing [2], we already know it in the form of load balancer, NAT, caching, and others. However, it can be more than that, such as processing raw data within network equipment e.g.

© Springer Nature Switzerland AG 2021
H. Elbiaze et al. (Eds.): UNet 2021, LNCS 12845, pp. 186–198, 2021.
https://doi.org/10.1007/978-3-030-86356-2_16

switches or routers, by doing that, it reduces the consumption of cloud/edge servers' resources, and also reduces core network traffic. And finally, having as result less congestion and a better latency. Combining ICN and in-network computing most likely results in a very effective solution.

Indeed, an implementation of the combination of these two recent concepts has already been proposed in several research works. Named Function Networking (NFN) [3] allows the implementation of one or more functions on any node (as long as it can perform it) of an ICN architecture. For example, a consumer sends a request specifying that he wants to execute a function with or without parameters, the network then takes the following task: choosing the node that will execute the function, executing it in a reliable and secure way and finally forwarding back the result. All these operations are done by hiding to the end-user all the complexity it takes to make it all work.

The purpose of this paper is to implement a use case, that is going to show the advantages of Named Function Networking if implemented in a scenario where there is a low tolerance for high latency. Our scenario is based on the Covid-19 pandemic situation. Currently, there is a great need to detect infected persons to help reducing the spread of the virus. One of the gathering points that pose a risk to healthy persons is the airport. Since it represents a place where several persons meet from different countries around the world. Some persons might be carriers of the highly contagious virus inside the airport.

Therefore, we designed a use case which makes it possible to detect persons with Covid-19 inside an airport. The use case consists of placing microphones inside the airport corridors to record voices. The recordings are then filtered to extract only coughs for further analysis. Also, next to each microphone there is a surveillance camera placed so whenever an infectious cough is detected the suspicious person will be detected too by analysing the video streaming of the camera.

The motivation behind implementing the use case in a NFN architecture is to benefit from a quick processing of audios close to the sources in order to be as efficient as possible to detect infected persons who represent a risk for others. The processing also includes eliminating any speech present in the audios for privacy protection while retaining the cough sounds.

The rest of this paper is structured as follows: Sect. 2 presents in-network computing. We present in Sect. 3 the use case overview. Section 4 presents the performance evaluation. In Sect. 4.3 we present the Discussion. And finally, we conclude the paper in Sect. 5.

2   In-Network Computing

With the evolution of the Internet of Things, cloud computing has started to reach its limits. Objects such as sensors require ultra-fast processing to be able to react in a reasonable time. It is for this reason that edge computing was born. Edge computing pushes computation closer to end users. However, in-network computing which refers to computing within the network, might be more effective in IoT scenarios, for example within mobile network [16] or critical scenarios that require real-time processing such as AR/VR applications. Figure 1 depicts a 3-tier architecture [6]. The tier 1 includes IoT devices e.g. sensors or user's smart devices such as smart phone or smart watch. These devices request data recovery and services. The tier 2 comprises of edge servers responsible for serving end users requests. The tier 3 is the cloud and is located at multiple hops from the tier 1. The cloud has enough resources and high storage capacity but it takes longer to respond to end user requests. In-network computing can be performed in the core network by network devices or in the wireless access network by the access points. The network devices such as routers can process requests that require limited resources and send back the results in a short time.

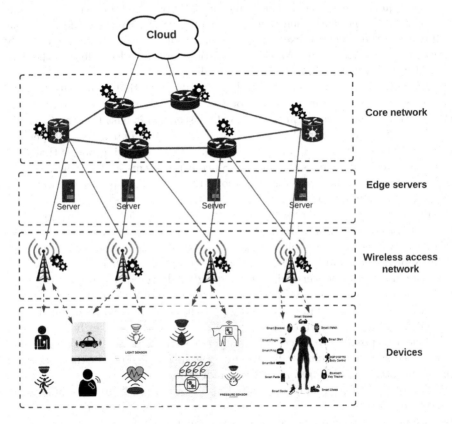

Fig. 1. In-network computing architecture

In the following subsections, we explain our motivation behind the use of in-network computing and we cite works that showed its effectiveness. In the second subsection, we introduce NFN and we explain how it works.

2.1 Motivation

Several works have been conducted to create a new extension of the ICN architecture which supports in-network computing, namely NFN [3], Compute First Networking (CFN) [4] and Named Function as a Service (NFaaS) [5]. The aim behind is to benefit from existing mechanisms in ICN, such as caching to cache the results already calculated, which prevents the redundancy of the calculation. Also, we can modify ICN forwarding strategies to do the processing in the best location and have a location-independent execution.

As claimed by [14], in a NFN network, the function code can be cached in the nodes and can move through the network according to the user's request. Also, a requestor can request the execution of a service without having to specify the exact node, which gives flexibility to the network to improve the quality of the service. Several evaluations of NFN have been done in [3], one in a small testbed topology in order to test how NFN distributes function execution tasks, and the benefit of caching results for reuse, as well as showing when is NFN doing network optimization and giving an overhead indication. Experiments have shown the effectiveness of NFN regarding decision making and optimization in different scenarios.

NFaaS [5] concerns the placement and execution of functions using unikernels. It is based on the two paradigms NDN and NFN. In NFaaS, other structures have been added to improve the NFN architecture. These structures are: Kernel store and score function. The Kernel store is responsible for storing functions i.e. unikernels as well as deciding which functions should be executed locally. On the other hand, the score function sort based on a calculated score the functions which are frequently requested in order to know which ones should be downloaded locally. The scenarios that were made to test the NFaaS framework confirmed the importance of performing functions within the network, especially when it comes to services that are sensitive to delay and bandwidth hungry.

Delay-sensitive applications [17] are applications that require processing with low latency, such as AR/VR applications, online games or others. In case the device where these applications run has limited resources, their tasks must be offloaded to a near entity such as a network equipment or an edge server.

2.2   Named Function Networking

NFN allows the orchestration of computation's tasks within the network dynamically, when an ICN client send a request for a computation task three scenarios can happen [3] as shown in Fig. 2:

(1), the result of the request has already been computed for a previous request, in this case the ICN node retrieve result from content source node.
(2), the result doesn't exist or it takes too much time to be retrieved, in this case the node will execute the requested function, and if it doesn't have the code, it will send a request to bring it from a code source node.
(3), the request precises a specific site where to address it e.g. due to policy, in this case the network forward the request to the specific site.

3   Use Case Overview

The main objective of the use case is detecting persons potentially infected with the corona virus in an airport since it represents a gathering place for different

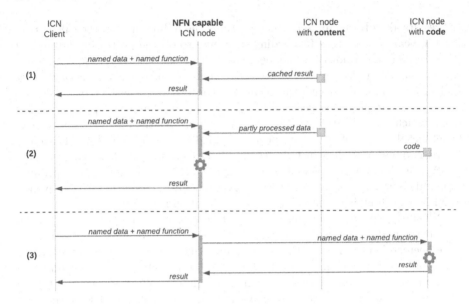

Fig. 2. NFN workflow

persons from different countries around the world. In this work, we are interested in a specific area of the airport which is the corridors because it is the first area through which the travellers pass after the landing of the plane. These corridors will be equipped with a control and detection system.

We consider Montréal-Pierre Elliott Trudeau International Airport [10]. Yul airport has three zones, a zone for domestic flights containing 26 gates, a zone for international flights other than the United States with 12 gates and a zone for flights to the United States containing 18 gates. Each gate is considered to be the opening of a corridor. Microphones with high sensitivity will be installed along the corridors as shown in Fig. 3. Among these types of microphones, we can use the long-range parabolic microphone MEGA EAR [7] designed by Endoacustica [8] Europe laboratories which have a range of 50 m and it can detects the sound of fingers rubbing. For a surface of 150 m long and 20 m wide, six microphones will be sufficient to cover the entire area. Near each microphone a camera is placed to record continuously in order to recognize the suspicious person. All these devices are connected to the edge server via an ICN network.

The sensors i.e. microphones and cameras are connected to the network via access points. The microphone records the voices and send continuously the audio data to the access point which forwards data to the NFN forwarder that is responsible to process these audios. Same operations are done on the side of the camera. Using access points provides multiple advantages as explained in [15]. They can be configured and set up easily, they provide better coverage, more flexible and adaptable compared to wired network, and since they are easy to install and don't require cables, the access points are relatively cost-effective.

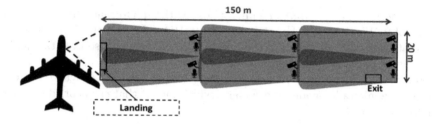

Fig. 3. Cameras and microphones placement in the corridor of the airport

However, the access points must be placed in an efficient manner in order to benefit from the previous advantages and to support maximum wireless performance. The access points placement and management are outside the scope of this paper.

3.1 Use Case Requirements

Figure 4 shows travelers walking through the corridor some of them are healthy (green circles), and others are infected with Covid-19 (red circles). The blue circle represents the agent who is going to arrest suspicious travelers. We assume that if a person leaves the corridor, he will be out of control. So, to deduce the RTT requirement, we decide to study the worst-case scenario which is when a person coughs when he arrives at the agent, in this case the agent should be alerted as soon as possible so that he can stop him before he leaves the corridor. For more details, the protocol of verifying people at the end of the corridor corresponds to: first, the agent checks the traveler's passport, after that he verifies the screen to see if there is any alert considering this person. Then, if this person is suspicious, the agent stops him for further testing. Otherwise, the agent will let him leave the corridor. This interaction takes at least 15 s i.e. time needed to proceed in a very fast way. So if the person has an infectious cough just at the moment before the agent started the checking, the system has a maximum of 15 s to send the alert to the screen of the agent, before he finishes the checking.

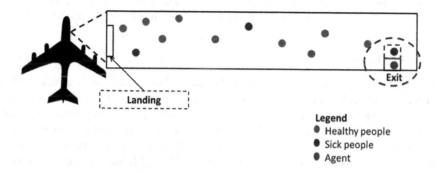

Fig. 4. Travelers walking through the corridor (Color figure online)

Furthermore, a recording of a microphone with mp3 format will need a bandwidth of 0.017 Mbytes/s. For the camera, an HD video camera 30 fps that consume at least 0.38 Mbytes/s of the bandwidth will be used, so that the quality will not be degraded. Considering the corridor shown in Fig. 3, for a surface of 3000 m^2 we deduce that we need a bandwidth of at least 0.4 Mbytes/s for each pair of one microphone and one camera, which means that each corridor of such an area will need 2,4 Mbytes/s.

3.2   Scenario Description

Let's assume we have a microphone M, a camera C, a ICN forwarder $F1$ with caching capability, a NFN forwarder $F2$ contains the code of the cough detection function and capable of executing it and an edge server E. M and C stream respectively the sounds and the videos recorded to $F1$.

In case we use in-network computing i.e. case (1) in Fig. 5: E sends a request asking for the execution of the cough detection function by specifying the microphone ID and the epoch.

$F2$ retrieve the audio of that epoch from $F1$ and then analyzes it and decides if it contains an infectious cough or not, by running a deep learning cough detection program. In the case $F2$ detects a cough it automatically sends the video recorded at the time when the cough was detected to E. Otherwise, if no cough was detected $F2$ responds with a message indicating that no cough was detected in the specific audio. If the response is a video, E runs a video analysis program to recognize the suspicious person.

In case we use only edge computing i.e. case (2) in Fig. 5: E sends a request asking for audio data. Then, it analysis the audio and in case it contains an infectious cough, it asks for video data corresponding to that time where the cough is detected to identify the suspicious person using a video analysis program.

4   Performance Evaluation

Our use case is simulated using PiCN library [13]. The evaluation is done with two different scenarios: First, using in-network computing i.e. the processing is done by the forwarder, and second, using the edge node for the processing.

4.1   Settings

The simulation consists of connecting the microphones and cameras with a forwarder via a wireless network. Each forwarder j with $j \in \{1, \ldots, N_c\}$ is a NFN forwarder with N_c is the number of corridors. The forwarder j represents the corridor j. As shown in Fig. 6, all these forwarders are connected to a core switch represented by forwarder C. The forwarders B and A insure packets routing between the corridors' network and the edge node. Additionally, each forwarder caches the paths of audios identified by the epoch of the time where they were recorded and the paths of videos corresponding to those audios. We use a sample

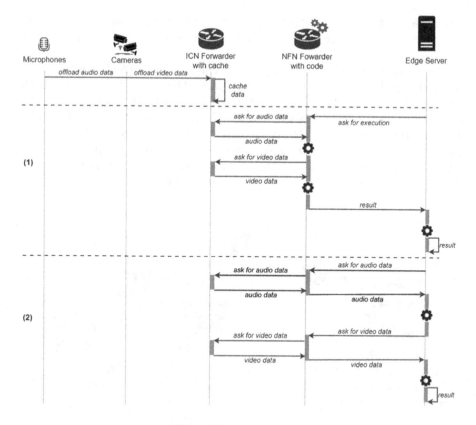

Fig. 5. Use case workflow

of fixed number of audios and videos, each one of them have a duration of 5 s. Some audios were recorded with coughs and others with simple talks. The videos consist of recordings of travelers walking throughout an airport.

The edge node asks for the execution of the function detectCough() on audio recorded at a specific epoch. The audio is recorded by the microphone i with $i \in \{1, \ldots, N_{mic}\}$ and N_{mic} is the number of microphones inside a corridor. The edge node sends an NFN interest to forwarders from 1 to n. The interest follows the path specified in the Forwarding Interest Base (FIB), until it reaches forwarders from 1 to n.

In in-network computing scenario, when the forwarders from 1 to n receive the interest message, they check in their Content Store (CS) if they have the function and the content of this naming on the CS: /mic$i$/epoch. Otherwise, the interest is forwarded to the next forwarder. After that, the forwarder starts the execution of the function which consists of a deep learning program that predicts if the audio contains a cough or not. When the execution is done, the forwarder sends to the edge server the result returned by the function. The result is in the case of "Cough detected", the video recorded at the time when the cough was detected. Otherwise, if "No cough detected", the forwarder responds with a message. The response follows the reverse path used to forward the interest message.

On the other hand, in edge computing scenario, the edge node sends interests to the forwarder A asking for the audio path. The forwarder A forwards the interest to the other forwarders. When a forwarder from 1 to n receive the interest message, it checks its CS, and send back the content to the edge server. The edge server will execute the cough detection program and if it finds a cough on it, it will send another interest to recover the video corresponding to the audio when the cough was detected, by sending an interest message to forwarder A. And finally, it brings the video for further analysis.

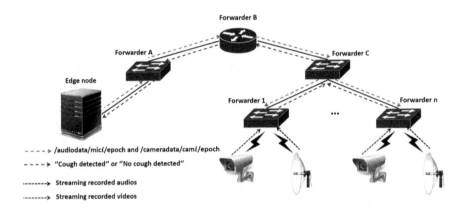

Fig. 6. Simulation topology

4.2 Deep Learning Based Cough Detector Mechanism

The cough detection program [11] consists of two python programs "Training.py" and "Inference.py". First, "Training.py" gets as inputs 162 non-cough sounds i.e. different environmental sounds, that we got from ESC-50 [9] dataset which is a publicly available dataset, and 53 cough sounds some of them are from Covid-19 [12] dataset. With the cough sounds we have a CSV file which contains for each audio file, the time laps where there is a cough. Then, we train the program and it generates a model. "Inference.py" will be based on this model to predict for each audio recording, if it has a cough or not. The audios giving as input to "Inference.py" were recorded by us, some of them contain a speech with coughs and others only speech.

Notice that the data used for the training might not be the optimal one, but we focused more on the network part of the simulation rather than the cough detection program.

4.3   Numerical Results

Round Trip Time (RTT). In the simulation we use six pairs of one microphone and one camera, each pair has a sample of 30 audios with cough sound of 5 s, and 30 videos each one related to one microphone of the same duration.

When a cough is detected, the RTT in case of in-network computing is calculated as the sum of the time needed to request for filtered audio data, run detectCough() function on forwarder near the microphone and response with the video captured in that time. In case of edge computing, the RTT is the sum of the time needed to request for audio data, run detectCough() function on the edge node, return a result specifying that a cough is detected, request for video captured in that time and recover video data.

Figure 7 depicts the RTT in milliseconds for each pair of one microphone and one camera in case of in-network computing. The RTT for all the pairs is increasing approximately the same way and it is mainly due to the processing time of the audios at the forwarder node. The processing is different from one audio to another as each audio has a particular speech with a different cough. The average of RTT for all pairs is less than 2.2 s which satisfies the requirements discussed in the Subsect. 3.1.

Figure 8 shows the RTT in milliseconds for each pair of one microphone and one camera in case of edge computing. We can clearly see that for the first audio and video identifier, the RTT is near 11 s and starts to exceed the required RTT i.e. 15 s from approximately the audio and video identifier 27. The increase of the RTT is very significant when asking for processing to the edge node. This increase is due to the processing of audios and the time taken for both the requests for the audio and the video related to.

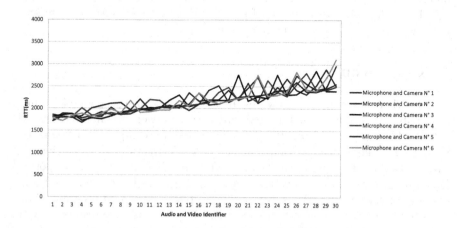

Fig. 7. RTT in in-network computing scenario

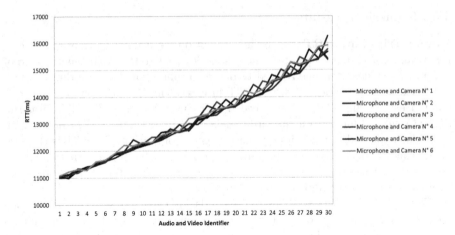

Fig. 8. RTT in edge computing scenario

Traffic Filtering and Memory Consumption. Referring to Subsect. 3.1, we concluded that each corridor equipped with 6 pairs of microphone and camera needs 2,4 Mbytes/s of bandwidth, due to audio and video data streaming. We notice that when we execute our function on the NFN forwarders near to corridors, the forwarder filter audio and video streaming data, and sends only videos of potentially infected people. Additionally, we did measure the memory consumption of our program executed in parallel on 6 audio/video data streaming input, and it has an average of 2,25 GBytes of memory allocated for the different processes. Assuming that we have an airport of only $N_c = 10$ corridors, it's almost 22,5 GBytes in terms of memory that can be gained on edge server, if we use in-network computing paradigm.

5   Conclusion

In-network computing is a new research area that brings a lot of promises, especially when applied in Information-Centric Networking architecture. NFN extends ICN to execute functions. In this work, we compare in-network computing with classical edge computing in ICN architecture, by designing a use case that allows to detect persons infected with Covid-19 inside an airport. We have implemented an architecture designed of sensors i.e. cameras and microphones, forwarders and edge server, and a deep learning based program which is executed within the network to detect suspicious coughs. The results show that in-network computing performs better than edge computing as the processing is done in a minimal delay and largely satisfies the use case requirements.

Acknowledgement. This work is partially supported by Chist-Era SCORING-2018 Project.

References

1. Jacobson, V., Smetters, D.K., Thornton, J.D., Plass, M.F., Briggs, N.H., Braynard, R.L.: Networking named content. In: Proceedings of the 5th International Conference on Emerging Networking Experiments and Technologies (CoNEXT 2009), pp. 1–12. Association for Computing Machinery, New York, NY, USA (2009). https://doi.org/10.1145/1658939.1658941

2. Zilberman, N.: In-Network Computing. SIGARCH, 25 April 2019. https://www.sigarch.org/in-network-computing-draft/

3. Sifalakis, M., Kohler, B., Scherb, C., Tschudin, C.: An information centric network for computing the distribution of computations. In: Proceedings of the 1st ACM Conference on Information-Centric Networking (ACM-ICN 2014), pp. 137–146. Association for Computing Machinery, New York, NY, USA (2014). https://doi.org/10.1145/2660129.2660150

4. Król, M., Mastorakis, S., Oran, D., Kutscher, D.: Compute first networking: distributed computing meets ICN. In: Proceedings of the 6th ACM Conference on Information-Centric Networking (ICN 2019), pp. 67–77. Association for Computing Machinery, New York, NY, USA (2019). https://doi.org/10.1145/3357150.3357395

5. Król, M., Psaras, I.: NFaaS: named function as a service. In: Proceedings of the 4th ACM Conference on Information-Centric Networking (ICN 2017), pp. 134–144. Association for Computing Machinery, New York, NY, USA (2017). https://doi.org/10.1145/3125719.3125727

6. Ullah, R., Rehman, M.A.U., Kim, B.: Design and implementation of an open source framework and prototype for named data networking-based edge cloud computing system. IEEE Access 7, 57741–57759 (2019). https://doi.org/10.1109/ACCESS.2019.2914067

7. Ultra-sensitive directional parabolic microphone — Endoacustica. Dans. www.endoacustica.com, https://www.endoacustica.com/parabolic-microphone.php

8. Microspie, Telecamere e App spia per cellulari. — Endoacustica. Dans. www.endoacustica.com, https://www.endoacustica.com/index.php

9. Piczak, K.J.: ESC: dataset for environmental sound classification. In: Proceedings of the 23rd ACM International Conference on Multimedia (MM 2015), pp. 1015–1018. Association for Computing Machinery, New York (2015). https://doi.org/10.1145/2733373.2806390

10. M-T Airport. Welcome to YUL. https://www.admtl.com/en

11. CobaltKite: Cobaltkite/dl-based-cough-sneeze-detector [Python] (2020). https://github.com/cobaltKite/DL-based-Cough-Sneeze-Detector (Original work published 2020)

12. Virufy/virufy-covid: [Jupyter Notebook]. virufy (2021). https://github.com/virufy/virufy-covid (Original work published 2020)

13. Cn-uofbasel/picn: [Python]. Computer Networks Group (2021). https://github.com/cn-uofbasel/PiCN (Original work published 2017)

14. Ullah, R., Ahmed, S.H., Kim, B.: Information-Centric networking with edge computing for IoT: research challenges and future directions. IEEE Access 6, 73465–73488 (2018). https://doi.org/10.1109/ACCESS.2018.2884536

15. Advantages and disadvantages of wireless communication. GeeksforGeeks, 20 April 2020. https://www.geeksforgeeks.org/advantages-and-disadvantages-of-wireless-communication/

16. Scherb, C., Grewe, D., Wagner, M., Tschudin, C.: Resolution strategies for networking the IoT at the edge via named functions. In: 2018 15th IEEE Annual Consumer Communications and Networking Conference (CCNC), pp. 1–6 (2018). https://doi.org/10.1109/CCNC.2018.8319235
17. Li, J., Liang, W., Xu, W., Xu, Z., Zhao, J.: Maximizing the quality of user experience of using services in edge computing for delay-sensitive IoT applications. In: Proceedings of the 23rd International ACM Conference on Modeling, Analysis and Simulation of Wireless and Mobile Systems (MSWiM 2020), pp. 113–121. Association for Computing Machinery, New York, NY, USA (2020). https://doi.org/10.1145/3416010.3423234

Artificial Intelligence-Driven Communications

DeepDDoS: A Deep-Learning Model for Detecting Software Defined Healthcare IoT Networks Attacks

Avewe Bassene$^{(\boxtimes)}$ and Bamba Gueye

Université Cheikh Anta Diop, Dakar, Senegal
{avewe.bassene,bamba.gueye}@ucad.edu.sn

Abstract. Internet of Things (IoT) brings major security challenges that have prominent social impact. Sensors diversity as well huge amount of generated data represent a big concern for handling security issues. Therefore, companies and organizations are exposed to increasingly aggressive attacks such as ransomware, denial of service (*DoS*), and distributed denial of service (*DDoS*). Although IoT devices bring a substantial socio-economic benefits, attacks can create drastically social problems within organizations like hospitals. According to healthcare-based IoT environment, attacks can impact real-time patient data monitoring/collection and consequently effect decision making with respect to critical healthcare IoT devices such as blood pressure, blood sugar levels, oxygen, weight, and even ECGs, etc. In this paper, we propose *DeepDDoS*, a stable framework that considers deep learning techniques to detect and mitigate, in real time, DoS/DDoS attacks within healthcare-based IoT environment. By leveraging the public available CICDDoS2019 dataset, we show that *DeepDDoS* outperforms previous studies and achieves a prediction model equals to 98.8%. In addition, *DeepDDoS* architecture gives an enhanced processing delay.

Keywords: Deep learning · Intrusion detection system · DDoS attacks · SDN · Healthcare Internet of Things · CICDDoS2019 dataset

1 Introduction

IoT networks are promising technologies where users, processes, data, and things are connected together via different kind of networks. For instance, medical IoT promotes real-time monitoring in order to enhance patient care. Therefore, remote advanced diagnostics can be done through telemedicine. A Healthcare-based IoT (or medical IoT) describes IoT networks and other technology gains used to monitor patient's physiological status.

Nevertheless, IoT devices are heterogeneous, and thus, they are more vulnerable to networks attacks [1–5]. It is worth noting that IoT networks suffer from several security issues with disastrous consequences. Health sector acts as the most targeted sector for cyber-attacks [1]. No doubt, healthcare-based IoT

© Springer Nature Switzerland AG 2021
H. Elbiaze et al. (Eds.): UNet 2021, LNCS 12845, pp. 201–209, 2021.
https://doi.org/10.1007/978-3-030-86356-2_17

network devices such as blood pressure, blood sugar levels, oxygen, weight, and even ECGs, etc. need robust security mechanisms that solely enable designated and authorized people to access to resources.

In 2018, Cisco estimated that the total number of DDoS attacks will double from 7.9 million to 15.4 million by 2023 [6]. According to an increasingly aggressive DDoS attacks, Senegal government developed cybersecurity strategies called "Digital Senegal 2025" (SN2025) [7]. The main objectives of SN2025 ("digital trust") are to guarantee necessary frameworks, tools, knowledge, resources and capacities in order to eliminate existing vulnerabilities within Senegalese information systems.

According to Healthcare-based IoT network, *DoS/DDoS* attacks target servers availability. As consequence, servers can be unreachable for a few hours to several days. Indeed, Senegalese government plans to leverage Healthcare-based IoT network in order to enhance the management of diseases such as hypertension and diabetes. For instance, 13.3% of adults are hypertensive and 41.6% do not know their status. Furthermore, blood sugar level is ignored by 84.7% of Senegalese population [7].

Indeed, understanding attacks types that are occurring are mandatory in order to mitigate their impact. To detect *DoS/DDoS* attacks types, machine learning or artificial intelligence based detection approaches have been proposed [2–5]. It should be noted that machine learning techniques present several limitations [3]. In contrast, Deep Learning (DL) techniques obtain good results in many different research fields.

The paper propose three main contributions. Firstly, we provide a DL-based DoS/DDoS intrusion detection techniques suitable for healthcare IoT network that leverages Long Short Term Memory (LSTM) and Convolutional Neural Network (CNN). Secondly, we describe a dataset preprocessing mechanism that tackles the problem of socket data and missing value by avoiding overfitting. Finally, we implemented and evaluated our *DeepDDoS* proposed solution according to released CICDDoS2019 dataset and edge computing scenarios within real-time scale.

The remainder of this paper is organized as follows. Section 2 illustrates literature review. Section 3 describes our *DeepDDoS* processing architecture whereas Sect. 4 evaluates *DeepDDoS* performance by leveraging public CICDDoS2019 dataset. Section 5 concludes and outlines our future work.

2   Related Work

In this section, we briefly discuss most recent DL mechanisms that have been used for DDoS detection attacks. In fact, [8] propose a feature extraction algorithm for maximizing CNN sensitivity to detect DDoS attacks. The obtained results show that DDoS attacks are recognized with an accuracy of 87.35%. However, none real-time detection system performance is proposed.

The authors of [2] propose *DeepDefense*, a deep learning based DDoS attack detection approach. Compared to ML algorithms, *DeepDefense* gives better performance and reduces error rate by at least 39.69%. However, the used dataset lacks most recent attacks patterns as well as diversity. Elsayed et al. [3] propose DDoSNet, an intrusion detection system (IDS) against DDoS attacks. It combines DL techniques and RNN with an autoencoder. Similarly to [2] any implementation is proposed. Moreover, models in [3] is compared with no equivalent learning algorithms like ML, despite the limitation ML techniques as representation models [2]. Furthermore, in [4] use various ML algorithms to identify potential malicious connections.

A *CNN+LSTM* [5] model is implemented and trained to detect newly *DoS* and *DDoS* attacks types. The *CNN+LSTM* model outperforms [4] as well as other studied DL models (1d – CNN, MLP, LSTM) with an accuracy of 97.16%. However, any online test and mitigation system is proposed.

In contrast to previous works [4,5], our *DeepDDoS* prediction model gives less processing delay and matches existing state of-the-art detection accuracy whilst ascertaining the healthcare-based IoT network security to save lives. In addition, *DeepDDoS* demonstrates consistent detection results across a range of newly sub-datasets and confirm the stability of proposed solution. To the best of our knowledge, *DeepDDoS* is the first attempt that leverages public available CICDDoS2019 dataset in order to detect real-time DDoS attack within SDN-based environments.

3   DeepDDoS Proposed Model

According to Healthcare-based IoT network, devices can be targeted by *DoS/DDoS* attacks in two different ways: *Standard* and *Reflection*. A large definition of these attacks is given in [9]. Since IoT servers are intended for very specific tasks [10], this paper focus on the second way of attack like *Reflection* one.

3.1   DeepDDoS Architecture

Figure 1 illustrates our proposed *DeepDDoS* framework architecture. After data processing, training and evaluation phases, the model is saved and scaled to deal with a resources-constrained device such as IoT gateway. A prediction is made based on real-time captured network traffic. Note that this online traffic can be converted to mimic the form of input that is compatible with training traffic traces. According to the prediction output ("Data Labeling" in Fig. 1), the traffic source device is either allowed to access server resources (potentially safe) or denied (header of the packet is sent through PACKET_IN message to the controller). Since the attacker can perform attacks through a different IP within the same subnet, rather than restricting the access of a single IP, we define blocking rules according to the entire subnet.

3.2   Model Training and Identification Approach

The *DeepDDoS* prediction model has the first 1d-CNN layer with ReLU [11] activation function, which is followed by Long Short Term Memory (LSTM) layer with respect to Adam activation function.

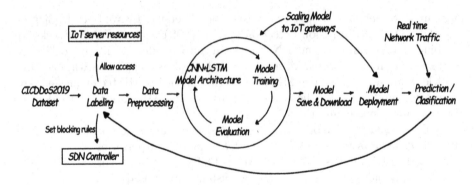

Fig. 1. DeepDDoS architecture for defining security rules on SDN controller

Since 1d-CNN accepts input shape of data in the 3D form as (batch, steps, channels), we use reshape function in *NumPy* to convert data in the following way {*data.shape(0), data.shape(1), 1*}. Used dataset has 12 training sub-datasets. Both target variable ("Label") and no socket data are encoded using sklearn *LabelEncoder* class. The socket categorical attributes are revoked because socket information can cause overfitting. In addition, traffic attributes such as the source and destination IP addresses can be usurped [12]. The missing values are imputed using the statistics mean (*strategy*). The input shape is fedded as {83, 1}. The LSTM output from the dropout layer is connected to a fully connected layer which provides input to a dense layer with *sigmoid* function to classify attack and normal data. A dropout layer with rate 0.2 is adopted to avoid the over fitting. A batch normalisation [13] is used to accelerate the training process.

Once the model is trained, it can be used to identify potential vulnerable hosts. We save then download our training model using *model.save()*. A set of tools, *joblib* is used to dump (*joblib.dump()*) the associated data transformer. The model is loaded in a flask-script custom code at the gateway to perform prediction. This application code, with high prediction ability, aims to predict then forward any suspicious traffic through the control layer. Figure 2 shows the overall *DeepDDoS* communication mechanism.

If a legitimate device located at, for instance at subnet 3, is attacked, generated traffic from this device would be predicted at edge as suspicious data ((1) in Fig. 2). The controller then defines the security rules (2) that aims to block the entire subnet within the same subnet IP range. Otherwise, the associated host is enabled to access to server resources (4). Since IoT devices are "predictable" thanks to generated traffic [10], any variation in its traffic can be important to take into account. Thus, we would rather get some attacked traffic labeled as attacked over leaving attacked traffic labeled not attacked. Moreover, convolutional neural networks (CNNs) that automatically extract features out of labelled input are also known as suited to reduce the false alarm rate.

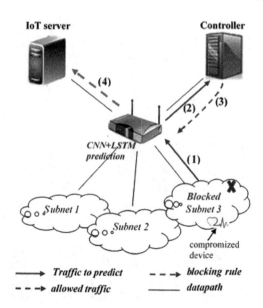

Fig. 2. A DoS/DDoS attack mitigation communication system

4   DeepDDoS Performance Evaluation

The performance of *DeepDDoS* prediction model is evaluated by considering standard well-known metrics such as Accuracy, Precision and Recall. The evaluation based on experimental results is done in two steps: determine proposed model efficiency in term of performance metrics and the ability to the predictor to process arrived traffic in real-time fashion.

The latest DDoS attack public CICDDoS2019 dataset [14] is considered for our extensive performance tests. The CICDDoS2019 dataset is formed by 12 DDoS attacks types categorized into 2 classes [15]. We evaluated our model by considering 10 time series. The mean performance value according to different series is selected.

Model Efficiency - We measured the performance of *DeepDDoS* prediction model by classifying unseen traffic flows as benign or malicious (DDoS). Obtained results are compared to the hybrid *CNN+LSTM* model [5].

The first experiment was conducted on CICDDoS2019 sub-datasets. Figure 3 shows that *DeepDDoS* prediction model outperforms *CNN+LSTM* proposal [5] with respect to different sub-datasets taken individually. It gives highest accuracy values between 96% (i.e. LDAP traces) to 99%. The WebDDoS traces gives the lowest accuracy value among all, near 49% (Fig. 3). Indeed, the positive class of this data is naturally be harder to detect due to the smaller number of captured samples. In fact, more WebDDoS samples are needed.

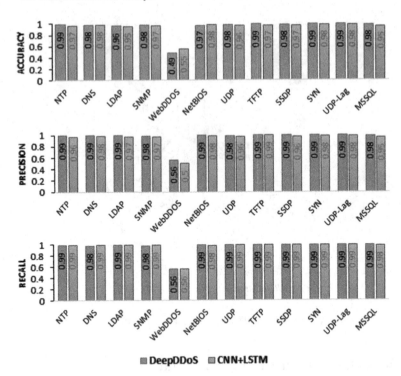

Fig. 3. Performance comparison between *DeepDDoS* and *CNN+LSTM*

When existing sub-datasets are gathered, Table 1 gives the ability of *Deep-DDoS* to obtain higher overall performance compared to *CNN+LSTM* [5]. This efficiency performance comes as an advantage of using both batch normalisation and dropout layers in our model. Indeed, when training Deep Neural Networks, the distribution of each layer's inputs changes and makes it hard to train models with saturating nonlinearities.

Based on Table 1, one can see that *DeepDDoS* prediction model outperforms *CNN+LSTM* [5] approaches according to accuracy metric. Also, we observe that the performance accuracy of the well-known DL-based *CNN+LSTM* is correlated with dataset size. Indeed, the accuracy increases with the size of the dataset and it is proportional with the training time. We expect that if CICDDoS2019 raw dataset was collected within an interval of 24 h instead of 7 h, *DeepDDoS* will be able to achieve an accuracy upper than 98.8%. Nevertheless, *DeepDDoS* obtained precision value outperforms the hybrid *CNN+LSTM* model [5] roughly 1.59%. However, *DeepDDoS* model struggles to adapts itself from new types of attacks that have not been already classified.

Processing Time - To gauge *DeepDDoS* online prediction delay, we provide an indication about the required time needed to classify several number of flows. Based on testing day traces, we randomly collected traffic flows for each

Table 1. Overall accuracy comparison when merging sub-datasets

Overall Accuracy (%)				
Datasets	Unique		Merged	
Models	DeepDDoS	CNN+LSTM	DeepDDoS	CNN+LSTM
Performance	98.25	97.16	98.8	97.23

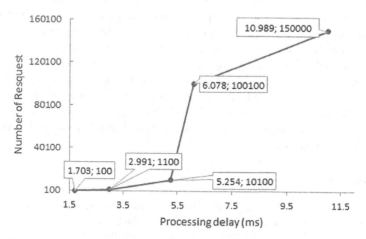

Fig. 4. Required time to classify at a glance different traffic flow requests

application and with different sizes from 100 to 150000. This data collection process exhibits the model stability with consistent detection results across a range of sub-datasets.

Figure 4 depicts the impact of requests number with respect to prediction delay. Let t_p and t_d to be the transmission time with and without predictor, respectively. The prediction time p_t is given by Eq. 1.

$$p_t = t_p - t_d \qquad (1)$$

Figure 4 illustrates that the flow processing are in correlation with respect to the number of requests. Nevertheless, whatever the number of collected requests, it can be predicted within a reasonable delay. For instance, within an interval of 10.989ms, 150000 requests are classified. The obtained time frame fits perfectly with IoT network scale transmission time.

5   Conclusion

We designed and evaluated *DeepDDoS* which an intrusion detection system that mitigates DoS/DDoS attacks within software defined healthcare IoT networks. *DeepDDoS* uses historical data in order to train an hybrid DL models. Afterwards, the obtained model is used to identify potential vulnerable IoT devices based on real-time generated traffic features. Furthermore, *DeepDDoS* embeds a SDN controller which defines security rules that aim to enable or block traffic as per the prediction output of the DL model.

DeepDDoS is evaluated using a newly comprehensive variety of DDoS attacks provided by CICDDoS2019 dataset. *DeepDDoS* prediction model outperforms the hybrid *CNN+LSTM* model [5] with an overall accuracy of 98, 8%. In contrast to previous studies, *DeepDDoS* provides a DDoS mitigation model that is able to classify up to classify 150000 requests within a interval time of 10.989ms.

As future work, we plan to simulate more WebDDoS attacks and other attacks types that can be seen according to current Internet traffic. As consequence, we will be able to address a large variety of attacks.

Data in intrusion detection system is mixed with a large amount of false alarm data, which brings great interference for network managers to analyze attack behavior. We plan to use Deep belief network (DBN) of Boltzmann Machines to avoid false alarm detection since it is shown that the DBN model is suitable to identify false alarm data in IDS system.

References

1. https://www.vectra.ai/news/vectra-networks-identifies-healthcare-as-the-industry-most-targeted-by-cyber-attacks. Accessed: 6 May 2020
2. Yuan, X., Li, C., Li, C.: DeepDefense: identifying DDoS attack via deep learning. In: Proceedings of the SMARTCOMP, pp. 1–8, China (2017)
3. Elsayed, M.S., Le-Khac, N. -A., Dev, S., Jurcut, A.D.: DDoSNet: a deep-learning model for detecting network attacks. In: IEEE 21st International Symposium on WoWMoM, pp. 391–396, Ireland (2020)
4. Nanda, S., Zafari, F., DeCusatis, C., Wedaa, E., Yang, B.: Predicting network attack patterns in SDN using machine learning approach. In: IEEE NFV-SDN, pp. 167–172 (2016)
5. Roopak, N., Tian, G.Y., Chambers, J.: Deep learning models for cyber security in IoT networks. In: Proceedings of the IEEE CCWC, pp. 0452–0457 (2019)
6. Cisco annual internet report. https://www.cisco.com/c/en/us/solutions/collateral/executive-perspectives/annual-internet-report/white-paper-c11-741490.htm. Accessed: 6 Oct 2020
7. http://www.numerique.gouv.sn/sites/default/files/SNC2022-vf.pdf.Accessed: 6 Oct 2020
8. Ghanbari, M., Kinsner, W.: Extracting features from both the input and the output of a convolutional neural network to detect distributed denial of service attacks. In: IEEE ICCI*CC (2018)
9. Guide to DDoS Attacks November (2017). https://www.cisecurity.org/white-papers/technical-white-paper-guide-to-ddos-attacks.Accessed: 06 Oct 2020
10. Bassene, A., Gueye, B.: A group-based INT devices classification through network traffic analysis based on machine learning approach. In: Zitouni, R., Phokeer, A., Chavula, J., Elmokashfi, A., Gueye, A., Benamar, N. (eds.) AFRICOMM 2020. LNICSSITE, vol. 361, pp. 185–202. Springer, Cham (2021). https://doi.org/10.1007/978-3-030-70572-5_12
11. Hahnloser, R.H., Sarpeshkar, R., Mahowald, M.A., Douglas, R.J., Seung, H.S.: Digital selection and analogue amplification coexist in a cortex-inspired silicon circuit. Nature **405**, 947–951 (2000)

12. Doriguzzi-Corin, R., Millar, S., Scott-Hayward, S., Martínez-del-Rincón, J., Sira-cusa, D.: Lucid: a practical, lightweight deep learning solution for DDOS attack detection. IEEE TNSM **17**(2), 876–889 (2020)
13. Ioffe, S., Szegedy, C.: Batch normalization: Accelerating deep network training by reducing internal covariate shift. In: Proceedings of the 32nd International Conference on International Conference on Machine Learning (2015)
14. Sharafaldin, I., Lashkari, A.H., Ghorbani, A.A. : Toward generating a new intrusion detection dataset and intrusion traffic characterization. In: International Conference on Information Systems Security and Privacy (ICISSP), pp. 108–116, January 2018
15. CICDDoS2019 dataset. http://205.174.165.80/CICDataset/CICDDoS2019. Accessed 20 Feb 2021

A General Survey on Plants Disease Detection Using Image Processing, Deep Transfer Learning and Machine Learning Techniques

Houda Orchi[✉], Mohamed Sadik, and Mohammed Khaldoun

EST Research Group ENSEM, Hassan II University, Casablanca, Morocco
{houda.orchi,m.sadik,m.khaldoun}@ensem.ac.ma

Abstract. The agricultural field is one of the mainstays of the Moroccan economy, with the growth of the human population, it becomes extremely difficult to meet the food needs of everyone. So, to meet the growing demand, the agricultural sector needs a boost to increase agricultural productivity. However, the agro-industrial part in Morocco is facing serious problems due to lack of water, common disasters and insect infestations as well as plant diseases. The presence of vermin and plant diseases is a major consideration that causes heavy losses in the country's economy. Thus, health surveillance and the early detection of plant diseases are crucial tasks to contain the spread of disease and protect the crop. As a result, several pest control methods against diseases have been exploited by farmers to increase yield. In this paper, we provide a general survey of several studies conducted and methods used with their advantages and disadvantages over the past decade in the field of plant disease recognition using image processing techniques, deep learning, transfer learning, hyperspectral image analysis, machine learning and IoT system. Also, this survey presents the challenges to be overcome in the process of automatic identification of plant diseases. Therefore, these gaps that need to be filled form the basis for future work to be undertaken and which we will discuss later.

Keywords: Image processing · Hyperspectral image analysis · Deep learning · Transfer learning · Machine learning · IoT system and plant disease recognition

1 Introduction

Agriculture is an important source of economic growth in most developing countries. The agricultural sector generates 14% of Morocco's gross domestic product and also remains the country's leading provider of jobs. So, early detection of plant diseases is the key to stopping the spread of disease and preventing food shortages and will also allow farmers to apply the right treatment at the right time to save the crop. To counter these challenges, it is imperative to develop automatic methods capable of reliably, accurately and rapidly detecting diseases at an early stage. Indeed, the automatic identification of plant diseases has become a matter of significant concern. In this regard, several systems and methods have been proposed for the automatic detection of diseases. In fact, the methods of automatic recognition of plant diseases are divided into two groups, the indirect based

© Springer Nature Switzerland AG 2021
H. Elbiaze et al. (Eds.): UNet 2021, LNCS 12845, pp. 210–224, 2021.
https://doi.org/10.1007/978-3-030-86356-2_18

on optical imaging techniques as well as direct methods serological and molecular. But they require time for processing and analysis. In particular, hyperspectral imaging and fluorescence are among the most widely used indirect methods in the early detection of disease. Although hyperspectral images may contain more information than normal photographs [1] except that these hyperspectral devices are expensive, bulky and not easily accessible to ordinary growers. While ordinary digital photographs are available everywhere in electronics stores at reasonable prices. Hence, the majority of automatic detection methods proposed up to now are based on visible range images, which makes it possible to exploit very fast and precise algorithms and techniques. Therefore, the scope of this review extends to several approaches based on spectroscopy and image processing for the automatic detection of plant diseases using different techniques and algorithms of machine learning, deep learning, transfer learning and fuzzy logic. In this paper, we have established a comparative study in order to understand the different techniques used in the process of plant disease identification. Thus, we will present their advantages and limitations. In addition, we will discuss recent research gaps among the existing techniques. Moreover, the primary objective of our paper manifests itself on the one hand in the identification of certain important challenges that have not yet been properly studied and which affect all previous studies on the automation of the disease detection process and on the other hand to highlight future directions that could help circumvent these challenges.

2 Scope of the Literature Review

Visual identification of leaf diseases is both tedious and imprecise and can only be done on small farms. Hence the need to use automatic disease detection, as it is much more accurate and requires less time and effort.

2.1 Application of Image Processing and Machine Learning in Disease Recognition

Image processing plays a fundamental role in the diagnosis and analysis of leaf diseases. Thus, the procedure followed in this process of identifying leaf diseases is illustrated in Fig. 1, which gives an overview of the different methodologies used by the authors to detect the disease using artificial intelligence and the treatment of the picture. The first step involved in the process of recognizing diseases is acquiring the images. In most cases, images can be acquired either from an imaging system or from a digital camera and since the raw images contain noise, it is necessary to remove these impurities. This leads to the second step called image preprocessing which consists of removing unwanted distortions and improving contrast. Then image segmentation involves separating the image from its background while segmenting the region of interest (ROI) the extraction of the characteristics, this one makes it possible to reveal the information and the details of an image. This brings us to the final step in the disease identification process which is classification. It should be noted that the choice of the correct classifier depends on the researcher. The objective of the classifier is to recognize the images by classifying them into different predefined groups based on the vector of features resulting from the fourth step. In this regard, there are two phases in the classification stage, namely training and testing. The training phase is to train the classifier from a training data set, and the higher the number of training sets, the better the accuracy obtained.

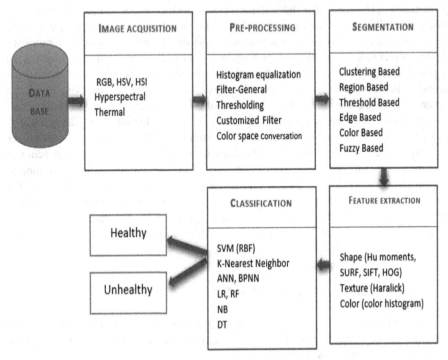

Fig. 1. Different approaches for the detection and classification of leaf diseases

2.2 Application of Transfer Learning and Deep Learning in Disease Recognition

In the last decade, the applications of TL, NN, and DL in agriculture have seen great success and have shown very promising results due to their ability to reliably learn and distinguish visual features. Thus, many fascinating studies have been published on the use of these promising approaches for the identification of diseases, in particular, the TL approach is a trend that is gaining more and more strength and which is used by researchers Too et al. [2], Ramcharan et al. [3]. Moreover, transfer learning is not a unique technique, but rather a set of fine-tuned methods, which allows the development of very precise models, on a specialized and more restrictive dataset such as those containing plant diseases and it was shown by Mohanty et al. [4], that fine-tuning was much better than training a deep CNN model from scratch. In addition, another promising tool is NN, which is widely used and recommended for the purpose of analyzing hyperspectral data for the early detection of diseases, in fact, its mechanism is inspired by the human nervous system. In addition, another similar comparative study was performed by Zhu et al. [5] in which, BPNN was tested with ELM, SVM, LS-SVM, Random Forest (RF), LDA and Partial Least Squares Discrimination Analysis (PLS-DA) for pre-symptomatic detection and classification of tobacco mosaic virus disease TMV using hyperspectral imaging. From the same perspective, Zhu et al. [6] investigated the ability of hyperspectral imaging as a non-invasive technique to detect TMV disease rapidly, combined with machine learning classifiers and the variable selection technique. The results showed that the BPNN backward propagation neural network model was able to achieve 95% accuracy while the chemometric models had 80% accuracy. It should be noted that it is possible to apply pattern recognition techniques such as SVM, RF, CA and linear regression using a new approach to recognizing patterns, which is called the artificial smart nose. Cui et al. [7] reviewed the different invasive and non-invasive techniques with their advantages and disadvantages, so they reported that the smart nose is a non-invasive and rapid method for diagnosing plant diseases. Ultimately, NNs guarantee very high-quality, unmodified spectral information for analyzing hyperspectral data. Notably, the study of the artificial neural network ANN gave rise to the concept of deep learning, which has recently become very popular in agricultural applications. Indeed, deep learning has attracted more and more interest from many researchers and especially since 2018 as indicated in the table below (Table 1). So, the most representative and typical models are the CNN convolutional neural network, auto-encoder (AE), restricted Boltzmann machine (RBM), and the recurrent neural network (RNN). In fact, several fascinating studies have been published on DL as it applies to the detection or classification of crop diseases. Among these works, those of Ma et al. [8], presented a DCNN model capable of detecting four types of cucumber diseases and by comparing it to other traditional methods like SVM, RF, and AlexNet, the DCNN was able to identify with great accuracy up to 93.41% the various diseases of cucumber. Similar to this research, Tran et al. [9] have proposed a system to monitor the growth of tomatoes and to increase the yield of tomatoes. This system was able to classify diseases and nutritional deficiencies during growth.

Table 1. A summary of various research being considered on deep and transfer learning since 2018 to detect plant diseases.

Year	Authors	Model	Crop	Classes	N°. images	Accuracy
2020 [10]	Davinder Singh	MobileNet R-CNN	13 Types	27	2598	70.53%
2020 [11]	J.S.H. Al-bayati et al	DNN, SURF, GOA	Apple	6	2539	98.28%
2019 [12]	Andre Abade et	CNN Multichannel	14 Species	38	54000	99.59%
2019 [13]	Joana Costa et al.	CNN V3 Inception	Tomato, apple, peach	16	24000	97.74%

2.3 Application of Hyperspectral Imaging in Disease Recognition

The hyperspectral imaging technique has developed strongly [14], and has been used for the identification and non-destructive detection of abiotic and biotic stresses in cultivated plants Mananze et al. [15]. Infection of the disease results in changes in the biochemical and biophysical properties of plants, these variations can influence properties of plants, Rumpf et al. [16]. These changes can influence the spectral properties of plants, and the hyperspectral system can capture these characteristics spectral Zhu et al. [5] and Zhu et al. [6], conducted a similar study, they reported that hyperspectral reflectance was collected in the visible and near-infrared range to discriminate between healthy and TSWV infected tobacco leaves using the methods of analyzing statistically to detect the growth of TSWV infection in tobacco. Mainly, the existence of the TSWV was determined to be 14 DPI. Zhu et al. [6] have proven that the use of hyperspectral imaging can detect tobacco mosaic virus (TMV) before showing symptoms while using SPA for length selection effective wave EW and the most important for the identification of different diseases. Due to a large number of highly correlated spectral values in the hyperspectral data set, multi-collinearity and high dimensionality often occur in hyperspectral data Ng et al. [17] and Wei et al. [18]. Hence, for hyperspectral analysis, the EW selection is crucial so as to reduce the complexity of the computation. Hence, to solve this multi-collinearity problem, various methods and approaches have been presented such as the SPA successive projection algorithm Xie et al. [19], Zhu et al. [6], the genetic algorithm GA, and partial least squares regression models PLSR [20].

2.4 Application of IoT in the Field of Plant Disease Recognition

Truong et al. [21] have proposed an IoT-based system composed of several devices capable of providing environmental information in real-time and sending it to the cloud for storage then this data is processed and analyzed to predict climatic conditions using an SVM machine learning algorithm deployed in the cloud to detect fungal diseases in crops. Krishna et al. [22] made an IoT system with an SMS alert that allows disease detection and automatic spraying of pesticides using the NodeMCU. Indeed, once the presence of the disease is detected, the information is transmitted to NodeMCU, then an SMS alert is sent to the farmer where the pesticides are sprayed automatically.

3 Comparative Study of Various Techniques for Detecting Plant Diseases

This section provides an overview of the research conducted over the decade to identify plant diseases. Table 2 below provides us with a picturesque idea of the different methodologies used by researchers using image processing, artificial intelligence, transfer and deep learning techniques. Furthermore, we find that the K-mean algorithm was the most common and widely used technique for the segmentation of diseased plants and classification. Indeed, there is no generalizable algorithm to solve all the problems, which is why the choice of an adequate training algorithm for a particular problem is a very crucial step for the efficiency of the model. It should be noted that the extracted texture features are the most useful to represent the regions affected by diseases in the images, which are subsequently used to train the SVM and NN classifier. Moreover, it is pointed out that these texture features are arithmetic parameters and are automatically calculated using the gray level co-occurrence matrix as follows:

a) *ASM:* Second angular momentum which represents the total quantity of squares in GLCM.

$$Energy = \sum_{i,j=0}^{N-1} \left(P_{i,j}\right)^2 \tag{1}$$

b) *Contrast:* It indicates the sum of the local intensity difference, where $i \neq j$.

$$Contrast = \sum_{i,j=0}^{N-1} P_{i,j}^{(i-j)^2} \tag{2}$$

c) *Entropy:* This is the amount of image information required for compression.

$$Entropy = \sum_{i,j=0}^{N-1} -\ln\left(P_{i,j}\right)P_{i,j} \tag{3}$$

d) *Correlation:* It represents the linear dependence of the gray levels of the adjacent pixels.

$$Correlation = \sum_{i,j=0}^{N-1} P_{i,j}(i - \mu)(j - \mu)/\sigma^2 \tag{4}$$

Table 2. Related work in the field of leaf disease detection

Title	Methodology	Advantages	Disadvantages
Pothen et al. 2020 [23]	The initial step in the workflow sequence, images are acquired, then preprocessed to ensure image characteristics are improved and unwanted distortions are removed, then images are segmented using the Otsu thresholding method. From the segmented area, various features are extracted using LBP + HOG, classified using SVM	– SVM + HOG with polynomial kernel function can be used to detect other plant diseases – The proposed work is relevant by offering better precision 94.6% compared to other work	– One of the drawbacks of the fundamental LBP operator is that it is unable to capture certain dominant characteristics

(continued)

Table 2. (*continued*)

Title	Methodology	Advantages	Disadvantages
Mugithe et al. 2020 [24]	They used IP techniques that involved 6steps, namely, the leaf images were first acquired in real-time under a webcam connected to Raspberry-Pi, then preprocessed, segmented and clustered using the K-Mean clustering algorithm, then the characteristics (are light intensity, perimeter) were extracted from the images and finally, these were evaluated to make the classification and categorization of leaf diseases	– For Alternaria Alternata disease, the results were 95.16313% accurate in the GUI	– In this study, they did not treat any other disease and even the established results are not entirely clear
Usman et al. 2020 [25]	Firstly, a computerized framework was developed to determine whether the plant is healthy or not secondly, an automated framework that includes the determination of the proximity of the disease in the plants and thirdly, a mechanical framework is created to identify diseases using temperature, humidity, and shade sensors, so thanks to its sensors the progress of the plants are recorded and then dissected, then this collected information is transferred to the cloud via WIFI for further processing and analysis to determine the plant state	– The proposed model based on IoT is low cost – Income farmers can buy it and take advantage of it to limit the spread of disease	They limited their model to just three parameters, and they took a range of properties from those parameters that could fluctuate suddenly depending on climatic conditions – Plant leaf disease has not been classified, so the types of disease are unknown
Reddy et al. 2020 [26]	First, the conversion of the RGB images to the HSI model was performed for the division, then the boundary detection algorithm and the median filter were used in the preprocessing phase for the clamor evacuation. Finally, the K-means clustering algorithm was used to partition the images into clusters	– K-means clustering takes into consideration the high precision compared to different advances and spends less time for the process	– Very common and ancient methods have been discussed

(*continued*)

Table 2. (*continued*)

Title	Methodology	Advantages	Disadvantages
Khan et al. 2020 [27]	The proposed algorithm is applied to a dataset of 148 images that includes 5 types of leaves with diseases. In particular, the images of plants are divided into two sets. A training set consists of 73 images and a test set consisting of 75 images. Indeed, 13 texture features of the image were extracted and calculated using the segment affected by diseases in the RGB color space	– The results obtained for the detection and classification of plant diseases demonstrate that the proposed method gives a very high accuracy rate of 92.8571%	– User intervention is essential in choosing the segment affected by the disease as this task in the system is not automatic and is done by visual inspection of the three segments
Al-bayati et al. 2020 [12]	A deep neural network is used for the detection of apple leaf diseases, using the accelerated robust function (SURF) and Grasshopper Optimization (GOA) algorithm. To note that, GOA was used for feature optimization and SURF for feature extraction	– Experiments have shown that the DNN optimized with SURF gives a very high mean value of 98.28% compared to other techniques designed	– Only apple leaf diseases have been discussed in this article
Karthikeyan et al. 2020 [28]	This research used IP techniques, the SVM classifier to identify plant diseases and the AHE adaptive color histogram as well as the GLCM co-occurrence matrix	– The system makes it possible to reveal the disease in the leaves at a lower cost and time compared to conventional methods	– The rate of precision is not given moreover the algorithm structure is a little complex
Simon et al. 2020 [29]	A plant disease identification system is presented based on IP techniques and CNN for automatic extraction and classification of leaf diseases. First, the start of convolution for each image of the dataset was performed using three different input matrices. Then, each of these matrices was convoluted and then the RLU grouping and activation function was involved in the output matrix	– The proposed method efficiently and accurately identifies different types of leaf diseases and gives an accuracy of 88% with a minimum number of parameters	– Creating and training the CNN model is a very tedious process and so due to its complexity and large size, it cannot be used in mobile applications

(*continued*)

Table 2. (*continued*)

Title	Methodology	Advantages	Disadvantages
Sawant et al. 2020 [30]	An approach based on DL and IP techniques is proposed for the identification and classification of plant diseases. To note that histogram equalizer, CLAHE and image resizing are applied, furthermore, the characteristics of the leaf are extracted and broadcast to CNN using the SoftMax function for the classification	– The CNN method allows us to identify and classify with great precision various plant diseases using IP techniques	– No results were given in this paper
Afifi et al. 2020 [31]	A Triplet network and deep adversarial Metric Learning approach were built using three CNN architectures (ResNet18, 34 and 50) and from a large dataset, the approaches were formed and then adjusted from 5 to 50 images per disease to detect new diseases	– The basic model achieves 99% accuracy when the change from the source domain to targets was small	– The results show a significant error rate of 22.2 for 50 shots and 42.6 for 5 shots for the DAML methods
Fulari et al. 2020 [32]	This paper presents an efficient method for the identification of an infected or healthy leaf using IP techniques and ML. Indeed, the data was collected using the Kaggle website containing over 12,949 images. This method involves different steps such as image preprocessing, segmentation, feature extraction (color, shape and texture) by using GLCM and the classification using SVM	– The SVM classifier is effective in large dimension spaces, even in cases where the number of dimensions is greater than the number of samples. The SVM gave an accuracy of 80% while CNN gave 97.71%	– The proposed method based on CNN gives a very good precision, however, it is tedious and requires a lot of time for training the model
Ouhami et al. 2020 [33]	In this paper, a study is conducted in order to find the most adequate ML model to identify tomato diseases in RGB images of leaves divided into 6 types of infections and pest attacks. Therefore, two DL models DensNet161 and 121 layers and VGG16 with TL were considered to carry out the study	– The DensNet 161 model with 20 training periods gave promising results and outperformed the other two architectures with an accuracy of 95.65%	– The negative transfer can occur and this could significantly decrease the accuracy of the model

4   Unresolved Challenges in the Field of Plant Disease Detection

There are a number of unresolved challenges that still need to be addressed and overcome in order to design robust and practical leaf disease detection systems capable of operating with high accuracy in a variety of field conditions. The challenges selected as the most convincing are:

4.1   Image Acquisition: Image Capture Conditions (Lighting, Wind, Spatial Location, Device)

Lighting Problem: Plants grow in highly fluctuating natural environments and images are influenced by many factors. Thus, lighting problems are unavoidable and it is almost impossible to completely eliminate variation, nevertheless, some attempts have been made to minimize them, for example, Pourreza, Lee et al. [34] have proposed a method using a custom-made high-power narrow-band LED lighting system and a set of polarizing filters for real-time detection of Huanglongbing disease in citrus leaves. The phenomenon of specular lighting can be minimized by changing either the position of the leaf or the angle of capture except that almost all the time, some degree of reflection occurs. In addition, shadows and specular reflections have been reported by Zhou et al. [35] as a major source of error.

Camera: The better resolution will allow the detection of small spores and lesions. Furthermore, the equipment used to take the image also influences these characteristics. Optimally the images should be taken under the same conditions, yet in practice, this can only be done in a laboratory as it is very difficult to control these capture conditions, which have been shown to be a thorny problem in measuring the severity of citrus leaf canker [36] and the recognition of citrus diseases [34]. Consequently, several efforts have been made to develop invariant [37] illumination methods, however, their success to date remains very modest.

4.2   Pretreatment

When processing and storing leaves images, the higher the compression ratio, the greater the loss of information. Compression should be minimized or even avoided, especially if the symptoms are small.

4.3   Segmentation and Discrimination of Symptoms

The problem of subjective delineation of diseased areas was initially tackled by Olmstead et al. [38] and then by Moya et al. [39] who pointed out that some kind of external reference should be created to properly validate the disease identification methods, but if a reference is not used, Oberti et al. [40] observed for powdery mildew on leaves that the number of false positives or negatives found in the discolored areas of the symptoms is too high. In short, there are not many proposed solutions to the problem because the inconsistencies are inherent in the process.

4.4 Selection and Extraction of Characteristics

The symptoms do not appear all the time in easily accessible areas, indeed they can often be under the leaves or masked by other obstacles and even diseases can occur on the stems, flowers, or even the fruits and these have not received enough attention from researchers. Moreover, we observe from the existing literature that up to now, they have focused more on detecting diseases on the upper surface of the leaves. However, Fuentes et al. [41] proposed the use of the Faster R-CNN network to detect several diseases on tomato plants in different locations.

4.5 Classification

1) Differences in symptoms caused by the disease: Depending on the stage of disease development, location on the plant, a specific disease can have very different characteristics causing serious problems for identification.

2) Diseases can be concomitant with many disorders (Nutritional deficiency, diseases and pests): Usually, many algorithms assume that there is only one disease in each image, except that in reality other diseases can occur simultaneously and even other types of disorders like the presence of pests and nutritional deficiencies and their simultaneous symptoms can be physically combined or separated which makes the identification of diseases a real challenge to overcome.

3) The similarity of symptoms between different types of disorders: Several authors have reported that certain disorders have strong similarities that can lead to serious differentiation problems. In this context, Ahmad et al. [42] found that the resulting symptoms of Alternaria, Fusarium, mosaic potyvirus and Phomopsis in soybeans were so similar that their algorithm could not discriminate between them. For this reason, the majority of studies up to now have chosen to treat only diseases with quite dissimilar symptoms, because even their choices still pose a great challenge to overcome.

5 Future Work and Possible Solutions to Current Restrictions

Future work should initially target the collection of diverse and large datasets to further encourage research in this direction. In addition, it is essential to develop compact models based on CNN that can on the one hand achieve higher accuracy and on the other hand promote the use of these technologies in embedded platforms. Second, future research should focus more on developing reliable methods and techniques for background suppression and integration of other forms of data such as weather trends, spatial location, and disease occurrence history to improve the reliability and accuracy of disease identification systems. Moreover, recognition of diseases in different places of trees and plants such as stems, flowers and fruits should attract more attention of researchers because of its great importance. Some of the major difficulties can be alleviated by using more sophisticated methods and techniques borrowed from the fields of machine learning and computer vision, such as Graph Theory, Mean Shift, Markov Random Fields, Deep Learning and Large Margin Nearest Neighbor (LMNN) classification, which are among many other methods that have not yet been properly exploited. Besides, future research efforts can be devoted to the automatic estimation of the severity of detected diseases and can also be extended to achieve high precision and faster speed, by developing hybrid algorithms like the algorithms genetics and NNs in order to increase the rate of disease recognition, the combination of PSO with other methods such as the gradient search technique which allows providing a much higher speed. Training and test data should be partitioned to avoid underfitting and overfitting. Furthermore, consideration should be given to optimizing the feature vectors in order to improve the rate of disease recognition at these different stages and since RNN models and long-term memory function to extract temporal and memory dimensions. So, they can be exploited with the intention of estimating plant growth. Finally, a web application can be developed with various functionalities such as the display of diseases recognized in crops from images of leaves taken by the camera of a smartphone.

6 Conclusion

Plant diseases are one of the major problems in the agricultural sector. Hence, the need to identify and detect plant diseases at an early stage to reduce the severity of the disease and stop its spread in the agricultural field. Therefore, significant and advanced research has been carried out in recent years on different types of disease recognition techniques that we have presented in this paper. Thus, the technical and in-depth analysis of each article and all the approaches that have been used up to now in this regard is the main difference between the other surveys and our article, and this to provide a guideline and references to research communities. This paper provides readers with an overview of the process of automatic detection of plant diseases and the major factors namely, variation in imaging conditions, absence of clear edges around symptoms, diseases that produce symptoms variables and different disorders that produce similar symptoms, besides the simultaneous presence of symptoms caused by various disorders, which have a significant impact on the efficiency of image processing techniques and analysis tools introduced up to now. Through this investigation, we concluded that image preprocessing has a direct impact on the segmentation step, moreover, it was found that the K-mean clustering algorithm is the most appropriate technique to segment the leaves affected by the disease. Moreover, it has been proven that CNNs are very powerful and effective in finding visual patterns in images. It should be noted that the use of computer vision and digital image processing in plant diagnosis is still new in the agricultural field, which implies that there are still many avenues and alternatives to be explored with the potential to reduce some of the problems mentioned above. Furthermore, with more computing power available, strategies that were previously demanding can now be easily applied. So, after a very thorough study of the existing literature on automatic detection of leaf plant diseases, we plan to develop an accurate, efficient, inexpensive and fast system to identify plant diseases using leaf images. In addition, this identification system will be deployed in a mobile application, so once the disease is detected, an alert is sent to the farmer so that he can intervene as quickly as possible.

References

1. Mishra, P., Polder, G., Vilfan, N.: Close range spectral imaging for disease detection in plants using autonomous platforms: a review on recent studies. Current Robot. Rep. **1**, 43–48 (2020)
2. Too, E.C., Yujian, L., Njuki, S., Yingchun, L.: A comparative study of fine-tuning deep learning models for plant disease identification. Comput. Electr. Agric. **161**, 272–279 (2019)
3. Ramcharan, Baranowski, K., McCloskey, P., Ahmed, B., Legg, J., Hughes, D.P.: Deep learning for image-based cassava disease detection. Front. Plant Sci. **8**, 1852 (2017)
4. Mohanty, S.P., Hughes, D.P., Salathé, M.: Using deep learning for image-based plant disease detection. Front. Plant Sci. **7**, 1419 (2016)
5. Zhu, H., Cen, H., Zhang, C., He, Y.: Early detection and classification of tobacco leaves inoculated with tobacco mosaic virus based on hyperspectral imaging technique. In: 2016 ASABE Annual International Meeting. American Society of Agricultural and Biological Engineers, p. 1 (2016)
6. Zhu, H., Chu, B., Zhang, C., Liu, F., Jiang, L., He, Y.: Hyperspectral imaging for presymptomatic detection of tobacco disease with success- sive projections algorithm and machine-learning classifiers. Sci. Rep. **7**(1), 1–12 (2017)
7. Cui, S., Ling, P., Zhu, H., Keener, H.M.: Plant pest detection using an artificial nose system: a review. Sensors **18**(2), 378 (2018)
8. Ma, J., Du, K., Zheng, F., Zhang, L., Gong, Z., Sun, Z.: A recognition method for cucumber diseases using leaf symptom images based on deep convolutional neural network. Comput. Electr. Agric. **154**, 18–24 (2018)
9. Tran, T.-T., Choi, J.-W., Le, T.-T.H., Kim, J.-W.: A comparative study of deep cnn in forecasting and classifying the macronutrient deficiencies on development of tomato plant. Appl. Sci. **9**(8), 1601 (2019)
10. Singh, D., Jain, N., Jain, P., Kayal, P., Kumawat, S., Batra, N.: Plantdoc: a dataset for visual plant disease detection. In: Proceedings of the 7th ACM IKDD CoDS and 25th COMAD, pp. 249–253 (2020)
11. Al-bayati, J.S.H., Ustundag, B.B.: Evolutionary feature optimization for plant leaf disease detection by deep neural networks. Int. J. Comput. Intell. Syst. **13**(1), 12–23 (2020)
12. Arsenovic, M., Karanovic, M., Sladojevic, S., Anderla, A., Stefanovic, D.: Solving current limitations of deep learning-based approaches for plant disease detection. Symmetry **11**(7), 939 (2019)
13. Costa, J., Silva, C., Ribeiro, B.: Hierarchical deep learning approach for plant disease detection. In: Morales, A., Fierrez, J., Sánchez, J.S., Ribeiro, B. (eds.) Pattern Recognition and Image Analysis. LNCS, pp. 383–393. Springer, Cham (2019). https://doi.org/10.1007/978-3-030-31332-6
14. Bioucas-Dias, J.M., Plaza, A., Camps-Valls, G., Scheunders, P., Nasrabadi, N., Chanussot, J.: Hyperspectral remote sensing data analysis and future challenges. IEEE Geosci. Remote Sens. Mag. **1**(2), 6–36 (2013)
15. Mananze, S., Pocas, I., Cunha, M.: Retrieval of maize leaf area index using hyperspectral and multispectral data. Remote Sens. **10**(12), 1942 (2018)
16. Rumpf, T., Mahlein, A.-K., Steiner, U., Oerke, E.-C., Dehne, H.-W., Plumer, L.: Early detection and classification of plant diseases with support vector machines based on hyperspectral reflectance. Comput. Electron. Agric. **74**(1), 91–99 (2010)
17. Ngugi, L.C., Abelwahab, M., Abo-Zahhad, M.: Recent advances in image processing techniques for automated leaf pest and disease recognition-a review. Inf. Process. Agric. (2020)
18. Wei, C., et al.: Hyperspectral characterization of freezing injury and its biochemical impacts in oilseed rape leaves. Remote Sens. Environ. **195**, 56–66 (2017)

19. Xie, C., Shao, Y., Li, X., He, Y.: Detection of early blight and late blight diseases on tomato leaves using hyperspectral imaging. Sci. Rep. **5**, 16564 (2015)
20. Ng, W., Minasny, B., Malone, B.P., Sarathjith, M., Das, B.S.: Optimizing wavelength selection by using informative vectors for parsimonious infrared spectra modelling. Comput. Electron. Agric. **158**, 201–210 (2019)
21. Truong, T., Dinh, A., Wahid, K.: An IoT environmental data collection system for fungal detection in crop fields. In: 2017 IEEE 30th Canadian Conference on Electrical and Computer Engineering (CCECE), pp. 1–4. IEEE (2017)
22. Krishna, M., Sulthana, S., Sireesha, V., Prasanna, Y., Sucharitha, V.: Plant disease detection and pesticide spraying using DIP and IoT. J. Emerg. Technol. Innov. Res. (2019)
23. Pothen, M.E., Pai, M.L.: Detection of rice leaf diseases using image processing. In: 2020 Fourth International Conference on Computing Methodologies and Communication (ICCMC), pp. 424–430. IEEE (2020)
24. Mugithe, P.K., Mudunuri, R.V., Rajasekar, B., Karthikeyan, S.: Image processing technique for automatic detection of plant diseases and alerting system in agricultural farms. In: 2020 International Conference on Communication and Signal Processing (ICCSP), pp. 1603–1607. IEEE (2020)
25. Nawaz, M.A., Khan, T., Mudassar, R., Kausar, M., Ahmad, J.: Plant disease detection using internet of thing (IoT). Plant Disease **11**(1) (2020)
26. Reddy, K.A., Reddy, N.M.C., Sujatha, S.: Precision method for pest detection in plants using the clustering algorithm in image processing. In: 2020 International Conference on Communication and Signal Processing (ICCSP), pp. 894–897. IEEE (2020)
27. Khan, M.A.: Detection and classification of plant diseases using image processing and multiclass support vector machine. Int. J. Comput. Trends Technol. **68**, 5–11 (2020)
28. Karthikeyan, N., Anjana, M., Anusha, S., Divya, R., Vinod, A.: Leaf disease detection using image processing
29. Simon, J., Kamat, S., Gutala, V., Usmani, A.: Plant disease identification using image processing.
30. Sawant, C., Shirgaonkar, M., Khule, S., Jadhav, P.: Plant disease detection using image processing techniques (2020)
31. Afifi, Alhumam, A., Abdelwahab, A.: Convolutional neural network for automatic identification of plant diseases with limited data. Plants **10**(1), 28 (2021)
32. Fulari, U.N., Shastri, R.K., Fulari, A.N.: Leaf disease detection using machine learning. J. Seybold Rep. ISSN NO, vol. 1533, p. 9211
33. Ouhami, M., Es-Saady, Y., Hajji, M., Hafiane, A., Canals, R., Yassa, M.El.: Deep transfer learning models for tomato disease detection. In: El-Moataz, A., Mammass, D., Mansouri, A., Nouboud, F. (eds.) ICISP 2020. LNCS, vol. 12119, pp. 65–73. Springer, Cham (2020). https://doi.org/10.1007/978-3-030-51935-3_7
34. Pydipati, R., Burks, T., Lee, W.: Identification of citrus disease using color texture features and discriminant analysis. Comput. Electron. Agric. **52**(1–2), 49–59 (2006)
35. Zhou, R., Kaneko, S., Tanaka, F., Kayamori, M., Shimizu, M.: Image- based field monitoring of cercospora leaf spot in sugar beet by robust template matching and pattern recognition. Comput. Electron. Agric. **116**, 65–79 (2015)
36. Bock, C., Cook, A., Parker, P., Gottwald, T.: Automated image analysis of the severity of foliar citrus canker symptoms. Plant Dis. **93**(6), 660–665 (2009)
37. Guo, W., Rage, U.K., Ninomiya, S.: Illumination invariant segmentation of vegetation for time series wheat images based on decision tree model. Comput. Electron. Agric. **96**, 58–66 (2013)
38. Olmstead, J.W., Lang, G.A., Grove, G.G.: Assessment of severity of powdery mildew infection of sweet cherry leaves by digital image analysis. HortScience **36**(1), 107–111 (2001)

39. Moya, E., Barrales, L., Apablaza, G.: Assessment of the disease severity of squash powdery mildew through visual analysis, digital image analysis and validation of these methodologies. Crop Protection **24**(9), 785–789 (2005)
40. Oberti, R., Marchi, M., Tirelli, P., Calcante, A., Iriti, M., Borghese, A.N.: Automatic detection of powdery mildew on grapevine leaves by image analysis: optimal view-angle range to increase the sensitivity. Comput. Electron. Agric. **104**, 1–8 (2014)
41. Fuentes, Yoon, S., Kim, S.C., Park, D.S.: A robust deep-learning- based detector for real-time tomato plant diseases and pests recognition. Sensors **17**(9), 2022 (2017)
42. Ahmad, S., Reid, J.F., Paulsen, M.R., Sinclair, J.B.: Color classifier for symptomatic soybean seeds using image processing. Plant Dis. **83**(4), 320–327 (1999)

Energy-Efficient Spike-Based Scalable Architecture for Next-Generation Cognitive AI Computing Systems

Ogbodo Mark Ikechukwu[1](✉), Khanh N. Dang[1,2],
and Abderazek Ben Abdallah[1]

[1] Adaptive Systems Laboratory, Graduate School of Computer Science and
Engineering, The University of Aizu, Aizu-Wakamatsu, Fukushima 965-8580, Japan
{d8211104,benab}@u-aizu.ac.jp
[2] SISLAB, University of Engineering and Technology, Vietnam National University
Hanoi, Hanoi 123106, Vietnam
khanh.n.dang@vnu.edu.vn

Abstract. In recent years, neuromorphic computing systems have taken
a range of design approaches to exploit known computational principles
of cognitive neuro-biological systems. Profiting from the brain's event-
driven nature modeled in spiking neural networks (SNN), these systems
have been able to reduce power consumption. However, as neuromorphic systems require high integration to ensemble a functional silicon
brain-like, moving to 3D integrated circuits (3D-ICs) with the three-
dimensional network on chip (3D-NoC) interconnect is a suitable approach that allows for scalable designs, lower communication cost, and
lower power consumption. This paper presents the design and evaluation
of an energy-efficient spike-based scalable neuromorphic architecture.
Evaluation results on MNIST classification, using the K-means-based
multicast routing algorithm (KMCR), show that the proposed system
maintains high accuracy with a small spike arrival window over various
configurations.

Keywords: Spiking neural network · Scalable architecture ·
Energy-efficient · Next-generation AI

1 Introduction

Spiking neural network (SNN) has gradually gained awareness by reason of its
ability to process and communicate sparse binary signals in a highly parallel
manner similar to that of the biological brain. Spike-based neuromorphic systems have leveraged this to exhibit rapid event-driven information processing
and low power consumption. SNNs are modeled after the biological information processing of the brain, where information is communicated via spikes, and

This work is supported by the University of Aizu, Competitive Research Funding
(CRF), Ref. UoA-P6-2020.

the processing of these spikes depends on their timing and the identity of the synapses used in communicating them. In contrast to multi-layer perceptrons where all neurons communicate by firing at every propagation cycle, SNN communication takes place only when the membrane potential of neurons are stimulated beyond a threshold [19]. Various ways can be employed when encoding information as spikes in SNN, and some of them include rate coding, population coding, and temporal coding [25]. There are various models of spiking neurons, and they describe the dynamics of a biological neuron at different levels. Some models which are broadly used include: the integrate and fire (IF) model [9], leaky integrate and fire (LIF) [9], and Hodgkin Huxley (HH) [14]. In general, their operation can be summarized as integrating currents from arriving spikes and the generation of new spikes whenever a threshold is exceeded. Typical spikes irrespective of their amplitude and shape are handled as similar events, and from the outset to finish, they last about two milliseconds [1] traveling down axonal lengths. The IF and LIF neuron models can easily be found in neuromorphic systems because of their simplicity and ease of implementation. However, the HH neuron model is not usually employed because its complexity makes it less suitable for large-scale simulation and hardware implementation.

SNN has successfully been used for tasks that range from vision systems[15] to brain-computer interfacing [27]. Performing software simulation of SNN has shown to be a flexible approach to exploring the dynamics of neuronal systems. However, as SNNs become deeper, simulating it in software becomes slow and consume more power, making it less suitable for large scale and real-time SNN simulation. As an alternative approach, Hardware implementation (neuromorphic system) provides the potential for rapid parallel real-time simulation of SNN, and holds an edge of computational acceleration over software simulations. Moreover, multi-neurocore neuromorphic systems can leverage the structure, stochasticity, parallelism, and spike sparsity of SNN to deliver rapid fine-grained parallel processing with low energy cost.

Over the years, Neuromorphic processors such as Loihi [7], MorphIC [11] and TrueNorth with two-dimensional (2D) architecture have been proposed. Loihi is a manycore 14-nm processor with on-chip learning capability. It occupies a silicon area of 60-mm^2 and communicates off-chip in a hierarchical mesh manner using an interface. MorphIC [11] is a quad-core processor with 512 LIF neurons per core and 528k synapses. It conducts learning using its on-chip stochastic spike-driven synaptic plasticity learning module. TrueNorth is the largest of these processors, with one million neurons and 256 million 1-bit synapses.

For three-dimensional (3D) architectures, the works in [31] and [30] both proposed multi-core 3D architectures, achieved by stacking several Stratix III FPGA boards. Inter-neuron communication was implemented using tree-based topology. This architecture, however, is not suitable as ASIC implementation, and because of the drawbacks of its topology, it seldom gets deployed in embedded neuromorphic systems [8].

The complexity of neural networks have increased over the years to inculcate multiple layers, each of which are expressed in 2D. These layers, when considered together, form a 3D structure. Mapping such structure on a 2D circuit generally results in several lengthy wires occurring between layers, or the occurrence of congestion points in the circuit [4,5,28]. 3D packet-switched NoC (3D-NoC), however, enables such structure to be mapped efficiently with communication between layers enabled via short through-silicon vias (TSVs). 3D-NoC also allows SNN to be scaled and parallelized in the third dimension by combining NoC and 3D ICs (3D-ICs) [2].

In designing a neuromorphic architecture that will support such deep SNN with many synapses, some challenges require attention. First, there is a need for a densely parallel multicore architecture with low-power consumption, light-weight spiking neuro processing cores (SNPCs) with on-chip learning, and efficient neuron coding scheme. Another major challenge that requires attention is on-chip neuron communication. Furthermore, we need to keep in mind that the number of neurons to be interconnected is immensely larger than the number of cores that require interconnection on recent multicore systems on chip platforms [12]. These challenges make the design of such a neuromorphic integrated circuit (IC) a demanding task [3].

This paper presents the design and evaluation of an energy-efficient spike-based scalable neuromorphic architecture. An extended version of this paper with fault-tolerant support and real hardware design is presented in [22]. The rest of this paper is organized as follows: Sect. 2 describes the architecture of the system's main building blocks. In Sect. 3, we present the evaluation, and in Sect. 4, we present the conclusion and future work.

2 System Architecture

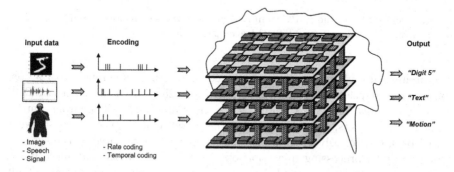

Fig. 1. High Level View of the System Architecture: (a) System architecture illustrated in a 4 × 4 × 4 configuration.

A high-level view of our proposed 3D-NoC-based neuromorphic architecture [29] in a 4 × 4 × 4 configuration is presented in Fig. 1. This architecture integrates several nodes in a 3D-NoC interconnect to provide a scalable neuromorphic architecture. Each node consists of a spiking neuron processing core (SNPC) [23], Network Interface (NI), and a multicast 3D router (MC-3DR). The nodes are arranged in two-dimensional (2D) mesh layers stacked to form a 3D architecture. Communication between layers is enabled via through-silicon-vias (TSVs).

2.1 Spiking Neuron Processing Core (SNPC)

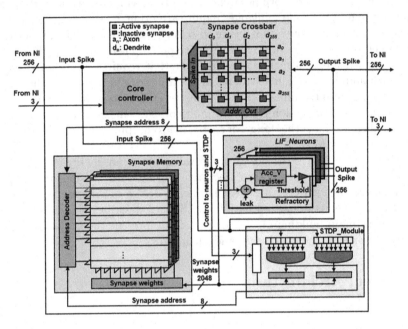

Fig. 2. Architecture of the SNPC comprising of the synapse memory, synapse crossbar, LIF neurons, control unit, and STDP learning module

The architecture of the SNPC is described in Fig. 2. It is composed of a core controller, synapse Crossbar, Synapse memory, 256 LIF neurons, and STDP learning module. The SNPC multiplexes the state of all 256 neurons onto a single bus of 256 bits, each bit signifying the presence or absence of a spike event with 1 or 0, respectively. A total of 65k synapses are represented at the synapse crossbar. Spike processing operation on the SNPC is carried out in response to the core controller's control signals. The SNPC assumes an initial default state of idle. At the arrival of a presynaptic spike array which is preceded by a spike arrival signal, it downloads the presynaptic spike array to the synapse crossbar. At the synapse crossbar, the presynaptic spike array is checked for the presence of spike events. If present, the crossbar determines the postsynaptic neuron and the synapse memory address of the associated synapses. This is done by performing one hot operation on the presynaptic spike array. When the synapse memory addresses are determined, the synapse weights stored at those addresses are fetched from the synapse memory and sent to the postsynaptic neurons for update. At the LIF neuron described in Fig. 3, the synaptic weights

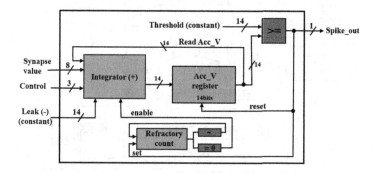

Fig. 3. Illustration of the Leaky Integrate and Fire Neuron Design.

received from the synapse memory are accumulated as the membrane potential. At the end of the accumulation, a leak operation that causes slight decay in the membrane potential value occurs. After that, the value of the membrane potential is compared with the neuron threshold value. If it exceeds the threshold, an output spike is fired. If not, no spike is fired. In the event of an output spike, the membrane potential value is reset to zero, and the neuron enters a refractory period that lasts a few time steps. While in the refractory period, the neuron cannot accumulate synaptic weights but resumes accumulation once the refractory period is over. The output spike array from the postsynaptic neuron is sent to the NI to be encoded into packets. The SNPC design enables the 256 neurons to be updated in one cycle. The accumulation of synapse weights by the LIF neuron is described in Eq. 1 as:

$$V_j^l(t) = V_j^l(t-1) + \sum_i w_{ij}{}^* x_i^{l-1}(t-1) - \lambda \tag{1}$$

where V_j^l is the membrane potential of a LIF neuron j in layer l at a time-step t. w_{ij} is the synaptic weight from neuron i to j, λ is the leak and x_i^{l-1} is pre-synaptic spike from previous layer $l-1$.

On-chip learning in each of the 65k synapses of the SNPC is achieved with an efficient implementation of the trace-based spike-timing-dependent plasticity (STDP) Learning rule [24]. As described in Fig. 4, the STDP module requires 16 presynaptic spike trace arrays, and the presence of postsynaptic spike arrays to carry out a learning operation. After an output spike array from the LIF neurons has been sent to the MC-3DR, the SNPC checks if learning conditions have been met. If met, learning begins, if not, learning is skipped, and the SNPC returns to the idle state. The presence of 16 presynaptic spike traces, and postsynaptic spike trace arrays are verified to begin learning. If present, the presynaptic spike trace arrays are grouped into two, 8 *Before* and 8 *After*, based on their arrival

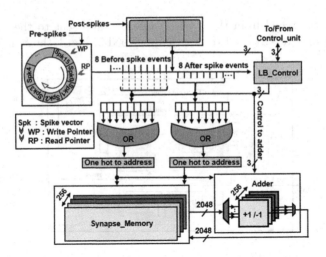

Fig. 4. Architecture of the STDP learning module.

time relative to the postsynaptic spike trace array(s). An OR operation is further performed on the groups to obtain two arrays. Using one hot operation and the postsynaptic spike trace array, the associated synapses' memory addresses are obtained from the two arrays. The corresponding synapse values are then fetched from the synapse memory, increased for the *Before* spike events, decreased for the *After* spike events, and then written back to the synapse memory. The trace-based STDP design utilizes 256 adders, which enables parallel update of synapses.

2.2   Neurons Interconnect

The MC-3DR is responsible for spike communication among SNPCs in the 3D architecture. As described in Fig. 5, it has 7 inputs and 7 output ports. Four of those ports connect to neighboring routers in the east, west, north, and south direction, two connect to the neighboring routers in the layers above and below, and the last connect to the local SNPC. The MC-3DR routes packets using four pipeline stages: buffer writing (BW), routing calculation (RC), switch arbitration (SA), and crossbar traversal (CT) [6]. It begins the first pipeline stage BW by storing the packet in the input buffer when it receives a packet from the NI or other routers. When BW is complete, the second pipeline stage RC begins. The packet's source address is obtained from the packet itself, and the next destination is calculated to arbitrate the right output port. After the right output port has been determined, the third pipeline stage begins. In this stage, the switch arbiter grants permission for the output port to be used. In the final stage, the packet is sent to the right output port through the crossbar.

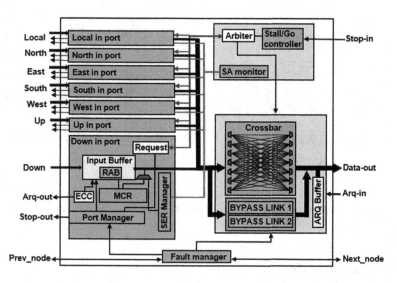

Fig. 5. Multicast 3D router (MC-3DR) [29] architecture, illustrating its ports and internal modules

The architecture of the NI is described in Fig. 6. It is made up of two modules: Encoder and Decoder. The architecture of the encoder is described in Fig. 6a, and its task is to pack spike arrays received from the SNPC into packets and send them to the router for transmission. The encoder packs spikes into flits of packet using an 81-bit flit format. The first two bits indicate the "*Type* of the flit: "00" for configuration and "11" for the spike. The next 9-bits (3-bits each for X, Y, and Z dimensions) are used to represent the address of the source neuron. The following 6-bits are a record of the time in which the source neuron fired the spike. The last 64-bits are used for the spike array from presynaptic neurons. In contrast to the encoder, the decoder, which is described in Fig. 6b unpacks packets that are received from the router into spike arrays before sending them to the SNPC.

To ensure efficient operation, we adopt and explore the shortest path k-means based multicast routing algorithm (KMCR) presented in [29]. In routing packets, the KMCR first partition destination nodes into subgroups, and from these subgroups, nodes with the least mean distance to other nodes in the subgroup are chosen to act as centroids. When the centroids have been chosen, the packets are routed from source node to the centroids, and then from the centroids to the destination nodes using a spanning subtree.

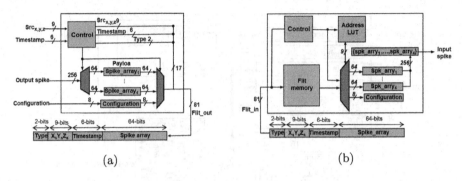

Fig. 6. Diagram of the Network Interface modules: (a) Encoder: packs presynaptic spikes into flits before routing to the destination SNPC, (b) Decoder: decodes flits received from source SNPCs into presynaptic spikes.

3   Evaluation Results

The proposed system was designed in Verilog-HDL, and synthesized with Cadence Genus. The NANGATE 45nm open-cell library [20] was used as the standard cell, the system memory was generated using OpenRAM [13], and TSV from FreePDK3D45 [21] was employed for inter-layer connection. To explore the efficiency of our proposed system, we evaluate it by carrying out MNIST data set [18] classification with on-chip and off-chip learning using SNN size of 784:400:10 and 784:100, respectively. The MNIST benchmark which contains 60K training and 10K testing images was used for evaluating the system because it is widely used, and therefore provides a basis for comparison with existing works (Fig. 1).

3.1   Performance Evaluation

We evaluate the system performance by classifying MNIST dataset. The classification was done on our proposed system using 3 different network configuration sizes of $3 \times 3 \times 3$ with a layer-based mapping scheme described in Fig. 7. The input layer of 784 neurons is mapped to the first layer of the system. The hidden layer of 400 neurons is also mapped onto the second layer. Finally, the output layer of 10 neurons is mapped to the third layer. The evaluation focused on classification accuracy and average classification time (ACT) on different configurations using the KMCR and the XYZ-UB algorithms, over various spike arrival windows (SAWs). The ACT is the average time taken to classify one MNIST image, and the SAW is the number of cycles allowed for all flits (spikes) from source SNPCs to arrive destination SNPC. After the first flit arrives, the SAW starts counting down till zero, and flits that do not arrive by the end of the countdown are not decoded. When the SAW countdown is over, the flits that arrived before the end of its countdown are decoded and sent to the destination SNPC, and it's value is reset.

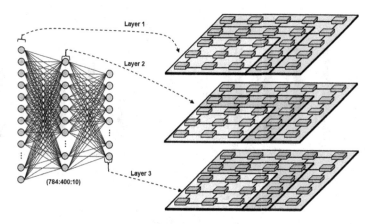

Fig. 7. SNN mapping for MNIST classification on $3 \times 3 \times 3$, $4 \times 4 \times 3$, and $5 \times 5 \times 3$ configurations: The first layer of 784 neurons without neural computation is mapped to Layer one, the second layer of 400 neurons is mapped to layer 2, and the third layer of 10 neurons is mapped to layer 3).

The accuracy and ACT of the evaluated system configurations over various SAWs are described in Fig. 8. For the $3 \times 3 \times 3$ configuration described in Fig. 8a and b, the KMCR shows better accuracy from SAW of 10 to 14 with 24.8%, 5.2%, and 9.9% better accuracy. However, as the SAW reaches 16, both algorithms reach same accuracy 98.2%. This is because the KMCR algorithm is able to service more spikes at lower SAW compared to the XYZ-UB, which reflects in the ACT, where the KMCR is lower than the XYZ-UB from SAW 10 to 12, due to the increased time taken by the KMCR to process more spikes that arrived within the SAW.

For the second configuration of $4 \times 4 \times 3$ described in Fig. 8c and d, the KMCR and XYZ-UB show similar accuracy at SAW 46, 54 and 62. This is because the similar number of spike packets were able to reach the destination SNPC for both algorithms. However, a slight difference can be seen in SAW 50 and 58, where the KMCR was able to utilize the little timing difference between it and the XYZ-UB, to deliver more spikes, which resulted in better accuracy compared to the XYZ-UB. However with more spike delivered at SAW 50 and 58, KMCR utilized more classification time compared to XYZ-UB. At SAW of 62, when the accuracy of 98.2% was reached, the KMCR utilizes 2.3% less ACT compared to XYZ-UB.

In the third configuration of $5 \times 5 \times 3$ described in Fig. 8e and f, both the KMCR and the XYZ-UB show similar performance in Accuracy and ACT over all the SAWs. It was observed that the performance of both algorithms gradually becomes similar as the size of system configuration increases.

With the SNPC able to update all neurons in parallel, the time taken to update neurons given same SNN size and number of spikes across the utilized system configurations are the same. The difference in the ACT and accuracy

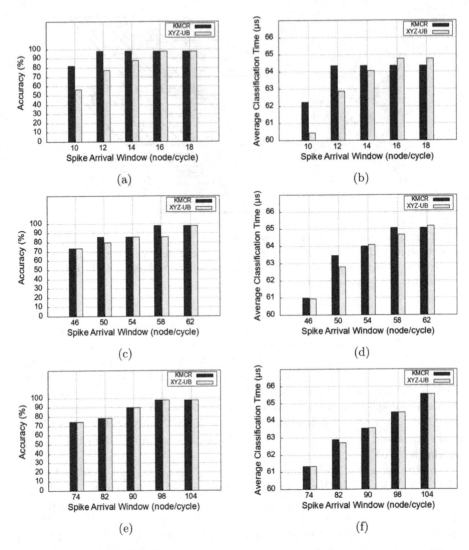

Fig. 8. MNIST classification (with off-chip learning) on different system configurations over various SAW: using the KMCR and XYZ-UB algorithms. (a) Accuracy on a $3 \times 3 \times 3$ system configuration. (b) Average classification time on a $3 \times 3 \times 3$ system configuration. (c) Accuracy on a $4 \times 4 \times 3$ system configuration. (d) Average classification time on a $4 \times 4 \times 3$ system configuration. (e) Accuracy on a $5 \times 5 \times 3$ system configuration. (d) Average classification time on a $5 \times 5 \times 3$ system configuration.

among the configurations result from the time taken to route spike packets, and the number of packets delivered to the destination SNPCs. As can be observed in Fig. 8, the $4 \times 4 \times 3$ and $5 \times 5 \times 3$ configurations requires 3.5 and 5.8 times more SAW respectively, compared to the $3 \times 3 \times 3$.

In conclusion, we evaluated different configurations of the proposed system by classifying MNIST hand written digits. We show that with off-line training, the system can successfully deliver reasonable accuracy across different configurations with increased SAW and ACT.

A comparison of the architecture and evaluation result of our proposed system and some existing works [10,17,26] is also performed. Compared to other works, our system utilizes a scalable 3D architecture which helps to provide increased parallelism and reduced communication cost. Also, the SNPC design utilizes parallel neuron and synapse update approach rather than the serial approach employed in other works. This enables all neurons to be updated in one cycle and synapses in two.

At an on-chip STDP learning accuracy of 79.4% on the MNIST dataset classification, our system achieved a higher accuracy than *Seo et al.* [26]. The higher accuracy is a consequence of the higher synapse precision utilized by our system. *ODIN* [11] and *Kim et al.* [16] nonetheless achieved a higher accuracy, but employed some form of supervision and image pre-processing, to achieve it.

Table 1. Comparison between the proposed system and existing works.

Parameters/Systems	Kim et al. [16]	ODIN [10]	Seo et al. [26]	This work
Accuracy (%)	84	84.5	77.2	79.4
Neurons/core	64	256	256	256
Neuron Model	IF	LIF and Izh.	LIF	LIF
Neuron Update	Serial	Serial	Serial	Parallel
Synapses/core	21k	64K	64k	65k
Synapse Precision	4, 5, 14	4-bit	1-bit	8-bits
On-chip Learning Rule	Stoch. grad. desc.	Stoch. SDSP	STDP	STDP
Memory Technology	SRAM	SRAM	SRAM	SRAM
Interconnect	2D	2D	2D	3D

4 Conclusion

In this work, we presented architecture and evaluation of an energy-efficient spike-based scalable neuromorphic architecture for next-generation cognitive AI computing systems. The proposed approach immensely benefits from the scalability, high parallelism, low communication cost, and high throughput advantages that 3D-NoC provides. Leveraging these benefits, our system can support large-scale SNN with an enormous amount of synapses. Evaluating with MNIST dataset classification, our method achieved 98.2% and 79.4% accuracy with off-chip and on-chip learning, respectively. The evaluation results show that with different configurations, our system can maintain high accuracy. Although the energy merit cannot be clearly seen in this evaluation due to the type and size of the used benchmark, we expect a higher energy efficiency and accuracy when the proposed system is benchmarked with large biological application.

References

1. Bear, M.F., Connors, B.W., Paradiso, M.A.: Neuroscience: Exploring the Brain, 4th edn., pp. 81–108. Lippincott Williams and Wilkins, Baltimore (2016)
2. Ben Abdallah, A.: Advanced Multicore Systems-On-Chip: Architecture, On-Chip Network, Design, chap. 6, pp. 175–199. Springer, Singapore (2017)
3. Carrillo, S., et al.: Scalable hierarchical network-on-chip architecture for spiking neural network hardware implementations. IEEE Trans. Parallel Distrib. Syst. **24**(12), 2451–2461 (2013). https://doi.org/10.1109/tpds.2012.289
4. Dang, K.N., Ahmed, A.B., Okuyama, Y., Abdallah, A.B.: Scalable design methodology and online algorithm for TSV-cluster defects recovery in highly reliable 3D-NoC systems. IEEE Trans. Emerg. Top. Comput. **8**(3), 577–590 (2017). https://doi.org/10.1109/TETC.2017.2762407
5. Dang, K.N., Ahmed, A.B., Okuyama, Y., Abdallah, A.B.: Scalable design methodology and online algorithm for TSV-cluster defects recovery in highly reliable 3D-NoC systems. IEEE Trans. Emerg. Top. Comput. **8**(3), 577–590 (2020)
6. Dang, K.N., Ahmed, A.B., Tran, X.T., Okuyama, Y., Abdallah, A.B.: A comprehensive reliability assessment of fault-resilient network-on-chip using analytical model. IEEE Trans. Very Large Scale Integr. (VLSI) Syst. **25**(11), 3099–3112 (2017). https://doi.org/10.1109/tvlsi.2017.2736004
7. Davies, M., et al.: Loihi: a neurophic manycore processor with on-chip learning. IEEE Micro **38**(1), 82–99 (2018). https://doi.org/10.1109/MM.2018.112130359
8. Ehsan, M.A., Zhou, Z., Yi, Y.: Modeling and analysis of neuronal membrane electrical activities in 3D neuromorphic computing system. In: 2017 IEEE International Symposium on Electromagnetic Compatibility Signal/Power Integrity (EMCSI), pp. 745–750, August 2017. https://doi.org/10.1109/ISEMC.2017.8077966
9. Fourcaud-Trocmé, N.: Encyclopedia of Computational Neuroscience: Integrate and Fire Models, Deterministic, pp. 1–9. Springer, New York (2013)
10. Frenkel, C., Lefebvre, M., Legat, J.D., Bol, D.: A 0.086-mm^2 12.7-pj/SOP 64k-synapse 256-neuron online-learning digital spiking neuromorphic processor in 28-nm CMOS. IEEE Trans. Biomed. Circ. Syst. **13**(1), 145–158 (2019). https://doi.org/10.1109/TBCAS.2018.2880425
11. Frenkel, C., Legat, J.D., Bol, D.: Morphic: a 65-nm 738k-synapse/mm 2 quad-core binary-weight digital neuromorphic processor with stochastic spike-driven online learning. IEEE Trans. Biomed. Circuits Syst. **13**, 999–1010 (2019). https://doi.org/10.1109/TBCAS.2019.2928793
12. Furber, S., Temple, S.: Neural systems engineering. J. Royal Soc. Interf. **4**(13), 193–206 (2006). https://doi.org/10.1098/rsif.2006.0177
13. Guthaus, M.R., Stine, J.E., Ataei, S., Chen, B., Wu, B., Sarwar, M.: OpenRAM: an open-source memory compiler. In: 2016 IEEE/ACM International Conference on Computer-Aided Design (ICCAD), vol. 34, pp. 1–6 (2017). https://doi.org/10.1145/2966986.2980098
14. Hodgkin, A.L., Huxley, A.F.: A quantitative description of membrane current and its application to conduction and excitation in nerve. Bull. Math. Biol. **52**(1), 25–71 (1990). https://doi.org/10.1007/BF02459568
15. Hopkins, M., García, G., Bogdan, P., Furber, S.: Spiking neural networks for computer vision. Interface Focus **8**(4), 128–136 (2018). https://doi.org/10.1098/rsfs.2018.0007

16. Kim, J.K., Knag, P., Chen, T., Zhang, Z.: A 640m pixel/s 3.65mw sparse event-driven neuromorphic object recognition processor with on-chip learning. In: 2015 Symposium on VLSI Circuits (VLSI Circuits), pp. C50–C51 (2015). https://doi.org/10.1109/VLSIC.2015.7231323

17. Kim, Y., Zhang, Y., Li, P.: A reconfigurable digital neuromorphic processor with memristive synaptic crossbar for cognitive computing. ACM J. Emerg. Technol. Comput. Syst. 11(4), 1–25 (2015). https://doi.org/10.1145/2700234

18. LeCun, Y., Cortes, C., Burges, C.: MNIST handwritten digit database. http://yann.lecun.com/exdb/mnist/. Accessed 23 Feb 2021

19. Maass, W.: Networks of spiking neurons: the third generation of neural network models. Neural Netw. 10(9), 1659–1671 (1997). https://doi.org/10.1016/s0893-6080(97)00011-7

20. NanGate Inc.: Nangate Open Cell Library 45 nm. http://www.nangate.com/. Accessed 05 May 2021

21. NCSU Electronic Design Automation: FreePDK3D45 3D-IC process design kit. http://www.eda.ncsu.edu/wiki/FreePDK3D45:Contents. Accessed 05 May 2021

22. Ogbodo, M., Dang, K., Abdallah, A.: On the design of a fault-tolerant scalable three dimensional NoC-based digital neuromorphic system with on-chip learning. IEEE Access 9(1), 64331–64345 (2021). https://doi.org/10.1109/ACCESS.2021.3071089

23. Ogbodo, M., Vu, T., Dang, K., Abdallah, A.: Light-weight spiking neuron processing core for large-scale 3D-NoC based spiking neural network processing systems. In: 2020 IEEE International Conference on Big Data and Smart Computing (Big-Comp), pp. 133–139 (2020). https://doi.org/10.1109/BigComp48618.2020.00-86

24. Rahimi Azghadi, M., Iannella, N., Al-Sarawi, S.F., Indiveri, G., Abbott, D.: Spike-based synaptic plasticity in silicon: design, implementation, application, and challenges. Proc. IEEE 102(5), 717–737 (2014). https://doi.org/10.1109/JPROC.2014.2314454

25. Rodrigues de Oliveira Neto, J., Cerquinho Cajueiro, J.P., Ranhel, J.: Neural encoding and spike generation for spiking neural networks implemented in FPGA. In: 2015 International Conference on Electronics, Communications and Computers (CONIELECOMP), pp. 55–61 (2015)

26. Seo, J., et al.: A 45nm CMOS neuromorphic chip with a scalable architecture for learning in networks of spiking neurons. In: 2011 IEEE Custom Integrated Circuits Conference (CICC), pp. 1–4, September 2011. https://doi.org/10.1109/CICC.2011.6055293

27. Valencia, D., Thies, J., Alimohammad, A.: Frameworks for efficient brain-computer interfacing. IEEE Trans. Biomed. Circuits Syst. 13(6), 1714–1722 (2019). https://doi.org/10.1109/TBCAS.2019.2947130

28. Vu, T.H., Ikechukwu, O.M., Ben Abdallah, A.: Fault-tolerant spike routing algorithm and architecture for three dimensional NoC-based neuromorphic systems. IEEE Access 7, 90436–90452 (2019)

29. Vu, T.H., Okuyama, Y., Abdallah, A.B.: Comprehensive analytic performance assessment and k-means based multicast routing algorithm and architecture for 3D-NoC of spiking neurons. ACM J. Emerg. Technol. Comput. Syst. 15(4), 1–28 (2019). https://doi.org/10.1145/3340963

30. Yang, S., et al.: Scalable digital neuromorphic architecture for large-scale bio-physically meaningful neural network with multi-compartment neurons. IEEE Trans. Neural Netw. Learn. Syst. **31**(1), 148–162 (2020). https://doi.org/10.1109/TNNLS.2019.2899936

31. Yang, S.: Real-time neuromorphic system for large-scale conductance-based spiking neural networks. IEEE Trans. Cybern. **49**(7), 2490–2503 (2019). https://doi.org/10.1109/TCYB.2018.2823730

Deep Neural Network Descriptor for Anomaly Detection in the Screening Unit of an Open Pit Phosphate Mine

Laila El Hiouile[1,2,3(✉)], Ahmed Errami[1], Nawfel Azami[3],
and Radouane Majdoul[3,4]

[1] Engineering Research Laboratory (LRI), Networks Embedded Systems
and Telecommunications Team (NEST), National and High School of Electricity
and Mechanic (ENSEM), Hassan II University of Casablanca,
B.P 5366, Maarif, Casablanca, Morocco
`leila.elhiouile@ensem.ac.ma`
[2] Research Foundation for Development and Innovation in Science and Engineering,
16 469 Casablanca, Morocco
[3] Innovation Lab for Operations, Mohammed VI Polytechnic University,
43150 Benguerir, Morocco
[4] Laboratory of Structural Engineering, Intelligent Systems and Electrical Energy,
ENSAM, Hassan II University, Casablanca, Morocco

Abstract. The screening unit is a critical step in the phosphate beneficiation process. However, the phosphate screening process encounters several problems and malfunctions that impact the entire production chain. Therefore, real-time visual inspection of this unit is very essential to avoid abnormal situations and malfunctions that affect production yield. Since image description is the most challenging stage in any machine vision system, this paper presents the evaluation of the performance of the convolutional neural network descriptor and three popular traditional descriptors (HOG, SIFT, and LBP), each coupled to the support vector machine classifier. The goal is to detect anomalies that may occur in the Benguerir open pit mine screening unit. Comparing these classification models shows the robustness of the deep neural network approach that gives the best tradeoff between both accuracy and runtime.

Keywords: Deep neural network · Anomaly detection · Convolutional neural network · Support vector machine

1 Introduction

Phosphorus is a limited resource that cannot be replaced in agriculture. More than 80% of the phosphorus produced is used in fertilizers to help crop production [1–3], as its use can increase yields by up to 50% [4]. With population

---

Supported by OCP.

H. Elbiaze et al. (Eds.): UNet 2021, LNCS 12845, pp. 239–251, 2021.
https://doi.org/10.1007/978-3-030-86356-2_20

growth, the demand for food will also increase, and is expected to be around 59% and 89% by 2050 [5]. This proportionally affects the demand for phosphorus fertilizers since it has increased from less than 1 Mt per year in 1850 to 22 Mt per year in 2012 [6]. Hence, it is essential that the resource is adequately managed to avoid, or at least mitigate any future supply limitations.

Once phosphate rock has been mined, the actual phosphate ore is beneficiated to separate it from the unwanted materials. Effective beneficiation can be achieved by various processes depending on the liberation size of phosphate, gangue minerals and other ore specifications. Different processes like screening, scrubbing, heavy media separation, washing, roasting, calcination, leaching and flotation may be used. Screening technique utilizes the differences in differential friability between phosphate minerals and associated gangue and cementing matrix (carbonates, silica, and silicates) [7]. The main problems occurring in the screening unit are related to the presence of sterile stones that negatively impact the quality of the final product and the rejection of high-grade Phosphate. Hence, it is essential that the screening operation of Phosphate ore could be managed adequately in order to avoid critical situations in the production.

Part of this management plan is to carry out real-time, on-site surveillance using cameras. Indeed, manual surveillance is not only monotonous and typically leads to overlooked errors by humans but it is quite not possible especially in production chains in large areas such as in mining sectors, without mentioning the cost.

The data captured every second by artificial sensors, once analyzed and classified, are used to detect any kind of anomaly that may arise during production in order to be fixed. This requires powerful techniques and object recognition algorithms. Thus, it is a question of developing algorithms that are able to process and describe captured images in order to be able to classify them.

Since the description and feature extraction of the image is the most challenging stage in image recognition pipeline, we propose in this paper to evaluate the performance of convolutional neural networks descriptor coupled to Support Vector Machine classifier for the detection of abnormal situation occurring in the screening unit of the open-pit mine of Benguerir. The classification model's performance is compared to classic manual descriptors to point out the most robust descriptor.

This work is organized as following: after introduction, Sect. 2 describes our problem and illustrates anomalies in screening unit. Section 3 presents some previous works having the same issue and details our working principal with algorithms that will be used. In Sect. 3, we present Data-Set, implementation of tested models, and obtained results. Finally, we propose a conclusion and future work (Sect. 5).

2   Problem and Method

In the phosphate industry, the screening operation is one of the most important and critical phases in the production process. This being mentioned, any malfunction in this phase has a direct impact on the performance of the entire process. The abnormal presence of pebbles sterile mixed with the transported material is an example that influences the production process in several ways. Indeed, machines cannot completely rid the pebbles mixed with the phosphate during the de-stoning operation. As a consequence, stones that cannot be removed could block the opening of the hoppers. This creates a blockage in the production chain that can last up to eight hours. Moreover, the situation is even worse when a poor layer of phosphate ore is extracted. Screens are thus overflowing with waste rock contained in low phosphate ore concentration. The grids could be unable to re-screen the product since the meshes are blocked. Also, the screening rejection of high-grade Phosphate is another malfunction which results in a loss in production. Indeed, in some cases, the screens do not allow filtering all the material due to the high flow rate of the material passage, which causes important losses of the product.

Figure 1 presents some examples of anomalies described above. The Infiltrated sterile stones directly influence (i) the safety (ii) the yield of production due to machine stops and micro-stops (iii) the lifetime of the machines by the effect of vibrations produced by large stones that impact on maintenance costs and (iv) loss of production caused by the passage of sterile material to the beneficiation process. In this paper, the images captured from the surveillance videos installed at the screening unit are used to automate the detection of anomalies based on computer vision techniques.

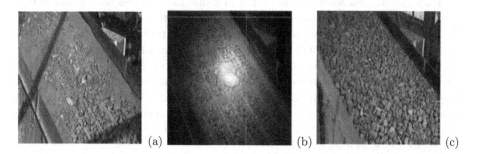

(a)   (b)   (c)

Fig. 1. (a) Passage of the phosphate at the screen to rejection. (b) Big sterile pebbles are blocking the screening hoppers. (c) A lot of sterile pebbles extracted from a poor phosphate layer.

The image recognition pipeline described in Fig. 2 is followed to approach this problem with supervised classification. As the description is the most sensitive step in artificial vision systems, we propose to evaluate the performance of two image description methods based on real databases of mages annotated by us. The first method is based on manual descriptors such as SIFT and HOG algorithms, and the second, the automatic one, uses convolutional neural networks as a descriptor. We propose to use the same classifier for both methods.

Thus, the classification mechanism will be the same and the analysis of the results will focus on the description stage to justify the differences. So, each one of the algorithms will be coupled with the famous SVM classifier in order to evaluate and compare the robustness of the descriptors used.

3   Theoretical Background

Anomaly detection is the problem of finding non confirming patterns relative to the image normality [8]. There exist several reviews on this issue. In its review [9], Pimentel et al. distinguishes between 5 methods: probabilistic, distance-based, reconstruction-based, domain-based, information-theoretic. Among anomaly detection methods there is the classification approach as Chandola described [8]. To classify images, it is first necessary to recognize the existing objects in those images. This is a very challenging issue because objects can be similar but have some subtle details, and they can appear differently in the image based on the light, viewing angle, distortion, and occlusion. A minor change in pixels leads to a major change in the image [10]. So, the objective of image recognition is to find a set of pertinent properties (or features) in the image that is stable even the pixels (location or values) are changing. It can be manual or automatic extraction. Manually extraction is a big challenge in image recognition, that's why the automatic feature extraction using deep neural networks is generally preferred as proven in [11].

There are many examples that demonstrate that the deep approach is successfully working for anomaly detection in industrial surfaces as [12–14]. While those works yield satisfactory results for specific problems, they may not be the best choice for different problems because each problem has its own characteristics that only respond to a certain kind of feature extractor. Thus, we investigate the two methods of feature extraction in order to choose the best feature extractor for our problem. Computer vision systems, whatever their field of application, are based on an image recognition pipeline that always goes from a simple image acquired by a camera to high-level information (image description) allowing the classification of particular objects or class of objects in the image [15] (as shown in Fig. 2).

After image acquisition, pre-processing is a step that maximizes the probability of successful recognition, by applying processing techniques to improve the quality of the inputs. Image description extract a set of typical features that faithfully describe each input. Then, the classification step tries to match each entry to its correct label or class using a classification algorithm already trained with a knowledge-base. The feature vector extracted should maximize

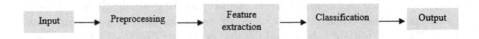

Fig. 2. General image recognition pipeline

the probability of mapping each input to its correct output and also minimize the probability of incorrect labeling of each input. Therefore, an analysis of types of features to be used for each recognition problem should be performed. So, what is a good feature descriptor in a mining context?

The description of the image can be done manually or automatically [16]. Manual description methods are hand-engineered-based methods that try to extract by hand a distinctive aspect in the image either globally, as color histogram and pixel count, or locally such as edges or key points [10,16]. Automatic description methods are feature learning-based methods that rely on a deep neural network architecture that automatically learns and extracts features via a convolution filtering succession.

3.1 Feature Extractor Using Artificial Neural Networks

Inspired by the working principle of the visual cortex in the brain, Artificial Neural Network (ANN) generally is a collection of trainable mathematical units (neurons) that learn collectively. CNN is one of the most famous models of feedforward ANNs. It's used particularly for high dimensional data (e.g. images and videos). Unlike standard neural networks, CNN takes a high dimensional filter convoluted with the input layer in favor of learning patterns and generating automatically powerful features by hierarchical learning strategies from massive amounts of training data with a minimum of human interaction or expert process knowledge [16]. So, the main process step of a CNN is that convolution layer.

The architecture is composed of multiple feature extraction stages. Each stage has three principal operations: convolution layer, non-linear neuron activation layer and feature pooling layer. The convolution layer performs convolution operation between the input image and a set of filters to generate a set of outputs feature maps. Each feature map corresponds to the output of a filter convoluted with the input image. The filter is a grid of discrete numbers called weights. The weights of each filter are randomly initialized at the start of the training of CNN, then they are updated during this learning procedure via the back-propagation method. The non-linear activation function is a very important operation that allows a neural network to learn nonlinear mapping. Generally, after each convolution layer, we apply the ReLU non-linear activation function which has a simple and quick computation.

$$ReLU(input) = max(0, input) \tag{1}$$

Afterward, the pooling layer is used to reduce the size of a feature map while preserving the most important information it contains. It can be an average, sum or max-pooling operation with a defined kernel size. The defined kernel browses the feature map (filtered image) and applies one of the tree operations, usually the max-pooling operation that selects the maximum value in the kernel. After many feature extractions stage the resulting feature maps are passed to the classification stage. Here we introduce one or many fully connected layers (FC). Each FC layer is an ANN with a number of neurons densely connected.

However, the last FC layer contained a number of neurons equal to the number of final classes with an activation function as the SoftMax function that allows the final classification. It's important to mention that instead of this final layer, many studies prove the performance of SVM as a classification algorithm [16].

In this work, we investigate this possibility of coupling CNN with SVM in order to compare CNN as an automated descriptor with manual descriptors. SVM is used mainly to solve classification problems but also regression problems. The concept of this algorithm consists of projecting the data into a space of n dimensions (n corresponds to the number of features) [16]. Then it performs the classification by searching for the hyperplane that effectively separates the projected data into two classes while maximizing the distance between the hyperplane and the nearest data (support vectors). SVM can be extended to non-linearly separable problems, by extending the original projection space into a large space. This is done using what is called a kernel function.

3.2   Comparison with Manual Feature Descriptors

Here we introduce some of the most popular manual feature extractors algorithms that have shown good results in different applications. We highlight, Histogram of oriented gradient (HOG) that has proven its efficiency in many works [17–19], Scale Invariant Features Transform (SIFT) and Local Binary Pattern (LBP) [20]. Histogram of Oriented Gradient is a feature descriptor proposed by Navneet Dalal and Bill Triggs in 2005 [17], and it's used in computer vision for object detection. It's based on the edge detection technique by computing the gradient intensity distribution for the entire image. Scale Invariant Feature Transform, is a feature extractor proposed by the researcher David Lowe in 2004 [21]. The general idea of this algorithm is to extract characteristic points, called "features points", on an image in such a way that these points are invariant to several transformations: rotation, illumination and especially invariant to scale. Local Binary Pattern is a texture descriptor proposed by Ojala et al. in 1996 [22]. It is used for detecting and tracking moving objects in an image sequence. This operator has the advantage of robustness against monotonous changes in gray levels such as illumination variations. Its general principle consists in comparing the luminance level of a pixel with those of its neighbors.

4   Experiments

4.1   Data

The captured images from surveillance cameras are pre-processed in order to prepare a dataset of learning. For each captured image, a $32°$ rotation, a cropping, and a resizing operation was introduced in order to eliminate the non-functional parts of the image. Thus, the resulting dataset consists of 3224 images each of $180 \times 120 \times 3$ color images having three classes. One class corresponds to the normal situation of screens labeled as good functioning with 1064 images.

The other classes refer to abnormal situations. Indeed, there is a sample of 1225 images represents the situation where an important quantity of phosphate is passed to the screen rejection labeled as phosphate loss class, the 3rd class correspond to the situation of high sterilization rate with 935 images, that represents the existing of high rate of stones on screens.

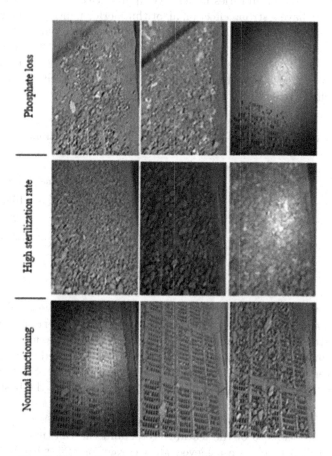

Fig. 3. Examples of dataset images after pre-processing

4.2   Implementation and Hyper-parameter

In this study, we follow the recognition pipeline described in Fig. 2. So, after pre-processing step, manual feature extractors HOG, SIFT, LBP are used to extract features that will train SVM classifier, as well as features learned by CNN during the training phase should be taken as training data for SVM. Each model, HOG-SVM, SIFT-SVM, LBP-SVM, and CNN-SVM is implemented and trained separately. In the testing stage, test samples should be fed to each of the feature extractors in order to get features. Then, the trained SVM in each model will be used to classify its corresponding testing features (see the general flowchart in Fig. 4).

Images used in this experiment are all gray-scale. The cross-validation method is used to split data into two sets. The train set contains 80% from the initial dataset and 20% for the test set. The implementation of all algorithm was doing with python libraries under a computer with CPU of 2.20 GHz.

Parameters have a strong effect on algorithm performance; therefore, we have tested different parameters for each descriptor. HOG has 3 parameters as showing in Table 1. It's clearly seen that accuracies of different HOG parameters are nearly equal, but fewer pixels per block gives a large feature vector and requires more time. We choose 16×16 pixels per block and 2×2 cells per block as the best trade-off between both, accuracy and runtime.

Table 1. Classification results with different HOG parameters

Pixels per cell	Cells per block	Orientation	Accuracy	Run-time of a single image (ms)	Feature dimension
8×8	2×2	9	0.996	114	10584
8×8	1×1	9	0.995	105	2970
16×16	2×2	9	0.996	27.7	2160
16×16	1×1	9	0.984	27.5	639

LBP has three parameters: R the radius of the circle, P the number of circularly symmetric neighbor set points and the method to determine the pattern. We have tested different parameters to generate LBP features, for $R = 1, 2, ...,5$, $P = R \times 8$ and two methods (uniform, default), but we noticed that all combinations give very low accuracy. Table 3, presents results of LBP-SVM model with $R = 1$, $P = 8*R$ and uniform method, these parameters give the best executing time.

For SIFT we tried to test different steps to space between key-points this allows reducing the size of the feature vector and the run-time (see Table 2). With a step of 6 pixels, we achieved an accuracy of 81% with 76800 feature dimensions for each image.

Table 2. Classification results with different SIFT parameters

Step	Accuracy	Runtime of a single image (ms)	Feature dimension
5	0.809	510	110592
6	0.811	350	76800
10	0.768	140	27648

Our CNN architecture is illustrated in Fig. 5. It's composed of 1 input layer with size $180 \times 120 \times 1$, 2 feature extraction stages and a fully connected layer FC of 128 neurons densely connected. Each feature extraction stage is composed of a convolutional layer followed by the ReLu activation function, a max-pooling layer with size 2×2 and a dropout layer. Convolutional layers have 64 and 128 filters respectively, the first one has padding "same" otherwise all of them have filter sizes of 4×4. A Bach normalization step is applied after the input layer. The description block ends with a feature vector of dimension 128. After the last FC layer, an SVM model is introduced in order to be trained with the resulting feature maps produced by the CNN. Our SVM in all models is a soft-margin classifier with a C value of 100 and the radial basis function as the kernel.

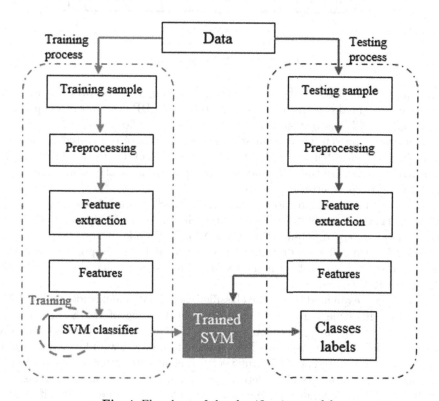

Fig. 4. Flowchart of the classification models

4.3   Results

Table 3 presents the accuracies of the different models tested. We note that the CNN-SVM and HOG-SVM models give better accuracies followed by the SIFT-SVM model which gives an average accuracy. However, the model based on the LBP texture descriptor is not efficient since it gave low accuracies despite the

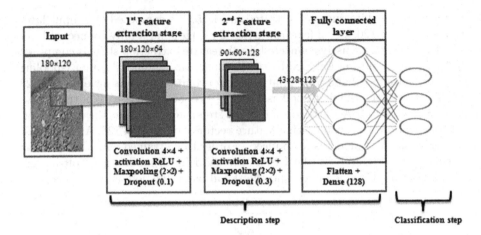

Fig. 5. Our CNN architecture

different configuration of its parameters as explained in the previous section. Relative to manual descriptors specially SIFT and LBP descriptors, deep learning descriptor CNN is very accurate in detecting anomalies in the screening unit. This is clearly proven when comparing the accuracies of the tested models. In fact, the SVM classifier is coupled to the three manual descriptors HOG, SIFT and LBP as well as to the CNN model in order to compare the robustness of the manual and deep description approach.

It is very interesting to notice that the HOG-SVM model has given a good accuracy that achieve 99.6%. This accuracy is very close to that of CNN-SVM model with the key difference that the CNN-SVM model is very fast since the classification time of a single image with each model is an important criterion. We can justify this result with the feature dimension of each descriptor; 2160 (HOG) vs 128 (CNN).

As we have explained below the classifier used in all model is identical (SVM) and it has the same parameters. So, after the training of the SVM classifier model, we suppose that a decision boundary that separate the classes is already set via the RBF kernel function. The classification of a new unlabeled image in test phase will be based on its feature vector. The feature vector will be projected into the space to find its class depending to the decision boundary. Thus, the smaller the feature dimension, the faster the execution time for classifying an image will be. This would explain the fast CNN-SVM model, in fact, as shown in Fig. 5 the CNN model used outputs a feature vector of dimension 128 which is very small compared to that of the HOG descriptor (see Table 1).

Table 4 presents the confusion matrices of the four models tested. The confusion matrix allows detailed analysis than just the proportion of correct classifications because it will give misleading results if the dataset is unbalanced and it makes it easy to see if the system is confusing two classes. C1, C2 and C3 are the three classes of the dataset, Phosphate loss, High sterilization rate and normal functioning respectively. The results of the confusion matrix justify the accuracy score of each model. CNN-SVM classifies the three classes most perfectly, giving high precision, while LBP-SVM and SIFT-SVM confuse classes which explain the low accuracies they achieve.

Table 3. Accuracies of tested models.

	HOG-SVM	SIFT-SVM	LBP-SVM	CNN-SVM
Overall Accuracy	0.996	0.811	0.392	0.998
Test time of a single image (ms)	27.7	296.5	86.12	0.04

Table 4. Confusion matrix of tested models.

	HOG-SVM			SIFT-SVM			LBP-SVM			CNN-SVM		
	C1	C2	C3	C1	C2	C3	C1	C2	C3	C1	C2	C3
C1	245	0	0	218	27	0	245	0	0	245	0	0
C2	0	186	0	29	148	9	182	4	0	0	186	0
C3	0	2	212	6	50	158	214	0	0	1	0	213

This comparison shows that the best model is the model of CNN coupled with SVM. This model presents the best trade-off between both accuracy and runtime. Thus, the CNN as a descriptor outperforms the manual descriptors, as the SVM parameters are the same in all models.

5 Conclusion

In this work, the performance of CNN's automatic descriptor was compared to that of some traditional manual descriptors for the detection of abnormal situations in the screening unit of the Benguerir open pit mine. This evaluation was carried out using the Support Vector Machine classifier which was coupled with each of the descriptors in order to compare classification accuracy and execution time.

The results show that the CNN descriptor coupled with the SVM classifier is the most robust model for detecting two major anomalies occurring in the phosphate ore screening unit. Indeed, it offers a high level of accuracy and a very short processing time, which underlines the robustness of the deep neural network approach used as automatic descriptor.

The robustness of the model will be studied in more detail in future work. In particular, the question of the influence of image noise on prediction performance, which is a major problem due to the open pit mining environment, which is subject to various severe weather conditions (fog, dust, rain, ...) that deteriorate image quality.

References

1. Steen, I.: Phosphorus availability in the 21st century: management of a non-renewable resource. Phosphorus Potassium **217**, 25–31 (1998)
2. Cordell, D., Drangert, J.-O., White, S.: The story of phosphorus: global food security and food for thought. Glob. Environ. Change **19**, 292–305 (2009)
3. Van Vuuren, D.P., Bouwman, A.F., Beusen, A.H.W.: Phosphorus demand for the 1970–2100 period: a scenario analysis of resource depletion. Glob. Environ. Change **20**, 428–439 (2010)
4. Stewart, W.M., Dibb, D.W., Johnston, A.E., Smyth, T.J.: The contribution of commercial fertilizer nutrients to food production. Agron. J. **97**, 1–6 (2005)
5. https://onlinelibrary.wiley.com/doi/abs/10.1111/agec.12089
6. Kremer, M.: Population growth and technical change, one million B.C. to 1990. Q. J. Econ. **108**, 681–716 (1993)
7. Gharabaghi, M., Irannajada, M., Noaparastb, M.: A review of the beneficiation of calcareous phosphate ores using organic acid leaching. Hydrometallurgy **103**(1–4), 96–107 (2010)
8. Chandola, V., Banerjee, A., Kumar, V.: Anomaly detection: a survey. ACM Comput. Surv. **41**, 1–58 (2009). https://doi.org/10.1145/1541880.1541882
9. Pimentel, M.A.F., Clifton, D.A., Clifton, L., Tarassenko, L.: A review of novelty detection. Signal Process **99**, 215–249 (2014). https://doi.org/10.1016/j.sigpro.2013.12.026
10. Gad, A.F.: Practical Computer Vision Applications Using Deep Learning with CNNs: With Detailed Examples in Python Using TensorFlow and Kivy. Apress, Berkeley (2018)
11. Chalapathy, R., Chawla, S.: Deep Learning for Anomaly Detection: A Survey (2019)
12. Anomaly detection with convolutional neural networks for industrial surface inspection - ScienceDirect. https://www.sciencedirect.com/science/article/pii/S2212827119302409. Accessed 31 Dec 2019
13. Anomaly Detection Using Deep Learning Based Image Completion - IEEE Conference Publication. https://ieeexplore.ieee.org/document/8614226. Accessed 31 Dec 2019
14. Weimer, D., Scholz-Reiter, B., Shpitalni, M.: Design of deep convolutional neural network architectures for automated feature extraction in industrial inspection. CIRP Ann. **65**, 417–420 (2016). https://doi.org/10.1016/j.cirp.2016.04.072
15. Awad D Vers un système perceptuel de reconnaissance d'objets. 162
16. Khan, S., Rahmani, H., Shah, S.A.A., Bennamoun, M.: A guide to convolutional neural networks for computer vision. Synth. Lect. Comput. Vis. **8**, 1–207 (2018). https://doi.org/10.2200/S00822ED1V01Y201712COV015
17. Patel, H.A., Rajput, R.D.: Smart surveillance system using histogram of oriented gradients (HOG) algorithm and Haar cascade algorithm. In: 2018 Fourth International Conference on Computing Communication Control and Automation (ICCUBEA), pp. 1–4 (2018)
18. Kapoor, R., Gupta, R., Son, L.H., et al.: Detection of power quality event using histogram of oriented gradients and support vector machine. Measurement **120**, 52–75 (2018). https://doi.org/10.1016/j.measurement.2018.02.008
19. Morphological analysis for automatized visual inspection using reduced HOG - IEEE Conference Publication. https://ieeexplore.ieee.org/document/7333435. Accessed 27 Dec 2019

20. A face recognition method based on LBP feature for CNN - IEEE Conference Publication. https://ieeexplore.ieee.org/document/8054074. Accessed 31 Dec 2019
21. Lowe, D.G.: Distinctive image features from scale-invariant keypoints. Int. J. Comput. Vis. **60**, 91–110 (2004). https://doi.org/10.1023/B:VISI.0000029664.99615.94
22. Ojala, T., Pietikäinen, M., Harwood, D.: A comparative study of texture measures with classification based on featured distributions. Pattern Recogn. **29**, 51–59 (1996). https://doi.org/10.1016/0031-3203(95)00067-4

Data Engineering, Cyber Security and Pervasive Services

A Novel Approach to Manage Ownership and VAT Using Blockchain-Based Digital Identity

S. M. Maksudul Alam[1], Md Abdullah Al Mamun[1], Md Shohrab Hossain[2(✉)], and M. Samiruzzaman[3]

[1] Department of CSE, Bangladesh University of Business and Technology,
Dhaka, Bangladesh
{1405087.smma,1405077.muam}@ugrad.cse.buet.ac.bd
[2] Department of CSE, Bangladesh University of Engineering and Technology,
Dhaka, Bangladesh
mshohrabhossain@cse.buet.ac.bd
[3] BioNanoTech, London, UK

Abstract. Blockchain is a revolutionary technology due to its security and transparency. A digital identity system based on blockchain technology can play an important role in securing the asset ownership information and protecting it against any discrepancy. However, there has been no work that combines the advantages of blockchain technology and an individual's biometric information in creating a digital identity that can be used for ownership system, thereby preventing any fraud in ownership system. In this paper, a Blockchain-based Ownership and Value Added Tax (VAT) management system have been proposed depending on a digital identity system that is implemented on blockchain technology using individuals' biometric information. The Ownership system along with VAT management was implemented using Ethereum smart contract. The experimental results of testing our system indicate that an intruder cannot perform any modification illegally to ownership data in the system. Any adversarial attempt is aborted instantly and thereby the security of citizen's ownership information is ensured. Moreover, appropriate amount of VAT is automatically assigned to the owner while changing the ownership of suitable products. Our proposed system can be very useful for protecting the digital ownership information of citizens of a country and ensuring fair payment of VAT for suitable products.

Keywords: Blocks · Blockchain · SHA-256 · Distributed network · Smart contract · VAT

1 Introduction

Blockchain is one of the major components that is driving the fourth industrial revolution. It is renowned for its capability of providing privacy and security to

© Springer Nature Switzerland AG 2021
H. Elbiaze et al. (Eds.): UNet 2021, LNCS 12845, pp. 255–268, 2021.
https://doi.org/10.1007/978-3-030-86356-2_21

information. Blockchain is a decentralized [8] system that hinders the encroachment of data. In abstraction, Blockchain refers to the chain of blocks that contains information. Tampering the information inside the blocks of a blockchain seems to be impossible. The property makes the system highly secured and trustworthy. Blockchain-based system has been used in several important contexts [25–30] that imply the reliability of blockchain in security and privacy aspects. Online has become an inseparable part of human life in this modern era of communication. People cannot but depend online because of their day-to-day needs. But there hardly exists a reliable and secured digital identity for an online user which can uniquely identify him. Dealing with ensuring the security and privacy of digital identities along with other crucial user information that is maintained by a central authority can not stay beyond the questions of being corrupted, unsecured and easily accessed. Serving a large number of users protecting information regarding the crucial aspects, i.e., identity, property ownership should be immutable to unauthorized access. Elena Karafiloski et al. [12] have provided a solution to deal with the data on large scale using Blockchain technology. Gradually, the usages of Blockchain technology is enhancing [13] because of its security and privacy. So, in the scenarios of dealing with the big data which needs to be kept secured and private Blockchain will suit at the best.

Blockchain is basically a chain of blocks that are cryptographically linked with each other. The cryptographic hash of a block is built by combining the information inside the block. Whenever a bit of information gets changed in a block, the overall hash of the block gets changed and the cryptographic linkage with its next blocks is disrupted. This is how a blockchain achieve immutability. Moreover, reproducing the blocks that follow an intruded block is somewhat impossible as the special conditions, termed as *proof of works*, of producing a block need to be fulfilled perfectly. Additionally, *consensus protocol*, applied in the distributed blockchain network, plays its role in reviving the disrupted blockchains ensuring robustness and security of the network.

The main *difference* of this work is the uniformity, integrity, and neutrality of the secured service systems. Our proposed Blockchain-based digital ownership and VAT management system has been developed depending on the Blockchain-based digital identity that uses the biometric information such as finger print and iris pattern of an individual along with a private key that belongs to him. As an user is identified by his digital identity in all of the systems, there will be consistency and integrity between the systems. Again, All of the systems are built on the smart-contract which performs autonomously in the Blockchain network. As no human is involved in the execution of the actions related to the services, there will be no chance of corruption. Rather, the systems will be secured and function fairly.

The main *objective* of this work is to develop a blockchain-based digital ownership and VAT management system using a blockchain-based digital identity [1]. Our proposed system can effectively manage the property ownership along with fairly enforcing the payment of VAT. The system will ensure transparency regarding property ownership and VAT payment in different aspects not only to the Government but also to the citizen of a country. The developed VAT management system can also be used as the Goods and Services Tax (GST) management system. The main *contributions* of our work are as follows:

- We have proposed a blockchain-based ownership system along with VAT management system using the digital identity produced from [1]. Our result shows that It is impossible to tamper the data of ownership and VAT management of an individual in the blockchain.
- We have examined the robustness of our systems by exposing the systems to different adversarial scenarios. The results have been presented with detailed explanations.

Results show that our proposed system performs better in terms of security than the previous related works. In all of the adversarial situations, the performance of the systems was vigorous and no inconvenience has been detected.

2 Previous Works

There existed only a few relevant research works [2,6,7,31,32] for blockchain-based ownership. Nevertheless, no work covers the idea of a blockchain-based Ownership and VAT management system which is built upon blockchain-based digital identity and manages the ownership information along with ensuring the collection of VAT for products or properties. Again, the existing ownership systems are not compatible with the blockchain-based digital identity and can not ensure the autonomous enforcement of VAT for the products or property. Toyoda et al. [2] has proposed a product ownership management system following a supply chain using blockchain. Perry Haldenby et al. [32] have described the methods for tracking and transferring ownership of connected devices. Cankal Altun et al. [7] proposed a reference model which grants the absolute ownership of the fog-located digital twin of an owner's home appliance. Nishant Baranwal Somy et al. [6] implemented a system using Hyper-ledger Fabric that ensures the privacy of data along with retaining the ownership of the data owner. Poonam Ghuli et al. [31] describe a unique method for peer to peer identification of ownership of IoT devices in a cloud environment.

To the best of our knowledge, there exists no earlier work that uses the digital identity along with ownership and VAT management system. However, there are some existing research works regarding VAT. Georges Bell et al. [5] have provided the Implementation of VAT Collection in blockchain technology. Ahmad et al. [4] have proposed a VAT system in Saudi Arabia. Van-Cam et al. [3] have proposed a blockchain-based method using smart contact to digitize invoice along with VAT management. The novelties of our work in comparison to the previous works can be described as follows:

- Our work has integrated the digital identity with the digital property ownership and the VAT management system. As a result, the system provides us a secure way that is hassle-free, user-friendly, and efficient to perform our tasks.

- Digitizing the ownership management system combining autonomous and fair procedures.
- Ensuring the enforcement of VAT automatically while transferring, i.e., buying or selling the ownership of property.

3   Proposed Blockchain-Based Ownership and VAT Management System

The records of any valuable properties and the owners whom the properties belong to should be stored in most efficient and secured way. As we are moving toward the digital era, the land and other expensive properties like car, bike, house, etc. ownership digitization is our situation demand. If these properties' ownership can be recorded in a proper way in the blockchain with the help of the owner's digital identity, we can ensure the privacy and legality of our documents. If the records of the ownership of property are kept in a naive method, then the data for the ownership of the property can be tampered further which is unfortunate. There are some problems in the current established naive method of ownership management. They are given below:

- Documents can be damaged with the passage of time or by natural calamities.
- Signature can be copied and the information can be modified.
- The government property and often other's personal property can be ousted by the potents.
- Legacy of the ownership is not easily verifiable and it creates confusion in the subsequent generation.
- Information is not easily accessible when people need to access it legally.
- Inefficient methods are used as files are stored in a room and people need to manually search for a relevant files while transferring the ownership of property or any expensive products
- The officials are often involved in corruption while processing the ownership transfer manually.

A blockchain-based digital ownership management system using the blockchain-based digital identity [1] prevents the information of ownership from being damaged. The property ownership will be much more secured, feasible, and transparent than before. On the other hand, VAT payment for a property or product is so important for the government. That's why there should be a system that will track all of the information regarding the VAT associated to the properties or products so that there will be no discrepancy in paying VAT to the government. Our proposed digital VAT payment system will provide the following advantages given below:

- Enforces people to pay the legal VAT while maintaining ownership legacy.
- Proves the legality of the properties or products easily.
- Keeps the track of VAT paid for the properties or products of individuals so that government can take a proper step against those who avoid paying VAT.

The system can play an important role in ensuring the appropriate payment of VAT to the Government and thus, will be beneficial to the national betterment of a country.

3.1   Interaction Diagram of Digital Ownership and VAT Management System

To manage the ownership and VAT management system, a citizen of a country will have to follow a sequence of procedures to maintain the ownership legacy for the properties or products. Figure 1 shows the interaction diagram of ownership and VAT management system using a digital identity.

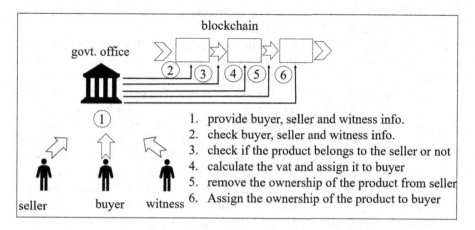

Fig. 1. Interaction diagram of ownership and VAT management system

Firstly, the buyer, seller, and witness provide their bio-information. **Secondly,** the local government office verifies each individual whether he is a citizen or not of the country. **After that,** the local government office checks whether the products or properties belong to the seller or not. **Then,** if there is no error on checking and verification, the VAT is calculated based on property type and it is assigned to the buyer. **Finally,** The ownership of the product or property is removed from the seller and the ownership is assigned to the buyer.

3.2   Assumption of Our Ownership and VAT Management System

We have considered those properties or products under the ownership and VAT management system which are expensive, have high longevity, and whose ownership can be changed legally. For example land, Flat, Television, Bike, Car etc. The products or properties of our frequent usage with a lower durability, i.e., soap, food, cosmetics, etc. are out of our scope. We are mainly concerned about ensuring the considerable amount of VAT that can be corrupted. While buying any property or product, the VAT information will be automatically assigned to the digital identity of the buyer.

3.3   Proposed Algorithm for the Ownership and VAT Management System

We have used blockchain-based digital identity in our ownership system. The followings steps will be performed while changing the ownership of a property.

Step 1: Provide the buyer's, seller's, witness's and product's information: The government official will provide the identity of the seller, owner and the witness to the smart contract which will have to be deployed finally to make our proposed system workable.

Step 2: Verify the identity of the buyer, seller and witness: The smart contract will check if the identities are correctly defined or not in the digital identity system [1] of buyer, seller, and witness. If there arises any inconvenience, the process will be aborted.

Step 3: Be sure about the product's validity (if the product belongs to the seller or not): With the help of digital identity system, each product will be assigned to its owner. So it can easily be checked if the product belongs to the person or not. If the seller does not own the product, the buyer can easily be notified and obviously, the buyer will not buy an invalid product.

Step 4: Assign the VAT based on property or product type to the buyer's digital identity: Different VAT is applicable for different property. When a buyer buys a property then the predefined VAT on that property, set by the Government, will be charged to the buyer. This VAT amount will be assigned to the corresponding buyer identity. So, there is no way to avoid the payment of VAT because it is automatic and has no explicit control. If anyone owns or buys somethings he must pay the proper amount of VAT.

Step 5: Delete the ownership of the property entry from the seller ownership list: While transferring the ownership, the smart contract will delete the ownership of the buyer from the seller property list.

Step 6: Add a new entry of the ownership of the product to the buyer ownership list: After transferring the ownership, the property belongs to the buyer. So, a smart contract will create the ownership of the buyer at the buyer property list.

If there any discrepancy occurs while completing the process, it will be terminated and there will be no update on stored data because of an incomplete process. The steps of the process have been described in detail as follows:

4   Implementation and Results

To implement our secured Ownership and VAT management systems, ethereum *smart-contract* were used. The smart-contracts were developed analyzing the functionalities and the vulnerabilities of the systems. The smart-contracts were coded with *solidity* programming language using the *Remix* online IDE. The test-net was used as an experimental blockchain network.

4.1   Implementation of the Ownership and the VAT Management System

In our implementation of smart contract, the structure "propertyInfo" keeps the record of the type of a property and property description. The structure "transferRecord" keeps the record of seller, buyer, witness, and property information. The structure "personProperties" keeps the array of structure "propertyInfo".

The modifier "onlyAdmin" is used to confine the access only to the admin. We can get the address of the admin by calling the function "getAdmin". The mapping "citizensProperties" keeps the track of the property ownership of the citizens. An admin can set the property information by calling "setPropertiesInfo" and if needed can also see the validity of the property ownership by passing the parameter mentioned above to the function "getPropertiesInfo". The function "deletePropertiesInfo" deletes the information of the property ownership from the database. and the function "vatPayment" calculates the VAT automatically for property transaction and add the VAT to the buyer total amount of VAT. While changing property ownership, "transferProperty" function is used. As the VAT varies property to property and it is fixed by the Government of a country, function "initializeVat" has been used to set the VAT percentage based on the property type. It can be changed further by the proper authority.

In our system, the "isValidPropertyTransfer" function is used to check the validity of the property transfer and the function can be used to see the amount of VAT assigned to a person. The details of this implementation is available in this Github repository: https://github.com/Mamun5011/Blockchain-Based-Ownership-and-VAT-Management-System.git.

4.2   Results of Ownership and VAT Management System

Our developed smarts contract for Ownership and VAT management system were successfully deployed in a test net. While deploying, the admin address and the contract address were '$\beta 1$' and 'S' respectively. To test the functionalities of our system, all the functions of the smart contracts were called. In order to check the vulnerability and robustness of our system, adversarial attempts were triggered. In all of the phases, our system's performance was well satisfactory.

The addresses and the hashes, used while testing the system, are given below:

The addresses are:

$\beta 1$: Admin Address
$\beta 2$: Intruder address
S: contract Address

The hashes are:

X: A random Seller hash with a private key
Y: A random Buyer hash with a private key
W: A random Witness hash with a private key
Z: The combined hash of seller, buyer and witness with a private key
ψ: Hash provided by an intruder

Proof of Successful Deployment of Our Smart Contract. In Fig. 2, we have successfully deployed the smart contract "propertyTransaction" in the test net holding the admin address 'β1' to test the functionality of our proposed system. The address of the contract is 'S'. In Fig. 3, we can see that our functions are working properly.

Fig. 2. The smart contract has deployed our proposed model into a test net from admin address 'β1'

Fig. 3. Functions of the contract 'S' have been executed successfully

Initializing the VAT Percentage for a Property. Figure 4, shows that the admin can initialize VAT percentage based on property. Here, the admin has assigned 17% VAT on the "land" property value.

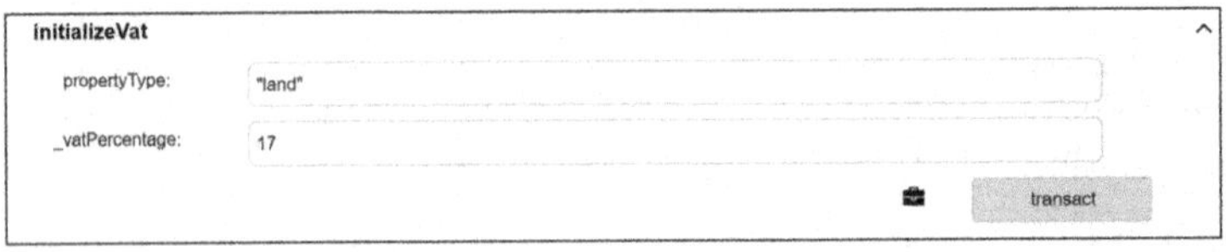

Fig. 4. Admin initializes the percentage of VAT for a type of property

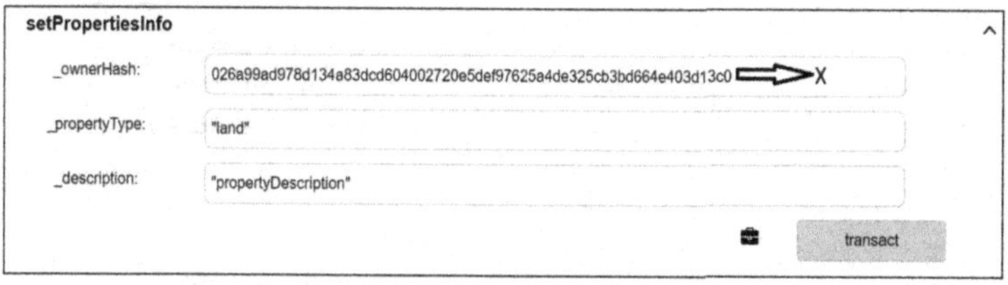

Fig. 5. Property ownership has been assigned to the person having hash 'X'

Assigning the Ownership of Property. In Fig. 5, the admin has assigned the ownership of the property of type "land" and described by "propertyDescriptipon" to the person with hash 'X'.

Verifying the Ownership of a Property. Figure 6 shows that the function "getPropertiesInfo" has been called by the admin to check the validity of the ownership if the property of type "land" and described by the "propertyDescription" belongs to the person with hash 'X'. The function returns *true*, which means the ownership is valid.

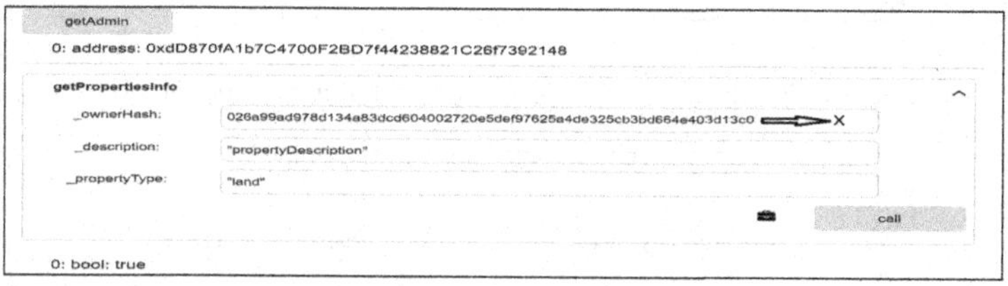

Fig. 6. Check whether the owner of land is the person having hash 'X' or not

Changing of Ownership. In Fig. 7, the ownership of a property has been changed. In this property transfer, the buyer hash was 'Y', seller hash was 'X', witness hash was 'W', property type was "land", property description was "propertyDescriptipon", combined hash was 'Z' and the value of the property was 100.

Verification for Property Transfer. The validity of a property transfer has been checked in Fig. 8. In the given information, the buyer's hash was 'Y', seller's hash was 'X', witness's hash was 'W', property type was "land", property description was "propertyDescriptipon" and combined hash was 'Z'. The function verified that it was a valid property transfer.

Transparent VAT Information. In Fig. 9, by calling the "getVatAmount" function, we can get the total amount of VAT assigned to a person. The person with hash 'Y' has the total amount of VAT 17 to pay.

Fig. 7. Property transfer from seller to buyer

Fig. 8. Check whether a property transfer is valid or not

Fig. 9. Get total amount of VAT assigned to a person having hashWithPrivatekey 'Y'

4.3   Attack by an Intruder

An intruder (the person but admin) tried to modify the ownership in Fig. 10. The intruder with address '$\beta2$' has tried to assign the ownership of the property of type "land" and described by "intruder'sDescription" to the person having hash 'ψ'.

Unauthorized Access Has Been Aborted. In Fig. 11, the adversarial attempt is successfully aborted by the system, thereby ensuring the security and robustness of our system. An intruder with the address '$\beta2$' (not the admin. Admin's address is '$\beta1$') tried to call the function "setPropertyInfo" to modify the property information. But our system denied the request.

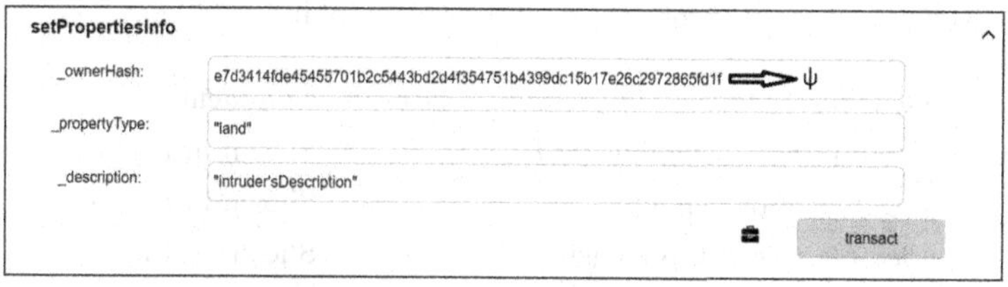

Fig. 10. Intruder's attempt to modify ownership of property

Fig. 11. System denied the intruder's request

5 Results Summary

5.1 Findings of the Ownership and VAT Management System

Smart contract "propertyTransaction" can successfully fulfil the criteria of the Digital Ownership and VAT management system building upon the digital identity. The system can successfully store the Property Ownership records in the ledgers. Property ownership can be successfully transferred from seller to buyer. VAT payment is ensured based on the property type. It is impossible to modify the ownership of a property with an unauthorized access. Table 1 illustrates the main key points of our work.

By observing the key point described above, Our proposed digital Ownership and VAT management system can be described as follows:

- All the ownership records of the citizens can be stored in a handily way. The owner of a property can easily be identified.
- It provides a valid and hassle-free way to transfer property ownership.
- The system ensures the payment of the legal amount of VAT associated to the property or products.
- The process of changing the ownership is much easier than the existing analog processes.

Table 1. Key points of our proposed digital ownership and VAT management system

Features	Result	Comments
Flexibility in assigning VAT	Yes	Shown in Fig. 4
Legality of ownership	Yes	Shown in Fig. 6
Flexible ownership transfer	Yes	Shown in Fig. 7
Property transfer validation	Yes	Shown in Fig. 8
Fair VAT payment	Yes	Shown in Fig. 9
Attack performed by an intruder	No	Shown in Fig. 10
Fraud Detection	Yes	Shown in Fig. 11

6 Conclusion

Digital identities are very crucial for every citizen and the government can integrate ownership management with digital identity. Blockchain technology can play its role to resolve security concern. There is lack of research works that integrate ownership and VAT management system with blockchain-based digital identity. In our work, a blockchain-based system has been developed to create reliable and secured digital identities for the citizen of a country using their biometric information. The ownership system has been also digitized with the help of blockchain-based digital identity through the deployment of smart contract. At the same time, VAT management system has also been developed. We have verified the robustness of our blockchain-based system. Our empirical analysis implies that the intruders can neither attack our system nor tamper the existing data in the blockchain. Our work ensures the authenticity of ownership for a property of a citizen in a country. Our blockchain-based systems are highly reliable than traditional systems. The important services of the government can be digitized merging with the blockchain-based digital identity in the future.

References

1. Mamun, M.A.A., Alam, S.M.M., Hossain, M.S., Samiruzzaman, M.: A novel approach to blockchain-based digital identity system. In: Arai, K., Kapoor, S., Bhatia, R. (eds.) FICC 2020. AISC, vol. 1129, pp. 93–112. Springer, Cham (2020). https://doi.org/10.1007/978-3-030-39445-5_9
2. Toyoda, K., Mathiopoulos, P.T., Sasase, I., Ohtsuki, T.: A novel blockchain-based product ownership management system (POMS) for anti-counterfeits in the post supply chain. IEEE Access **5**, 17465–17477 (2017)
3. Nguyen, V.-C., Pham, H.-L., Tran, T.-H., Huynh, H.-T., Nakashima, Y.: Digitizing invoice and managing VAT payment using blockchain smart contract. In: IEEE International Conference on Blockchain and Cryptocurrency (ICBC), pp. 74–77. IEEE (2019)
4. Alkhodre, A., Jan, S., Khusro, S., Ali, T., Alsaawy, Y., Yasar, M.: A blockchain-based value added tax (VAT) system: Saudi Arabia as a use-case. Int. J. Adv. Comput. Sci. Appl. **10**(9), 708–716 (2019)

5. Bitjoka, G.B., Edoa, M.M.N.: Blockchain in the implementation of VAT collection. Am. J. Comput. Sci. Technol. **3**(2), 18–26 (2020)
6. Somy, N.B., et al.: Ownership preserving AI market places using blockchain. In: 2019 IEEE International Conference on Blockchain (Blockchain), pp. 156–165 (2019)
7. Altun, C., Tavli, B., Yanikomeroglu, H.: Liberalization of digital twins of IoT-enabled home appliances via blockchains and absolute ownership rights. IEEE Commun. Mag. **57**(12), 65–71 (2019)
8. Blockchain: The Meaning of Decentralization. https://medium.com/@Vitalik Buterin/the-meaning-of-decentralization-a0c92b76a274?fbclid=IwAR0e2zSjubCj zM25PMsb3Y-G5g490Vpsv7U9GBnHPu5Xion-4dWzMMhIQYI. Accessed 12 Feb 2019
9. The Most Corrupt Countries in the World. https://www.ranker.com/list/the-most-corrupt-countries-in-the-world/info-lists. Accessed 22 Jan 2019
10. Rivera, R., Robledo, J.G., Larios, V.M., Avalos, J.M.: How digital identity on blockchain can contribute in a smart city environment. In: International Smart Cities Conference (ISC2), pp. 1–4. IEEE (2017)
11. Mudliar, K., Parekh, H., Bhavathankar, P.: A comprehensive integration of national identity with blockchain technology. In: International Conference on Communication information and Computing Technology (ICCICT), pp. 1–6. IEEE (2018)
12. Karafiloski, E., Mishev, A.: Blockchain solutions for big data challenges: a literature review. In: 17th International Conference on Smart Technologies (EUROCON), pp. 763–768. IEEE (2017)
13. Dai, F., Shi, Y., Meng, N., Wei, L., Ye, Z.: From bitcoin to cybersecurity: a comparative study of blockchain application and security issues. In: Systems and Informatics (ICSAI), pp. 975–979. IEEE (2017)
14. Abe, R., Watanabe, H., Ohashi, S., Fujimura, S., Nakadaira, A.: Storage protocol for securing blockchain transparency. In: 2018 IEEE 42nd Annual Computer Software and Applications Conference (COMPSAC), pp. 577–581. IEEE (2018)
15. Zheng, Z., Xie, S., Dai, H.-N., Chen, X., Wang, H.: Blockchain challenges and opportunities: a survey. Int. J. Web Grid Serv. **14**(4), 352–375 (2018)
16. Watanabe, H., Fujimura, S., Nakadaira, A., Miyazaki, Y., Akutsu, A., Kishigami, J.: Securing a blockchain applied to smart contracts. In: Consumer Electronics (ICCE), pp. 467–468. IEEE (2016)
17. ETHEREUM, a next generation of blockcahin and working mechanism of ethereum as a virtual machine. http://www.ethdocs.org/en/latest/introduction/what-is-ethereum.html. Accessed 24 Apr 2019
18. ETHEREUM development Tutorial. https://github.com/ethereum/wiki/wiki/Ethereum-Development-Tutorial. Accessed 24 Apr 2019
19. SOLIDITY- solidity 0.5.6 documentation. https://solidity.readthedocs.io/en/v0.5.6/. Accessed 24 Apr 2019
20. REMIX- solidity IDE. https://remix.ethereum.org/. Accessed 24 Apr 2019
21. Antipova, T.: Using blockchain technology for government auditing. In: 2018 13th Iberian Conference on Information Systems and Technologies (CISTI), pp. 1–6. IEEE (2018)
22. Chen, Y.-H., Chen, S.-H., Lin, I.-C.: Blockchain based smart contract for bidding system. In: 2018 IEEE International Conference on Applied System Invention (ICASI), pp. 208–211. IEEE (2018)

23. Meng, Z., Morizumi, T., Miyata, S., Kinoshita, H.: Design scheme of copyright management system based on digital watermarking and blockchain. In: 2018 IEEE 42nd Annual Computer Software and Applications Conference (COMPSAC), pp. 359–364. IEEE (2018)
24. Kshetri, N., Voas, J.: Blockchain in developing countries. IT Prof. **20**(2), 11–14 (2018)
25. Cheng, J.-C., Lee, N.-Y., Chi, C., Chen, Y.-H.: Blockchain and smart contract for digital certificate. In: 2018 IEEE International Conference on Applied System Invention (ICASI), pp. 1046–1051. IEEE (2018)
26. Hanifatunnisa, R., Rahardjo, B.: Blockchain based e-voting recording system design. In: 2017 11th International Conference on Telecommunication Systems Services and Applications (TSSA), pp. 1–6. IEEE (2017)
27. Yuan, C., Xu, M., Si, X., Li, B.: Blockchain with accountable CP-ABE: how to effectively protect the electronic documents. In: 2017 IEEE 23rd International Conference on Parallel and Distributed Systems (ICPADS), pp. 800–803. IEEE (2017)
28. Savelyev, A.: Copyright in the blockchain era: promises and challenges. Comput. Law Secur. Rev. **34**(3), 550–561 (2018)
29. Zhao, H., Bai, P., Peng, Y., Xu, R.: Efficient key management scheme for health blockchain. CAAI Trans. Intell. Technol. **3**(2), 114–118 (2018)
30. Dorri, A., Kanhere, S.S., Jurdak, R.: Blockchain in Internet of Things: challenges and solutions. arXiv preprint arXiv:1608.05187 (2018)
31. Ghuli, P., Kumar, U.P., Shettar, R.: A review on blockchain application for decentralized decision of ownership of IoT devices. Adv. Comput. Sci. Technol. **10**(8), 2449–2456 (2017)
32. Haldenby, P., Mahadevan, R., Lee, J.J.S., Chan, P.M., Del Vecchio, O.: Systems and methods for tracking and transferring ownership of connected devices using blockchain ledgers. Adv. Comput. Sci. Technol. (2017). Google Patents. US Patent App. 14/936,833

Predicting Type 2 Diabetes Through Machine Learning: Performance Analysis in Balanced and Imbalanced Data

Francisco Mesquita and Gonçalo Marques[(✉)][iD]

Polytechnic of Coimbra, ESTGOH, Rua General Santos Costa,
3400-124 Oliveira do Hospital, Portugal
lei193025@alunos.estgoh.ipc.pt, goncalosantosmarques@gmail.com

Abstract. Type 2 diabetes is a lifelong disease that causes a substantial increase of sugar (glucose) in the blood. Nowadays, diabetes type 2 is a major public worldwide health challenge. Therefore, it is necessary to automate the process of predicting diseases. The dataset used was the "PIMA Indians Diabetes Data Set". This dataset is imbalanced. Consequently, the authors have randomly selected 268 cases from each class to create a new balanced dataset. The objective is to analyse the impact of imbalanced data for predicting diabetes type 2. Four different machine learning methods have been applied to the original and balanced dataset. Neural network, k-nearest neighbors, Logistic Regression, and AdaBoost have been implemented with 10-fold cross-validation. Detailed information concerning the proposed model's parameters is presented. The results recommend the use of Neural Networks for predicting diabetes type 2. This method presents 71.4% and 82.3% of accuracy for the original and balanced dataset, respectively. Furthermore, the proposed method has been compared with other studies available in the state of the art. Neural Networks presented 85.9% for AUC, 82.2% for F1-Score, 82.6% for Precision, 82.3% for Recall/sensitivity and 77.6% for specificity when applied in balanced data.

Keywords: Type 2 diabetes · Data mining methods · Balanced dataset · Neural Networks

1 Introduction

World Health Organization (WHO) presents critical facts about diabetes [1]. The number of people with diabetes has risen from 108 million in 1980 to 422 million in 2014. Diabetes is a major cause of blindness, kidney failure, heart attacks, stroke, and lower limb amputation. In 2016, an estimated 1.6 million deaths were directly caused by diabetes. Furthermore, 2.2 million deaths were attributable to high blood glucose in 2012. Therefore, this subject was chosen to be studied due to its tremendous impact on public health. The before mentioned diseases are chronic and affect the way the body regulates blood sugar or glucose.

© Springer Nature Switzerland AG 2021
H. Elbiaze et al. (Eds.): UNet 2021, LNCS 12845, pp. 269–279, 2021.
https://doi.org/10.1007/978-3-030-86356-2_22

Patients with type-1 diabetes do not produce insulin. On the other hand, people with type 2 diabetes do not respond to insulin as well as they should and later in the disease often do not produce enough insulin [2].

The highest prevalence of diabetes in Europe concerning the adult population in 2019 occurred in Germany with 15.3% diagnosed with diabetes. Portugal followed with the second-highest share at 14.2 %. On the other hand, the lowest prevalence of diabetes in Europe corresponds to Ireland with at 4.4% [3]. One in two (50.1%) people living with diabetes do not know that they have diabetes [4].

Predicting diseases is essential to prevent them. This is critical for all diseases and especially for type 2 diabetes. Traditional methods of predicting whether a person may or may not have type 2 diabetes are time-consuming and are becoming increasingly inefficient when compared to machine learning. Consequently, the authors propose a machine learning approach for predicting diabetes.

The dataset chosen to study diabetes was "PIMA Indians Diabetes". Other studies have been carried out in this dataset. However, the great difference of this study is the creation of a new balanced dataset from the original data source, which is imbalanced. The number of negative cases is very different from the number of positive cases. On the one hand, the main objective of this study is to efficiently automate the recognition of possible cases of type 2 diabetes using machine learning methods in a balanced dataset. On the other hand, the main contribution of this paper is the comparison between the results of 4 different methods to predict type 2 diabetes and show the difference and importance of using balanced data.

This paper is structured as follows. In Sect. 2, a review of existent studies in the literature is presented. In Sect. 3, the authors present the dataset analysis and the methods are detailed in Sect. 4. The results and discussion is described in Sect. 5. Finally, Sect. 6 presents the main conclusions of this work.

2   Related Work

Several researchers have studied datasets for predicting type 2 diabetes, especially the PIMA dataset [5].

Rajni et al. [6] used RB-Bayes techniques. Data imputation were handled by replacing the missing values with the mean values. Cross-Validation was used. The results achieved accuracy was 72.9%.

Deepti et al. [7] used Naive Bayes (NB), Support Vector Machine (SVM), and Decision Tree (DT). They also used cross-validation through the usage of Accuracy, F-Measure, Recall, Precision, and ROC (Receiver Operating Curve) measures. By comparing the results it was concluded that Naive Bayes was the best of the three methods with 76.30% of accuracy.

Smith et al. [8] used an adaptive algorithm (adap) in a non-learning mode. In this mode, the algorithm predicted the values but did not learn or correct them if they were wrong. This study had 576 instances in the training set and 192 instances in the test set. Sensitivity and specificity were analysed as performance measures and both gave a result of 76%.

Sehly et al. [9] compared the accuracy of k-nearest neighbors (kNN), SVM, Linear SVM, Sigmoid SVM, Logistic Regression (LR), CART and NB models. They also used MSE statistic method to calculate the average error between the estimated value and the actual value by squaring them. This study uses the 10-fold cross-validation. The best results are provided by Linear discriminant analysis (LDA) with an accuracy of 77.35%.

Kayaer et al. [10], used general regression neural networks (GRNN), which is a variation to radial basis neural networks. Two other different neural network structures were used: a Multilayer Perceptron (MLP) and a radial basis function (RBF). The best result was achieved through the GRNN structure with 80.21% accuracy.

3   Dataset Analysis

We have used the PIMA Indians Diabetes Database [5]. The source for this data was the National Institute of Diabetes and Digestive and Kidney Diseases. All patients considered in the dataset are PIMA-Indian women which have at least 21 years old and live close to Arizona, Phoenix, USA. The binary response variable takes the values '0' or '1', which means that a patient may or may not have diabetes. The '0' is used when the pathology is nonexistent (test negative) and the '1' is used when the pathology is present (test positive). The attributes of the dataset are listed below:

1. Number of times pregnant
2. Plasma glucose concentration after 2 h in an oral glucose tolerance test
3. Diastolic blood pressure (mm Hg)
4. Triceps skin fold thickness (mm)
5. 2-Hour serum insulin (mu U/ml)
6. Body mass index (weight in kg/height in m^2)
7. Diabetes pedigree function
8. Age (years)
9. Target variable (0 or 1) - positive or negative

The authors do not implement feature selection methods since the main objective is to evaluate the impact of imbalanced data in the prediction of diabetes. Table 1 and Table 2 shows the feature importance on the original and balanced dataset, respectively. The features are evaluated according to Information Gain and Gain ratio as suggested by [11,12]. K. Alpan et al. used the Gain ratio to select the best 9 features out of 17 in total when using diabetes data as well [11]. Zdravevski et al. proposed a parallel implementation of the metric information gain that can be used for feature selection [12].

Table 1. Information Gain and Gain Ratio on original dataset

Attribute	Information Gain	Gain Ratio
1	0.0425	0.0215
2	0.1704	0.0852
3	0.0148	0.0007
4	0.0364	0.0183
5	0.0547	0.0302
6	0.0787	0.0394
7	0.0220	0.0110
8	0.0813	0.0407

Table 2. Information Gain and Gain Ratio on balanced dataset

Attribute	Information Gain	Gain Ratio
1	0.0605	0.0303
2	0.2083	0.1042
3	0.0362	0.0182
4	0.0473	0.0238
5	0.0742	0.0411
6	0.0675	0.0337
7	0.0159	0.0079
8	0.0850	0.0425

The most important attributes in both datasets are Plasma glucose concentration after 2 h in an oral glucose tolerance test (2) and age (8). On the other hand, the less significant attributes are Diastolic blood pressure (mm Hg) (3) and Diabetes pedigree function (7). When we statistically analyze the data we are able to have a better idea about the data distribution presented in the datasets. The statistical analysis for the original dataset is presented in Table 3.

Table 3. Original dataset statistics

Attribute	Min	Max	Mean	Standard deviation
1	0	17	3,85	3.37
2	0	199	120.89	31.95
3	0	122	69.11	19.34
4	0	99	20.54	15.94
5	0	846	79.80	115.17
6	0	67.10	31.99	7.88
7	0.08	2.42	0.47	0.33
8	21	81	33.24	11.75

This dataset is imbalanced with the value of negatives being higher than the positives. The original dataset has 768 samples. In total, 500 are negative and 268 are positive. The imbalance-ratio is 0.536. Consequently, the authors have created a new dataset that was made from this with 268 negative cases randomly selected and 268 positive cases (total positive cases). Table 4 presents the statistical analysis for the balanced dataset.

Table 4. Balanced dataset statistics

Attribute	Min	Max	Mean	Standard deviation
1	0	15	4.22	3.54
2	0	199	124.10	31.20
3	0	122	69.78	18.96
4	0	63	20.46	16.12
5	0	744	83.18	117.26
6	0	67.10	32.26	7.69
7	0.08	2.42	0.49	0.35
8	21	72	34.23	11.28

When we compare the statistical analysis with the original one, small differences are reported. Differences have more impact on the most important attributes such as attributes 2 and 8. In attribute 2, we have the same Min and Max, an increase of 3.21 on Mean and a decrease of 0.75 in the Standard deviation. In attribute 8, we have the same Min, a decrease of 9 in Max, an increase of 0.99 in Mean, and a decrease of 0.47 in Standard deviation.

4 Methods

In this study, we used KNN, Neural Network, LR and AdaBoost methods. To start obtaining the results a test environment was created through the following steps:

1. Create a new random dataset from the original
2. Test each dataset with the selected models
3. Evaluate each model with the defined evaluation methods
4. Analyse the results and find the best model

The machine used to run the experiments has the following specifications: Intel(R) Core(TM) i7-7700HQ CPU @ 2,80 GHz, 16 Gb RAM, NVIDIA GeForce GTX 1050. We used a Python based tool, Orange Data Mining Version 3.26 [13].The complete and summarized description of the parameters used in each method are presented in Table 5.

Table 5. Parameters of each method

Method	Parameters
kNN	Neighbours: 16 Metric: Euclidean Weight: Distance
Neural Network	Hidden layers: 50 Activation: ReLu Solver: L-BFGS-B Alpha: 0.005 Max iterations: 50 Replicable training: True
Logistic Regression	Regularization: Lasso (L1) Strengh (C): 8
AdaBoost	Base estimator: tree Estimators: 13 Classification: SAMME.R Regression: Linear

4.1   KNN

KNN finds the distances between a sample and all the remaining examples in the data, selecting the specified number of examples (K) closest to the query. Then, this method votes for the most frequent label (in the case of classification) or averages the labels (in the case of regression) [14]. We choose these parameters when implementing kNN: the number of neighbors used was 16, the Metric is Euclidean and the Weight is Distance.

4.2   Logistic Regression

LR is a classification model that is used when the dependent variable (output) is in the binary format such as 0 (False) or 1 (True). The logistic function, also called as sigmoid function was initially used by statisticians to describe properties of population growth in ecology. The sigmoid function is a mathematical function used to map the predicted values to probabilities. Logistic Regression has an S-shaped curve and can take values between 0 and 1 but never exactly at those limits. It has the formula of $1/(1 + e^{-value})$ [15]. The regularization used was Lasso (L1) and C = 8.

4.3   Neural Network

Neural networks are an ML technique, where the structure of the human brain inspires the algorithms. Neural networks use input data, train themselves to recognize patterns found in the data, and then predict the output for a new data [16]. We choose the following parameters when implementing Neural Networks. Hidden layers: 50, Activation: ReLu, Solver: L-BFGS-B, Alpha: 0.005, Max iterations: 50 and Replicable training: True.

4.4   AdaBoost

AdaBoost defines weights to both classifiers and data points (samples) and allow the classifiers to concentrate on observations that are difficult to be correctly identified. This method works sequentially in that the two weights are adjusted at each step as iterations of the algorithm. AdaBoost is a sequential ensemble method. Ensemble refers to a type of learning that combines several models to improve the final predictive performance [17]. The base estimator is a tree, the number of estimators is 13, the Algorithm (classification) is SAMME.R, and the Loss (Regression) is Linear.

5   Performance and Validation

5.1   Performance Metrics

Classification accuracy was the most valued metric although the Area Under Roc Curve (AUC), Precision, Recall, and F1 Score were also considered. These methods are suggested by several studies to analyse the performance of machine learning models. Deepti et al. used Accuracy, F-Measure, Recall, Precision, and ROC (Receiver Operating Curve) as performance metrics [7].

5.2   K-Fold-cross-validation

K-Fold-cross-validation consists of, for a given dataset, dividing it into K sections. Each section is used for testing at a given time. For example for K = 5, in the first iteration, the first section is used for testing and the rest for training the model, in the second iteration the second section is used for testing and the rest for training. The process is repeated until reaching the last section, in this case, Sect. 5.

Breiman, Friedman, Olshen and Stone in 1984 [18] and Kohavi in 1995 have shown that the optimal number for K is equal to 10. To test the model we are using K-Fold-cross-validation with K = 10 as suggested by Breiman et al. [18], Kayaer et al. [10], Deepti et al. [7] and Sehly et al. [9].

6   Results and Discussion

The dataset initially had imbalanced data. To analyse the performance in balanced and imbalanced data we randomly create a balanced dataset. Chawla et al. [19] mention the problems of mining in imbalanced datasets and Qiong Wei et al. The authors of [20] has a presented relevant discussions on why is critical to use balanced data. Considering this, we randomly joined the same number of positive and negative cases (268 of each) to create a balanced dataset. We can see the results for each dataset in Table 6 and Table 7.

Regarding diabetes, the most important is to identify true positive cases. If an actual negative is identified as positive it is not a critical problem. However, if an actual positive case is classified as negative presents a relevant failure.

Table 6. Imbalanced dataset results

Model	AUC	CA	F1	Precision	SE*	SP*
NN	0.745	0.714	0.712	0.711	0.714	0.790
AdaBoost	0.681	0.708	0.709	0.709	0.708	0.772
kNN	0.793	0.751	0.744	0.744	0.751	0.860
Logistic	0.828	0.777	0.771	0.772	0.777	0.882

[a]SE = Sensitivity and SP = specificity

Table 7. Balanced dataset results

Model	AUC	CA	F1	Precision	SE*	SP*
NN	0.859	0.823	0.822	0.826	0.823	0.776
AdaBoost	0.806	0.806	0.805	0.810	0.806	0.750
kNN	0.919	0.785	0.782	0.802	0.785	0.668
Logistic	0.832	0.746	0.746	0.747	0.746	0.772

[a]SE = Sensitivity and SP = specificity

Table 8 shows that it was possible to obtain better accuracy than the ADAP, GRNN, Naive Bayes, RB-Bayes and LDA methods.

This study uses a balanced dataset, 50% negative cases and 50% positive cases. Therefore, its results are more reliable than the original imbalanced dataset with a proportion of 65% negative cases to only 35% positive cases. A high sensitivity means that there are few false-negative results. Consequently, fewer cases of type 2 diabetes are miss-classified. In this case, sensitivity is more significant than specificity because is essential to predict all true positive cases or in other words, we need to avoid false negatives.

In this paper, we show all the scoring metrics and parameters for each method. However, the other analysed studies do not provide detailed information concerning the proposed model's parameters. Therefore, we can not reproduce their methods in the created balanced dataset and present a more reliable comparison.

Table 8. Other results comparison

Method	Author	CA	SP	SE
GRNN [10]	Kayear et.al	0.802	–	–
ADAP [8]	Smith et al.	–	0.760	0.760
Naive Bayes [7]	Deepti et al.	0.763	–	0.763
RB-Bayes [6]	Rajni et al.	0.729	–	–
LDA [9]	Sehly et al.	0.773	–	–
Proposed (NN)	**This study**	**0.823**	**0.776**	**0.823**

[a]SE = Sensitivity and SP = specificity

Kayear et al. used GRNN with the same validation (k-cross-validation with K = 10) in the original dataset [10]. This study only presents the accuracy metric. The authors report 80.2% of accuracy, 0.021 (2.1%) below comparing with the obtained in this study.

Deepti et al. obtain their best result using Naive Bayes in the original dataset [7]. They used k-cross-validation with k = 10 as well and he used practically the same metrics that we used in this study. Their results are below compared with the method we propose. Their model had 76.3%, 0.06 (6%) below in accuracy and sensitivity compared with the proposed model.

The ADAP model implemented by Smith et al. used an adaptive algorithm with 576 instances in training and 192 instances in test [8]. They achieved 76%, 0.016 (1.6%) below in specificity, and 0.060 (6%) below in sensitivity compared with the proposed model.

Rajni et al. implemented an RB-Bayes model in the original dataset and used cross-validation as well [6]. Their results report 72.9%, 0.094 (9.4%) below in accuracy comparing to our results.

LDA model was implemented by Sehly et al. and verified by MSE statistical method [9]. They used k-cross-validation with K = 10, however, the authors only presented the accuracy value. The authors report 77.3% of accuracy, 0.05 (5%) below comparing with the proposed method in this study.

7   Conclusion

Type 2 diabetes is a chronic condition that affects the way your body metabolizes sugar (glucose). The importance of better predictions on whether a person may or may not have type 2 diabetes is essential. In this study, we had analyzed the PIMA dataset. This dataset is imbalanced (65%/35%). This work focuses on a dataset which is imbalanced in a different way transforming it into a new balanced dataset. Therefore, we created a new balanced dataset (50%/50%). The results suggest that balanced data could perform better with the same parameters applied in the imbalanced dataset. The authors tested 4 different methods, Neural network, kNN, LR, and AdaBoost using 10-fold cross-validation. This study recommends Neural Networks and outperformed other studies which use this dataset. However, these studies were made in a created balanced dataset. Neural Networks presented 85.9% for AUC, 82.3% for Accuracy, 82.2% for F1-Score, 82.6% for Precision, 82.3% for Recall/sensitivity and 77.6% for specificity. Nevertheless, this work has limitations. Firstly, the dataset used does not consider important factors to predict diabetes. According to the National Institute of Diabetes and Digestive and Kidney Diseases, other important factors include family history, physical activity, and depression. Hyper-parameter choices can also be a limitation because we only do one random sample to balance data when we could do more independent runs to pick-up different samples from the dataset. Another limitation is that we only tested the models on PIMA dataset. Therefore, we can not ensure if it will maintain the accuracy in other datasets. We use this dataset with these limitations because it is a public one since collecting diabetes data is very challenging due to GDPR regulation.

As future work, we aim to create a new dataset containing features that have been proved to be essential on predicting type 2 diabetes. Moreover, the authors aim to study the impact of oversampling methods such as SMOTE and their respective variants.

Acknowledgements. This work was supported by the Polytechnic of Coimbra (EST-GOH). We thank Polytechnic of Coimbra (ESTGOH) for their continuous support in this work.

References

1. "Diabetes" World Wealth Organization 8 June 2020, 27 December 2020. https://www.who.int/news-room/fact-sheets/detail/diabetes
2. Osborn, C.O.: Type 1 and Type 2 diabetes: what's the difference? Healthline 28 October 2020, 27 December 2020. https://www.healthline.com/health/difference-between-type-1-and-type2-diabetes
3. Stewart, C.: Prevalence of diabetes in adult population in Europe 2019, by country. Statista, 24 Jun 2020, 2 January 2021. https://www.statista.com/statistics/1081006/prevalence-of-diabetes-in-europe/
4. Saeedi, P., et al.: Global and regional diabetes prevalence estimates for 2019 and projections for 2030 and 2045: results from the International Diabetes Federation Diabetes Atlas, 9th edn. Diabetes Research and Clinical Practice, vol. 157, p. 107843, November 2019, https://doi.org/10.1016/j.diabres.2019.107843
5. Smith, J.W., et al.: Using the ADAP learning algorithm to forecast the onset of diabetes mellitus. In: Proceedings of the Annual Symposium on Computer Application in Medical Care. American Medical Informatics Association (1988)
6. Rajni, B., Bagga, A.: RB-Bayes algorithm for the prediction of diabetic in Pima Indian dataset. Int. J. Electr. Comput. Eng. **9**(6), 4866 (2019)
7. Sisodia, D., Sisodia, D.S.: Prediction of diabetes using classification algorithms. Proc. Comput. Sci. **132**, 1578–1585 (2018)
8. Smith, J.W., Everhart, J.E., Dickson, W.C., Knowler, W.C., Johannes, R.S.: Using the ADAP learning algorithm to forecast the onset of diabetes mellitus. In: Proceedings Symposium on Computer Applications and Medical Care, pp. 261–265. IEEE Computer Society Press, Piscataway (1988)
9. Sehly, R., Mezher, M.: Comparative analysis of classification models for pima dataset. In: 2020 International Conference on Computing and Information Technology (ICCIT-1441), Tabuk, Saudi Arabia, pp. 1–5 (2020). https://doi.org/10.1109/ICCIT-144147971.2020.9213821
10. Kayaer, K., Yildirim, T.: Medical diagnosis on Pima Indian diabetes using general regression neural networks. In: Proceedings of the International Conference on Artificial Neural Networks and Neural Information Processing (2003)
11. Alpan, K.,, İlgi, G.S.: Classification of diabetes dataset with data mining techniques by using WEKA approach. In: 2020 4th International Symposium on Multidisciplinary Studies and Innovative Technologies (ISMSIT), Istanbul, Turkey, pp. 1–7 (2020). https://doi.org/10.1109/ISMSIT50672.2020.9254720
12. Zdravevski, E., et al.: Feature ranking based on information gain for large classification problems with mapreduce. In: 2015 IEEE Trustcom/BigDataSE/ISPA, vol. 2. IEEE (2015)

13. Demšar, J., et al.: Orange: data mining toolbox in Python. J. Mach. Learn. Res. **14**(1), 2349–2353 (2013)

14. Kramer, O.: K-nearest neighbors. In: Dimensionality Reduction with Unsupervised Nearest Neighbors, pp. 13–23. Springer, Heidelberg (2013). https://doi.org/10.1007/978-3-642-38652-7_2

15. Kleinbaum, D.G., et al.: Logistic Regression. Springer, New York (2002). https://doi.org/10.1007/b97379

16. Yegnanarayana, B.: Artificial Neural Networks. PHI Learning Pvt. Ltd. (2009)

17. Schapire, R.E.: Explaining AdaBoost. In: Schölkopf, B., Luo, Z., Vovk, V. (eds.) Empirical Inference, pp. 37–52. Springer, Heidelberg (2013). https://doi.org/10.1007/978-3-642-41136-6_5

18. Breiman, L., Friedman, J.H., Olshen, R.A., Stone, C.J.: Classification and Regression Trees. Wadsworth & Books/Cole Advanced Boks & Software, Monterey (1984)

19. Chawla, N.V.: Data mining for imbalanced datasets: an overview. In: Maimon, O., Rokach, L. (eds.) Data Mining and Knowledge Discovery Handbook, pp. 875–886. Springer, Boston (2009). https://doi.org/10.1007/978-0-387-09823-4_45

20. Wei Q, Dunbrack RL Jr. The role of balanced training and testing data sets for binary classifiers in bioinformatics. PLoS ONE **8**(7), e67863 (013). PMID: 23874456, PMCID: PMC3706434. https://doi.org/10.1371/journal.pone.0067863

Follow Recommendation in Social Networks

Ferdaous Affan[✉], Dounia Lotfi, and Ahmed Drissi El Maliani

LRIT, Rabat IT Center, Faculty of Sciences, Mohammed V University in Rabat, Rabat, Morocco
{ferdaous.affan,d.lotfi,a.elmaliani}@um5r.ac.ma

Abstract. Social Networks (SN) constitute a major component of our daily lives. Not only do they allow users to stay in touch with friends and family, but they also allow them to follow their favorite celebrities or people of interest. Such relationships within the social graph are most of the time one-directional and SN where this type of relations exists are directed networks. Link Prediction (LP) is used to analyze these networks and predict the creation of links in the future. However, most of LP metrics that have been proposed consider only undirected graphs, and leave out the most relevant aspect of a directed network which is the asymmetrical nature of its edges. In this work, we review proposed adaptations of LP measures for directed graphs and propose our own adaptation of a novel LP metric, which takes into account path depth and in-degrees and out-degrees of nodes. Using Area Under Curve (AUC), we compare the accuracy of all these measures on 3 directed social networks.

Keywords: Social Networks · Link Prediction · Directed Networks

1 Introduction

Social interactions of human beings have come a long way from their ancient primitive form to the highly developed technologies of the present age. The advent of new means of communication, and especially Social Networks (SN), has revolutionized the way we communicate. The importance of SN is such that research has emerged from different fields studying their evolution, dynamics, global structure, and other characteristics that may be useful. SN offer a way for people to share different types of content (text, image, video, etc.) and to easily interact with each other, individually or through groups and communities. These interactions create complex and evolving relationships within the SN, which can be represented and analyzed through graphs, where nodes represent users and the edges between them determine the relationships of interest that exist between these individuals [1]. Depending on the type of relationship and social networks, the edges between nodes may be undirected or directed. For example, friendship between users on Facebook is mutual: both users have to agree to share a relationship, thus making Facebook an undirected network. Instagram or Twitter on the other hand, allow users to follow other users without the need for the relationship to be mutual. These kinds of networks are therefore directed. The discovery of patterns or relationships within the network represents a major challenge of SN analysis. When these patterns consider the identification of links that may occur in the future, we speak of Link Prediction (LP).

© Springer Nature Switzerland AG 2021
H. Elbiaze et al. (Eds.): UNet 2021, LNCS 12845, pp. 280–292, 2021.
https://doi.org/10.1007/978-3-030-86356-2_23

Link prediction can be defined as the problem of estimating the probability of creation or disappearance of a link between two nodes in the near future, based on links that occurred in the past [2]. LP has many applications. In E-commerce, it is mostly used for building recommendation systems [3, 4]. LP can also be used as a tool to discover hidden groups and links within criminal networks [5–7]. In Bioinformatics, Link Prediction has been used to predict protein-protein interactions (PPI) [8]. In the context of social networks, LP can be applied to predict and recommend friendships or users to follow [9–11].

Depending on the structure of the social graph, many LP approaches have been proposed, generally classified in 3 categories [12]: Probabilistic models [13–16], Maximum likelihood methods [17], and Similarity-based [18]. Probabilistic methods base link prediction on an abstract model of the network. Assuming that the network fits a particular model, the parameters of the model are estimated and the probability of formation of each possible link is calculated. As for maximum likelihood methods, the probability of link existence is calculated based on a set of extracted rules. The likelihood of the observed structure is maximized and the likelihood of non-observed links can be calculated through the extracted rules. One of the major drawbacks of these first two methods is that they can be hard to compute when networks are very large. It is argued [12] that the simplest approach to link prediction is similarity-based methods, where a S_{xy} score is assigned for each pair of nodes x and y. This score is defined as the similarity (or proximity) between x and y. All unobserved links are ranked according to their scores: the higher the score the higher the chance of those nodes being linked. Similarity-based methods have the advantage of being more scalable, especially the ones that use the structural property of the network (local and global, node-dependent and path-dependent, etc.)

However, many of the existing LP studies and measures analyze networks in the same way, assuming that they are undirected, disregarding asymmetrical relations that exist in directed networks [12]. While these measures allow the prediction of a link being created between two nodes, they fail to consider its direction. There are many SN where the connections between users have an asymmetrical nature. For example, it is usual in SN such as Instagram, Youtube or Twitter, for a person to follow a celebrity without them following her back, thus making the relationship in the social graph one-directional. To predict the creation of links in such networks, metrics that have been designed for undirected graphs can be adapted [19] to take into account the direction of the edges.

In this work, we focus on Link Prediction in directed networks and specifically, on the adaptation of existing Similarity-based measures to take into account the direction of edges in the social graph. Our key contributions are as follow:

- We investigate and compare Link Prediction metrics for directed networks.
- We propose an extended measure for directed graphs based on paths and in-degrees and out-degrees.
- We compare between 3 datasets (Wiki-Vote, Twitter and Google+) in terms of in-degree distribution.
- We test all of the presented metrics for directed networks and compare their results using AUC.

This work is structured along these lines: In Sect. 2, we present different Similarity-based metrics for undirected, unweighted graphs. We then introduce the adaptation of these indexes for directed networks. In Sect. 3, we propose an adaptation of a novel parameter free similarity measure that was recently proposed for undirected and unweighted graphs [20]. This adaptation considers path length between a source node and a destination node, and also the in and out neighbors of these nodes, thus allowing as well the prediction of link direction. We then evaluate on 3 directed social networks the performance of ranking of this metric and 10 existing ones using Area under Curve (AUC), and compare their results.

2   Related Works

The aim [18] of link prediction algorithms is to analyze existing nodes, links and their attributes to predict the possibility of potential links, which are likely to happen over a period of time. In this section, we first present the similarity-based link prediction measures for undirected and unweighted networks. Next, we review the adaptation of these measures for directed graphs.

2.1   Similarity-Based LP Measures for Undirected Graphs

Let $G(V, E)$ be an undirected and unweighted graph where V is the set of vertices and E is the set of edges. Throughout this section the symbols x and y, denote nodes, N denotes the number of nodes in the network. $\Gamma(x)$ and $\Gamma(y)$ denote the neighbor sets of these nodes and kx and ky denote the degree of nodes x and y, respectively. Table 1 resumes the most notable node-based similarity measures.

Node-Based Similarity Measures

Table 1. Node-based similarity measures

Metric	Equation	Comment
Common Neighbor (CN) [21]	$\lvert \Gamma(x) \cap \Gamma(y) \rvert$	Intuitively, two nodes x and y are more likely to have a link if they have many common neighbors
Jaccard coefficient (JC) [22]	$\frac{\lvert \Gamma(x) \cap \Gamma(y) \rvert}{\lvert \Gamma(x) \cup \Gamma(y) \rvert}$	The importance is given to the nodes that are strongly connected, rather than those having a lot of neighbors
Sørensen Index (SI) [23]	$\frac{2\lvert \Gamma(x) \cap \Gamma(y) \rvert}{k_x + k_y}$	Proposed by Sørensen in 1948 to measure similarities between species. Nodes with common neighbors have higher similarity when they have fewer neighbors in total
Preferential attachment (PA) [24]	$k_x \times k_y$	It is based on the idea that the more neighbors a node has, the higher the probability of it generating links

(continued)

Table 1. (*continued*)

Metric	Equation	Comment
Hub Promoted Index (HP) [25]	$\frac{\|\Gamma(x) \cap \Gamma(y)\|}{min\{k_x, k_y\}}$	HP is defined as the ratio of the common neighbors of nodes x and y with the minimum of nodes x and y degrees
Hub Depressed Index (HD) [25]	$\frac{\|\Gamma(x) \cap \Gamma(y)\|}{max\{k_x, k_y\}}$	Similarly to the previous index, a measure with the opposite effect on hubs was also considered
Leicht-Holme-Newman Index (LHN) [26]	$\frac{\|\Gamma(x) \cap \Gamma(y)\|}{k_x \times k_y}$	This index assigns higher similarity to pairs of nodes with more common neighbors than the maximum possible
Salton Index (SA) [27]	$\frac{\|\Gamma(x) \cap \Gamma(y)\|}{\sqrt{k_x \times k_y}}$	This metric considers that the similarity between two nodes is given by the common cosine measure
Adamic-Adar coefficient (AA) [28]	$\sum_{z \in \Gamma(x) \cap \Gamma(y)} \frac{1}{log k_z}$	This index assigns weight to common neighbors that have low degree
Resource Allocation Index (RA) [29]	$\sum_{z \in \Gamma(x) \cap \Gamma(y)} \frac{1}{k_z}$	Considering a pair of nodes, x and y, that are not directly connected, node x may send some resource to y, with their common neighbors playing the role of transmitters
Path depth and node degree similarity measure [20]	$\frac{\left\| path_{x,y}^{length \leq l} \right\|}{k_x + k_y + 1}$	This topological, node attributes-based method considers the number of simple paths from a source to a destination node and also the degree of both nodes. $\left\| path_{x,y}^{length \leq l} \right\|$ is the number of paths from x to y with $length \leq l$, l is the depth of the path, k_x and k_y the degrees of x and y respectively

All of the metrics presented above were designed for undirected networks. There are, however, many instances where a social graph is directed, meaning that links that may occur in the future may be one-directional: for example a user on Twitter choosing to follow a celebrity. The likelihood of this user being followed back (making the relationship in the graph mutual), is very low, thus the link created is directed. To predict the existence of such links and their direction, new metrics adapted for the specificity of directed graph should be used.

2.2 Link Prediction in Directed Graphs

To extend link prediction algorithms to directed networks, the characteristics of directed networks should be taken into account. The most relevant aspect of a directed graph is the asymmetrical nature of its edges.

Yan Yu et al. [30] describe in their work link prediction for directed networks based on a directed graph $G(V, E)$, where V represents a set of nodes and E represents a set of asymmetric links among these nodes. They state in their research that the analysis of links becomes more complex when applied to directed graphs. For undirected networks a link is symmetric: the link is either present or absent.

When links are asymmetric or directed, there are four states between two nodes: node x towards node y (x → y), y towards x (y → x), x and y are mutually connected (x ↔ y), or x and y are not connected. If a directed link exists from x to y, it could be said that y is more important for x than x is for y, and that the directed link functions as an indicator of the direction in which information flows within the network. Thus, it can be naturally deduced that, in such networks, LP will not only estimate the probability that a link will connect two nodes x and y, but will be adapted to estimate the probability of a link going from node x to node y, this probability being different from that of a link going from node y to node x.

Considering the above, [30] introduce the definitions of the sets of in and out neighbors, and in degrees and out degrees of a node, which result from the adaptation of the concepts of neighbors and node degree, respectively, defined for link prediction in directed networks.

The set of out-neighbors of a node (x) is composed of the nodes that are connected to that node through an out-link: $\Gamma_{out}(x) = \{v \in V | (x, v) \in E\}$. The set of in-neighbors of a node (x) is composed of the nodes that are connected to that node through an in-link: $\Gamma_{in}(x) = \{v \in V | (v, x) \in E\}$. The out-degree k_x^{out} of a node corresponds to the number of edges or links connected to that node through an out-link: $k_x^{out} = |\Gamma_{out}(x)|$. The in-degree k_x^{in} of a node corresponds to the number of edges or links connected to that node through an in-link: $k_x^{in} = |\Gamma_{in}(x)|$. Taking these specifications as a starting point it becomes possible to adapt similarity-based link prediction metrics for directed networks.

In their work, Xue Zhang et al. [19] attempt to adapt classical link prediction measures used in undirected networks for directed ones, to predict both the existence and the direction of an edge between two nodes. Adapted metrics are given in Table 2. The authors argue that from the perspective of information diffusion, the more out-neighbors x has the greater its capacity to transmit information; the more in-neighbors y has the greater its aptitude to attract or collect information, making it more likely that a link between x and y might be created in the future. The effect of in-neighbors is thus considered insignificant.

Table 2. Local similarity measures and their corresponding adaptation for directed networks

Metric	Undirected graph	Directed graph
Common neighbor	$|\Gamma(x) \cap \Gamma(y)|$	$|\Gamma_{out}(x) \cap \Gamma_{in}(y)|$
Jaccard	$\dfrac{|\Gamma(x) \cap \Gamma(y)|}{|\Gamma(x) \cup \Gamma(y)|}$	$\dfrac{|\Gamma_{out}(x) \cap \Gamma_{in}(y)|}{|\Gamma_{out}(x) \cup \Gamma_{in}(y)|}$
Sørensen	$\dfrac{2|\Gamma(x) \cap \Gamma(y)|}{k_x + k_y}$	$\dfrac{2|\Gamma_{out}(x) \cap \Gamma_{in}(y)|}{k_x^{out} + k_y^{in}}$
Preferential attachment	$k_x \times k_y$	$k_x^{out} \times k_y^{in}$
Hub promoted	$\dfrac{|\Gamma(x) \cap \Gamma(y)|}{min\{k_x, k_y\}}$	$\dfrac{|\Gamma_{out}(x) \cap \Gamma_{in}(y)|}{min\{k_x^{out}, k_y^{in}\}}$

(continued)

Table 2. (*continued*)

Metric	Undirected graph	Directed graph
Hub depressed	$\dfrac{\|\Gamma(x)\cap\Gamma(y)\|}{max\{k_x,k_y\}}$	$\dfrac{\|\Gamma_{out}(x)\cap\Gamma_{in}(y)\|}{max\{k_x^{out},k_y^{in}\}}$
Leicht-Holme-Newman index	$\dfrac{\|\Gamma(x)\cap\Gamma(y)\|}{k_x\times k_y}$	$\dfrac{\|\Gamma_{out}(x)\cap\Gamma_{in}(y)\|}{k_x^{out}\times k_y^{in}}$
Salton	$\dfrac{\|\Gamma(x)\cap\Gamma(y)\|}{\sqrt{k_x\times k_y}}$	$\dfrac{\|\Gamma_{out}(x)\cap\Gamma_{in}(y)\|}{\sqrt{k_x^{out}\times k_y^{in}}}$
Adamic adar	$\displaystyle\sum_{z\in\Gamma(x)\cap\Gamma(y)}\frac{1}{\log k_z}$	$\displaystyle\sum_{z\in\Gamma_{out}(x)\cap\Gamma_{in}(y)}\frac{1}{\log k_z^{out}}$
Resource allocation	$\displaystyle\sum_{z\in\Gamma(x)\cap\Gamma(y)}\frac{1}{k_z}$	$\displaystyle\sum_{z\in\Gamma_{out}(x)\cap\Gamma_{in}(y)}\frac{1}{k_z^{out}}$

3 DiPaDe: Path Depth and Node Degree Similarity Measure for Directed Networks

We introduced above a new parameter-free measure proposed by Jibouni et al. [20]. This index takes into consideration the number of paths between two nodes and their degree. The authors proved through their work that this new metric achieved a high performance of ranking for path lengths l = 2 and l = 3. However, as most existing works in LP, [20] assumed the network to be undirected, thus failing to consider the orientation of the edges, which may lead to loss of accuracy in link prediction in case of directed graphs. We propose DiPaDe, an extension of the metric to directed networks, based on in-degrees and out-degrees. Let G(V, E) be a directed, unweighted graph where V represents a set of nodes, E represents a set of directed links between these nodes, and where self-connections are not allowed. While in [19] calculation takes into account only out neighbors and the effect of in neighbors is considered insignificant, we believe that to accurately predict the orientation of a link, both in and out neighbors should be included in calculation. Therefore, DiPaDe calculates the probability of both in-coming and out-going links of a node.

3.1 Out-Going Link Prediction Measure

To predict the probability of an out-going link being created form a node x to a node y (x → y), the adapted measure for directed networks is given as follows:

$$DiPaDe_{xy}^{out} = \frac{\left|path_{x,y}^{length\leq l}\right|}{k_x^{out} + k_y^{out} + 1} \qquad (1)$$

Where:

- $\left|path_{x,y}^{length \leq l}\right|$ is the number of paths from x to y with $length \leq l$,
- l is the depth of the path.
- k_x^{out} and k_y^{out} the out-degrees of x and y respectively.

3.2 In-Coming Link Prediction Measure

To predict the probability of an in-coming link being created form a node x to a node y ($x \leftarrow y$), the adapted measure for directed networks is given as follows:

$$DiPaDe_{xy}^{in} = \frac{\left|path_{x,y}^{length \leq l}\right|}{k_x^{in} + k_y^{in} + 1} \tag{2}$$

Where:

- $\left|path_{x,y}^{length \leq l}\right|$ is the number of paths from x to y with $length \leq l$,
- l is the depth of the path
- k_x^{in} and k_y^{in} the in-degrees of x and y respectively.

3.3 Experimental Results

To evaluate the performance of ranking of the adapted measures for directed networks, we test them on 3 different real-world datasets and using AUC, we compare their results.

Evaluation Metric

To test the adapted metrics, first the datasets used are split into a training graph $G_{train}(V, E_{train})$ and a testing graph $G_{test}(V, E_{test})$. G_{train} consists of 90% of links and all nodes, and G_{test} consists of 10% of edges, where $E = E_{train} \cup E_{test}$ and $E_{train} \cap E_{test} = 0$. To evaluate and compare the measures, we will use AUC (Area Under Curve), the most commonly used metric to evaluate the quality results of Link Prediction [31]. This index can be interpreted as the probability that a randomly selected positive instance appears over a randomly selected negative instance in the score space [32]. In the context of link prediction, given all unobserved links, the value of AUC can be interpreted as the probability that a randomly chosen link excluded from the test set will have a higher score than a randomly chosen non-existent link. To calculate the value of the indicator, at each time point an excluded link and a non-existing link are randomly selected to compare their scores, if among n independent comparisons, there are n' times when the excluded link has a higher score and n'' times they have the same score, the value of AUC is:

$$AUC = \frac{n' + 0.5\, n''}{n} \tag{3}$$

Datasets

3 directed real-life networks are used for empirical test and validation. A brief introduction of each dataset is introduced as follows:

Wiki-vote [33]: Wikipedia voting data from the inception of Wikipedia till January 2008. The dataset contains 7115 nodes and 103,689 edges. Nodes in the network represent Wikipedia users and a directed edge from node *x* to node *y* represents that user x voted on user *y*. The in-degree distribution of this network is given in Fig. 1.

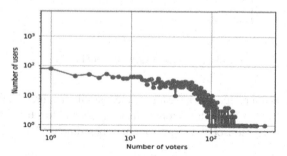

Fig. 1. In-degree distribution of Wiki-Vote

The average degree of the network is $|k| = 14, 57$. Compared to the other networks used in our experimentation, Wiki-Vote has more edges but fewer nodes. This is due to the nature of the network and its purpose, which is to elect Wikipedia administrators.

Twitter [34]: A directed network containing a subset of Twitter user–user following information (23,370 nodes and 33,101 edges). A node represents a user. A directed edge indicates that the user represented by the left node follows the user represented by the right node. The in-degree distribution of this network is given Fig. 2.

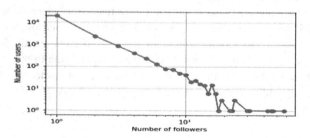

Fig. 2. In-degree distribution of Twitter

Compared to Wiki-Vote, this network has fewer edges, but more nodes, due to the fact that Twitter has more users than Wiki-Vote has voters. Also, the average degree of Twitter is $|k| = 2, 83$, which is less than Wiki-Vote's, mostly because this dataset is a subset of a larger Twitter-based network.

Google+ [34]: A directed network containing a subset of Google+ user–user links (23,628 nodes and 39,242 edges). A node represents a user, and a directed edge denotes that one user has the other user in his circles. Figure 3 depicts the network's in-degree distribution.

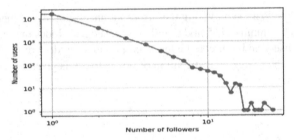

Fig. 3. In-degree distribution of Google+

Google+ and Twitter networks have more or less similar features. The average degree of Google+ is $|k| = 3,32$, which is more than Twitter's and less than Wiki-Vote. Once again, this network is a subset of a larger Google+ based network.

Path Depth l Influence on LP

As explained above, our proposed adapted metric takes as a parameter l the number of paths from a source node to a destination node. However, in the case of a directed network, the paths have the added restriction that the links are all directed in the same direction. We tested the metric on the 3 datasets introduced above, to evaluate the impact of the parameter l on the performance of the measure for the prediction of both out-going and in-coming links, for different lengths ranging from 0 to 10.

Figure 4 and 5 show the results of the impact of path depth on the accuracy of the proposed metric. For Wiki-Vote, path length $l = 3$ is where the AUC score is the highest, anything beyond that and AUC starts to decrease. However, as it happens, on both out-going and in-coming link prediction for datasets Google+ and Twitter, DiPaDe performed best for paths $l = 6$ and $l = 7$. This can be tied to the "algorithmic small-world hypothesis" [35] that relies on the "six degrees of separation" assertion. It is assumed that a user can be connected to another with many paths of different length, through human chains [36]. Taking into consideration longer paths expands the user's "neighborhood horizon" where other patterns might be discovered. Note that the accuracy of the metric for both out-going and in-coming links remains stable, whatever the length of the path chosen.

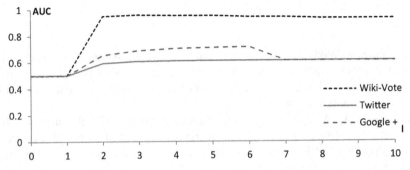

Fig. 4. AUC Scores of in-coming links for different path lengths on 3 networks

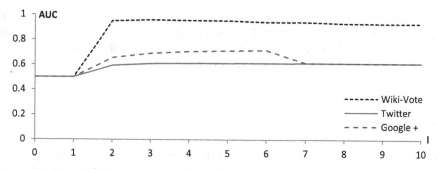

Fig. 5. AUC Scores of out-going links for different path lengths on 3 networks

Comparison with other LP Measures

In this section we compare the AUC results of the adapted LP measures in directed graphs.

Table 3. AUC Score for compared link prediction measures

	Out-going link prediction			In-coming link prediction		
	Wiki-Vote	Twitter	Google+	Wiki-Vote	Twitter	Google+
CN	0.7449	0.5198	0.5871	0.7452	0.5836	0.6140
PA	0.6994	0.5245	0.4267	0.7438	0.3212	0.4308
AA	0.2549	0.4801	0.4932	0.2545	0.4163	0.3850
SA	0.7403	0.5179	0.5783	0.7443	0.5835	0.6103
SI	0.7413	0.5198	0.5792	0.7442	0.5843	0.6103
LHN	0.7339	0.5197	0.5667	0.7396	0.5835	0.6095
RA	0.7447	0.5196	0.5856	0.7455	0.5836	0.6148
HD	0.7413	0.5198	0.5792	0.7441	0.5838	0.6103
HP	0.7377	0.5197	0.5785	0.7430	0.5837	0.6112
Jaccard	0.7412	0.5198	0.5793	0.7440	0.5835	0.6102
DiPaDe	**0.9583**	**0.6124**	**0.7159**	**0.9583**	**0.6124**	**0.7159**

In Table 3, we can see that Link Prediction measures that were adapted for directed networks have different performances on the 3 datasets. All of them, except DiPaDe, have varying AUC scores for out-going and in-coming link prediction. It can be noted that AA is the least performing in all 3 datasets. However, it is obvious that DiPaDe, which takes into account simple paths between two nodes, and their in-degree and out-degree, has the highest AUC value. It out-performs all of the metrics in all of the tested datasets especially in Wiki-Vote (tested dataset with the biggest volume), where it achieves a high AUC result. This proves that the proposed measure performs well in large scale networks. The lowest scoring of the metric was in the Twitter network. Unlike other measures, our proposed metric's performance of ranking in both out-going and incoming links remains stable. DiPaDe has a clearly significantly higher performance than the other metrics. While more tests need to be done to ascertain that, it seems to us that considering path depth can also add to the performance of ranking of Link Prediction in directed networks.

4   Conclusion

We focused in this paper on Link Prediction in directed networks. We first introduced LP metrics that were mainly proposed for undirected and unweighted graphs, and then presented the adaptation of these measures to directed graphs. Finally, we proposed DiPaDe, an adaptation to directed networks of a novel index based on path depth and node similarity. DiPaDe takes into account the in-neighbors and out-neighbors of a node, therefore allowing the prediction of two nodes being connected and the orientation of the edge. We investigated the impact of length l on the results of the proposed metric and found that for Wiki-Vote the best performance was for $l = 3$, while for Twitter and Google+ it was for $l = 7$ and $l = 6$. When we compared DiPaDe with 10 other metrics on 3 real-world social networks, AUC scores proved that it achieved the best results.

Acknowledgement. This research is carried out as part of the project «Plateforme logicielle d'intégration de stratégies d'immunisation contre la pandémie COVID-19» funded by the grant of the Hassan II Academy of Sciences and Technology of Morocco.

References

1. Hasan, M., Chaoji, V., Salem, S., Zaki, M.: Link Prediction Using Supervised Learning (2006)
2. Liben-Nowell, D., Kleinberg, J.: The link-prediction problem for social networks. J. Am. Soc. Inf. Sci. Technol. **58**, 1019–1031 (2007)
3. Li, J., Zhang, L., Meng, F., Li, F.: Recommendation algorithm based on link prediction and domain knowledge in retail transactions. Procedia Comput. Sci. **31**, 875–881 (2014)
4. Zhu, C., Li, J., Somasundaram, S.: Global Link Prediction for E-commerce using Deep Networks 10 (2019)
5. Berlusconi, G., Calderoni, F., Parolini, N., Verani, M., Piccardi, C.: Link prediction in criminal networks: a tool for criminal intelligence analysis. PLOS ONE **11**, e0154244 (2016)
6. Lim, M., Abdullah, A., Jhanjhi, N.Z., Supramaniam, M.: Hidden link prediction in criminal networks using the deep reinforcement learning technique. Computers **8**, 8 (2019)
7. Calderoni, F., Catanese, S., De Meo, P., Ficara, A., Fiumara, G.: Robust link prediction in criminal networks: a case study of the Sicilian Mafia. Expert Syst. Appl. **161**, 113666 (2020)
8. Lei, C., Ruan, J.: A novel link prediction algorithm for reconstructing protein–protein interaction networks by topological similarity. Bioinformatics **29**, 355–364 (2013)
9. Parimi, R.: LDA based approach for predicting friendship links in live journal social network (2010). https://krex.k-state.edu/dspace/handle/2097/4624
10. Papadimitriou, A., Symeonidis, P., Manolopoulos, Y.: Friendlink: link prediction in social networks via bounded local path traversal. In: 2011 International Conference on Computational Aspects of Social Networks (CASoN), pp. 66–71 (2011)

11. Junuthula, R., Xu, K., Devabhaktuni, V.: Leveraging friendship networks for dynamic link prediction in social interaction networks. In: Proceedings of the International AAAI Conference on Web Social Media, p. 12 (2018)
12. Lü, L., Zhou, T.: Link prediction in complex networks: a survey. Phys. Stat. Mech. Its Appl. **390**, 1150–1170 (2011). https://doi.org/10.1016/j.physa.2010.11.027
13. Wang, C., Satuluri, V., Parthasarathy, S.: Local probabilistic models for link prediction. In: Seventh IEEE International Conference on Data Mining (ICDM 2007), pp. 322–331 (2007)
14. Ninagawa, A., Eguchi, K.: Link prediction using probabilistic group models of network structure. In: Proceedings of the 2010 ACM Symposium on Applied Computing, pp. 1115–1116. Association for Computing Machinery, New York (2010)
15. Luna, J.E.O., Revoredo, K., Cozman, F.G.: Link prediction using a probabilistic description logic. J. Braz. Comput. Soc. **19**(4), 397–409 (2013). https://doi.org/10.1007/s13173-013-0108-8
16. Das, S., Das, S.K.: A probabilistic link prediction model in time-varying social networks. In: 2017 IEEE International Conference on Communications (ICC), pp. 1–6 (2017)
17. Clauset, A., Moore, C., Newman, M.E.J.: Hierarchical structure and the prediction of missing links in networks. Nature **453**, 98–101 (2008)
18. Srilatha, P., Manjula, R.: Similarity index based link prediction algorithms in social networks: a survey **2016**, 87–94 (2016)
19. Zhang, X., Zhao, C., Wang, X., Yi, D.: Identifying missing and spurious interactions in directed networks. In: Cai, Z., Wang, C., Cheng, S., Wang, H., Gao, H. (eds.) WASA 2014. LNCS, vol. 8491, pp. 470–481. Springer, Cham (2014). https://doi.org/10.1007/978-3-319-07782-6_43
20. Ayoub, J., Lotfi, D., El Marraki, M., Hammouch, A.: Accurate link prediction method based on path length between a pair of unlinked nodes and their degree. Soc. Netw. Anal. Mining **10**(1), 1–13 (2020). https://doi.org/10.1007/s13278-019-0618-2
21. Newman, M., Newman, M.E.J.: Clustering and preferential attachment in growing networks. Phys. Rev. E **64**, 025102 (2001). Phys. Rev. E Stat. Nonlin. Soft Matter Phys. 64, 025102
22. Jaccard, P.: Etude de la distribution florale dans une portion des Alpes et du Jura. Bull. Soc. Vaudoise Sci. Nat. **37**, 547–579 (1901)
23. Sørenson, T.: A Method of Establishing Groups of Equal Amplitude in Plant Sociology Based on Similarity of Species Content and Its Application to Analyses of the Vegetation on Danish Commons. I kommission hos E. Munksgaard (1948)
24. Barabási, A.L., Jeong, H., Néda, Z., Ravasz, E., Schubert, A., Vicsek, T.: Evolution of the social network of scientific collaborations. Phys. Stat. Mech. Appl. **311**, 590–614 (2002)
25. Ravasz, E., Somera, A.L., Mongru, D.A., Oltvai, Z.N., Barabási, A.L.: Hierarchical organization of modularity in metabolic networks. Science **297**, 1551–1555 (2002)
26. Leicht, E.A., Holme, P., Newman, M.E.J.: Vertex similarity in networks. Phys. Rev. E Stat. Nonlin. Soft Matter. Phys. **73**, 026120 (2006)
27. Salton, G., McGill, M.J.: Introduction to Modern Information Retrieval. McGraw-Hill, New York (1983)
28. Adamic, L.A., Adar, E.: Friends and neighbors on the Web. Soc. Netw. **25**, 211–230 (2003)
29. Zhou, T., Lü, L., Zhang, Y.-C.: Predicting missing links via local information. Eur. Phys. J. B. **71**, 623–630 (2009)
30. Yu, Y., Wang, X.: Link prediction in directed network and its application in microblog. Math. Probl. Eng. **2014**, 1–8 (2014)
31. Chen, B., Hua, Y., Yuan, Y., Jin, Y.: Link prediction on directed networks based on AUC optimization. IEEE Access. **6**, 28122–28136 (2018)
32. Yang, Y., Lichtenwalter, R.N., Chawla, N.V.: Evaluating link prediction methods. Knowl. Inf. Syst. **45**(3), 751–782 (2014). https://doi.org/10.1007/s10115-014-0789-0

33. SNAP: Network datasets: Wikipedia vote network. https://snap.stanford.edu/data/wiki-Vote. html. Accessed 14 Apr 2021
34. The KONECT Project. http://konect.cc/. Accessed 13 Apr 2021
35. Goel, S., Muhamad, R., Watts, D.: Social search in "Small-World" experiments. In: Proceedings of the 18th International Conference on World Wide Web, pp. 701–710. Association for Computing Machinery, New York (2009)
36. Papadimitriou, A., Symeonidis, P., Manolopoulos, Y.: Fast and accurate link prediction in social networking systems. J. Syst. Softw. **85**, 2119–2132 (2012)

A CNN Based 3D Connectivity Matrices Features for Autism Detection: Application on ABIDE I

Fatima Zahra Benabdallah[1](✉), Ahmed Drissi El Maliani[1], and Mohammed El Hassouni[2]

[1] LRIT - CNRST URAC 29, Rabat IT Center, FS, Mohammed V University in Rabat, Rabat, Morocco
fatimazahra_benabdallah@um5.ac.ma
[2] LRIT - CNRST URAC 29, Rabat IT Center, FLSH, Mohammed V University in Rabat, Rabat, Morocco

Abstract. Autism spectrum disorder (ASD) is a neurodevelopmental disorder with no clear information about its origin or development. Its occurrence is going in increasing but no cure was found. However, early diagnosis can improve the autistic's life. Hence, understanding the mechanisms of this disorder is of high importance. Previously, methods theoretically comparable to some autism theories were tested and proved the existence of these latter. In this paper, we propose a framework that takes into account the properties of over and under-connectivity in the autistic brain by constructing images alike matrices that incorporate the aforementioned properties into their layers. Then, extract features from these matrices using transfer learning and finally classifying these latter to detect the autistic patients from the non-autistics. Furthermore, since deep learning is used, to test the effectiveness of corroborating autism theories into the tests, other 3D matrices were also constructed by simply dividing the information by 3 and fed into deep learning models to extract features. The overall objective is to facilitate the early diagnosis of autism. The tested dataset is the large multi-site Autism Brain Imaging Data Exchange I (ABIDE I). The results show that this approach provides accurate prediction up to 80%.

Keywords: Autism spectrum disorder · Transfer-learning · Features extraction · ABIDE · Rs-fMRI · Over-connectivity · Under-connectivity

1 Introduction

ASD is a neurodevelopmental disorder that have been gaining a lot of interest in the last decades. It touches more children with the passing of the years and still has no definite cure. Moreover, this disorder's symptoms are varied and include at least two qualitative impairment in social interactions, one qualitative impairment in communication and one of the restricted, repetitive, and

H. Elbiaze et al. (Eds.): UNet 2021, LNCS 12845, pp. 293–302, 2021.
https://doi.org/10.1007/978-3-030-86356-2_24

stereotyped patterns of behavior, interests, and activities [1]. Additionally, its development is highly correlated with age and environment [2].

Currently, the diagnosis of Autism is conducted through a behavioral test around the age of 2 years old. However, according to [3], the average age of autism detection is 5 years old, due to many factors as parental awareness and availability of diagnosis centers. It also can co-occur with other disorders which render its detection more difficult.

On the bright side, early diagnosis permit to put the autistic children through adapted programs that can lessen the impact of autism on their everyday life [4]. However, with the aforementioned detection problems, this might not be possible for all autistic children. Thus, the need of early diagnosis methods.

For an alternative detection method that can be conducted in the early days of childhood, new approaches based on studying the brain function have emerged. From them we can cite [5], where authors applied deep learning algorithms to identify patients from large datasets based solely on the brain activation patterns. They achieved 70% accuracy and found an anticorrelation of brain function between anterior and posterior areas of the brain.

Later, in [6], Multi-atlas functional connectivity was used as an original feature representation for ASD detection. The approach began by calculating multiple functional connectivity based on different brain atlases from the ABIDE fMRI database. Then, to get the more discriminative features, authors proposed a multi-atlas deep feature representation method based on stacked denoising autoencoders. For the final identification, authors applied a multilayer perceptron and an ensemble learning method to achieve an accuracy of 74.52% (sensitivity of 80.69%, specificity of 66.71%, AUC of 0.8026).

Nevertheless, most of the literature approaches are not theoretically adapted to ASD, i.e. they do not consider the known theories about autistic brains in the process of detection.

In this paper, we approach autism detection from a different angle, by combining methods that can be said to be autism specified, as they extract information related to previous autism theories, with machine learning and deep learning tools. The proposed approach is divided into three important steps that are:

- The creation of the entry data where we create 3-dimensional image alike connectivity matrices to feed into the deep learning models.
- The extraction of features is the step where we use deep learning to explore the 3D entry data to extract new features for the last step.
- The classification which is the last step categorizes the data into autistics and non-autistics and through the results we measure the efficiency of our autism detection approach.

All these steps will be more detailed in the Proposed approach section down below. Experiments are conducted on resting state FMRI images available in the ABIDE I database. This latter is part of the ABIDE program that groups images from multiple international sites around the world with a vast range of characteristics.

2 Materials and Methods

2.1 Data

The base data of this work are fMRI images proposed by ABIDE I in [7]. ABIDE I is a dataset of ABIDE, a base dedicated to autism. This base regroups brain images from different sites around the world. Its main objective is to increase the availability of data to forward the autism research. In this paper, from the images that account for 1112 images we only use 871 images proved free of damage according to [8]. But the actual used data is a component representing the time series of these images by the parcellation of specific atlases. The time series are available through ABIDE preprocessed [9]. As the name suggest the data in ABIDE preprocessed is preprocessed using different pipelines and strategies. The most used preprocessing pipeline in the state of art is C-PAC mainly because of its better results when compared to the other strategies. Hence, in this paper, we also extract the data preprocessed with C-PAC.

2.2 Connectivity Matrices

The base of this work are the brain connectivity matrices that compute the force of interaction of the different regions of the brain. These matrices are computed based on the time series extracted from fMRI images. The fMRI images are 4-dimensional images that capture blood fluctuations that reflect the brain activities on a certain lap of time [10]. There are two types of fMRI images, but the most adapted to autism are the resting state type (rs-fMRI) that does not require any participation from the patient.

The time series permit to transform the 4-dimensional information of the fMRI into a 1-dimensional signal that is simpler to manipulate. Another mean of complexity reduction is the use of parcellation. Parcellation permits to divide the brain into a small number of regions with the same specifications. Its use has been proven more informative. Because the number of synapses composing the brain go beyond millions which induces humongous connectivity matrices with a high order of complexity. Parcellation, on the other hand, permits the construction of connectivity matrices that are simpler and easy to study. For this we use two different atlases, the AAL [11] that divides the brain into 116 regions and the DosenBach atlas [12] that divides the brain into 161 regions of interest (ROIs).

The correlation matrices are computed from the time series using the correlation method that allocates weights by comparing the different regions signal and deciding the likelihood of communication between these regions, with 1 highly correlated.

2.3 Proposed Approach

As mentioned in the introduction, our approach consists of three essential steps that are:

Creation of the Entry Data. Where we simulate the RGB image format which is the base entry of the Convolutional Neural Networks (CNN) models by creating 3D connectivity matrices. These latter are composed by dividing connectivity matrices computed from the rs-fMRI images' time series via two approaches:

- Division by 3: divides the connectivity matrices information by 3 and puts every third of the information on a layer.
- Division by STs: is based on the maximum and minimum spanning trees which are autism adapted. They permit to extract connections related to over and under-connectivity in the autistic brain.
  In this approach, the first layer incorporates the original connectivity matrix minus the highest and lowest weights extracted using the maximum and minimum spanning trees, respectively. The second layer contains the high weights (over-connectivity information), while the third layer contains the lowest weights (under-connectivity information).
  The STs were extracted from graphs constructed with the connectivity matrices weights using the Kruskal algorithm as Fig. 1 shows.

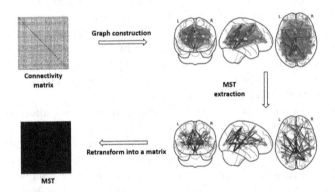

Fig. 1. Extraction of the spanning trees. Example of the minimum spanning tree.

The kruskal algorithm is a greedy algorithm that orders the vertices connections according to their weight. Then, constructs the spanning trees by extracting information from the ordered vertices connections list according to a set condition. In this work, the conditions are the lowest weights for the minimum spanning tree and the highest weights for maximum spanning tree.

The overall steps of the data entry creation are summed in Fig. 2.

Extraction of Features. In the second step, we use deep learning in the form of CNN models from Keras [13] with transfer learning to extract features from our 3D entry data. Transfer learning provides better outcomes when comparing

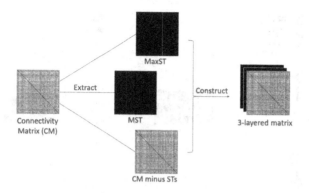

Fig. 2. 3D Connectivity matrices construction. Example of the Spanning trees division strategy.

to end-to-end models. It also solves the problem of the training phase since it uses the weights of existing classification models that have been trained on big databases as imageNet, an image database with millions of images [14], that we also use in this work. For the CNN models we test-compare two widely used models that are Inception and ResNet50 and also their combination model InceptionResNet. The objective of using these models is only to extract features. Hence, the process stops before the fully connected layer that originally gives the final classification result. Then we store the features the models constructed into vectors for the final step.

Classification. Finally, the classification step uses SVC an implementation of SVM by scikit-learn library [15] to classify the features extracted by deep learning to categorize the subjects into autistics and non-autistics. It calculates the approximation of the decision boundary between the autistic subject and non-autistic subjects in the space of the deep learning extracted features vectors. The classification is a 10-fold cross-validation with a p-values of 0.01.

Figure 3 showcases all the steps that come after the creation of the data entry. The validation of the classification performance is measured by three metrics, that includes the accuracy, a test's ability to differentiate autistic and non-autistic subjects correctly, the sensitivity, the ability to determine the autistic subjects correctly and the specificity which is the ability to determine the non-autistic subjects correctly [16].

These metrics are defined as follow:

$$Accuracy = \frac{TP + TN}{TP + TN + FP + FN} \tag{1}$$

$$Sensitivity = \frac{TP}{TP + FN} \tag{2}$$

$$Specificity = \frac{TN}{TN + FP} \tag{3}$$

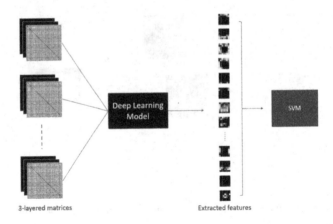

Fig. 3. Schema of the proposed approach.

With:

TP (True positive) is the number of cases correctly identified as autistics.

FP (False positive) is the number of cases incorrectly identified as autistics.

TN (True negative) is the number of cases correctly identified as non-autistics.

FN (False negative) is the number of cases incorrectly identified as non-autistics.

3   Results

As mentioned before, the features extracted with different models were flattened to one-dimensional vectors for the SVM classification. In this classification, we used a 10-fold cross-validation strategy with a p-value of 0.01, that repeatedly leaves one-fold for test while learning from the remaining ones.

To extend the tests and verify the efficiency of the tested approach, we used two atlases-based time series for the creation of the connectivity matrices. Hence, we got two different connectivity matrices (the AAL matrices and the DosenBach matrices). Then, using the two methods of the entry data creation we created two batches of 3D images-alike matrices to be fed in the deep learning models.

After feeding these newly created 3D matrices separately into the deep learning models, we extracted different arrays of features. These features sizes go from 2×2 to 6×6 depending on the fed matrices size and their number changes according to the deep learning model. Table 1 groups all the different features sizes in correspondence with the deep learning model. The separate classification of every atlas-model combination extracted features gave interesting results.

First, the AAL atlas connectivity matrices classification was over all very low. As can be seen in Table 2, the highest accuracy 46.04% was achieved by the classification of the features extracted with the InceptionResNet model. The ResNet features classification gave even lower results that can be due to an impairment in the learning phase of the classification model. Since the number of wrongly identified autistics and non-autistics is very high. On the other hand,

Table 1. Sizes of the features extracted by the different models from the two atlases' connectivity matrices

	Inception	ResNet50	InceptionResNet
AAL	2×2	4×4	2×2
Dosenbach	3×3	6×6	3×3

the results of the DosenBach atlas stored in Table 3, are very different, as a high accuracy number showed up with a value of 80.48%. The other models' features' classification results did not differ much from the AAL atlas.

Table 2. Results of the classification of the features of the AAL atlas connectivity matrices

		Inception	ResNet50	InceptionResNet
Division by 3	Accuracy	40.18	26.64	44.09
	Sensitivity	45.73	31.84	46.58
	Specificity	33.75	20.60	41.19
Division by STs	Accuracy	43.05	19.75	46.04
	Sensitivity	47.01	22.44	48.93
	Specificity	38.46	16.63	42.68

Another point worth signaling is the fact that the ST division did not add any advantage in this classification.

Table 3. Results of the classification of the features of the DosenBach atlas connectivity matrices

		Inception	ResNet50	InceptionResNet
Division by 3	Accuracy	41.68	80.48	43.17
	Sensitivity	46.15	63.68	50.00
	Specificity	36.48	100.00	35.24
Division by STs	Accuracy	43.97	38.81	41.79
	Sensitivity	45.94	63.68	45.51
	Specificity	41.69	9.93	37.47

Finally, a comparison with the state of arts methods is stored in Table 4 and shows the different best results of accuracy, sensitivity and specificity achieved in this paper and the state of art when deep learning is used on the ABIDE dataset.

Table 4. Comparison with the state of art's methods of ASD detection with deep learning

	Accuracy	Sensitivity	Specificity
ResNet-Division by 3	80.48	63.68	100.00
DNN [5]	70	74	63
Multi-atlas [6]	74.52	80.69	66.71

4   Discussion

With the goal of finding a new mean of early diagnosis we proposed an approach that combines machine learning and deep learning to detect autism based on connectivity matrices of the brain. To make this approach more autism adapted, alongside a simple division, we proposed another method for data entry creation that uses tools previously verified to affect autism detection, i.e., the spanning trees.

In a previous work [17], the elimination of minimum spanning trees showed proof of the existence of under-connectivity of the autistic brain. Later, in [18] using the same approach, we tested the over-connectivity and also found proof of its existence in the autistic brain.

However, in this paper, we did not explore those eliminated connections. But used the aforementioned method to construct image alike 3D matrices to give as entry to deep learning models to extract features that will permit the detection of autism. Taking into consideration the fact that since the previously eliminated connections proved their relationship with the autism disorder, we divided our connectivity matrices into layers that incorporate these special connections. For this, we added two new layers containing the connections with the over-connectivity specifications and the under-connectivity specifications that we extracted from the original connectivity matrices computed using different atlas's ROIs. Then, we combined deep neural networks with SVM for the classification by extracting features with transfer learning and classifying these extracted features separately with SVM.

We also tested matrices constructed by dividing the connectivity weights by 3 to keep the original information intact and fill the layers of the 3D matrices.

The results achieved showed a great difference with [8] and [17]. The best results achieved in this test reached 80,48% accuracy 63,68% sensitivity and 100.00% specificity. They were achieved using the ResNet50 model combined with the division by 3 method with a 0.01 p-value, and using 3D matrices of the DosenBatch atlas.

The results of this paper led us to different conclusions. First, from comparing the results of all tests, we found that when working with heterogeneous data, many factors can have an impact on the accuracy of detection. As the results showed, the accuracy with the two atlases tested gave different results. In the other hand, we have the deep learning models used for extracting features.

In general, all models performed poorly and produced very low accuracy except the ResNet50. Which means that the depth and structure of the deep learning model has an important impact on the quality of the extracted features. Therefore, even though, these models' accuracy in detecting images was good but in our case, where we mimic images using connectivity matrices, it was not fit to extract features that can differentiate autistics from controls. However, ResNet50 permitted to extract features that increased the accuracy of detection to 80%. Finally, incorporating autism theories in this test led to a change in the matrices' structure that did not improve the accuracy of detection when compared to the state of art. But the approach based on dividing the information onto three equals layers was more fit and highly increased the accuracy of detection.

5   Conclusion

In this work, we approached autism detection from a new angle based on an approach that combines deep learning with machine learning. In this approach, 3D images alike matrices were constructed by using different types of connectivity matrices with two different strategies for building these latter. Then we fed these newly formed 3D matrices into deep learning models to extract features that we classified separately with SVM.

The results achieved reached 80% accuracy and almost 64% sensitivity, proving that this method is effective in detecting autism to some point. However, more tests with other combinations of tools and methods might lead to better results in the future.

References

1. Herbert, M.R.: 52 - autism. In: Gilman, S. (ed.) Neurobiology of Disease, pp. 581–591. Academic Press (2007). ISBN: 9780120885923. https://doi.org/10.1016/B978-012088592-3/50054-2
2. Simonoff, E., et al.: Trajectories in symptoms of autism and cognitive ability in autism from childhood to adult life: findings from a longitudinal epidemiological cohort. J. Am. Acad. Child Adolesc. Psychiatry (2019). ISSN: 0890-8567. https://doi.org/10.1016/j.jaac.2019.11.020. http://www.sciencedirect.com/science/article/pii/S0890856719322312
3. Daniels, A.M., Mandell, D.S.: Explaining differences in age at autism spectrum disorder diagnosis: acritical review. Autism 18(5), 583–597 (2014). https://doi.org/10.1177/1362361313480277
4. Johnson, C.P., Myers, S.M.: Autism spectrum disorders. In: Wolraich, M.L., Drotar, D.D., Dworkin, P.H., Perrin, E.C. (eds.) Developmental-Behavioral Pediatrics, Mosby, pp. 519–577 (2008). ISBN: 9780323040259. https://doi.org/10.1016/B978-0-323-04025-9.50018-0
5. Heinsfeld, A.S., Franco, A.R., Craddock, R.C., Buchweitz, A., Meneguzzi, F.: Identification of autism spectrum disorder using deep learning and the ABIDE dataset. NeuroImage Clin. 17, 16–23 (2018). ISSN: 2213-1582. https://doi.org/10.1016/j.nicl.2017.08.017

6. Wang, Y., Wang, J., Wu, F.-X., Hayrat, R., Liu, J.: AIMAFE: autism spectrum disorder identification with multi-atlas deep feature representation and ensemble learning. J. Neurosci. Methods **343**, 108840 (2020). ISSN: 0165-0270. https://doi.org/10.1016/j.jneumeth.2020.108840

7. Di Martino, A., et al.: The autism brain imaging data exchange: towards a large-scale evaluation of the intrinsic brain architecture in autism. Mol. Psychiatry **19**(6), 659–667 (2014). https://doi.org/10.1038/mp.2013.78

8. Abraham, A., et al.: Deriving reproducible biomarkers from multi-site resting-state data: an autism-based example. Neuroimage **147**, 736–745 (2017)

9. Craddock, C., et al.: The neuro bureau preprocessing initiative: open sharing of preprocessed neuroimaging data and derivatives. In: Neuroinformatics 2013, Stockholm, Sweden (2013)

10. Nierhaus, T., Margulies, D., Long, X., Villringer, A.: fMRI for the assessment of functional connectivity, neuroimaging - methods. In: Bright, P. (ed.) InTech (2012)

11. Rolls, E.T., Joliot, M., Tzourio-Mazoyer, N.: Implementation of a new parcellation of the orbitofrontal cortex in the automated anatomical labeling atlas. Neuroimage **122**, 1–5 (2015)

12. Dosenbach, N.U.F., et al.: Prediction of individual brain maturity using fMRI. Science **329**(5997), 1358–1361 (2010). https://doi.org/10.1126/science

13. Chollet, F., et al.: Keras. GitHub (2015). https://github.com/fchollet/keras

14. Deng, J., Dong, W., Socher, R., Li, L.-J., Li, K., Fei-Fei, L.: ImageNet: a large-scale hierarchical image database. In: 2009 IEEE Conference on Computer Vision and Pattern Recognition, pp. 248–255 (2009)

15. Pedregosa, F., Varoquaux, G., Gramfort, A., Michel, V., et al.: Scikit-learn: machine learning in Python. J. Mach. Learn. Res. **12**, 2825 (2011)

16. Baratloo, A., Hosseini, M., Negida, A., El Ashal, G.: Part 1: simple definition and calculation of accuracy, sensitivity and specificity. Emergency **3**(2), 48–49 (2015)

17. Benabdallah, F., El Maliani, A.D., Lotfi, D., Jennane, R., El Hassouni, M.: Analysis of under-connectivity in autism using the minimum spanning tree: application on large multi-site dataset. In press

18. Benabdallah, F.Z., El Maliani, A.D., Lotfi, D., El Hassouni, M.: Analysis of the over-connectivity in autistic brains using the maximum spanning tree: application on the multi-site and heterogeneous ABIDE dataset. In: 2020 8th International Conference on Wireless Networks and Mobile Communications (WINCOM), Reims, France, pp. 1–7 (2020). https://doi.org/10.1109/WINCOM50532.2020.9272441

Catadioptric Omnidirectional Images Motion Deblurring

Brahim Alibouch[1][(✉)] and Mohammed Rziza[2]

[1] LabSIV, Faculty of Science, Ibn Zohr University, Agadir, Morocco
`b.alibouch@uiz.ac.ma`
[2] LRIT URAC 29, Faculty of Sciences, Mohammed V University, Rabat, Morocco
`rziza@fsr.ac.ma`

Abstract. Unlike conventional perspectives cameras, omnidirectional cameras allow to capture images with a large field of view. However, the resulting images contain important distortions that need to be taken into account in any image processing task. In this paper, we introduce a novel approach for omnidirectional images motion deblurring. We propose to adapt the Wiener deconvolution technique in order to takes into account the omnidirectional images geometry. We present a reformulation of the motion deblurring problem on the sphere which is considered as the most appropriate space for omnidirectional image processing. For this purpose, we develop a spherical Wiener filter using the necessary mathematical tools for spherical images processing and we model the motion blur using the velocity fields estimated via our omnidirectional optical flow estimation method. Experimental results show that our approach performs well on real and synthetic omnidirectional images.

Keywords: Omnidirectional images · Motion blur · Spherical Wiener filter · Deblurring

1 Introduction

Image acquisition is a main step in computer vision and image processing. It is the process in which imaging systems try to capture a faithful representation of the perceived scene. However, the acquired images may be affected by certain degradations caused by the intrinsic properties of the imaging systems. A common form of these degradations is the motion blur which is caused by the imaging systems shake or the fast movement of objects in the perceived scenes. The theoretical model of the motion blur generally describes the degraded image as a convolution between the original sharp image and a blurring kernel commonly known as the point spread function (PSF).

To address the motion blur problem, various deblurring methods have been proposed in literature. They can be organized into two categories, blind restoration approaches [1–4] and non-blind restoration approaches [5–7]. Blind restoration is the process of recovering the original sharp image when the degradation is

© Springer Nature Switzerland AG 2021
H. Elbiaze et al. (Eds.): UNet 2021, LNCS 12845, pp. 303–312, 2021.
https://doi.org/10.1007/978-3-030-86356-2_25

unknown. In contrast, non-blind restoration algorithms such as recursive Kalman Filtering [8], Least Square Filtering [9,10] and Wiener Filtering [11], assume that the motion blur kernel is known or computed elsewhere.

In this paper, we introduce a new motion deblurring method adapted to omnidirectional images. We first consider a sequence of blurred omnidirectional images on which the optical flow has been estimated, using our previously published method dedicated to omnidirectional images [12], to estimate the corresponding spherical motion blur kernel. Then, we define the spherical Wiener deconvolution to reduce the blur while taking into account the particular geometry of omnidirectional images.

2   Preliminaries

The general degradation model discussed in this paper is the linear and shift-invariant model. As shown in Fig. 1, the output of this model is the convolution of the original sharp image $f(x, y)$ with a degradation function (PSF) $h(x, y)$ to which is added an additive noise $b(x, y)$. The degraded image is given by:

$$f_d(x, y) = f(x, y) * h(x, y) + b(x, y) \tag{1}$$

In frequency domain, Eq. (1) becomes:

$$F_d(u, v) = F(u, v)H(u, v) + B(u, v) \tag{2}$$

The restoration process attempts to recover the original image by solving Eq. (2). In the non-blind restoration case, the system model estimates the original image $f(x, y)$ when the degradation function $h(x, y)$ and the additive noise $b(x, y)$ are assumed to be known. The main goal of this process (Fig. 2) is to find the filter $k(x, y)$ that attenuate the degradation so that the produced image $f_r(x, y)$ is restored as close as possible, given a degraded image $f_d(x, y)$. This constraint can be expressed as:

$$f_r(x, y) = f_d(x, y) * k(x, y) \tag{3}$$

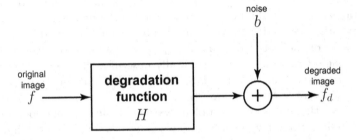

Fig. 1. Image degradation model.

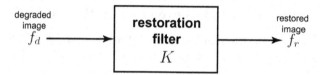

Fig. 2. Image restoration model.

Wiener filtering is one of the most used non-blind techniques to solve the image degradation problem. The Wiener filter $k(x, y)$ is designed in such a way to minimize the mean square error between the original image $f(x, y)$ and the restored image $f_r(x, y)$:

$$\xi = \mathbb{E}(\|f(x, y) - f_r(x, y)\|^2) \tag{4}$$

The transfer function of the Wiener filter is given by:

$$K(u, v) = \frac{H^*(u, v)}{|H(u, v)|^2 + \rho} \tag{5}$$

where ρ is the regularization term.

The Wiener filter can also be considered as an inverse filter cascaded with an adaptive filter who depends on the local content of the image [13]. Equation (5) can be rewritten as:

$$K(u, v) = \frac{1}{H(u, v)} \frac{|H(u, v)|^2}{|H(u, v)|^2 + \rho} \tag{6}$$

An adaptation of the Wiener filter on the sphere was introduced by Bigot et al. in [14]. The proposed filter, used by authors for denoising purposes, is invariant by rotation and take into account the particular geometry of omnidirectional images. However, the degradation and restoration model considered by the authors in this work does not take into account the blur. We propose in this paper an extension of the spherical Wiener filter for omnidirectional images motion deblurring based on the work of Bigot et al. [14–16].

3   Proposed Method

Early works on omnidirectional vision have shown that the sphere is the most appropriate domain for omnidirectional images processing. In this section, we present a reformulation of the motion deblurring problem in this domain. Therefore, we consider the omnidirectional image as a function of the sphere and we use necessary mathematical tools for spherical image processing.

3.1   Fourier Transform and Convolution on the Sphere

The frequency representation on the sphere of a function $f \in L^2(\mathbb{S}^2)$ is obtained by decomposition on the spherical harmonics Y_ℓ^m basis [17]:

$$f = \sum_{\ell \geq 0} \sum_{|m| \leq \ell} \hat{f}(\ell, m) Y_\ell^m(\theta, \varphi) \tag{7}$$

where $\hat{f}(\ell, m)$ are the function f spherical Fourier coefficients, which are obtained from the inner product of f and Y_ℓ^m on the sphere:

$$\hat{f}(\ell, m) = \langle f, Y_\ell^m \rangle \tag{8}$$

$$= \int_0^{2\pi} \int_0^\pi f(\theta, \varphi) \overline{Y_\ell^m(\theta, \varphi)} \sin(\theta) d\theta d\varphi \tag{9}$$

Spherical harmonics of order m and degree ℓ $\{Y_\ell^m : m \in \mathbb{Z}, |m| \leq \ell \in \mathbb{N}\}$ are given by:

$$Y_\ell^m(\theta, \varphi) = \sqrt{\frac{(2\ell + 1)(\ell - m)!}{4\pi(\ell + m)!}} P_\ell^m(\cos\theta) e^{im\varphi} \tag{10}$$

where P_ℓ^m is the associated Legendre polynomial.

In [17], Driscoll and Healy introduced the convolution on the sphere between two functions f et h as follow:

$$(f * h)(\omega) = \int_{g \in SO(3)} f(g\eta) h(g^{-1}\omega) dg \tag{11}$$

where ω is a point of the unit sphere $\mathbb{S}^2$, η it's north pole and $SO(3)$ is the group of rotations which acts on the sphere.

The Fourier transform of the convolution of two function f and h in the Hilbert space $L^2(\mathbb{S}^2)$ is given by:

$$\widehat{(f * h)}(\ell, m) = 2\pi \sqrt{\frac{4\pi}{2\ell + 1}} \hat{f}(\ell, m) \hat{h}(\ell, 0) \tag{12}$$

where $\hat{f}$ and $\hat{h}$ are respectively the Fourier transform of f and h.

3.2   Spherical Wiener Filtering

In the context of omnidirectional vision, the degradation and restoration processes remain the same as in traditional vision (Figs. 1 and 2). However, original image f and degraded image f_r are function in the Hilbert space $L^2(\mathbb{S}^2)$ and therefore Eqs. (1) and (3) respectively become:

$$f_d(\theta, \varphi) = \frac{1}{2\pi} f(\theta, \varphi) * h(\theta, \varphi) + b(\theta, \varphi) \tag{13}$$

and

$$f_r(\theta, \varphi) = \frac{1}{2\pi} f_d(\theta, \varphi) * k(\theta, \varphi) \tag{14}$$

Considering Eq. (12), the Fourier transforms of the degraded image f_d and the restored image f_r are respectively given by:

$$\hat{f}_d(\ell, m) = \sqrt{\frac{4\pi}{2\ell + 1}} \hat{f}(\ell, m)\hat{h}(\ell, 0) + \hat{b}(\ell, m) \tag{15}$$

and

$$\hat{f}_r(\ell, m) = \sqrt{\frac{4\pi}{2\ell + 1}} \hat{f}_d(\ell, m)\hat{k}(\ell, 0) \tag{16}$$

The Wiener filter results from the minimization of the mean square error between the original image f and the restored image f_r:

$$\Psi = \mathbb{E}(\|f(\theta, \varphi) - f_r(\theta, \varphi)\|^2) \tag{17}$$

Using the Riesz-Fischer's theorem [14], Eq. (17) becomes:

$$\Psi = \mathbb{E}\left(\sum_{\ell \geq 0} \sum_{|m| \leq \ell} \left|\hat{f}(\ell, m) - \hat{f}_r(\ell, m)\right|^2\right) \tag{18}$$

$$= \mathbb{E}\left(\sum_{\ell \geq 0} \sum_{|m| \leq \ell} \left|\hat{f}(\ell, m) - \sqrt{\frac{4\pi}{2\ell + 1}} \hat{f}_d(\ell, m)\hat{k}(\ell, 0)\right|^2\right) \tag{19}$$

In order to achieve good performance on every region of the omnidirectional image, the filter k should be invariant by rotation which is equivalent to:

$$k(\theta, \varphi) = \sum_{\ell \geq 0} \hat{k}(\ell, 0)Y_\ell^0(\theta, \varphi) \tag{20}$$

The minimisation problem can be solved using the following constraint on the partial derivative of Ψ with respect to $\hat{k}(\ell, 0)$:

$$\frac{\partial \Psi}{\partial \hat{k}(\ell, 0)} = 0 \tag{21}$$

$$\mathbb{E}\left(\frac{\partial}{\partial \hat{k}(\ell, 0)}\left(\sum_{|m| \leq \ell} \left|\hat{f}(\ell, m) - \sqrt{\frac{4\pi}{2\ell + 1}} \hat{f}_d(\ell, m)\hat{k}(\ell, 0)\right|^2\right)\right) = 0 \tag{22}$$

since $(|z|^2)' = 2\bar{z}$, where $\bar{z}$ is the conjugate of z, we obtain:

$$\mathbb{E}\left(\sum_{|m| \leq \ell} 2 \times \overline{\left(\hat{f}(\ell, m) - \sqrt{\frac{4\pi}{2\ell + 1}} \hat{f}_d(\ell, m)\hat{k}(\ell, 0)\right)}\left(-\sqrt{\frac{4\pi}{2\ell + 1}} \times \hat{f}_d(\ell, m)\right)\right) = 0 \tag{23}$$

namely:

$$\sqrt{\frac{4\pi}{2\ell+1}}\hat{k}(\ell,0)\mathbb{E}\left(\sum_{|m|\leq\ell}\hat{f}_d(\ell,m)\overline{\hat{f}_d(\ell,m)}\right) = \mathbb{E}\left(\sum_{|m|\leq\ell}\overline{\hat{f}(\ell,m)}\hat{f}_d(\ell,m)\right) \quad (24)$$

therefore:

$$\hat{k}(\ell,0) = \sqrt{\frac{2\ell+1}{4\pi}}\frac{\mathbb{E}\left(\sum_{|m|\leq\ell}\overline{\hat{f}(\ell,m)}\hat{f}_d(\ell,m)\right)}{\mathbb{E}\left(\sum_{|m|\leq\ell}\hat{f}_d(\ell,m)\overline{\hat{f}_d(\ell,m)}\right)} \quad (25)$$

replacing $\hat{f}_d(\ell,m)$ in the previous equation, we get:

$$\hat{k}(\ell,0) = \sqrt{\frac{2\ell+1}{4\pi}}\frac{\mathbb{E}\left(\sum_{|m|\leq\ell}\left(\sqrt{\frac{4\pi}{2\ell+1}}\left|\hat{f}(\ell,m)\right|^2\hat{h}(\ell,0) + \overline{\hat{f}(\ell,m)}\hat{b}(\ell,m)\right)\right)}{\mathbb{E}\left(\sum_{|m|\leq\ell}\left(\frac{4\pi}{2\ell+1}\left|\hat{f}(\ell,m)\right|^2\left|\hat{h}(\ell,0)\right|^2 + \left|\hat{b}(\ell,m)\right|^2\right)\right)} \quad (26)$$

$\mathbb{E}(\left|\hat{f}(\ell,m)\right|^2)$ and $\mathbb{E}(\left|\hat{b}(\ell,m)\right|^2)$ are respectively power spectral densities of the original image $f(\theta,\varphi)$ and the noise $b(\theta,\varphi)$.
Let $\mathbb{E}(\left|\hat{f}(\ell,m)\right|^2) = W_f(\ell,m)$ and $\mathbb{E}(\left|\hat{b}(\ell,m)\right|^2) = W_b(\ell,m)$. We assume that the original image and the noise are independent, namely $\mathbb{E}(\overline{\hat{f}(\ell,m)}\hat{b}(\ell,m)) = 0$.
Eq. (26) becomes:

$$\hat{k}(\ell,0) = \frac{2\ell+1}{4\pi}\frac{\hat{h}(\ell,0)}{\left|\hat{h}(\ell,0)\right|^2 + \frac{2\ell+1}{4\pi}\frac{W_b(\ell,m)}{W_f(\ell,m)}} \quad (27)$$

the Spherical Wiener Filter is therefore given by:

$$k(\theta,\varphi) = \sum_{\ell\geq0}\frac{2\ell+1}{4\pi}\frac{\hat{h}(\ell,0)}{\left|\hat{h}(\ell,0)\right|^2 + \frac{2\ell+1}{4\pi}\frac{W_b(\ell,m)}{W_f(\ell,m)}}Y_\ell^0(\theta,\varphi) \quad (28)$$

3.3   Experiments

In this section, we conduct several experiments to test the performance of our approach. We evaluate our method on real and synthetic omnidirectional sequences degraded by motion blur. On these sequences, the blur was simulated using the image averaging technique and the optical flow was estimated by applying our motion estimation method [12]. We use the resulting velocity fields to model the blur and generate the PSF in each pixel of the image to deblur using the spherical Wiener filter.

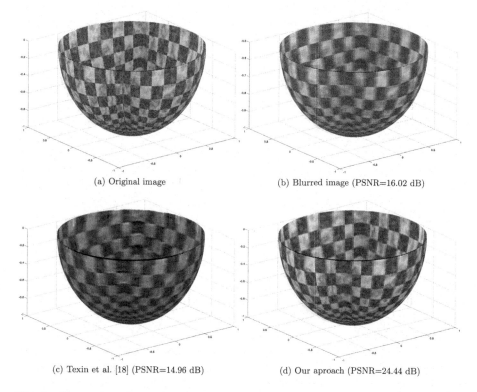

(a) Original image

(b) Blurred image (PSNR=16.02 dB)

(c) Texin et al. [18] (PSNR=14.96 dB)

(d) Our aproach (PSNR=24.44 dB)

Fig. 3. Comparison between the original synthetic image, the image degraded by motion blur, the restored image using Texin et al. method [18] and the restored image using our approach.

The main goal here is to show the importance of using the sphere as the most appropriate space for omnidirectional image deblurring. Therefore, we compare our method with the motion deblurring method of Texin et al. [18] developed for classical perspective images. This method is based on Wiener deconvolution and apply, on each point of the perspective image, a regularization filter using the velocities generated by the optical flow calculations to create the PSF that represent the motion blur. In order to quantify our experiments, we report the widely used PSNR (Peak Signal to Noise Ratio) metric between the original image and the degraded image.

Figure 3 shows the experimental results obtained on a synthetic omnidirectional images of size 250×250 pixels, representing a scene where a parabolic camera, initially at the origin of the three-dimensional Cartesian coordinate system, looking in the y-axis. This camera observes two planes at the same distance of the origin and parallel to yzplane. They observe also two other planes at the same distance of the origin and parallel to xy-plane [12]. As we mentioned above, this degraded image is a frame of an omnidirectional image sequence degraded by motion blur which is simulated by averaging three consecutive frames.

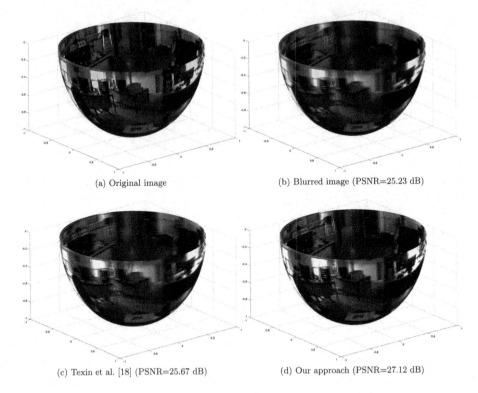

(a) Original image   (b) Blurred image (PSNR=25.23 dB)

(c) Texin et al. [18] (PSNR=25.67 dB)   (d) Our approach (PSNR=27.12 dB)

Fig. 4. Comparison between the original real image, the image degraded by motion blur, the restored image using Texin et al. method [18] and the restored image using our approach.

In visual comparison, we can observe that our method outperforms Texin et al. method [18]. The calculated PSNR confirm the efficiency of our approach.

We also evaluate our method using real omnidirectional images of size 1280×960 pixels captured using a catadioptric camera performing a rotational movement. As for synthetic images, the blur was simulated by averaging three consecutive frames. The results are shown in Fig. 4. We can notice that our deblurring approach provides a restored image of good visual quality as well as a better PSNR compared to Texin et al. method [18].

4   Conclusion

In this paper, we have proposed to adapt the image restoration technique by Wiener deconvolution for omnidirectional images. We have introduced an approach which allows a reformulation of the problem on the sphere and which takes into account the geometry of omnidirectional images. Therefore, we have developed a spherical Wiener filter using the necessary mathematical tools for spherical images processing. The experimental results show that our adapted method improves the correction of motion blur on omnidirectional images.

References

1. Bascle, B., Blake, A., Zisserman, A.: Motion deblurring and super-resolution from an image sequence. In: Buxton, B., Cipolla, R. (eds.) ECCV 1996. LNCS, vol. 1065, pp. 571–582. Springer, Heidelberg (1996). https://doi.org/10.1007/3-540-61123-1_171
2. Stern, A., Kopeika, N.S.: Analytical method to calculate optical transfer functions for image motion using moments and its implementation in image restoration. In: Proceedings of SPIE 2827, Digital Image Recovery and Synthesis III, 25 October 1996. https://doi.org/10.1117/12.255083
3. Yitzhaky, Y., Boshusha, G., Levy, Y., Kopeika, N.S.: Restoration of an image degraded by vibrations using only a single frame. Opt. Eng. **39**(8) (2000). https://doi.org/10.1117/1.1305319
4. Zhang, Y., Wen, C., Zhang, Y.: Estimation of motion parameters from blurred images. Pattern Recogn. Lett. **21**(5), 425–433 (2000). https://doi.org/10.1016/S0167-8655(00)00014-3. ISSN 0167–8655
5. Levin, A., Durand, R.F.F., Freeman, W.T.: Image and depth from a conventional camera with a coded aperture. ACM Trans. Graph. **26**(3), 70-es (2007). https://doi.org/10.1145/1276377.1276464
6. Krishnan, D., Fergus, R.: Fast image deconvolution using hyper-Laplacian priors. In: Advances in Neural Information Processing Systems 22 - Proceedings of the 2009 Conference, pp. 1033–1041 (2009). https://doi.org/10.1145/1531326.1531402
7. Schmidt, U., Rother, C., Nowozin, S., Jancsary, J., Roth, S.: Discriminative non-blind deblurring. In: IEEE Conference on Computer Vision and Pattern Recognition 2013, pp. 604–611 (2013). https://doi.org/10.1109/CVPR.2013.84
8. Woods, J., Ingle, V.: Kalman filtering in two dimensions: further results. IEEE Trans. Acoust. Speech Signal Process. **29**(2), 188–197 (1981). https://doi.org/10.1109/TASSP.1981.1163533
9. Miller, K.: Least squares methods for ill-posed problems with a prescribed bound. SIAM J. Math. Anal. **1**, 52–74 (1970)
10. Tikhonov, A.N., Arsenin, V.Y.: Solutions of Ill-posed Problems. John Wiley Sons, Washington, D.C.: V. H. Winston Sons, New York (1977)
11. Wiener, N.: Extrapolation, interpolation, and smoothing of stationary time series: with engineering applications. MIT Press **113**(21), 1043–54 (1949)
12. Alibouch, B., Radgui, A., Demonceaux, C., Rziza, M., Aboutajdine, D.: A phase-based framework for optical flow estimation on omnidirectional images. SIViP **10**(2), 285–292 (2014). https://doi.org/10.1007/s11760-014-0739-z
13. Surin, I., Fety, L.: Filtrage de Wiener adaptatif appliqué á la restauration d'images. In: 15eme colloque sur le traitement du signal et des images, Juan-Les-Pins, France, 18–21 septembre 1995, September 1995
14. Bigot-Marchand, S., Kachi, D., Durand, S., Mouaddib, El.M.: Spherical image denoising and its application to omnidirectional imaging. In: International Conference on Computer Vision Theory and Applications, Spain (2007)
15. Bigot, S., Kachi, D., Durand, S.: Spherical edge detector: application to omni-directional imaging. In: Blanc-Talon, J., Bourennane, S., Philips, W., Popescu, D., Scheunders, P. (eds.) ACIVS 2008. LNCS, vol. 5259, pp. 554–565. Springer, Heidelberg (2008). https://doi.org/10.1007/978-3-540-88458-3_50

16. Bigot-Marchand, S.: Image processing tools for omnidirectional vision. Theses, Université de Picardie Jules Verne, Octobre 2008

17. Driscoll, J.R., Healy, D.M.: Computing Fourier transforms and convolutions on the 2-Sphere. Adv. Appl. Math. **15**(2), 202–250 (1994). https://doi.org/10.1006/aama.1994.1008. ISSN 0196–8858

18. Texin, C.: Optical flow using phase information for deblurring. Thesis (M. Eng.)-Massachusetts Institute of Technology, Department of Electrical Engineering and Computer Science (2007)

Author Index

Printed in the United States
by Baker & Taylor Publisher Services

Printed in the United States
by Baker & Taylor Publisher Services